THE
NEPTUNE
FACTOR

THE
NEPTUNE
FACTOR

ALFRED THAYER MAHAN
and the Concept of
$EA POWER

NICHOLAS A. LAMBERT

Naval Institute Press
Annapolis, Maryland

Naval Institute Press
291 Wood Road
Annapolis, MD 21402

Library of Congress Cataloging-in-Publication Data

Names: Lambert, Nicholas A., 1967–author.
Title: The neptune factor : Alfred Thayer Mahan and the concept of sea
  power / Nick Lambert.
Other titles: Alfred Thayer Mahan and the concept of sea power
Description: Annapolis, Maryland : Naval Institute Press, [2023] | Includes
  bibliographical references and index.
Identifiers: LCCN 2023040387 (print) | LCCN 2023040388 (ebook) | ISBN
  9781612511580 (hardcover) | ISBN 9781612511597 (ebook)
Subjects: LCSH: Sea-power—History. | Sea-power—Economics. | Mahan, A. T.
  (Alfred Thayer), 1840-1914—Influence. | Mahan, A. T. (Alfred Thayer),
  1840-1914. Influence of Sea Power upon History. | United States.
  Navy—History. | Naval history, Modern.
Classification: LCC V25 .L36 2023 (print) | LCC V25 (ebook) | DDC
  359/.03—dc23/eng/20230901
LC record available at https://lccn.loc.gov/2023040387
LC ebook record available at https://lccn.loc.gov/2023040388

31 30 29 28 27 26 25 24 23   9 8 7 6 5 4 3 2 1
First printing

To the 848 graduates of the U.S. Naval Academy Class of 1957,
and the SS *John W. Brown*

Contents

FOREWORD

Adm. James Stavridis, USN (Ret.)

WHEN WRITING MY own book on sea power, I was deeply conscious of the fact that I was following in distinguished footsteps. More than a century ago, Capt. Alfred Thayer Mahan developed the concept of "sea power" to explain to the American people why the United States needed a powerful navy. His name acquired such mystique that, in the famous words of Henry Stimson, the United States' secretary of war during World War II, the U.S. Navy sometimes "seemed to retire from the realm of logic into a dim religious world in which Neptune was God, Mahan his prophet, and the United States Navy the only true church."

Like the messages of so many prophets, however, Mahan's has become garbled over time. In this marvelous new book, Nicholas A. Lambert takes us back to the very essence of his original message. Surveying the whole of Mahan's writings—not just his best-known early work—Lambert provides, for the first time, a complete account of Mahan's concept of sea power and its development over time.

This historical Mahan is even more impressive—and ironically, more relevant today—than I had realized. For many readers, it may come as a surprise to learn Mahan was a serious student of international economics. If their education was anything like mine, the Mahan they learned about was an advocate of building a big fleet that could defeat an enemy fleet in decisive battle. Yet as shown in the pages that follow, in his later work Mahan modified his concept of sea power. A pioneering student of the era of globalization before World War I, he came to argue that economics and commerce were as important, and possibly more important, than combat. The power to regulate the flows of commerce at sea, Mahan believed, allowed the Navy to apply decisive strategic pressure, both in peace and in war. Battle remained important, but only insofar as it advanced a higher strategic end.

This makes a great deal of sense to me, not least because it makes Mahan resonate much more closely with what I wrote in my 2017 book *Sea Power: The History and Geopolitics of the World's Oceans.* In surveying the strategic environment confronting our Navy five years ago, I was struck over and over by the old British expression that "The Sea is One." On ships and through undersea cables, goods and information are flowing constantly over and under the world's waters, which makes them the Navy's business. These transoceanic flows still vastly exceed the volumes that travel by air or land. Mahan understood, as all sailors instinctively do, that the sea is its own domain and paramount. We live on a blue planet covered by water over 70 percent of its surface, not a green one.

Expanding the concept of sea power beyond combat and wartime to include economics and peacetime offers a valuable framework for thinking about the challenges that confront our Navy today. When I was a young officer, the world was very different. For one thing, our rival was the Soviet Union, which for all its bristling exoskeleton was not a peer competitor in the way China is today. For another thing, the global economy did not seem terribly important—and why should it have? International trade levels were nothing like what they are now, nor was the Soviet Union anywhere near as dependent on the global economy as China is. Our Navy's ability to inflict economic pressure on an enemy was negligible. It then made sense to think of sea power almost exclusively in terms of combat.

No longer. Of course, the ability to fight remains critically important. But we must not lose sight of the fact that strategic opportunity and vulnerability now may come in other guises. If the recent past of supply-chain disruptions and inflation has taught us anything, it has been that the international trading system in our era of globalization is fragile and vulnerable to disruption, whether inadvertently, as in the case of the COVID-19 pandemic, or deliberately, as in the case of Russia's blockade of Ukrainian wheat.

Indeed, I am no fan of Mr. Putin, on whose sanctions list I am proud to appear, but I am grateful that he has offered the world an important reminder of the influence of sea power. Mahan would have found our recent past unsurprising, since his study of history convinced him of the same thing that the headlines make so clear today: the ability to regulate access to the global trading system was both a sword of tremendous potency and a vital shield, which is the essence of sea power. A maritime nation like ours, which depends on access to the global trading system for our economic security, our place in the world, and indeed our very way of life, forgets this lesson at its peril.

We are fortunate to have this new book to remind us of this lesson, and equally fortunate to have the Naval Institute Press (NIP) publish it. The U.S. Naval Institute was founded in 1873, an outgrowth of the same post–Civil War intellectual ferment and reform movement from which Mahan himself emerged. The Institute's press, established in 1898, was one of the first university presses in the United States. For more than a century, the Naval Institute has been at the forefront of building bridges between the study of history and the analysis of contemporary policy problems. At a time of renewed intellectual ferment within the Navy over its future direction, it is therefore altogether appropriate that this attempt to resurrect Mahan's arguments for a new era is published by NIP.

Finally, I look at Dr. Lambert's brilliant new book as a jumping-off point for scholars and mariners alike to expand the idea of Mahan's strategy for this volatile twenty-first century. In addition to bringing geoeconomic issues to the fore in our strategic planning, we need to meld new concepts of cybersecurity, integration of space assets, and underwater and surface maritime unmanned vehicles into maritime technology. The environmental issues that increasingly damage the oceans—pollution, unregulated and illegal overfishing, global warming, melting ice, plastics, and all the rest—must be addressed. The challenges are manifest, and it will take all of us thinking together to craft a strategy worthy of Mahan for this century. *The Neptune Factor* is a superb beginning to that voyage. Let's get underway.

—JS
Vice Chairman, Global Affairs, Carlyle Group
Chair, Board of Trustees, the Rockefeller Foundation
Supreme Allied Commander, NATO, 2009–13
Dean, the Fletcher School of Law and Diplomacy,
Tufts University, 2013–18

Preface

A Prophet's Rise and Fall

*To our fathers, Alfred Thayer Mahan was a name to conjure with.
The world's foremost authority on all matters of naval warfare
and strategy, as well as one of the most brilliant and influential
interpreters of contemporary developments, he was the writer in
whose words that age found perhaps the clearest conscious expression
of its aspirations, its problems, its ideologies. Today, less than a
generation since his death, that influence has practically disappeared,
and his name has become little more than a dim historical
reminiscence. . . . His memory is still invoked on all solemn occasions
and his teachings continue to be considered the foundation of official
doctrine. But that invocation has long since become an empty ritual.*

—HERBERT ROSINSKI, 1941[1]

CAPT. ALFRED THAYER MAHAN remains one of the most important thinkers on geostrategy and international politics that the United States has produced. His signature contribution was the concept of sea power. He is widely supposed to have defined sea power in strictly naval and combat terms: the importance of attaining command of the sea through decisive battle against the enemy fleet. As indicated by the epigraph, although he was highly regarded in his own day and acclaimed as the apostle of naval power, within the space of a single generation his reputation for sagacity had evaporated. Well before the end of the twentieth century, his standing had so deteriorated that he became derided as a simplistic thinker and his conceptions dismissed as mostly irrelevant.

This book immodestly argues that the conventional wisdom about Mahan's beliefs is not only wrong, but that neglect of its finest thinker has had a deleterious effect on the U.S. Navy, whose persistent misreading of Mahan has handicapped its own strategic thinking to the present time. For decades, Mahan and his concept of sea power have been misunderstood by naval writers, and this misunderstanding has contributed materially to the impoverishment of thinking about naval policy in the United States. In effect, the Navy has projected its own crude conception of what navies are for onto Mahan, whose ideas were far more sophisticated than most then or since. Yet if we actually read all his words, his usefulness to current strategists might equal and perhaps even surpass the eminence that Professor Rosinski saw as long gone, even before the apogee of the Navy during World War II. That is to say, the recovery of what Mahan really thought and argued has the potential to improve U.S. naval policy formulation in the present, offering the prospect of enhancing the role of sea power in support of peace and world security in a new era.

It will be helpful to explain up front the main argument of this book. Far from defining sea power in terms of combat, Mahan defined it in terms of economics. Indeed, his worldview—his understanding of how the world worked and conception of general causation—was profoundly economics-centric. He wrote from a national strategic rather than a naval operational perspective. Proceeding from the conviction that historically, international trade carried across the world's oceans was the single greatest driver of national wealth (and thus power), Mahan defined sea power essentially as the ability to regulate access to and influence the flows of transoceanic trade. A nation possessing sea power could not only ensure access to international trade for itself and its allies but might also endeavor to deny such access to its enemies and competitors as well. Mahan distinguished himself by not merely gesturing at or paying lip service to the connections between sea power and economics. He went to the trouble of studying the day-to-day conduct of international trade in sufficient detail to draw the mechanism of coercion by which action at sea could generate significant pressure against adversaries. What is more, thus defined in terms of economics rather than combat, sea power for Mahan operated as strongly, if not more strongly, in times of peace than it did in times of war. Much as Clausewitz regarded war (on land) as the continuation of politics by other means, Mahan regarded sea power as the continuation of economics by other means.

Fundamentally, for Mahan, the sea was a separate and equal domain to the land, not an extension of it. Unlike theorists of land power and amphibious operations, Mahan viewed the sea not as the zone that armies must cross to get to the land, where the really decisive action was, but as the zone where nations might most readily generate sufficient pressure on an enemy to force him to sue for peace. Mahan further came to believe that the nature of the mechanism by which this pressure was generated against and felt by an enemy depended on the relationship between national economies and international trade. As the character and structure of the international trading system altered, moreover, the precise pressure points shifted. A pioneering student of what is now referred to as the first era of globalization, lasting from the late nineteenth century until World War I, Mahan also identified the growing dependence of national economies on uninterrupted access to an interconnected global trading system built on the invisible scaffolding of sea power. This growing dependence, he thought, increased rather than decreased the potency of sea power.

Notably, Julian Corbett, the other most prominent naval thinker of the day, thought the exact opposite. Blind to the contemporaneous process of globalization that so intrigued Mahan, and uninterested in the day-to-day conduct of international trade in earlier eras (or his own), Corbett viewed actions at sea as subsidiary to events on land, and that sea power was becoming less potent at the turn of the century. In his words, "Since men live upon the land and not upon the

sea, great issues between nations at war have always been decided—
except in the rarest cases—either by what your army can do against
your enemy's territory and national life or else by the fear of what the
fleet makes it possible for your army to do."[2] In these respects, Corbett's thinking on navies paralleled not Mahan's but that of Halford
Mackinder, the primary theorist of land power at the turn of the century, whose interest lay in the geopolitical effects of industrialization
as distinct from the forces of globalization.

To better understand the relationship between navies and international economics is not the only reason why Mahan's ideas remain—
or rather have once again become—so important. For one thing, he
wrote in, and of, a multipolar world, when the reigning hegemon (the
British Empire) faced new challengers, and confusion and uncertainty
reigned as the result of rapid social and technological change. For
another, he abhorred the sense of entitlement to public resources,
often found among senior naval officers, understanding that the U.S.
Navy must justify its existence and funding against competing domestic priorities. In other words, he did not take the support of the American people for granted. Going far beyond naval matters, he carefully
studied the domestic issues, largely economic in character, which
dominated the American politics in his day. At a time of profound
social upheaval and greater government spending on welfare, Mahan
believed that the Navy owed the American people a compelling explanation for its imposition on finite public funds. He devoted his life to
this mission. His extensive, deeply informed, and highly sophisticated
body of work on sea power constituted his attempt to supply such an
explanation. Both his goal and his message are as relevant today as
they were then.

To be clear, this book is not a call for the Navy to abandon its
organizational focus on combat. On the contrary, it is crucial that the
Navy maintain its ability to fight and defeat enemy warships. Rather, it
is a call to rebalance by adding a new focus on the Navy's role within
the global economy. The Navy needs to broaden its perspective without abandoning its old one. If this seems paradoxical, that is because
it is. Yet such paradoxes will be familiar to any reader of Clausewitz,

who perceived that both combat and politics were central to war while at the same time being in tension with each other. Mahan understood that combat, the realm of the military spirit, must remain at the heart of what navies did. At the same time, he saw that commerce and politics, the realms of the civilian spirit, must also remain at the heart of what navies did. He was fond of recalling that "a saying has been attributed by Thiers to the great Napoleon that the difficulty of the art of war consists in concentrating in order to fight, and disseminating in order to subsist. There is no other, he [Napoleon] said, aphoristically. The problem is one of embracing opposites."[3] Antinomies lay at the heart of Mahan's concept of sea power, and, in his mind, were intrinsic to strategic problem solving.

This book is divided into three parts. Part I acts as the foundation for the second and third parts, and the pace of argument is slow but steady. Readers will be reminded of much they already know but at the same time will be introduced to new material showing that many conventional interpretations cannot be right. After the introduction, chapter 1 focuses on the history of the U.S. Navy during the 1880s. It argues that naval reform proceeded much more slowly than generally thought, and that at the close of this decade there remained no consensus as to the best path forward. Chapter 2 explores the relationship between Captain Mahan and the famous Rear Adm. Stephen B. Luce. It demonstrates that their ideas diverged far more than previously appreciated, and consequently it is important to differentiate between the two. It also reveals that, in the early days, Luce pressured Mahan (his subordinate) to tell the story that he wanted told. The result was an unhappy compromise. Chapter 3 offers a dissection of Mahan's first monograph, *The Influence of Sea Power upon History, 1660–1783*, demonstrating the many tensions and contradictions within. Basically, it was a hot mess, reflecting a combination of Mahan's own ideas and ambitions for the book, Luce's influence, and various publishing imperatives; as a result, its message was more ambivalent, for better or worse, than caricatures of the text suggest.

In part II, the narrative pace accelerates. Chapter 4 looks at the development of the U.S. Navy during the early 1890s, when Benjamin Harrison was president and Benjamin Tracy his Secretary of the Navy, in order to correct several misconceptions of U.S. naval history that have warped understandings of Mahan. Chapter 5 explains the significance of Mahan's second book on sea power, discussing the wars of French Revolution and Empire. It shows the ways in which his understanding of sea power was already beginning to change and economics becoming steadily more important in his conceptualization. Chapter 6 shows how Mahan's interest in economics deepened after the financial Panic of 1893, which brought in its train one of the deepest depressions in U.S. history. At the same time, he developed an appreciation of the changes in the world around him, and increasingly saw that these changes had implications for the future application of sea power. Chapter 7 documents Mahan's service during the Spanish-American War, including his active participation in high-level strategic decision making and the lessons he drew from his practical experiences.

Part III consists of three chapters plus what might be termed an afterword. Chapter 8 lays out Mahan's revised (version 2.0) concept of sea power as well as his views on the importance in war of systematic commerce interdiction. Chapter 9 charts Mahan's efforts to persuade the Theodore Roosevelt administration to change the position of the U.S. government respecting the rights of belligerents to capture private property at sea and reveals not only that his exhortations had an impact and changed minds but also came far closer to ultimate success than even he realized. Chapter 10 briefly details the collapse of Mahan's health and his struggle to regain the world stage and explains how his efforts to do so considerably tarnished his reputation. Chapter 11 is premised on the conviction that in order to understand what Mahan said, it is helpful to understand fully why and how the conventional wisdom about him got to be so wrong in the first place and why the misinterpretations have endured.

   The book closes with a short essay arguing that Mahan's concept
of sea power, by explaining the importance of understanding the structure of the global trading system, is more relevant today than ever.
To underscore this point, it also includes a comparative analysis of
Mahan's concept of sea power versus Samuel P. Huntington's famous
1954 essay on transoceanic navies. Huntington's ideas, brilliant and
appropriate during the Cold War, were premised on the existence of
an international economic and geopolitical order that no longer exists
and yet still, almost invisibly, shapes U.S. naval policy today. The wheel
of history has turned back to Mahan; perhaps the Navy should turn
with it.

ACKNOWLEDGMENTS

MY INTEREST IN Alfred Thayer Mahan, and the conviction that his writings have been misunderstood, owes much to conversations during the 1990s with two renowned Mahan scholars, the late Donald M. Schurman (1924–2013) and Jon T. Sumida. I began this book in 2011 and was grateful for the opportunity to present some of my early thoughts to a conference held at the U.S. Naval War College (USNWC) in March 2014. Shortly after, I set aside my Mahan studies in order to complete another project. In 2016, during a two-year stint at the U.S. Naval Academy as the "Class of 1957 Chair in Naval Heritage," my interest in Mahan was rekindled thanks in no small part to Capt. Dr. Scott Mobley, USN (Ret.), my Class of 1957 colleague. Scott not only shared my enthusiasm for the subject (the essential ingredient in writing a book) and knew the sources (making for an informed critic) but acted as a sounding board for many of the ideas advanced in this book. So did (albeit unwittingly) several of my former midshipmen; for their enthusiasm and willingness to entertain new ideas, I especially thank Lts. (USN) Sam Siprelle, Ben Blakeslee, and Thomas Wolfe, and Capt. (USMC) Matthew Suarez.

For scrutinizing draft chapters and making valuable criticisms and suggestions, I thank Adm. James Foggo, USN (Ret.), as well as Steve Deal, Katherine Epstein, Kevin Farrell, Lloyd Gardner, Cameron Hazlehurst, Andrew May, Scott Mobley, Jon Sumida, and Bruce Taylor. It was Jon Sumida who came up with the title for this book. For helping track down articles from the periodical literature, I am grateful to Sam Biddle, another former student. Particular thanks are owed to C. Lee Walker (Class of 1957) for identifying structural errors in my original introductory chapter and convincing me to start afresh. Evidently submariners make for excellent book editors.

All Mahan scholars are indebted to Doris D. Maguire and Robert Seager II for their painstakingly edited three volumes of Mahan's papers and correspondence, though it is curious that their work did not include an editorial essay. For permission to quote from these volumes I thank the board of directors of the U.S. Naval Institute. Equally invaluable is John B. and Lynn C. Hattendorf's *A Bibliography of the Works of Alfred Thayer Mahan* (Naval War College Press, 1987). Bruce Taylor not only helped me think through the events of the Spanish-American War, but also allowed me to see the manuscript of his soon-to-be-published translation of Agustín Ramón Rodríguez González's *The Spanish-American War of 1898: The Spanish Perspective*, a work that will compel the English-speaking world to rethink what it knows about this conflict.

In the course of my research, I received much help from archivists. Especially deserving of mention are Bruce Kirby of the Library of Congress Manuscripts Division, Mike Macan of the Nimitz Library at the U.S. Naval Academy, and Elizabeth Delmarge at the USNWC. For making the publication process swift, painless, and surprisingly fun, I am grateful to Adam Kane, the director of the Naval Institute Press, and to Brennan Knight, the production editor. For the second time, John Donohue did a wonderful editing job, rescuing my thoughts from my words. Most of all, I should like to express my thanks to and admiration for Vice Adm. Pete Daly, USN (Ret.), the CEO of the Naval Institute; he persuaded me that the Naval Institute Press was the natural home for this book.

As ever, none of the above is responsible for what follows, and any errors of fact or interpretation are my own.

INTRODUCTION
The Origins of Sea Power

*The only word I can be said to have coined is sea power, which is rather
a phrase than a word. It was born of my preference for the English
"sea" over the Latin adjective "maritime," although I recognized the
incongruity of marrying "sea" to a Latin word, "power." There was,
however, no handy equivalent, and I have heard the Germans have
been puzzled to find one in their tongue. Afterward, I stuck to the
expression, because I thought its very roughness—over "maritime
power"—would arrest and fix attention and so give vogue,
at which I aimed. The result has justified the expedient.*

—ALFRED THAYER MAHAN, AUGUST 25, 1901[1]

IN MAY 1890, Alfred Thayer Mahan, a captain in the U.S. Navy,
leaped in one bound from obscurity to center stage in world affairs.
In his first major monograph, *The Influence of Sea Power upon History,
1660–1783*, he introduced his concept of "sea power" into the lexicon
of foreign policy elites around the globe. Based on a close reading of
naval history and consideration of the relationship of that history to
larger political and economic issues, he argued that in order to comprehend the shape of the modern world, it was necessary to understand the hitherto ignored history of events on the sea—the Neptune
Factor. In his own words: "Control of the sea was an historic factor

which had never been systematically appreciated and expounded."[2] At the same time, Mahan insisted that the sea must be understood as a domain separate from the land and not a mere subsidiary thereof. He further maintained that national action on the sea had in the past, and *could again*, decisively affect events on land.

What Mahan argued subsequently is less well known, if not generally unknown. A couple of years later, he followed up *Influence*, as we shall henceforth refer to his first and most famous monograph, with a pair of volumes taking the story of sea power forward to the year 1812. These simultaneously buttressed his reputation as an authoritative historian and a prophet of the future course of great-power relations. Actually, these two volumes may well have had a greater impact than his first book, though they have received far less attention from historians. Not only were they were more fluently written and told an intrinsically more interesting story, but they were read more widely and by important people. At home, during congressional debates, senators and congressmen began holding aloft blue-penciled copies of Mahan and to hail his wisdom and insight. Abroad, kings, admirals, and emperors sought his company; Queen Victoria invited him to tea. Universities around the world showered him with honorary degrees.

After forty years of service and within months of an automatic step to the rank of commodore, Mahan announced his retirement from the U.S. Navy in November 1896. Already a celebrated historian and much sought after by the editors of newspapers and periodicals as a pundit, Mahan looked forward to supplementing his modest naval pension by writing more serious books and paid commentary on a range of geopolitical subjects of general interest. Writing then was considerably more lucrative than it is today, and afforded newspaper by-liners the kind of incomes that helped build lives and homes. In May 1898, however, the Spanish-American War interrupted his literary ambitions. Mahan was recalled to duty and appointed a member of the Navy's strategy board, in which capacity he participated actively in meetings of President William McKinley's "war council." During his brief stint in Washington, moreover, his duties within the Navy Department extended a good deal further than generally realized.

After the close of hostilities, Mahan returned to his writing possessing even greater stature than before, his horizons broadened and his mind stocked with fresh insights from his experience.

At the turn of the twentieth century, Mahan was at the height of his powers. For the next several years his output was prodigious. In addition to honing his concept of sea power and applying it in his second career as a commentator on geopolitical affairs, he embarked on a quixotic crusade aimed at changing U.S. government policy on a vital point of international maritime law: he opposed the "American" principle of Freedom of the Seas. Belying his reputation as a theorist fixated on battle and dismissive of attacking enemy commerce in time of war, explaining the importance of the belligerent's right to seize private property at sea quickly became the primary focus of his writings. With the assistance of his friends, including Arthur Twining Hadley (professor of economics at Yale) and John Bassett Moore (professor of international law at Columbia)—*the* leading American scholars of the day in their respective fields—Mahan polished his arguments.[3] From 1904, he tried to persuade President Theodore Roosevelt and his administration that the ability to interdict international trade in wartime—not the ability to win a decisive battle against the enemy battle fleet—was the principal mechanism of coercion against an enemy, and that possession of this capability would be of immense value to the United States in the future. Far from looking on him as a midnight scribbler, leading policy makers took his opinions very seriously.

Midway through his campaign, however, Mahan's health collapsed. In the spring of 1907, aged sixty-six, he suffered what today would be classified as a minor stroke, prompting him to remove himself and his family from New York City to the quiet seaside town of Quogue at the far extremity of Long Island.[4] That same year, in the fall, he was diagnosed with prostate cancer and underwent a series of operations. From these he never fully recovered. His mind slowed, his energy faded, and his writing thereafter lacked sparkle; he increasingly recycled old arguments with few revisions. In 1911, against his better judgment but in need of money, Mahan published *Naval Strategy*, probably his second most popular book but by his own admission the worst he ever produced, little more than a rehash of his oldest lecture notes penned twenty-five years earlier.[5] In other words, far from representing the final expression of his concept of sea power, the ideas and approach in his last book predated those found in even his earliest published work.[6] The beginning of World War I in August 1914 sparked a brief revival in Mahan's energy and fortunes, until quelched a week later by an executive order issued by President Woodrow Wilson that gagged him from commenting on the conflict. Shortly afterward, Mahan suffered a heart attack. Though he recovered sufficiently to return to work, he died three months later on December 1, 1914.

So what were Mahan's arguments about sea power, and just how did they develop over time? Contrary to popular opinion, *Influence* was not primarily concerned with the employment of naval forces in wartime; rather it explained the symbiotic relationship between trade, wealth, and power. State power, he held, was chiefly a function of national wealth and the sustained generation of new wealth through commerce; historically, the single most valuable font of commercially produced wealth was overseas trade. This, he always maintained, was because "both travel and traffic by water have always been easier and cheaper than by land."[7] Following this logic, he reasoned that access to the sea (the "common") was essential to national well-being, hence the need for a strong navy to guarantee access. Mahan further held that sea power worked continuously, not only in war but also in peace, because commerce and wealth generation (economic activity) was a continuous process. Thus *Influence* was less a tract about naval warfare than one about the importance of state coordination of national resources to achieve relative advantage in the maritime domain. In identifying the interrelationships between trade, wealth, and power—fundamentally economic propositions—Mahan was the first to articulate a coherent explanation for why a nation should invest in a navy.

Mahan's thesis gained traction as quickly as it did because his audience was not only prepared for his ideas but as yet undecided about the issues on which he wrote. During the 1880s, there had been a proliferation of debate on naval power that had prepared the potential audience, but thus far no one had managed to pull the many threads together. In the opinon of Jon Sumida, when writing *Influence* Mahan "for the most part had simply restated thoughts that had been put forward by others. That there had been much previous independent musing upon the sources and significance of naval power, however, meant that Mahan's first major book fell upon a reading public well primed to accept a coherent presentation of certain large issues."[8] This is true. Yet, in addition, *Influence* was published at a moment (in May 1890) when the question of increased naval spending comprised one of the major political issues of the day, and not just in the United States. There was considerable controversy over the purpose and character of the fleet, as well as over the amount of funds that would be needed, with ramifications not just for U.S. foreign policy but also—as is too often forgotten—for the federal budget and thus for domestic politics. In consequence, the debate over the future of the U.S. Navy was both politicized and protracted.

Naval reform remained a contentious issue throughout the 1890s because it occurred during a period of economic depression and social upheaval that bred competing demands on the federal purse. Some interests wanted the federal government to invest in national infrastructure (or the Panama Canal) instead. Others demanded more generous pensions (especially for Union Civil War veterans). A large number ("Populists") thought the money would be better spent fixing social problems at home, a down payment on a redistribution of wealth necessary to create a more equitable American society. Mahan followed these debates closely, understanding that his case for a larger naval funding necessarily had implications for the ability to pursue other public priorities with substantial political support. Accordingly, to comprehend Mahan's ideas, it is necessary to study the broader political, social, and economic issues that informed them.

While it is difficult to calculate *Influence*'s precise effect on public discourse in the United States, it is clear that Mahan intended his book to be an intervention. As chapter 1 shows, contrary to the view that Mahan merely put an exclamation point on a debate already settled, the debate was in fact ongoing, and *Influence* was not only central to that debate but helped to irreversibly shape it. Mahan's ideas had an effect because he successfully connected narrowly naval issues to politically important questions of more general public concern. Put more simply, his ideas resonated with a broad audience from across the political spectrum. The timing of his publication helped political and even business leaders make sense of, and coincided with, the changes unfolding around them—America's industrial progress, growing technological accomplishments, surging agricultural production and exports—and much else.

The elasticity of Mahan's concept of sea power as initially conceived aided his popularity. Though as more than one later detractor has complained, at no point did Mahan offer a sustained and coherent exposition of his theory of sea power or precise definitions of important terms such as command of the sea, such criticisms miss the point.[9] Mahan realized that the complexity of his subject militated against the sort of theoretical simplicity demanded by his critics. Moreover, the lack of precision in *Influence* redounded to Mahan's credit. It was precisely because his argument was so malleable that so many nonexperts (his target audience) embraced his concept. Commentators from across the political spectrum were able to claim that Mahan's conclusions vindicated their own proposals. In addition, Mahan's lack of clarity enabled him to make adjustments to his concept of sea power without inviting too much criticism of his lack of consistency. As we shall see, these adjustments, especially those made after he had witnessed the formulation and execution of policy firsthand in 1898 and digested the implications of what he had observed, were more numerous and extensive than has been realized.

In parallel with his historical work, in retirement Mahan enjoyed significant success as a pundit on contemporary foreign and geopolitical affairs. In the foreword to a compilation of articles on the

Spanish-American War published a year after the event, he openly declared that his mission was to educate the American public on the importance of sea power and to identify the forces shaping U.S. security policy more generally. "The study of the Art and History of War is pre-eminently necessary to men of the profession, but there are reasons which commend it also, suitably presented, to all citizens of our country. Questions connected with war—when resort to war is justifiable, preparation for war, the conduct of war—are questions of national moment, in which each voter—nay, each talker—has an influence for intelligent and adequate action, by the formation of sound public opinion; and public opinion, in operation, constitutes national policy."[10]

This striking formulation—"public opinion, in operation, constitutes national policy"—concisely expressed Mahan's understanding of its relationship to the Navy. He wanted his countrymen to understand better that the United States inhabited a dangerous world likely to become a good deal more dangerous, and that events outside the continental United States impinged on the nation's general economic security, as well as its long-term prosperity. Through education, Mahan hoped the electorate would more readily accept the necessity for a stronger and thus more expensive navy. He aimed to show citizens how *their* navy was essential to protecting *their* essential interests— *their* way of life. More than most naval officers of any generation, Mahan grasped the paramount necessity for naval policy to command not just public assent but also understanding in order to obtain the requisite levels of funding.

Because he so aggressively lobbied for a large increase in the current naval establishment, sometimes as asides within the pages of historical monographs, Mahan is often remembered today as a dyed-in-the-wool "navalist."[11] If meant descriptively—as one who advocates for the navy—then the term is accurate. Frequently, however, the term is employed pejoratively, often with a connotation of jingoism or extreme nationalism, and this is a mistake. Mahan did not advocate for a larger fleet simply to enhance the status of his institution or out of chest-thumping militarism, as the negative use implies; he instead argued that a properly established navy was not only a vital instrument of national statecraft but that it needed to be widely understood as such. "I think it a mistake to suppose that Mahan is a merely *naval* historian in any narrow or technical sense," thought Arthur James Balfour, the British prime minister, writing in 1902. "He is in truth *a historian of the British Empire from a military point of view*."[12] Equally powerful testimony for Mahan's broader perspective and intent comes from Theodore Roosevelt, who of course knew him very well. Shortly after Mahan's death, the former president recalled that "Mahan was the only great naval writer who also possessed in international matters the mind of a statesman of the first class. His interest was in the larger side of his subjects: he was more concerned with the strategy than with the tactics of both naval war and statesmanship."[13]

In alerting his fellow Americans to the perils that threatened the United States from without, and thus to the necessity of considering the position of the United States in the wider world, Mahan faced an uphill battle. In the words of George Baer, one of the leading historians of the U.S. Navy, "in 1900, few Americans thought that the United States was a maritime nation dependent for its security and its prosperity on control of its sea approaches."[14] Many questioned the connection between the nation's security and its prosperity; what did either (especially the latter), they asked, have to do with the sea? Was not by now the United States too large and too populous to invade, and anyway self-sufficient? By virtue of its strength, size, and distance from Europe, did not the United States effectively enjoy what the historian C. Vann Woodward famously termed "free security"?[15]

Mahan acknowledged the partial truth of such popular presumptions, but he also pointed to their limits. He warned in his writings that foreign powers over the sea could still hurt the United States and that the young American goliath was not invulnerable. It seemed to him that the nation was, in the words of his Boston-Brahmin friend Brooks Adams, grandson of John Quincy Adams, "opulent, aggressive and unarmed."[16] In order to be able to articulate precisely the form and nature of the danger, Mahan looked ever more closely at international economics, seeking to understand the strategic implications of the recent (post-1870) transformation in the global economic system. Mahan, in other words, deliberated on the strategic implications of what has since become known as globalization, defined by the growing interdependence of markets and interconnections between market and financial systems and reflected in the convergence of prices in hitherto different markets across the globe.[17]

The rising assertiveness of U.S. statesmen in matters of foreign affairs heightened Mahan's concern over what he perceived as widespread ignorance (in Congress and within the public at large) over defense issues. While he wholeheartedly approved of the broad thrust of America's new "imperial" policy, regarding it as essential for the nation's future economic security and thus its social stability, he worried that the nation's leaders, spurred on by the public, were moving too quickly and without adequate prior preparation. It troubled him whenever members of the executive or the legislature advocated taking an aggressive stance on the world stage, blind to the fact that the United States lacked the military wherewithal to maintain or enforce its position if its bluff were called and push came to shove. It alarmed him still more that so many American leaders complacently misjudged the republic's power relative to other empires, being too enthralled by its obvious strengths yet at the same time blind to its many weaknesses. In the words of the historian William A. Williams, a true expert on this period, there existed at that time an "assumption of overweening American Power."[18] Few American politicians really understood the international economic system (or accepted that the United States was slave to global market forces) or were skillful players in the game of international power politics.

Mahan despaired, with reason, that the nuance and qualification of his arguments were passing over the heads of his readers and that consequently his lessons were being misunderstood. In 1900, he toyed with the idea of rewriting his existing volumes on sea power to make his arguments more explicit. But on reflection, he found the thought of revisiting old ground unappealing. Instead he ventured into a parallel historical pasture to try and get his message across. *Sea Power in Its Relations to the War of 1812*, published at the end of 1905, was unquestionably Mahan's finest book. It was based on levels of archival research that far surpassed his earlier work and exceeded those of most contemporaneous historians. His research into the economic history of the early United States was pioneering and continued to be regarded as definitive by experts in the subject for decades. The arguments contained in this volume were far more sophisticated and subtle than anything else he wrote before or after. Thus *War of 1812* represents Mahan's mature thought on the meaning of sea power far better than does *Influence*, yet it is hardly read while the latter has received disproportionate attention from historians.

STUDYING MAHAN

In most books, and not just books on naval history, Mahan is presented as a theorist of naval power who preached a crude gospel about the paramount importance of battle, battleships, and battle fleets. Too often his concept of sea power is reduced to, or rather conflated with, his advocacy for securing command of the sea. Parts of his argument are mistaken for the whole, and his ideas are critiqued before they are understood. Confirmation bias and the rush to judge thus have fed each other in a vicious loop.

This begs a series of questions. Why is Mahan not remembered as the deep and erudite thinker he really was? More precisely, why have so few readers seemed to notice that, from the start, Mahan's concept of sea power was fundamentally about political economy, both domestic and international, and not about the application of naval power per se? Another of the constant themes throughout all of Mahan's writing was the necessity to relate naval affairs to larger political and economic issues. So why is it that most of those who write about Mahan invariably shear his arguments of their political and economic contexts? Most importantly, why has it escaped attention that, over time, Mahan attached less and less weight to the military (combat) dimensions of sea power in favor of commercial and economic factors?

For many of these questions there is an obvious answer. Truth be told, few modern readers have either the patience or the time to revisit Mahan's work in the original. As the historian James Field once pointedly remarked to an audience of naval officers, "Having attained the status of prophet, Mahan is more praised and quoted than read."[19] Anyone who has ever tried knows why: his books are tough to read. His overly qualified sentences, strung together in endless paragraphs, punctuated with frequent asides and apparent contradictions, make for turgid prose and thus impose a heavy demand on his students. Perhaps Mahan took too seriously the prophet's charge to be mystical and inscrutable. At the same time, examining the entire corpus of Mahan's work is a daunting undertaking. As the naval historian Geoffrey Till quipped, "Mahan sometimes suffers from having written more than most people are prepared to read."[20] To the extent that anyone today reads Mahan, moreover, they typically focus on his earliest writings. But of course this is a mistake. Stopping the clock on Mahan's output at *Influence* is akin to stopping the clock on Shakespeare's output at *The Taming of the Shrew*: it presents a wholly incomplete picture of a complex and protracted body of work. Moreover, unsurprisingly for a powerful intellect wrestling with a difficult subject, Mahan's ideas developed and changed over time. One cannot treat his scholarship as a singular or monolithic body of thought.

Yet those with the fortitude to attempt following in Mahan's footsteps will face multiple pitfalls. The first difficulty in reading Mahan is not the time it takes to read all of what he wrote but the passage of time itself, the gulf that separates our time from his. Mahan wrote not for posterity but for a well-educated contemporary audience. He could write in a sort of shorthand for his readers, who, reading the same things he read, recognized his references and allusions to the leading political issues of their day and, no less importantly, to the opinions of other commentators writing on the same subject (often in the same journals). To read every word that Mahan ever wrote, in other words, is to scale only half the mountain. To reach the summit of understanding, not only must one know a great deal of the history of the era in which he lived, but one must also read what Mahan read. It is necessary to begin at the beginning and not, as it were, at the end.

This is not all. Mahan's lax terminological habits further contributed to misreading of his ideas. As one scholar has well explained,

"Words convey concepts: if they are not defined, the thinking about them cannot be clear, and there is also the danger that one man's (or woman's) military strategy is another's policy, just as one man's naval strategy is another's maritime strategy. Such ambiguity creates confusion."[21] Mahan was unquestionably guilty of failing to define all of his terms. That said, there were mitigating circumstances. As will be shown in chapter 2 and again in chapter 3, he was grappling with a raft of new (and highly complex) subjects, and quite often the appropriate word had not yet been invented or did not exist in the contemporary lexicon—for instance, "Grand Strategy" or "Globalization." Sometimes he knowingly employed an old though inappropriate word, and sometimes he invented a new one. Perhaps the most famous term he ever coined was "the Middle East."

To give a more specific example, the words "strategy," "strategic," and "strategical" appear in *Influence* more than one hundred times, without clear definition or distinction. When he wrote the book, it is important to understand, the root word "strategy" was not a naval term but was borrowed from the military; further, it did not become commonplace in the sea service until the late 1890s. As will be demonstrated in the next chapter, when employing the word "strategy" Mahan was conscious that it did not quite fit. He employed it in connection with decision making both at the intersection of policy (the domain of politicians) and operations (the domain of admirals), and also at the intersection of operations and tactics.[22] In so doing, he expected his readers to infer his precise meaning from the surrounding context. Only in his later work, from around 1897, did he narrow his use of the term, coming to argue that for an action or thought to be termed strategic it must be clearly linked to some national policy, while at the same time he broadened his definition of what constituted national policy.[23]

If this is not complicated enough, Mahan created further interpretive difficulties for his readers by frequently employing metaphors, as was common with many nineteenth-century thinkers trying to make sense of the changing world around them. When tackling particularly complex subjects, he had a fondness for employing the language of evolutionary biology. Metaphors, however, can be tricky things; what may seem an obvious allusion in one place and time may not be apparent to a reader in another. More than one of Mahan's biographers have incorrectly interpreted these biological metaphors as references to his strong religious beliefs.[24] However, as other scholars more familiar with the intellectual milieu of the late nineteenth century have shown, it was commonplace to employ evolutionary biology metaphors to explain dynamic and complex systems, such as the structure of the international trading system. Moreover, as Suzanne Geissler has demonstrated, although Mahan was indeed deeply religious, much of his religious writing was highly technical and does not translate easily.[25] Correct interpretation requires both a specialized knowledge of old terminology as well as a detailed sense of the period in which he was writing, because the meanings of words and definitions of concepts can change over time.

For these reasons and others, it is far simpler to read the summaries of Mahan by others—accessing his ideas secondhand, so to speak. Yet in choosing this path the reader is at once confronted with a surfeit of options, which present their own difficulties. In one hundred years, Mahan's career has been the subject of four book-length biographies and more than a half dozen major biographical essays, as well as paragraphs and chapters in articles and books too numerous to count.[26] Opinions on what Mahan argued, or tried to argue, run the gamut, as do assessments of the level of influence he enjoyed with contemporary policy makers. Amid this Babel of opinion, it is difficult to know where to begin or what to trust. That said, as will be shown in chapter 11, it is striking how a relatively small number of studies has had an outsized influence on understandings of Mahan's thoughts. Most remarkably of all, though "sea power" is universally acknowledged to have been Mahan's signature idea, all scholars have struggled to explain what he meant by the term, how it was supposed to work, and how his views on it changed over time. This is the object of the present work and its core thread.

PART I

CHAPTER 1

MAHAN'S WORLD

(1865–84)

I am so heartily disheartened by our history of the past fifteen years that
I have left in me no expectations except to do my duty as I may best;
and trust that the Lord will look out for me. The country cares nothing
for the service nor will care, I think, till irredeemable disaster in that
quarter has over taken it. It will then be too late for that time.

—ALFRED THAYER MAHAN, AUGUST 14, 1883[1]

ALFRED THAYER MAHAN was born on September 27, 1840, at West
Point, New York. He was the eldest son of the famous Dennis Hart
Mahan, professor of military and civil engineering at the U.S. Military
Academy for more than forty years. A strict upbringing, combined
with spending his formative years at the remote academy, inculcated
into Alfred the habit of reading widely. In 1856, against the advice of
his father, who thought him temperamentally unsuited for a military
career, Mahan obtained a nomination to the U.S. Naval Academy
at Annapolis. Because he had already completed a year at Columbia
College, acting midshipman Mahan was allowed to skip his plebe
year. He graduated with nineteen others from the Naval Academy
class of 1859.[2]

Mahan joined the fleet in an era of American naval expansion and
at the twilight of the age of sail. His training in full-rigged ships gave

him an unrivaled practical understanding of their operation, which in his later literary years proved valuable. The beginning of the Civil War, in 1861, found the newly promoted Lieutenant Mahan as executive officer of a sloop that participated in the first important naval action of the conflict, the bombardment and subsequent capture of Port Royal, South Carolina. Over the next four years, he saw much service but little action. In 1862, Mahan was reassigned to teach seamanship at the Naval Academy, which had been relocated for the duration of the war from Annapolis to Newport, Rhode Island. There he served under Stephen B. Luce, a man who would become the lynchpin of his career. The following year, Mahan was posted to the southern squadron responsible for blockading the Texas coast, a notoriously grueling duty station. In July 1864, after a brief taste of command, he was reassigned to the staff of Rear Adm. John Dahlgren commanding the Southern Atlantic Blockading Squadron, which patrolled the Confederate coast from Cape Fear, North Carolina, to the Florida Keys. Though Mahan won no laurels, nor participated in any of the famous naval engagements of the war, he never failed in his duty. As officer who had served alongside him later recalled, "what he did was done well."[3]

Just before the Civil War ended in 1865, Mahan was fortunate to be advanced to the rank of lieutenant commander. This placed him near the front of the pack in the postwar promotion race. As is well known, advancement in the downsized postbellum navy was glacial, with appointments few and far between. Contrary to some historians' depictions of him as a substandard officer, Mahan favorably impressed his superiors. During the Civil War, Lt. Cdr. Luce had asked for Mahan to serve as his executive officer aboard the sloop *Macedonian* for a midshipman training cruise to Europe, the highest form of official approval. After the war, Capt. Robert Shufeldt invited him to join his high-profile expedition to survey the Isthmus of Tehuantepec in Mexico in a quest to find a route for a future canal, an opportunity that he declined.[4] Seen, in fact, as an above-average officer, Mahan survived the congressionally mandated cull of the officer list in 1870. More tangibly still, two years later, after just seven years in grade, he made commander.[5] The resulting bump in pay allowed him to marry.

In 1876, however, Mahan stood on the brink of quitting the service after being placed on involuntary administrative leave in retaliation for his testimony against the Navy Department before a congressional inquiry into corruption at the eight notoriously corrupt and inefficient navy yards. His income dropped by more than half, inducing him to flee the high cost of living in the United States and move his family to France, to join in-laws who were also sheltering abroad.[6] Although Mahan was restored to active duty in the summer of 1877, financial insecurity stemming from family obligations remained a perpetual concern for the rest of his life, influencing his choice of duty stations and (later) even what he wrote. Writing to a friend in 1882, Mahan alluded to his financial difficulties by way of mentioning that he could not afford housing close to the Brooklyn Navy Yard and consequently had to commute an hour each way.[7]

In 1883, Mahan was given command of the *Wachusett,* an elderly wooden-hulled steam sloop with full masts and canvas of just over 1,000 tons displacement. The ship was a veteran of the Civil War and had captured the confederate raider *Florida* off Brazil. When Mahan assumed command in August 1883, she was part of the Pacific Squadron, deployed to protect U.S. lives and property in South America during a period of intense political turmoil. Initially, Mahan was excited by the prospect of command (and doubtless pleased to be earning command pay), but on joining the ship he was dismayed to find her in a poor state of repair as well as short on stores and personnel. The *Wachusett* was an unhappy ship: Mahan's officers greeted him with requests for transfers out, and the men declined to reenlist as their engagements expired. Difficulties in finding replacements compounded his woes. All these troubles generated paperwork, which added to Mahan's already heavy administrative load as the commanding officer of a small warship in distant waters. Thus, when, after just a year in command, Commo. Luce invited him to join the faculty at the soon to be established Naval War College, Mahan leaped at the opportunity.[8] His career at Newport will be the subject of the next chapter.

At first glance, Mahan's letters predating his appointment to the Naval War College show a fairly conventional naval officer. "Although he read widely," one Mahan scholar concluded, "Mahan held the undisciplined opinions, prejudices and reflections of his naval contemporaries."[9] But if his professional opinions were ordinary, the way he viewed and understood the world was unusually broad. This comes across clearly in his correspondence with Samuel Ashe, a former Naval Academy classmate from North Carolina who dropped out before graduating. Until Mahan's death in 1914, the two conducted an extensive correspondence on a wide range of subjects. Historians have long known about this cache of lengthy letters and have mined them assiduously to construct montages of Mahan's thoughts on naval policy and international affairs—the twin pillars, it is conventionally thought, on which he built his concept of sea power. In the process, however, they have disregarded a number of other subjects that Mahan thought worthy of writing about. In his letters to Ashe, Mahan devoted as much space to domestic political issues as he did to discussing international affairs or naval policy, an interest that has gone previously unremarked.

Domestic politics mattered a great deal to Mahan; he marked time by elections. "So long a time has elapsed since we exchanged letters that I have almost forgotten whether it was before or after the nomination of the Presidential candidates," he apologized in one letter to Ashe.[10] And again, thirteen months later: "It has been my purpose to write to you for some time back, but first I put it off till after the election, and since then I have been prevented by one thing or another."[11] To discount or discard this strand of Mahan's thought is a mistake. Not only was it part and parcel of how he viewed the world and how it worked, but close reading of his letters reveals that he saw domestic political issues as inextricably intertwined with questions of foreign policy and the formulation of naval policy. Still more significantly, Mahan's interest in domestic politics fed and drove his growing appreciation for the study of economics. It is not difficult to see why: most of the leading political issues of his day—the tariff, monetary reform, pensions for veterans, and the building of an Isthmian Canal between the Atlantic and the Pacific through either Nicaragua or Panama—were all primarily economic in nature.

Mahan's appreciation of economic factors appears to date from his spell of involuntary leave for his whistleblowing over corruption in the Boston Navy Yard.[12] (One might add that this experience provided him with an object lesson in the importance of closely tracking domestic politics, and of their interconnectedness with naval policy.) During his nine-month sojourn in France, Mahan seems to have learned much from his father-in-law, a businessman, about commercial and financial matters. Directly afterward, in 1878, he wrote a remarkably intricate discourse on the meaning of money and the implications of the Bland-Allison Silver Act.[13] This piece of legislation, which obliged the Treasury Department to purchase silver and put it into circulation in the form of silver dollars, advanced farmers' campaign to get the United States off the gold standard.[14]

Mahan's perception of the interconnectedness between naval policy, international affairs, and domestic politics is most easily seen in his various writings on the importance of building an Isthmian Canal. This was a subject that captivated Mahan for more than thirty years, and he wrote extensively on its geopolitical significance until the canal's eventual completion in August 1914. It should be noted that Mahan always presented the significance of the canal in economic terms, not as a shortcut for the fleet to transit between the east and west coasts of the United States but as a facilitator of global trade. The building of an Isthmian Canal was the most ambitious infrastructure project of the age; experts the world over agreed that its construction would need stupendous amounts of capital but that the commercial dividends would be enormous. After the Civil War, the building of an Isthmian Canal was one of the two recurring overseas issues that provoked the most congressional debate (the other being the political instability in Cuba, where U.S. businessmen who had purchased sugar plantations at distressed prices were constantly demanding the government protect their property when social turmoil threatened).[15]

In February 1880, Ferdinand de Lesseps, the French engineer who had constructed the Suez Canal, arrived in New York and announced his intention to organize a company to build a canal through modern-day Panama. In Washington, interest turned rapidly to concern after the discovery that de Lesseps had the financial backing of the French government. This news brought back memories of the unwelcome French intervention in Mexico in 1862, when the United States had been distracted by its civil war. Americans feared that French economic involvement in Central America on such a large scale would induce the French government to seek political control over the surrounding territory in order to safeguard their investment, much as Britain would do in Egypt two years later over the Suez Canal and the United States would do throughout the twentieth century.[16]

Writing to Ashe on the subject in March 1880, a month after de Lesseps' arrival in New York, Mahan speculated about what might happen, and in so doing displayed his awareness that naval policy was intertwined with both foreign and domestic politics:

> Now the Canal at the Isthmus may bring our interests and those of foreign nations in collision—and in that case—which it is for statesmen to forecast—we must without any delay begin to build a navy which will at least equal that of England when the Canal shall have become a fact. We have for such a purpose *no* navy; it would probably be safe to say we have not two ironclads worthy in armor or guns to stand alongside those of Turkey or Spain. To control at the Isthmus we must have a very large navy—and we must begin to build as soon as the first spadeful of earth is turned at Panama. That this will be done I don't for a moment hope, but unless it is we may as well shut up about the Monroe doctrine at once. Our millions of men cannot get to or be fed at the Isthmus except by sea; but a popular government will never dare to spend the money necessary to prepare.[17]

The references here to the Monroe Doctrine and to popular government as a constraint on naval spending demonstrate Mahan's awareness of the Navy's political environment.

In the months and years that followed, U.S. interest in Latin America intensified. Writing in November 1880, for instance, the then–Secretary of the Navy frankly acknowledged that European ambitions near the isthmus conflicted with the United States' own expansive interests. "The commercial importance of the Central and South American States never attracted more universal attention than at present. Their tropical productions are a necessity for all the nations. And inasmuch as they are in such close proximity to us, and need to be supplied with many of our productions in exchange for theirs, our own interest demands that we should not suffer the trade with them to pass entirely out of our hands, as it is likely to do if we do not adopt prompt and vigorous measures to secure it."[18] Accordingly, "I have deemed it an imperative public duty to send our ships of war into as many of their ports as possible, with the view of enabling the authorities and people of those countries to understand that it is our desire to cultivate with them the most amicable commercial relations, and that both their own interest and ours would be thereby promoted."[19]

Early the following year, the U.S. government embarked on more active measures. In March 1881, ill-fated Gen. James Garfield assumed the presidency and appointed the arch-expansionist James Blaine as his secretary of state. Blaine, who at various times contemplated the annexation of various Caribbean islands and even the "liberation" of Canada from British rule, was particularly keen to establish U.S. leadership throughout the Western Hemisphere, which, as the historian Jay Sexton notes, he and his friends "increasingly referred to as 'our hemisphere' or 'our sphere of influence.'"[20] One of Blaine's first acts as head of the State Department was to intervene in the war between Chile and Peru, undertaking support for the latter against the former, claiming that the war was being sustained through British interference.

Mahan was horrified, viewing Blaine's diplomatic assertiveness as ill conceived to the point of recklessness. Never mind the risk of confrontation with European powers with powerful fleets: the administration failed to grasp that the United States lacked the naval wherewithal to face even the local regional powers of Argentina, Brazil, and Chile, who were none too happy at the pretensions of their northern neighbor.[21] Mahan judged that the U.S. Navy would have struggled to fight even the Chileans, and freely acknowledged that "Spain, a near and troublesome neighbor, is our superior."[22] Blaine's brash blustering threatened to embroil the Navy in a war it was ill equipped to fight. "Practically we have nothing," Mahan lamented to Ashe at the end of 1882. "Never before has the Navy sunk so low. Up to the war & for a short time after it we had always ships that could find equals & cope with them. Now it is not too much to say we have not six ships that would be kept at sea in war by any maritime power."[23] Within the service, Mahan was not alone in his pessimism.[24]

Fortunately for the United States, the fighting capability of its postbellum Navy was never put to the test. In September 1881, President Garfield was assassinated and Chester Arthur entered the White House. Wary of Blaine's ambition and power within the Republican Party, the new president promptly ejected him from the administration. Although the resulting change in leadership at the State Department produced no change in overall foreign policy direction, with the new head, Frederick Frelinghuysen, equally committed to hemispheric domination, he sought a less confrontational path.[25] He tried to weave a web of bilateral trade treaties with the various Central American countries in the hope of securing effective economic control over them without the burden of direct political control. For him, the prize was an American-built, American-controlled Isthmian Canal, and he was willing to pay a high price. In 1883, he negotiated a pact between the United States and Nicaragua whereby the two would share ownership (but not the revenues) of the canal. In return, the U.S. government promised not only to underwrite the construction but also to guarantee the territorial integrity of Nicaragua against any avaricious neighbors. In the eyes of many at home, the proposal resembled an "entangling alliance," one in which the United States undertook political and military obligations instead of merely commercial ones—and thus could be seen by the electorate as marking a dangerous shift in foreign policy. Although a majority of senators voted in favor of the draft treaty, it did not obtain the requisite two-thirds majority and thus failed to pass.

Mahan kept a close eye on these events, and they caused him much unease. "The strict construction of the constitution, the jealous maintenance of the rights and powers of the states . . . the vigilant limitation of the central government to simply what is granted it by the constitution; this is my dearest political wish," he confided to Ashe on July 26, 1884.[26] Like most Americans of his day, he was instinctively appalled by the thought of the United States entering into an alliance or becoming an imperial power, which he saw as contrary to the letter and the spirit of the U.S. Constitution. At the same time, however, again like most Americans, he regarded economic expansion overseas as a good idea and imagined that the United States could achieve commercial dominance in the Western Hemisphere without the necessity to extend formal political control over the region. Yet unlike most Americans, his nationalistic haughtiness had to contend with his awareness as a professional naval officer that competing aggressively for foreign trade ran the risk of confrontation with powerful rivals, which would require a larger navy that must in turn lead to a stronger federal government.

By this time, Mahan was off the west coast of South America on board the *Wachusett*, and thus in a position to see firsthand just how politically unstable the region was and how perilously close the United States stood to the precipice of direct intervention and possible conflict.[27] Writing to Ashe in July 1884, he expressed his concern:

> The air is rife with expected strife and revolution and the American squadron which, *pace* the Monroe doctrine, has the fewest interests and fewest people to protect is tied down to this place. We have here three out of the five ships composing it . . . yet I suppose each of these [foreign warships] have ten compatriots where we have one, for as yet Americans have ample opportunity enough in America. Luckily Mr. Blaine is not yet president so we will not probably interfere beyond taking refugees on board if necessary; but if that magnetic statesman were in office I fancy American diplomats would be running around in the magazine with lighted candles.[28]

Mahan was particularly troubled when ordered to land a party of blue-jackets ashore to protect American property. Although he complied with his orders, such action offended his political ideals, and he feared a slippery slope. "The question of landing troops in a foreign county is very delicate," he explained to Ashe.

> I trust it may be avoided. I don't know how you feel but to me the very suspicion of an imperial policy is hateful; the mixing of our politics with those of Latin republics especially. . . . I dread outlying colonies or interests, to maintain which large military establishments are necessary. I see in them the on-coming of a "strong" central government (as though any government could ever be strong enough to administer our vast territory on any other plan than leaving each part as free as may be from interference), of discontent in various sections, or attempted repression by force of arms, or perhaps subversion of really free government.[29]

Here again we see within Mahan's analysis the complex interweaving of naval, foreign, and domestic policies, each dependent on and determining the others. We can also see his worry that the U.S. government was pursuing a foreign policy that its military could not back. This begs the question: why were the Navy's fortunes so low?

THE NAVY ADRIFT
After the Civil War, the U.S. Navy found itself with few political friends or supporters, far fewer than it had possessed before the conflict. The inability of its postwar leaders (most notably David Dixon Porter) to articulate a clear and convincing purpose for the Navy undermined the service's claims on the public purse. It did not help that, in the eyes of many, the wartime performance of the Navy had been patchy at best. On the high seas, the Navy was judged to have performed poorly. A handful of Confederate commerce raiders had inflicted punishing losses on northern commercial shipping, and what the raiders did not sink, take, or burn was promptly transferred to the protection of the British flag. Though nearly all the Confederate raiders were eventually caught, the consensus was that the Navy had taken far too long to meet the threat, and the merchants who had suffered losses were slow to forgive.

At the same time, the Navy did a poor job at explaining to the public the magnitude and significance of its considerable wartime achievements. The Union blockade of the coast had disrupted the South's ability to import much needed foreign armaments and, much more importantly (and more successfully), to export cotton for the cash it required to pay for them.[30] The Navy's strangulation of the South's war economy was a major contributor to the victory of the North. But in the mind of the general public, the blockade lacked the romance of the great battles that had been fought on land. Similarly, although it had been the Navy that had led and made possible the capture of the critical southern seaports and river towns (including New Orleans in 1862 and Vicksburg in 1863), invariably it had been the Army that received the lion's share of the credit. Therefore, with no foreign threat to national security even on the remotest horizon, with a nation to reconstruct, expensive transcontinental railways to finance, and huge war debts to repay, once the war was over most Americans regarded the retention of a large fleet as a wasteful luxury.[31] To the extent that any thought was given to the defense of the republic from external aggression, the nation looked to the Army rather than the Navy.

Accordingly, the Navy's armada of ironclad monitors, technological triumphs of the day albeit of limited practical use outside of coastal waters, were docked at the back of the various navy yards and left to rust. A cadre of around two thousand officers—fifty for every warship on the books—was retained as insurance against future emergency (which over time appeared less and less likely) as well as to crew a flotilla of some forty cruisers and gunboats retained for constabulary duties. A cynic might suspect that the large number of officers also had something to do with that fact that since 1852, Congress reserved to itself the power to make nominations to the Naval Academy, an important source of political patronage. In any case, as a consequence of the superabundance of officers, over half of the Navy budget went to salaries and pensions, and roughly a quarter more was consumed by repairs to the steadily aging fleet in one of the eight navy yards. This left very little money for everything else.

Within little more than a decade, the rapid pace of technological change meant that the fleet that had fought the Civil War was reduced to obsolescence. Though naval officers pleaded for new warships and bewailed their falling behind in adopting new naval technologies, they struggled to explain how their current vessels were inadequate to the limited tasks required of them. Basically, the politicians in Washington did not expect the Navy would ever have to fight; they assumed that if it did, then warships could be built rapidly, as had been done during the late war. In the meantime, the Navy still possessed a large stock of serviceable wooden-hulled vessels, and no less importantly a substantial inventory of naval stores—seasoned timber, canvas, and miscellaneous ironmongery—to keep them in repair and thus in service at comparatively little cost. These vessels were cheap to run and perfectly capable of performing the service's core mission of showing the flag, safeguarding U.S. lives and property in Latin America by serving as a visual reminder of their northern neighbor's potential power. Unsurprisingly, naval officers, including Mahan, hated this thankless and irksome duty which, in effect, placed them at the beck and call of the State Department. It also mortified them to have to do the job in increasingly dilapidated warships, especially when more modern foreign warships were nearby.[32]

Besides the complete lack of any external threat, Congress had other reasons to deny the Navy Department any budgetary increase. Money was tight. Not only was there an overriding desire to pay down the national debt accumulated during the Civil War, but the years 1873–79 were a period of severe economic depression, stemming from the Panic of 1873. For one thing, federal tax revenues fell so sharply that Congress mandated cuts in naval salaries and pensions. For another, although the naval leadership was loud in demanding more ships, it was divided over the kind of warships it wanted. As Mahan remarked to Ashe in 1875, "naval policy throughout the world is at present in a very unsettled, transitional, state—and doctors differ greatly in the courses they advise."[33]

Probably the most important reason for congressional unwillingness to spend more on the Navy was the reluctance to flush good

money after bad. Back in 1873, Congress had authorized the building of eight new warships, but their construction had been so deeply
mired in malfeasance that the legislature became disinclined to fund
any more.[34] Throughout this period, there was a widespread and
amply justified public perception of the eight navy yards as cesspools
of corruption and graft. What is more, this stench (and the consequences) lingered well into the 1880s. No serious attempt was made
at reform until the appointment of William C. Whitney as Navy Secretary during the first Grover Cleveland administration (1885–89). But
this is to get ahead of the story.

Between 1865 and 1884, there was not a single plank in the plat-
forms of either political party on naval policy. By the beginning of
the 1880s, among the membership of the House naval committee
at least, there was cross-party consensus that new warships were necessary. But their voice carried little weight. Service on this committee was viewed more as a punishment than a reward. Many senior
congressmen refused point-blank to serve there, and those unlucky
enough to be appointed worked to get out as quickly as they could.
Membership turnover every two years exceeded fifty percent.[35] At the
end of 1881, the then Secretary of the Navy, William Hunt, warned
Congress that the fleet was, quite literally, falling apart at the seams
and that "unless some action be had in its behalf it must soon dwindle
into insignificance. From such a state it would be difficult to revive it
into efficiency without dangerous delay and enormous expense."[36] Yet
despite the backing of both naval committees and the White House,
by both Garfield and Arthur, Congress flatly declined to provide the
requested sums.[37]

So how was this congressional logjam broken? Alas, there is
no easy or concise answer to this important question; there was no
'Road to Damascus' imperative or moment. The generally accepted
explanation was first put forward as long ago as 1939 by Harold and
Margaret Sprout in their triumphalist account *The Rise of American
Naval Power*.[38] One year later, George Davis published a slightly
more detailed account that argued on very similar lines.[39] Both constructed their narratives largely based on the (unverified) claims made

by various interested politicians, either at the time in the congressional record or the press, or later in their memoirs, all keen to claim the title of "father of the new navy." Triumphalist histories tend to be replete with "founding fathers" and "founding moments," punctuated with milestones or events that add luster to the subject yet eschew discussion of the unsavory details (such as corruption in the navy yards) that can tarnish reputations. Although these historians provided coherent narratives, their explanations were neither complete nor convincing. Because their book has been and remains so influential, the Sprouts' interpretation requires particularly careful examination.

In the opening to the chapter titled "Beginnings of the New Navy," they boldly proclaimed that "the year 1881 was an historical milestone in the rise of American naval power. The process of naval reconstruction was commenced in that year."[40] They immediately qualified this statement by acknowledging that "this work proceeded haltingly at first, encumbered with strategic and technological prejudices" and that "a generation was to elapse before Mahan's capital-ship, or command-of-the-sea, theory finally and conclusively superseded the commerce-raiding and passive-coast-defense theory as the basic doctrine of American naval policy."[41] Reading on, however, it emerges that no new warships were actually ordered in 1881; however, the authors insist, "the process" had begun.

As best as can be determined—for it is difficult to pin down exactly what the Sprouts were arguing—the "milestone" of 1881 they had in mind was a decision by the Navy Secretary to appoint a committee of officers, known as the Rodgers board, to determine the needs of the Navy and make recommendations for future naval construction.[42] The timing, they insisted, was propitious. The economic upturn after 1880 caused the U.S. Treasury to become flush with tariff revenues, which, when combined with growing concerns over European encroachments into the Western Hemisphere, gave "a strong incentive to increased government expenditures."[43] This was tantamount to saying that Congress was happy to give the Navy more money because more money was available and because foreign ambitions had demonstrated the need for a larger fleet. All that was necessary, the Sprouts concluded, was for the Navy to advance a coherent building program. To say the least, this imposes a misleading coherence on the events of this period and thus on the direction of naval policy generally.

Two years later, in March 1883, Congress provided an appropriation to build four steel-hulled warships—the cruisers *Atlanta*, *Boston*, and *Chicago* and the dispatch vessel (or gunboat) *Dolphin*—that became popularly known as the ABCD ships, or the White Squadron (after their distinctive white-and-buff paint scheme). These four warships, the Sprouts averred, "provided tangible evidence of the physical rebirth of American naval power, and aroused the popular enthusiasm necessary to sustain further progress in naval reconstruction."[44] A page later, however, the Sprouts yet again qualified their assessment by admitting that "it would be a mistake to conclude that naval reconstruction proceeded smoothly, in accord with any prearranged plan. On the contrary, as already intimated, the work went forward spasmodically, with very little planning at all."[45] They then mentioned that before the decade was over, thirty additional warships had been ordered.[46] By the end of their chapter covering the 1880s, the attentive reader is left thoroughly perplexed by the tensions, if not outright contradictions, in their arguments.

Little supplementary research is required to reveal that the Sprouts achieved their narrative coherence only through bending certain facts to fit their chain of causality and ignoring ones that did not.[47] For instance, they neglected to mention that Congress roundly rejected the advice of the 1881 Rodgers Board, on its face a rather important detail. They also failed to account for the various successor advisory boards, perhaps because their official recommendations too received equally short shrift from Congress, thus further undercutting the asserted significance of these construction boards as instruments of progress. As will be shown below, moreover, suggestions that the ABCD ships represented some sort of landmark in the history of the U.S. Navy are equally difficult to sustain. So too is the Sprouts' suggestion that the Navy had forged internal consensus over a coherent building program.

But the most glaring weakness in the Sprouts' analysis (and this goes for Davis as well) was their explanation for the newfound willingness of Congress to spend more on the Navy.[48] The assertion that the money was provided because it was available ignores overwhelming evidence that other interests were competing for the same money; also that there were also calls (especially from the South) for the tariff (the federal government's main source of revenue) to be lowered. In short, the Sprouts failed to engage with the politics of government spending, as fatal and unrealistic a failure for understanding congressional appropriations in the late nineteenth century as it would be today.[49]

The errors and omissions by the Sprouts would not matter so much (and would not be dwelt on here) were it not for the fact that most subsequent naval historians have largely followed them in pivoting their analysis of postbellum naval policy on the formation of the Rodgers board and in trumpeting the construction of the ABCD ships as a "revolution in naval architecture" that heralded a "naval renaissance."[50] Furthermore, to the extent that they have considered how the congressional logjam was broken, too many have followed the Sprouts' lead in thinking that money was not a problem, that concern over European assertiveness in the Western Hemisphere was widespread, and therefore that all the Navy had to do was merely present a coherent program and ask nicely.[51] Such beliefs reflect the divorce of naval history from the best work on U.S. political economy, an estrangement that has fed and been fed by a tendency to study the U.S. Navy in isolation from its fiscal and political contexts.

There is another indicator that the standard explanations for U.S. naval policy during the 1880s cannot be relied on. These portrayals do not resonate at all with what Mahan wrote during this decade. That is to say, based on the letters he wrote at the time, Mahan most certainly would not have recognized the picture of a naval renaissance underway. Writing in 1883, just before the contracts for the ABCDs were announced, Mahan outlined to Ashe his vision of "a small capable Navy" that "shall be superior ship for ship to the same kind of vessels anywhere. This was our old policy."[52] He could see no financial impediment to achieving his modest vision, as "our coffers are full and with any amount of judicious reduction of taxes, we still have enough for this most necessary force."[53] The chief obstacle, Mahan averred, was Congress: disgust over naked corruption plus perceptions of incompetence continued to inhibit the majority of legislators from trusting the Navy Department with so much as another dime, while the crushing national apathy for naval issues meant there was little incentive to fix the underlying problems.[54] As Mahan eloquently explained it in his autobiography, the Navy "was accepted without much question as part of the necessary lumber that every adequately organized maritime state carried, along with the rest of a national establishment. Of what use it was, or might be, few cared much to inquire. There was not sufficient interest even to dispute the necessity of its existence."[55]

In 1885, by which time the construction of the ABCD ships was well underway, Mahan was still grumbling over the continued absence of direction in naval policy, which he attributed to general ignorance over the purpose of a navy.[56] He also remained frustrated at the lack of consensus within the service over force structure. "As regards the type of ships, opinions are very divergent. I give you mine. The surest way to maintain peace is to occupy a position of menace. I think that our geographical position will make war with us unlikely but the surest deterrent will be a fleet of swift cruisers to prey on the enemy's commerce. . . . This threat will deter a possible enemy, particularly if coupled with adequate defense of our principal ports."[57] These thoughts, however, were conditional and contingent. Overleaf, he clarified that "my theory however is based on the supposition that we don't have interests out of our own borders. If we are going in for an Isthmian policy we must have nothing short of a numerous and thoroughly first class iron clad navy—equal to either England or France."[58] Here, again, incidentally, is a through line of Mahan's thinking: that the formulation of naval policy was contingent on foreign policy, itself a function of myriad factors, including domestic politics. In any case, as late as 1887 (and arguably even in 1889), we find Mahan still complaining that the Navy lacked direction and purpose.[59]

Unlike the Sprouts, Mahan correctly identified the chief obstacle to naval expansion: the lack of congressional *willingness* to fund the Navy.

The mere existence of available funds did not equate to willingness to spend them on the Navy; there were competing priorities. Moreover, again unlike the Sprouts, Mahan accurately perceived the absence of consensus within the Navy over force structure and strategy—that is, of how to spend any funds that Congress might grace it with. The key questions, therefore, are: when and why did public attitudes toward the navy begin to change? To these questions we now turn.

THE NEW NAVY: REALITY OR RHETORIC?

In March 1881, President James Garfield appointed William H. Hunt of Louisiana to become Secretary of the Navy. After three months in office, finding the fleet in even worse disrepair than his predecessor had let on and the department rudderless, Hunt on his own initiative set up an advisory board of fifteen naval officers under Rear Adm. John Rodgers, charging them to review the Navy's materiel requirements and issue "a practical and plain statement" making specific recommendations on new construction.[60] In November 1881, the Rodgers board reported, recommending the immediate construction of thirty-eight new cruisers to replace worn-out vessels. Eighteen were to be made of steel and twenty of wood, for a total price of $29 million. Though Hunt energetically promoted the report, imploring his fellow southerners to vote for it, and also obtained the president's endorsement of a draft bill, his exhortations fell on deaf ears.

The main reason why the House naval committee so roundly rejected the advice of the Rodgers board was that its authority had been fatally compromised. The membership did not include any of the chiefs of bureaus—the bureaus being well known as the real centers of power within the Navy Department—but was drawn entirely from outside the bureaucracy. Fatally also, Adm. Rodgers failed to reconcile the conflicting opinions within the service, in particular the divergence between line and engineer officers over the practicality of building steel cruisers in U.S. yards, and the embarrassing upshot of the discord was a minority report. Mindful of congressional exasperation at the Navy's constant internal bickering, Secretary Hunt had tried to suppress this dissenting viewpoint; but, as was predictable, the news leaked and

ultimately the document was turned over to the House Naval Committee.[61] From this it further emerged that the board regarded the
thirty-eight warships requested only as a first installment: they envisioned the building over the next eight years of another seventy cruisers plus twenty-one ironclads (sometimes referred to as battleships).
In the political environment of the day these numbers were pure fan-
tasy, not to mention inflammatory.

In vain, the House naval committee trimmed the number of
requested warships from thirty-eight to a more modest fifteen; the
Ways and Means Committee whittled down the authorization to just
two cruisers, and ultimately Congress agreed to zero. In fact, that year
Congress imposed cuts on the Navy, again pruning the officer corps by
roughly 14 percent and closing the construction facilities at the Washington and Philadelphia Navy Yards. These cuts were not restored
until the mid-1890s. By any measure, this was a resounding defeat for
Secretary Hunt, who quit shortly afterward and was replaced (in April
1882) by William E. Chandler. Before he departed, however, Hunt
did obtain congressional approval for establishing an Office of Naval
Intelligence (ONI). Over the next several years, the ONI systematically and successfully plundered the intellectual property of foreign
shipbuilders, the significance of which will become apparent below.[62]

In October 1882, a new naval advisory board was established under the politically well-connected (now) Commo. Robert
Shufeldt. The new board proposed a more palatable program of five
steel warships, and in March 1883 Congress grudgingly appropriated
$1.3 million to begin work on what became the ABCD ships. The
Sprouts were not alone in failing to distinguish the (1882) Shufeldt
board from the previous (1881) Rodgers board or realized that there
was a critical difference in how they were constituted. Basically, the
Shufeldt board (consisting of five officers and two independent civilian constructors) was established not by the Navy Secretary but by
the Senate Naval Committee.[63] Further, the board was authorized to
invite private firms to submit plans for the projected new warships,
to choose the best sketch designs, to forward them to the Bureau of
Construction along with directions to work out detailed plans, to

superintend the building of said warships, and to oversee their acceptance into service. In effect, Congress gave the Shufeldt board the
power to dictate to the department and the bureaus. To say the least,
this was extraordinary.

The real significance of the 1882 board, therefore, lay far more
in the political and administrative spheres than the technical. Establishing the board independent of the Navy Department represented
a public censure of the naval bureaucracy—a vote of no-confidence
in the "expert" naval bureaus—and signaled a congressional wish to
exert tighter supervision. More interestingly still, and to the general
disgust of his staff, Navy Secretary Chandler publicly approved of
this effective rechanneling of authority.[64] Just how energetically the
Shufeldt board exercised their theoretical powers remains unclear.[65]
Doubtless there was some accommodation made by both sides, but
this is not the place for extended consideration of the issue. The main
point here is that neither the Rodgers board nor even the Schufeldt
board can plausibly be regarded as a stepping-stone in the triumphant
march toward a self-ordained naval renaissance.

Suggestions that the ABCD ships represented some sort of landmark in the history of the Navy are equally difficult to sustain. In
conception, they were merely steel versions of the wooden vessels
they replaced—backward-looking rather than forward-looking, so to
speak. In sporting masts and carrying sails, they even looked similar.[66]
"The immediate object should be at moderate expense to replace our
worn-out cruisers with modern constructions fitted for general service," Secretary Chandler explained when announcing the contracts.[67]
Far from heralding a new technological beginning for the U.S. Navy,
moreover, the ABCD ships proved more an embarrassment. Chandler had bragged they would represent "an example of the largest
and best unarmored cruising and fighting vessels now built, and will
have no superior in the world in the combination of speed, endurance, and armament."[68] In fact, the combat capabilities of *Chicago* and
her stepsisters were excruciatingly inferior to the latest European-built
cruisers, as the press quickly pointed out. Worse, U.S. firms proved
unable to supply many necessary components, such as armor plate

and forgings for the main armament, forcing the Navy reluctantly to source them from abroad.[69]

In another way too, the ABCD cruisers were linked more to the past than the future. The decision to award the contract for all four ships to John Roach & Sons of Philadelphia, a firm that contributed generously to the Republican Party, snared the Navy Department in yet another corruption scandal.[70] It emerged that Secretary Chandler was friends with Roach and had been previously employed by his firm as a lobbyist.[71] It was further alleged that several members of the Schufelt board were also close acquaintances.[72] Disappointed rival builders, like William Cramp & Sons of Philadelphia, added their criticisms to the din. The controversy might have subsided and been quickly forgotten, but for the fact that the Democrats won the elections of 1884, with Grover Cleveland defeating James Blaine to become the first Democratic president since before the Civil War. The new Democratic administration immediately launched an investigation into the awarding of the contracts.[73] Of course there was a partisan dimension to all this: after twenty-seven years of Republican rule, any malfeasance lay squarely at their door. Yet it is difficult to escape the supposition that there were solid grounds for an inquiry.

The Secretary of Navy in the new Democratic administration, William Whitney, initially tried to downplay the shortcomings with the ABCD ships (still under construction) by claiming that "it is unavoidable that some diversity of opinion should be found among professional constructors."[74] He further allowed that his predecessor's decision to award all four ships to a single yard might not have been as suspicious as it had first appeared.[75] Six months later, however, by mid-1885, these excuses were wearing thin, after the first of the ABCD ships failed her trials for the third time.[76] Whitney suspended making payments on the ships, causing Roach to declare bankruptcy. This placed the Navy in the rather awkward position of having to take over the construction of the other three cruisers and finish them in navy yards that had neither the experience nor the tools to work steel. Unsurprisingly, therefore, the work proceeded slowly. The *Chicago* was not finally commissioned until April 1889.

Certainly, Roach's firm was seriously undercapitalized and had underestimated the technological hurdles to be overcome in constructing steel warships. That said, the Navy Department bureaus bore a substantial share of the blame by constantly chopping and changing the design after the contract had been let and the price set, promising to settle up later—but never in fact doing so—a practice that continued and arguably still continues.[77] Secretary Whitney admitted as much in his annual report for 1885.[78] In fact, he went a good deal further. In the space of twenty pages (more than half of his report), he laid bare the shortcomings in the department's bureau system, cataloging his discoveries of administrative incompetence and accounting irregularities.[79] "It is a long time since the working of a department of the Government have been so thoroughly criticized by its own chief as are those of the Navy Department in the current report of Mr. Whitney," exclaimed the *New York Times* in an editorial. "The illustrations he gives of the extravagance and irresponsibility of the system are astonishing."[80]

Particularly significant was the revelation that the Navy Secretary possessed "very scant means of investigating" the inner workings of the bureaus, to establish what exactly they were working on and exactly where the money was being spent. The secretary's administrative staff consisted of just eighteen clerks, eight messenger boys, three laborers, and a carpenter.[81] This was doubtless sufficient to process routine paperwork (and to fix any shelves broken by their weight) but wholly insufficient to verify figures submitted by the bureaus. What Whitley was saying, in short, was that the Navy Secretary had no effective financial control over his department.

Acting on his conviction that his department could not be trusted to design anything more complex than a rowboat, and equally unimpressed by the Naval Advisory Board (now led by Rear Adm. Edward Simpson), Whitney looked abroad for help in designing the next cruisers for the U.S. Navy. He frankly told the chairman of the Senate naval committee that "I think our true policy is to borrow the ideas of our neighbors so far as they are thought to be in advance of ours."[82] Impressed (as was everyone) by the performance of the *Esmerelda*, a

British-designed cruiser sold to the Chilean Navy in 1884, Whitney purchased from the same firm the plans for an updated design to be built as the *Charleston* by Union Iron Works of San Francisco.[83] The *Charleston*, incidentally, would be the first U.S.-commissioned cruiser without sails. Another variant of the same British design was built as the *Baltimore* by William Cramp & Sons.[84]

Far from heralding a new beginning, therefore, the much-trumpeted ABCD ships demonstrated the backwardness of U.S. ship-building, steel manufacturing, and engineering, as well as of the Navy Department's procurement process.[85] Serious obstacles still lay in the way of creating a modern fleet.[86] For all the hype surrounding their construction and the ordering of additional warships, the fact is that the fleet did not grow and no new capabilities were added. In numbers of personnel, the Navy was actually 10 percent smaller at the end of the decade than it had been at the beginning. In money terms, real naval spending at the end of the 1880s was more or less the same as it had been twenty years before, albeit now on an upward trajectory. To all intents and purposes, the Navy still remained a cruiser navy organized to perform constabulary duties. At the end of the 1880s, U.S. naval policy was still trending toward a traditional cruiser navy—a trajectory that Mahan, whom the Sprouts described as the author of the Navy's "capital-ship, or command-of-the-sea, theory," substantially endorsed.

The foregoing shows that the Sprouts' influential account of a U.S. naval renaissance in the 1880s cannot be right, but it does not propose an alternative account. To that task we now turn.

ENTER THE WISCONSIN SCHOOL

In order to understand Congress' willingness to provide the Navy with larger appropriations in the late 1880s after the cuts of the previous decade, it is necessary to understand something more of U.S. political economy and its relationship with U.S. foreign policy. The best source on these subjects is the work of the Wisconsin School (so named because it was based out of the University of Wisconsin). By asking highly original and important questions about the relationships between domestic economic interest groups, the wider political economy at home, and decision making in U.S. foreign policy, better than any historians before or since they identified and mapped the leading issues of the day (which proved to be mostly economic in character) that drove American politics during the Gilded Age and the Progressive era. The road ventures far from the conventional path of naval history, but it is the only viable way to understand Congress's newfound willingness to fund naval expansion.

The most prominent figure of the Wisconsin School was William Appleman Williams, who, ironically, had been destined for a career in the U.S. Navy (Naval Academy class of 1944) but had been invalided out of the service for wounds sustained at Okinawa. Instead, he became one of the most influential historians of his day. Although he and his followers (chiefly Walter LaFeber, his student turned colleague) chose to address the expansion of the Navy only tangentially in their major writings, their chief object being to explain the growth of American expansionism at the end of the nineteenth century, their studies provide an essential analysis of the broad political and economic forces at work at the end of the nineteenth century, and in particular during the 1880s and 1890s. Their work remains unsurpassed. Yet for reasons that defy easy explanation, the scholarship of the Wisconsin School has been (and remains) largely ignored by naval historians.

Regardless, beginning with *The Tragedy of American Diplomacy*, published in 1959, Williams offered a new conceptual framework for understanding the burst of American expansionism at the end of the nineteenth century, what he described as the desire by the United States to extend its economic frontiers beyond its territorial frontiers.[87] During the fifteen years following the end of the Civil War, the U.S. population and national economic output more or less doubled, fueled mainly by a massive wave of postwar immigration. Absolute growth notwithstanding, national economic performance was sluggish, characterized by a cycle of boom and bust, and prices were depressed because of gluts in production in both agricultural and industrial goods. Few of those who lived through this period saw any significant increase in their standards of living or strengthening of their personal economic security. Social inequality at home was massive and highly visible.

Williams showed that political commentators of the day attributed the general economic malaise to various causes, but from around 1880 increasingly focused on the theory of "overproduction" (basically an excess of supply over demand). Proponents of this explanation argued that the obvious solution to America's domestic economic woes was to be found by expanding into overseas markets. Williams thus drew a connection between the nation's internal economic problems, growing public unhappiness toward their leaders for their failure to bring about a period of sustained prosperity, and increasing support for a more assertive foreign policy. Put more simply, as economic unhappiness grew, public opinion became more receptive to calls for overseas expansion, and to spending more on the Navy. In other words, where the Sprouts emphasized *foreign* developments, in the form of European incursions into the Western Hemisphere, as the main driver of congressional willingness to increase the Navy's funding, Williams emphasized a *domestic* crisis of capitalism. As he termed it, American citizens looked to "externalize" their internal economic problems by expanding into foreign markets.

At the beginning of the 1880s, there remained two substantial bulwarks holding in check general American public support for overseas expansion and for greater spending on the Navy. The first was that such ideas smacked of imperialism, associated with abhorrent European-style repression of political freedoms, irreconcilable with the nation's core values and traditional self-image. The second was the still deep-rooted public aversion to the creation of a strong federal government, which in practice meant that Congress was unwilling to supply the funds for the machinery—like a large navy—necessary for penetrating foreign markets. Williams and LaFeber showed that over the course of this decade, these bulwarks against overseas adventurism had been steadily crumbling before they finally collapsed in the wake of the Panic of 1893.

As Williams continued to study the period, he became convinced that the key factors in explaining U.S. economic expansionism (and naval growth) in the late nineteenth century were wheat and wheat farmers. Since he wrote, a rich literature (equally ignored by naval historians) on the so-called first era of globalization, lasting from roughly 1870 to the outbreak of World War I, has shed additional light on the development of the international wheat market and the place of U.S. grain therein. Reading Williams' work alongside this literature makes possible a new explanation of why Congress became more willing to fund the Navy in the late 1880s.

Williams found, based on an extraordinary volume of research in contemporary papers, that the "overproduction" theory originated not in the urban-industrial East, as he (and LaFeber) had first supposed, but in the rural agricultural Midwest.[88] The son of a farmer himself, Williams reminded his readers that the United States was a predominantly agricultural country—as late as 1900, three-fifths of the population still lived in rural as opposed to urban communities. Moreover, the vast majority of U.S. exports during the late nineteenth century were in primary products, the two most important being cotton and wheat. Only toward the end of the 1880s, Williams argued, did industrialists and financiers begin to entertain the concept of overproduction, and even then they did not fully embrace it until the mid-1890s.

Although cotton may have remained king, wheat grew rapidly in economic and political significance. After the Civil War, the combination of renewed westward expansion, a fresh railroad boom, and the spread of commercial as distinct from subsistence agriculture led to a steady increase in wheat production. The construction of the Northern Pacific Railroad, begun in 1870, progressively opened up the mid- and northwestern plains to the raising of wheat that could be profitably transported by rail or barge to the burgeoning cities on the East Coast and beyond.[89] Between 1873 and 1883, the cultivation of wheat in the United States surged from 29 million to 41 million acres, yielding an increase from 368 million bushels to 555 million bushels.[90] This enormous increase in supply proved to be highly destabilizing, both to the United States and the rest of the world. Yet although wheat supply increased faster than demand, thus placing downward pressure on prices, the adverse consequences for farmers' standards of living did not materialize immediately because of certain countervailing pressures in the global market.

Between 1876 and 1881, a series of bad harvests in Europe stimulated a threefold increase in demand for U.S. agricultural exports, propelling gross sales from $76 million to $226 million per annum. For many years after, Americans fondly recalled these years as ones of exceptional prosperity. The success of U.S. agricultural exports also encouraged other businessmen to think of selling abroad. As Williams explained, "the effect on all American thinking, therefore, was to extend and deepen the orientation towards overseas markets as a crucial element in the nation's well-being."[91] But there were also drawbacks. Whereas hitherto the United States had exported around 10 percent of its wheat harvest, by the mid-1880s the share approached 30 percent.[92] This meant that U.S. farmers—and the U.S. economy—were exposed to global market forces to a far greater degree than before. When the climatic pendulum swung back, therefore, American farmers were poised to be hit hard.

In Europe, farming interests viewed the influx of cheap American wheat with anger, an aspect that Williams did not explore. While cheap American wheat may have been good for European consumers, and certainly good for American farmers, it was decidedly bad for European farmers, agricultural workers, and especially the landed aristocracy whose political power rested on the sale of agricultural produce.[93] In other words, cheap American wheat threatened the established economic and political order, and it struck back. In Germany, for instance, Prussian agricultural interests whose wealth and political power were derived from raising cereals demanded protection. As early as 1879, despite another poor harvest, Germany introduced a tariff on imported cereals. Over the course of the following decade, as the cycle of bad weather came to an end and European agricultural output recovered, the tariff climbed steadily, by 1887 reaching 33 percent ad valorum on wheat. France, meanwhile, imposed a 22 percent duty on wheat; other Mediterranean countries applied rates upward of 40 percent.[94]

The steady recovery of European agriculture, combined with the raising of tariff barriers against the torrent of U.S. agricultural exports, caused U.S.-raised wheat to rebound back across the Atlantic. Now, instead of destabilizing European societies, the U.S. wheat surplus— the result of "overproduction"—destabilized U.S. society by producing a glut in the domestic market. Prices were driven down, much to the distress of the farmers who had raised and grown it.[95] The consequences were both painful and immediate. Depressed prices for agricultural produce (especially wheat) resulted in thousands of American farmers defaulting on their mortgages, forcing many into bankruptcy.

Not surprisingly, the farmers looked to the federal government to arrange the reopening of "their" European markets, or at least to punish the Europeans by imposing retaliatory tariffs on their agricultural produce.[96] The metropolitan-based political leadership in both parties hesitated, however. They feared that negotiating with their European counterparts for a reciprocal lowering of tariffs would alienate their core metropolitan supporters, producing unpredictable electoral consequences. Their failure to act provoked anger among the agricultural majority. From 1886, the farming lobby became noticeably more militant and politically active, with the movement that in the following decade would blossom into populism gaining traction in the agricultural midwestern swing states.[97]

In his later work, Williams explored some of the connections between this agricultural story and naval expansion. Summarily rejecting the assumption of naval historians that appropriations followed automatically from the availability of money, he argued that the decisive factor in changing political attitudes toward funding the Navy was the support from agricultural districts; farmers intuitively grasped the connection between the need to secure foreign markets and the need for a larger navy.[98] As Williams put it, voters in the agricultural districts saw that "American power had to be deployed and used to establish and maintain a strategic perimeter coincident with that wider American marketplace."[99] What is more, there were those in the Navy who saw this and exploited it. Williams was especially impressed with Commodore Shufeldt, who "pointed to the central importance of agricultural exports in the general economy as proof that America was becoming irrevocably involved and committed in the world marketplace, and argued that the Navy was the only military instrument capable of dealing with the new situation."[100]

Williams further showed that the agriculturalists in Congress had been willing to support a naval expansion much earlier but that chronic corruption had caused them to shrink from voting in favor of larger appropriations. Well into the 1880s, they continued to distrust the process of awarding government contracts to notoriously crooked East Coast (Republican) manufacturing interests, and also to doubt their capability (or of any American firm) to build effective warships. The fiasco over the ABCD ships amply confirmed their misgivings. As Williams argued, "agricultural attitudes on those issues have often been misunderstood because their critique of specific proposals has been misread as unequivocal opposition to the programs."[101] All this is to say that the agriculturalists were prepared to vote for naval expansion but first wanted to root out the corruption surrounding naval contracts. If correct—and on its face Williams' evidence is compelling—this would indicate that the largely unstudied naval administrative reforms of the 1880s (initiated by Secretary William Whitney) were far more important than has been previously allowed.[102]

Subsequent scholars have substantially confirmed Williams' claim that the Midwest constituted the key source of support for increased naval spending.[103] In an article scrutinizing voting patterns for naval appropriations during the period from 1880 to 1895, Thomas Coode disproved the notion that this support came from the South.[104] He found that although Navy Secretary William Hunt, who appointed the Rodgers Board, implored his fellow southerners to support his 1881 bill, "an overwhelming majority of their Dixie colleagues failed to heed the call."[105] Assertions that funding for the ABCD ships passed the House thanks to the support of the South have been demonstrated equally false. In fact, just 17 out of 103 southern congressmen voted in favor, all of whom lived in coastal districts and thus could be presumed to benefit directly.[106] The subsequent work of Massachusetts Institute of Technology political scientist Peter Trubowitz is practically conclusive. Support for the Navy was strongest in the Northeast and weakest in the South—except for Alabama, the home state of Hillary Herbert and of the Birmingham steel district. The pivotal votes came from the predominantly agricultural upper Midwest and Pacific states.[107]

█████████████████████████████

The traditional approach of naval historians, epitomized by the Sprouts and employed by many since, blinds them to key aspects of Mahan's writing and of U.S. naval history at the turn of the century. They typically treat external events (i.e., European incursions into the Western Hemisphere), the availability of money, and the existence of consensus within the Navy on a coherent building program as sufficient causes for the "renaissance" of U.S. naval power in the 1880s. They then narrate the story as one of unalloyed progress toward a practically preordained outcome of a seagoing capital-ship navy, marked by the milestone advisory boards and the ABCD ships. The upshot of such accounts is that by the time Mahan's *The Influence of Sea Power upon History* appeared in 1890, the U.S. Navy had already broken decisively with its past as a cruiser force organized around commerce raiding and was well on its way to becoming a powerful capital-ship navy organized around the search for decisive battle.

In fact, this representation of events is flawed, for reasons that Mahan understood and articulated at the time. The advisory boards cannot bear the interpretive weight placed on them, while the ABCD ships were ineffective and in any case belonged more to the old commerce-raiding paradigm than to a new battle-seeking one. There was no consensus within the Navy over force structure and strategy; the Rodgers board made an end run around the regular department bureaucracy, and such "consensus" as existed in the report of the Shufeldt board was forced on the Navy by Congress. Perhaps most importantly, European imperialism and the availability of funding are nowhere near sufficient to explain Congress's willingness to reverse the cuts of the 1870s and early 1880s, and not adequately supported by archival research. Changes in the domestic political economy, identified by the Wisconsin School, and in the international economy, identified by scholars of the first era of globalization, also must factor into the explanation.

Mahan's own keen interest in domestic politics and economics, clearly illustrated in his correspondence with Samuel Ashe, is itself an important clue that the traditional approach of naval historians cannot be correct. It is impossible to say which is the chicken and which the egg in the tendency to neglect these themes found in his early correspondence, or in the neglect of them in U.S. naval history. Regardless, the result has been a serious misunderstanding of both, which in turn has marred understanding of what Mahan wrote in *Influence* and of the book's effect on U.S. naval history. As we will see in chapter 3, *Influence* was a far more complex text than the Sprouts' characterization of Mahan's "capital-ship, or command-of-the-sea, theory" indicates, and it intervened in an ongoing debate over the future of the U.S. Navy, not a settled one. Before then, however, we must examine what Mahan did at the Naval War College.

CHAPTER 2

NAVAL INSTRUCTOR

(1884–89)

*I feel impelled to acknowledge my indebtedness to Admiral Luce. With
little constitutional initiative, and having grown up in the atmosphere
of the single cruiser, of commerce-destroying, defensive warfare, and
indifference to battleships; an anti-imperialist, who for that reason
looked upon Mr. Blaine as a dangerous man; at forty-five I was drifting
on the lines of simple respectability as aimlessly as one very well could.*

—ALFRED THAYER MAHAN, MAY 1908[1]

THERE COULD HAVE BEEN no Captain Mahan without Stephen B.
Luce. It had been Luce, it will be recalled, who had rescued Mahan
from his misery on board the *Wachusett* with an invitation to return
home and join the embryonic Naval War College. Although Mahan
was already a published author and had expressed his hope to write
a monograph on naval power, he was far from clear in his own mind
about how to go about it or even what he wanted to say. Above all
else, he lacked the necessary time and financial freedom to embark
on such a quest. By bringing him to Newport, Luce provided Mahan
with the opportunity to read, to think, and to write, and thus made
possible his first major monograph. The commodore was important
in another way as well. When Mahan arrived at Newport in 1885, his
ideas were still crystallizing. Luce, by contrast, had very clear ideas.

For the next four years, the forceful Luce pushed Mahan down certain avenues of thought; in so doing, he had a major effect on the direction of argument found in *The Influence of Sea Power upon History*—a direction the author was not entirely happy about taking. Untangling the similarities and dissimilarities between their ideas is important and requires close attention to detail.

We begin with Luce. In 1884, though not yet an admiral, Luce was one of the titans of the U.S. Navy: an officer of ideas and influence who enjoyed a significant following within the service, who possessed the ear of at least several important politicians, and whose opinion on important professional matters the Navy Secretary was sure to solicit. During the Civil War, Luce achieved his standing via the old-fashioned path of proficiency in seamanship, which endeared him to his seniors while also gaining him their respect. Directly after, between 1865 and 1868, Cdr. Luce served as commandant of midshipmen at the U.S. Naval Academy, where he attracted the attention of David Dixon Porter, who was then superintendent. The patronage of one of the Navy's two great heroes of the Civil War proved important for his career. On promotion to captain in 1872, Luce's career followed the conventional path, alternating between commands at sea and on shore for the next nine years.

At sea, Luce cemented his reputation as a superlative ship handler. He also developed the reputation as a "fighting" officer, derived from his advocacy of the need to prepare for war rather than achievements in combat. Like Mahan, his war record had been creditable rather than distinguished. On land, by contrast, Luce floundered, which explains why he was never appointed commandant of one of the navy yards or made chief of one of the bureaus inside the Navy Department.[2] This failure to check an administrative box was not insignificant: after the Civil War, the shortest path to advancement for officers of ambition and talent lay through the administrative or technical bureaus. All the leading officers of the day—including Francis Ramsey, Robert Shufeldt, Montgomery Sicard, William Sampson, and John G. Walker—served one or more tours inside the Navy Department.[3] Though Luce applied, he was always passed over in favor of other candidates and thus was denied the authority and access to resources necessary to initiate reform from within. This goes a long way to explaining why, as one authority has noted, Luce's contributions to the Navy were largely "intangible."[4] As Adm. Bradley Fiske described him in an obituary, Luce was "the prophet without honor in his own country."[5]

His seeming lack of administrative skills notwithstanding, Luce cleverly leveraged his sea experience and two tours at the Naval Academy to carve for himself a niche within the Navy's upper echelon as an expert in naval education. On his elevation to the rank of commodore in 1881, Luce was put in charge of the newly formed training squadron based at Newport—a grandiose title for the receiving ship responsible for inducting and providing basic training to lower-deck recruits. Even so, it served as a platform from which to agitate for reform and provided the status to make and cultivate friends in the political world. Although a proponent of educational reform, unlike most of his peers Luce did not want officers to be given yet more technical education. Luce was of the school, as was Mahan, which thought that naval officers were already spending far too much time in workshops or tinkering with mechanical devices and not enough thinking about command and combat. As Mahan once neatly explained it: "The present predominant tendency of the naval mind, as evidenced by the literature in which it finds expression and the work on which its practical energies are expended, is toward mechanical progress and development of materiel, rather than toward the study of military movements which that material is to subserve [*sic*]."[6] Luce was thus "the leader of the fight against technicism in the Navy."[7] Put another way, he wanted to put a stop to the Navy's technological tail wagging its warfighting dog.[8] It was this concern that lay behind the complaints by Luce and others that engineer officers (as distinct from line or seaman officers) enjoyed far too much influence within the service.[9] Instead of a navy organized for peace that in time of conflict would (hopefully) step up to perform war missions, as the U.S. Navy was then structured, Luce envisioned the Navy organized primarily for war, with the capability to step down to perform peace missions. In his own words, he wanted the Navy to recognize that proficiency in combat should be "the chief object and end of a fleet."[10] The implications of this creed extended far beyond naval training and ship design; they amounted to a call for a new U.S. Navy ethos.[11]

Since the end of the Civil War, it will be recalled, U.S. policy had been to maintain a peace navy, predicated on the assumption that the republic would never seek aggressive war, that its geographical isolation and territorial expanse made a European invasion logistically impossible, that it would maintain its traditional foreign policy of avoiding "foreign entanglements," and that it possessed limited interests overseas. When in January 1878 the Secretary of the Navy asked the chief of the Bureau of Equipment (Robert Shufeldt) to explain the logic behind the Navy's current force structure, he replied that "sea going foreign-cruising Iron Clads neither come within the limits of our probable means, nor is [*sic*] demanded by the foreign policy of this country. We neither wish to carry on an aggressive war, nor have we Colonies to defend."[12] That is to say, U.S. naval policy was to maintain a navy comprised of cheap cruising vessels built and organized for peacetime missions, such as showing the flag and protecting U.S. life and property overseas. The heterogeneous collection of warships that comprised the fleet seldom operated together, and even when they did, it was for administrative rather than tactical or training purposes.

Just in case, however, successive administrations permitted the Navy to retain a superabundance of officers to serve as a cadre in time of war and a reserve of ironclad monitors for port defense. Convinced that no foreign power could ever invade, and inspired more than they cared to admit by the success of Raphael Semmes and the Confederate sloop *Alabama* during the late war, the U.S. Navy's strategy in the event of war was to shield the nation's most important civilian seaports from capture or bombardment while waging a *guerre de course* (war against seaborne trade) against the enemy's merchant fleet. "It is only by destroying the commerce of a[n enemy] great nation that we could bring her to terms," declared David Dixon Porter in 1874, predicting that "one vessel like the *Alabama* roaming the ocean, sinking and destroying, would do more to bring about peace than a dozen unwieldy iron-clads cruising in search of an enemy of like character."[13] The nation's enormous productive potential and recent history bred confidence in this strategic policy. Within six months of the outbreak of the Civil War, the federal fleet had tripled in strength. It thus seemed reasonable to assume that the United States could again quickly commission warships by converting merchantmen to serve as corsairs, if and when needed.

Before the end of the 1870s, however, naval officers were questioning the practicality of improvising a fleet in time of crisis.[14] It was already apparent that the Navy could no longer be supplemented in an emergency by simply converting merchantmen into warships through fitting a few guns and hoisting naval ensigns fore and aft, as had been done during the Civil War. To stand any chance of success in combat, the ship required its machinery spaces to be protected from high-explosive shells (either by armor or carefully placed coal bunkers) and to be fitted with modern high-velocity guns, which required hard points on which to mount them so as to be structurally built into the ship. Then there was the matter of finding crews. For reasons unnecessary to elaborate on here, since 1865 the U.S. merchant marine had shrunk to almost insignificance. The continued usefulness of the old monitors kept in reserve for port defense duties was also becoming increasingly dubious. They were no match for new European iron-clads that the British (at Alexandria in 1882) and the French (at Fuzhou in 1884) had already demonstrated could operate in fleets at considerable distances from their bases, and both powers maintained naval bases in the Caribbean that were closer to the United States than Malta had been to Alexandria, or Saigon to Fuzhou.

To be clear, Luce and his associates were not questioning the Navy's strategy nor challenging its current force structure. They continued to promote the "short sword and buckler" approach, with a navy comprised of coastal defense craft on the one hand and cruising vessels in the other. All the reformers were asking for (at least at this stage) was the provision of modern warships: armored coastal defense ships with the fighting power to engage enemy ironclads with a reasonable prospect of success, plus purpose-built cruisers with the speed and range to serve as effective commerce raiders. Although Luce and his faction participated in the decades-long service arguments over warship design, they never pushed consistently for any particular design or offered a formula for the optimal fleet—certainly not before the 1890s. Luce in particular regarded such debate as sterile, or at any rate premature, until the Navy had first developed a clearer picture of how to wage naval combat in the age of steam. Put simply, Luce believed that the first step in the path toward naval renaissance was the development of practical naval tactics for steam-powered warships, something no navy in the world had yet accomplished. But who would be the officers to perform this vital task?

LUCE AND THE CREATION OF THE NAVAL WAR COLLEGE

In April 1883, at a gathering of the Naval Institute, Luce floated the idea (and not for the first time) of setting up a naval college "to prepare officers for the great business of their lives—the practical operation of war."[15] Such an educational matter fell within his area of competence. The idea gained traction. Over the course of the year, Luce added some flesh to the bones of his idea, and in March 1884 wrote to Secretary of the Navy William Chandler proposing the establishment of a new "war" college.[16] Chandler promptly set up a board of officers to formulate more specific proposals, inviting Luce himself to take the chair and pick his team. Only two officers were added: the high-flying Cdr. William Sampson (who would command the fleet during the Spanish-American War), then assigned to the Naval Torpedo Station but slated to become the next Superintendent of the Naval Academy (and thus an obvious choice). The other was Lt. Cdr. Caspar Goodrich, another well-regarded officer who was close to Luce and one of the original founders of the Naval Institute.

The report of the Luce board, dated June 13, 1884, was a model of deliberate ambiguity. It insisted that the new school be independent of the Naval Academy but offered no suggestions as to exactly where it should be built or under whose umbrella it should operate. In fact, Luce had already determined on Newport to be the site of his new school, and indeed had already secured the support of local Rhode Island politicians, but he was aware that talk of creating a new institution was already stirring up old jealousies and provoking squabbles. For instance, the current superintendent of the Naval Academy, Capt. Francis Ramsey, a notoriously prickly and opinionated officer, made known his expectation that the new college would be added to his command, and inside the department the bureau chiefs were bickering over which officer would supervise the new institution.[17] Ultimately, the plum went to the politically well-connected Commo. John G. Walker (the nephew of a sitting U.S. senator), who was bent on elevating the status of his Bureau of Navigation to become the first among equals. Whether Luce regarded this as a good thing or a bad thing is difficult to say.

The Luce report was similarly imprecise as to what the new college should teach. His report simply stated that "officers would not only be encouraged, but required to study their profession proper—war—in a far more thorough manner than had ever heretofore been attempted, and to bring to the investigation of the various problems of modern naval warfare the scientific methods adopted in other professions." Again, this opaqueness was quite deliberate and demonstrated that even if Luce was not a great administrator, he was well versed in the art of bureaucratic obfuscation. By eschewing all references to curriculum, moreover, Luce encouraged officers inside the technical bureaus to imagine the new institution as something many had long wanted, a graduate college for providing serving officers with further professional (largely technical) education.[18] While these bureaucratic machinations paid off in the short run, in that Luce obtained the authority and appropriation to establish his college, it stored up trouble for the future and fostered misunderstandings in the years ahead.

In fact, Luce was determined that his new college would have as little to do with technology as possible. For him, its primary focus lay elsewhere: to devise a practical system of naval tactics for employment by a squadron of steam-powered warships, defined as a group of at least four in company conforming to instructions issued from a flagship. To those who counseled waiting until the Navy actually possessed a squadron of modern warships—which as yet it did not—Luce replied that the unrelenting pace of technological change over the previous decades had resulted in nothing but confusion. Despite years of study and experiments, naval architects were no closer to penetrating the fog of uncertainty surrounding future trends. The lack of consensus within the service over the most important characteristics in warship design had induced Congress to refuse money for new vessels. What Luce proposed, therefore, was to break the construction logjam by tackling the problem from the opposite direction. Once the Navy possessed a coherent tactical doctrine, he reasoned, the best design characteristics of warships would become obvious; professional naval opinion would swiftly coalesce, allowing the Navy Department at last to speak with a single powerful voice when petitioning the legislature for new warships.

Equally distinctive were Luce's ideas on how to begin devising naval tactics. Rather than allowing the parameters of the technologically possible to govern the creation of tactics—or rather best guesses as to what future technology would make possible—Luce thought the Navy should seek inspiration through the rigorous study of naval history; in a sense, to look not forward but backward to the ages of sail and oar. This would be the mission of the Naval War College. Yet as one historian recently explained, "it was always Luce's intension to marry intellectual efforts at the shore establishment with practical work at sea."[19] That is to say, the task of the Naval War College would be to sketch out new tactical ideas, then pass them over to the North Atlantic Squadron for testing on the scale of twelve inches to the foot. That his vision did not come close to realization until long after he had retired from the service is another story that need not concern us here.

To understand Luce's intent correctly, it is critical to comprehend precisely what he meant by certain terms. For instance, when Luce demanded officers study naval history, he meant studying the history of naval tactics. He had little interest in the broader study of war, what today would fall under the heading of policy and strategy.[20] When he used the term "tactics," moreover, he applied it both to the *organization* of naval forces for combat operations and to the *employment* of those forces in battle. Whenever Luce employed the word "strategy," invariably he was referring to what today we would call "operations." Though he had read the writings of military theorist Carl von Clausewitz, for him the term "strategy" was devoid of any political/policy connotations.[21] More importantly still, when Luce called on naval officers to read naval history, he did not mean any old book. At that time, naval histories were little more than records of battles and the biographies of the men who fought them. No, Luce wanted them to read "scientifically" written history. What did that mean?

Luce outlined his thinking on the "scientific" approach, and his new college's role in developing it, in a paper titled "On the Study of Naval Warfare as a Science," a revised copy of which was later published in the U.S. Naval Institute's *Proceedings.*[22] Albeit in somewhat tangled prose, this paper opens a window on Luce's overarching aims and vision of naval reform better than any other paper he wrote. John Hattendorf and John D. Hayes, the leading authorities on Luce, agree that this paper was "the most complete expression of the intellectual concept behind the establishment of the Naval War College."[23] In the very first paragraph, Luce was deliberately provocative: "It must strike anyone who thinks about it as extraordinary that we, members of a profession of arms, should never have undertaken the study of our real business—war."[24] Though steam-propelled warships had been around for nearly forty years, Luce went on, even "the great naval powers of Europe still regard steam tactics as an unsolved problem."[25] Solving it was his objective.

The very model of a modern naval officer, Luce believed in the importance of tackling problems by employing a "scientific method." Like many leading nineteenth-century intellectuals, Luce believed that all human progress was regulated by discoverable scientific laws.[26] Naval officers of this era perceived themselves to be living in a (modern) scientific age, in much the same way as many officers today talk of a new digital age. But science had yet not acquired all the connotations that it would in the twentieth century, and the "scientific method" did not mean for Luce the iterative developing, testing, and revising of hypotheses that many now take it to mean. For him, "science" was "knowledge duly arranged, and referred to general truths and principles, on which it is founded, and from which it is derived."[27] In other words, science was the systematic arrangement of knowledge, something more akin to what would now be called taxonomy. After reviewing pages and pages of examples to illustrate his point, drawn from his reading of geology, chemistry, astronomy, and especially the scholarship of the English historian Henry Thomas Buckle, Luce pronounced science to be "the method of investigation pursued by the most advanced thinkers of the age."[28] Transparently he was trying to draw prestige to his work by associating it with the methods of scientists.

Luce brooked no disagreement. To those who dared to question his logic, he thundered that "to disregard such teachings is not merely to commit a great blunder by shutting our eyes to the lessons of history, but it is to be unscientific in one's own profession, which, in these days, is to be culpably ignorant, if not criminal."[29] Having defined his terms and forewarned his audience, Luce proceeded to assert that "Science is contributing so liberally to every department of knowledge, and has already done so much towards developing a truer understanding of the various arts, including that of the mariner, that is seems only natural and reasonable that we should call science to our aid to lead us to a clearer comprehension of naval warfare, as naval warfare is to be practiced in the future. Steam tactics and naval warfare under steam are comparatively new studies, and readily admit of modern and scientific methods of treatment."[30] In essence, therefore, Luce was calling for the application of the "scientific method" (the systematic arrangement of knowledge) to the study of naval history in order to permit officers to discern patterns within the organized data and so identify "principles." As indicated in the often-overlooked epigraph to his paper, for Luce "science is applied knowledge."

Warming to his theme, Luce turned to the critical importance of producing "scientific" naval history. He explained to his readers that

> naval history abounds in materials whereon to erect a science, as science has been defined and illustrated, and it is our present purpose to build up with these materials the science of naval warfare. We are far from saying that the various problems of war may be treated as rigorously as those of one of the physical sciences; but there is no question that the naval battles of the past furnish a mass of facts amply sufficient for the formulation of laws or principles which, once established, would raise maritime war to the level of a science.[31]

But, Luce cautioned, there was much preliminary work to be done. Presently there existed "no authoritative treatise on the art of naval warfare under steam" and "no recognized tactical order of battle," not even an agreed lexicon of "terminology of steam tactics."[32] How should the data gleaned from the study of naval history be organized "scientifically"?

Presuming a similarity between the conduct of war on land and by sea, Luce proceeded to argue that the solution to these related problems could be found through the simultaneous study of naval alongside military (army) history.[33] "The existence of fundamental principles, by which all the operations of war should be conducted," he asserted, "has been placed beyond doubts by the researches of [Gen. Baron Antoine-Henry] Jomini and other military writers. What has been done for military science is yet to be done for naval science."[34] He argued that to make sense of naval history, "we must, perforce, resort to the well-known rules of the military art with a view to their application to the military movements of a fleet, and, from the well-recognized methods of disposing troops for battle, ascertain the principles which should govern fleet formations. Thus from the known, we may arrive at something like a clear understanding of what is now mere conjecture. It is by this means alone that we can raise naval warfare from the empirical stage to the dignity of a science."[35] This construction of naval theory from military theory—not, as might be thought, the construction of naval theory from multiple naval examples—he called "the comparative method." His process of aligning the naval with the military also resulted in the Navy appropriating military terminology, like "object," "objectives," and "strategy."

Luce claimed there were precedents for taking this "comparative" approach. The French scientist George Cuvier, he argued, "applied to the study of generalizations of comparative anatomy, and coordinated the study of the strata of the earth with the study of the fossil animals found in them. Thus he was the founder of the science of geology."[36] Accordingly, "to elevate naval warfare into a science, as we now propose doing, we must adopt the comparative method; and, as Cuvier coordinated the study of geology with that of comparative anatomy, so must we coordinate the study of naval warfare with military science and art. That is the theory on which we are now to proceed."[37] In sum, Luce envisioned the codification of steam tactics through a two-step process: first, gathering data through the scientific study of naval history; second, analyzing that data through the lens of military theory (the comparative method) to arrive at the principles of naval tactics.

Why do these idiosyncratic ideas of an eccentric, long-dead admiral matter? There are two reasons. First, this was the original agenda for the establishment of the Naval War College—to study tactics and naval operations (not strategy). In Luce's scheme, it was to be the faculty's job to write the "scientific" naval history and identify the historical "lessons" required by the U.S. Navy. Second, students of Mahan's scholarship have long assumed that the captain was committed to the theory of scientific method and the teachings of Jomini. Close reading of the extant evidence suggests otherwise, however. These ideas were Luce's, and he pressed them on his subordinate. In other words, to the extent that Mahan borrowed from the Swiss theorist in his first book (far less than some have averred) this reflected more of Luce's push than of Jomini's pull. After the publication of *Influence* in 1890, moreover, Mahan's writing escaped from Luce's influence, and he progressively distanced himself from his mentor's ideas.

LUCE'S RECRUITMENT OF MAHAN

The Naval War College was formally established in October 1884, and Luce appointed as its first president. Already, however, the commodore had begun recruiting faculty. In July, directly after the Navy Secretary approved his recommendation and requested an appropriation from Congress, Luce wrote to Mahan, inviting him to join him at Newport.[38] His selection was no accident: their professional paths had crossed several times before. In 1862, the two had taught seamanship together at the Naval Academy. In 1863, as noted in chapter 1, on being given his first command, Luce had asked for Mahan to serve as his executive officer.[39] The following year the two came into contact again when Mahan joined Adm. John Dahlgren's staff; Luce commanded a ship in Dahlgren's squadron. In 1875, Luce and Mahan again overlapped at the Boston Navy Yard.

Luce would have approved of Mahan's willingness to testify before the congressional inquiry into corruption at the navy yards, an act that marked him as a zealous, if perhaps naive reformer.[40] In 1878, Mahan wrote an essay advocating an overhaul of naval education, another subject close to Luce's heart, which won third prize in a Naval Institute essay competition. Both felt strongly that officer education had become overly focused on scientific training in excess of what most naval offers required, or would ever use, to the detriment in teaching of command in war.[41] In 1883, the lure of $600 (20 percent of his annual pay) induced Mahan to write *Gulf and Inland Waters*, a slim volume describing the principal naval events during the late war where he had served. Though researched and written in the space of just five months, the book was competently written and reflected real effort and thought. It was well received, including by those who had fought for the Confederacy, and further burnished his service reputation as an intellectual officer.[42]

Despite these credentials, it is not clear whether Mahan was Luce's first choice for the chair in naval history at the War College. A letter written in 1906 from Caspar Goodrich, one of Luce's favorites and the officer who had served under him on the board that that had drawn up the recommendation to establish the War College, claimed

that "it was I who suggested Mahan's name as that of a person eminently fitted by temperament and acquirements to take the chair of
naval history."[43] This suggests that Mahan was the first choice, but that
the Navy Department flatly refused to consider curtailing him after
just four months in command of his sloop. In any case, in February
1884, Luce (subsequently?) offered the position to Goodrich himself. It evidently did not matter to him that Goodrich possessed no
credentials whatsoever as a historian. In declining the offer for family
and financial reasons, Goodrich advised Luce to approach Lt. Morris
R. MacKensie, currently assigned to the *Essex*, or failing him either Lt.
Richard Wainwright or Lt. Edward Very.[44] Whether Luce acted on this
advice remain unknown, but given that five months elapsed between
Goodrich's refusal and his offer to Mahan, it seems probable that he
did. By that time Mahan had held his command for a year, a more
respectable duration before reassignment.

First choice or not, Mahan immediately accepted Luce's invitation.
In so doing, he confessed to feeling daunted by the amount of work
ahead. "As I turn over in my mind the naval battles, and naval and
mixed expeditions, scattered through history, and think how little I
know about them in detail, the work assumes very great proportions,"
he replied to Luce on September 4, 1884.[45] He was painfully conscious of how much he did not know: "I do not on questioning myself
find that now I have the special accurate knowledge that I should
think necessary. I fear you give me credit for knowing more than I do,
and having given special attention to the subject which I have not."[46]
Mahan estimated that he would need at least a year in a proper library
to prepare his course: "to look out the authorities, master them, digest
and arrange the material thus acquired, bring together examples illustrating the same lessons, above all the criticism, every one of these
steps is big."[47] Mahan then gingerly floated the idea of Luce arranging
his early recall home.[48] Luce tried, but the Department declined his
curtailment.[49]

A couple of months later, however, in January 1885, Mahan was
ecstatic to receive unexpected word that the *Wachusett* would shortly
be ordered home. In anticipation of a prompt departure, the squadron

commander cannibalized his ship of personnel and stores, a standard practice at the time. While he awaited his official orders, Mahan scoured the local libraries and source-mined what he could find.[50] But as the days turned to weeks and then to months, Mahan became increasingly upset. After learning from an acquaintance just arrived on station that Luce wanted a lecturer that fall—allowing him no time at all to prepare his course—Mahan was reduced to despair. "As I wrote you eight months ago," he complained to Luce on May 13, 1885, "in order to do any good work I needed several months preparation at home, that there was little or no material, of the kind I needed, here."[51] Mahan was afraid the commodore would grow impatient and "swap horses"—in other words, find a replacement instructor.[52] In fact, Luce had already tried. In March he had approached Lt. William Mathews, who, fortunately for Mahan, proved even more daunted by the necessary study and consequently declined the position.[53]

Then, two days later, a letter from Luce arrived from out of the blue rekindling Mahan's hopes.[54] The same evening (May 15), desperate to catch a mail steamer due to depart the following morning, Mahan penned several letters in great haste, in places with little thought, and each dripping with emotion. The longest and most important was addressed to Luce. Mahan seemed euphoric that "it would appear that you do not expect to begin this fall," before beseeching the commodore not to forsake him, and assuring him that he had made considerable progress in conceptualizing his subject. Signaling his commitment to the cause of naval history, he boasted that "when I began to think that the College plan was to fall through indefinitely I determined, or rather I entertained the idea, of gathering the materials and writing a book on the general plan proposed to me."[55]

> As far as I can remember, and can now gather in a hurry from scanty notes made, I meant to begin with a general consideration of the sea as a highway for commerce and also for hostile attacks upon countries bordering on it, dwell upon principal commercial routes—then consider sources of maritime power or weakness—materiel, personnel, national aptitude, harbors with their positions

relative to commercial routes and enemy coasts. I proposed after to bring forward instances, from ancient and modern history, of the effects of navies and the control of the sea upon great or small campaigns. Hannibal for instance has to make that frightful passage of the Alps, in which he lost the quarter part of his original army, because he did not control the sea.

While it is possible to see something of Mahan's *Influence* in this 1885 letter—particularly the infamous first chapter—it contains important dissimilarities as well as similarities. For instance, elsewhere in the letter, Mahan envisioned structuring his book geographically rather than chronologically. He also imagined his text would span a much broader period of history, encompassing ancient as well as modern times. As is well known, Mahan subsequently maintained that he experienced an epiphany after reading Theodore Mommsen's volumes on the Carthaginian War, placing him firmly on the path to developing his concept of sea power—but later reading, as we will see below, seems to have had a still greater influence on his conception of the subject. It may be that Mahan had an inkling of what he wanted to say but that he remained far from clear as to how.

Desperate to escape his ship, Mahan wrote to the Secretary of the Navy formally requesting an early release and implored Luce to endorse it.[56] Two months later, Mahan received by telegram orders to bring *Wachusetts* home. Luce had indeed interceded on his behalf with the Navy Secretary, who told Luce, "On the 23d of July, the day of your letter seems to have been written, a cablegram was sent to Cdr. Mahan to proceed to San Francisco," going on to quip, "I suppose that answers your suggestion and is only another illustration of the fact that great men agree in their thoughts."[57] Luce clearly wanted Mahan.

LUCE'S INFLUENCE AND MAHAN'S TASK

For various reasons, Mahan did not finally report to the War College in Newport until mid-October 1885, after the end of the academic year.[58] Because no quarters were available locally and the War College as yet possessed no library, Luce granted the newly promoted Capt. Mahan permission to reside in New York City for the next ten months, until the beginning of the next academic year.[59] This is not to say that in the interim Mahan was left to his own devices. Luce was not that sort of commanding officer. Given his burning mission to codify naval tactics and his very clear idea of how to do so, combined with Mahan's admission to him that "on the subject of naval tactics I own that I am awfully at sea," it seems reasonable to assume that when they met in Newport, Luce provided his subordinate with guidance on how to proceed.[60] After all, Luce had recruited Mahan to assist him. Although he enjoyed the reputation of being a "progressive" officer, back in the day that meant a willingness to listen to the opinions of his subordinates. Luce may not have demanded his officers steer a straight course toward the destination he had charted—they might zig a bit here and zag a bit there—but they were expected to keep to the base course. So it proved to be with Luce and Mahan.

What general instructions did Luce give to Mahan about his teaching? This, alas, does not admit a ready answer and indeed has generated a great deal of confusion. Luce's original invitation to Mahan of July 1884 has not survived, but in any case was probably no more than an outline, since the reply to it shows a struggle to grasp the message.[61] "I take it," Mahan wrote, "the subject you propose to me involves an amount of historical narration, specially directed toward showing the causes of failure and success, and thus enforcing certain general principles. Whether to this is to be added any attempt at evolving a system of tactics applicable to modern naval warfare, I don't understand; but I suppose by Naval Tactics you scarcely mean a reproduction of [Commo. Foxhall] Parker."[62] Luce likely clarified his requirements in his next letter, but alas that too has not survived. The earliest surviving evidence of Luce's thoughts are found in a draft of his "Report of the Superintendent Naval War College" [sic] dated September 30, 1885, in which he noted that Capt. A. T. Mahan, USN, would "prepare to instruct in Naval History and Naval Tactics."[63]

This solitary line seems to have fueled the assumption that Luce tasked Mahan to teach not one but two courses, one on naval history and the other on naval tactics.[64] Yet a letter in February 1886 from Mahan to his old Naval Academy friend Samuel Ashe indicates that Luce had instructed him to prepare a single course consisting of two parts designed to dovetail: "I have had assigned to me the subject of Naval Strategy and Tactics involving of course to a considerable extent Naval History as affording lessons."[65] This sounds very much like the approach that Luce had prescribed in his *Proceedings* essay, of using the "lessons" of history, isolated from any particular technological context, to identify the ideal tactics, which modern technology could then be designed to advance. Subsequent back-to-back letters from Mahan to Luce also point toward this interpretation. In the first, Mahan spoke of his "glimmering of how to *hitch-on* [i.e., join] the history of the past to the theory of the present."[66] In the second, he wrote, "The first parts of my course relating to naval history &c are yet untouched, though prepared for."[67] "Course" singular, "parts" plural: this makes clear that Mahan had structured his course in the way that Luce had conceived it, as an idiosyncratic fusion of naval history and naval tactics, with the former illustrating and providing insight into the latter.

Their correspondence that winter (1885–86) shows that Luce indeed was constantly pressing Mahan to employ his unique methodology. At first, eager to please and uncertain in his own mind, the latter seemed happy to comply. Over time, however, Mahan became increasingly doubtful that Luce's model would serve. As his research progressed, he found himself heading in quite a different direction, both methodologically and in the way he conceptualized the subject of naval history. For one thing, he questioned whether Luce's notion of the "scientific method" married to the "comparative approach" could ever bear fruit. For another, whereas Luce was focused on tactics, Mahan was drawn outside the boundaries of naval battle toward the bigger question of how states employ navies to achieve their long-term political goals and how navies go about achieving them—that is, he was much more interested in what today fall under the headings of policy and strategy than in operations and tactics. The letters between the two men also show clearly that Mahan's research was not limited simply to looking for material to decorate his already formed thesis, as some have argued, but that his thesis was still very much under development.[68]

Mahan spent his first three months in New York trawling thorough the stacks of the Astor Library and the New York Lyceum (now the New York Public Library) before carrying his haul back to the University Club and devouring it either side of lunch. (The club boasted a fair library and a tolerable dining room.) He also was allowed to request material from the Navy Department library to be mailed to him. Throughout, he stayed in close contact with Luce, reporting his progress, suggesting titles of books to be added to the War College library, and asking for pointers to find answers to puzzling questions. All the while, Luce was constantly prodding Mahan to follow his direction and read the books he had already identified as fundamental, even offering to lend him his valuable personal copies.

At the end of October 1885, for instance, the commodore pressed Mahan to read Jomini's *Art of War*. The captain replied, on November 3 and again on November 19, that he was not yet ready, that he was fully occupied gathering historical facts. He nevertheless promised to use Jomini's book as "as a model possibly suggestive of *manner* of treatment"—for use as an analytical template, so to speak.[69] In fact, the captain was engrossed in reading Henri Martin's magisterial, multi-volume *History of France*.[70] It is not too much to say that Martin, one of the leading French historians of the nineteenth century, had a profound and hitherto unnoticed impact on Mahan's work. Indeed, in his autobiography he acknowledged his debt to the French historian, whose four volumes translated into English he discovered on the shelves of a friend. "The particular value of Martin to me was the attention paid by him to commercial and maritime policy," Mahan recalled.[71] The captain frankly admitted that hitherto he had not adequately considered the commercial and economic aspects of the subject. These two elements would form part of the core of Mahan's argument in *Influence*. In his autobiography he wrote,

> Whatever Martin's views on political economy, he was in profound sympathy with [Jean-Baptiste] Colbert [1619–83] as an

administrator, and enlarged much on his commercial policy as conducing to the financial stability upon which that great statesman sought to found the primacy of his country. To one as ignorant as I was of mercantile movement, the story of Colbert's methods, owing to their pure autocracy, was a kind of introductory primer to this element of sea power. Thus received, the impression was both sharper and deeper. New light was shed upon, and new emphasis given to, the commonplace assertion of the relations between commerce and a navy; civil and military sea power.[72]

To those who trouble to read Martin's oeuvre, the magnitude of Mahan's debt to him becomes instantly apparent. Not only did the four Martin volumes cover the period from 1643 to 1783—practically the same periodization that Mahan would use in *Influence* (1660–1783)—but more suggestively still, Martin's analysis was structured around the policy interplay between state finances, international trade, commercial development, and naval policy. The importance of Martin's work reinforces the argument made by Jon Sumida that Mahan did not focus on British success at sea as a model for emulation. Rather, Mahan "left little doubt that his chief interest was in the behavior of France, in spite of the attention that he paid to Britain," and he presented his arguments "largely in terms of French error or success."[73]

In the New Year 1886, Luce pushed Mahan harder to align his work with the theory of war on land. He sent him copies of the lectures of Lt. (later Gen.) Tasker Bliss, the Army officer he had recruited for the War College to teach military theory, a clear prompt to begin using his "comparative method." "I will keep the analogy between land and naval warfare before my eyes," Mahan assured his chief by return.[74] Luce was doubtless much relieved when a fortnight later Mahan wrote him that "I am now reaching a point at which I think the books of other writers on kindred subjects will be more suggestive to me than they would have been three months ago"—by kindred subjects he was referring to military theory.[75] Now "I shall be glad to have Hamley," he wrote—a reference to British Lt. Gen.Edward

Bruce Hamley's *Operations of War*, a contemporary (1866) textbook on military theory.

Four days later, however, clearly in response to yet another prod from Luce, Mahan provided a much fuller exposition of his views.

> With regard to my own course of lectures my ideas have not yet attained the precision which I would like to throw into any reply to you. In a general way they are these: I think to begin with a general consideration of the sea, its uses to mankind and to nations, the effect which the control of it or the reverse has upon their peaceful development and upon their military strength. This will naturally lead to, and probably embrace in the same lecture, a consideration of the sources of Sea Power, whether commercial or military; depending upon the [geographical] position of the particular country—the character of its coast, its harbors, the character and pursuits of its people, in its possession of military posts in various parts of the world, its colonies &c., its resources, in the length and breadth of the world. After such a general statement of the various elements of the problem, illustrated of course by specific examples—the path would be cleared for naval history.[76]

Readers familiar with Mahan's famous book will instantly see a clear resemblance between the passage above and the first thirty-odd pages of his 1890 book. Yet, external similarities aside, much more significant was Mahan's description of how he conceived his subject. After explaining why he had decided to drop the ancient history of the Punic Wars that had so fascinated and inspired him the year before, Mahan informed Luce he now intended to focus on "that period succeeding the peace of Westphalia, 1648, when the nations of Europe began clearly to enter on and occupy their modern positions." He reasoned: "I have carefully followed up this [modern] period both in respect of naval history and the general struggles of Europe; for it has seemed to me, with reference to my subject, that the attempt to violently separate the naval history from that context will be something like, to capsize a proverb, Hamlet with all but the part of Hamlet left out."[77] What Mahan was saying here was that in the course of his historical studies, he had come to realize that naval history could not be separated from the political and economic context; the naval history of one nation could not automatically be treated the same as that of another. In order to draw any meaningful lessons from any particular decision or course of action, it was necessary first to form a clear picture of contexts and circumstances.

If this reading is correct, then Mahan's statement represented a profound divergence from Luce's methodology and even an implicit repudiation of his conception of history. Whereas the commodore wanted to use history to identify timeless principles that would stimulate efforts to solve modern-day tactical problems, the captain cast doubt on the possibility of divorcing principles from particular historical contexts and advocated studying history in order to understand war on a higher plane—a different approach to a different set of questions.

Luce could have been no further reassured by the second point contained in Mahan's letter of January 22, informing him that, as yet, he had given no thought on how to interweave naval history with naval tactics. The captain hastened to assure his commodore that he remained committed to the "comparative method": "I expect to begin with Jomini &c, and, having naval conditions constantly before my mind, I shall hope to detect analogies—and with an admirable system of one kind of war before me to contribute something to the development of a systematic study of war in another [naval] field."[78] But in the next breath Mahan confessed that he remained "a little at sea" as to how this might be accomplished.[79] That is to say, he could see no way to make Luce's method work. A few days before, Mahan had told Ashe of his troubles at work and had admitted that "I am somewhat fearful of failure."[80] Ashe evidently asked his friend to elaborate, for three weeks later Mahan sent him a long letter outlining the function of the new War College, and his task to divine insights from the study of naval history. Or as he expressed it, "how to view the lessons of the past so as to mold them into lessons for the future, under such differing conditions, is the nut I have to crack."[81] In so doing, Mahan made clear his discomfort.

To excogitate a system of my own, on wholly *a priori* grounds, would be comparatively simple and I believe wholly useless. We are already deluged with speculations and arguments as to future naval warfare—more or less plausible and well considered; but I don't see any use in my adding to that clack. I want if I can to wrest something out of the old wooden sides and 24 pounder that will throw some light on the combinations to be used with ironclads, rifled guns and torpedoes; and to raise the profession in the eyes of its members by a clearer comprehension of the great part it has played in the world than I myself have hitherto had.

What we see here is Mahan's nervousness at the thought of mixing history with present-day conjecture. He did not dispute that history could be employed as a foundation for the study of contemporary problems, indeed he ardently believed it could be; but if that historical foundation was to bear any significant interpretative weight, such as Luce expected, then it would have to be built with much greater care than Luce appeared to realize and was demanding. History was not simply a collection of self-evident facts waiting to be plucked from the past and transported to the present for contemporary edification, as Luce seemed to assume: establishing the "facts" was far more problematic, requiring intensive research and command of context.

Possessing only one side of the correspondence, we can only speculate what Luce made of Mahan's letter of January 22. But reading between the lines of Mahan's subsequent letters to him suggests that the commodore firmly steered his wayward subordinate back onto his own preferred path of using history to derive lessons about naval tactics. Throughout February and March, the captain was too ill to work (with a bout of malarial fever that he had contracted in Ecuador) and so Luce stayed his hand.[82] From the beginning of April 1886, however, though their correspondence remained friendly, the tone of Mahan's letters change noticeably, now containing a certain defensiveness. Was Mahan perhaps reacting to criticism received from Luce, suggestions that he was not doing what had been asked of him and consequently that he was failing in his task? What else accounts for Mahan's apology to Luce on April 24 that "if I fail—the failure will be mine"? Why else did he confess that "if I confine myself to history the College would be blamed for not keeping me to things that were useful"?[83] Or are these comments merely a reflection of Mahan's worry that he was still unwell and falling behind in his work? One thing is certain: by this time he saw that the scale of the enterprise on which he had embarked was far greater than he—or Luce—had imagined it would be.

Around this time also, Luce made a point of sending the captain the latest redaction of his own "On the Study of Naval Warfare as a Science" with instructions to read it carefully.[84] By now, having taken the hint, Mahan had ceased his historical research and was focusing exclusively on naval tactics. A fortnight and a half later, the commodore apparently requested to see Mahan's notes on naval tactics, for the latter replied that he presently had "some 70 odd pages of foolscap—80 of which will about make two lectures."[85] On May 1, Mahan forwarded his notes along with an apology for the mess of erasures and marginalia they contained, "but it was desirable that you should judge as soon as possible whether the matter and manner of my treatment of the subject is likely to meet your views. There is as yet but a small fragment of that which that must be produced; but enough to know whether the lines on which I work—the method with which I approach the problem—gives hope of a probably satisfactory solution."[86] Luce, it seems, found the notes barely legible and had the manuscript pages typed, for a copy is found in the records of the Naval War College.[87] "I am anxious to get beyond the mere historical part if I can," a clearly anxious Mahan wrote him again several days later, "hence the attempt I have made which is now in your hands."[88] On May 31, the admiral finally replied, informing him that he found his notes "in the main satisfactory."[89] Mahan interpreted Luce's response as a passing grade and thanked him.

Mahan spent the summer of 1886 with his family at his mother-in-law's house at the summer resort town of Bar Harbor, Maine. Carrying with him as many essential texts as he could scrounge from friends or borrow from the War College's library, he sat down to transcribe his four-hundred-plus pages of notes on naval history into several lectures and to fashion a hitch to join them with a couple more on naval tactics drawn from his seventy-odd pages of jottings on that subject.[90] With the beginning of the academic term now just months away, Mahan was scrambling.

In June 1886, Mahan's life became further complicated after Secretary William C. Whitney unexpectedly appointed Commo. Luce as the next commander of the North Atlantic squadron—a prestigious rather than powerful command—and detached him from the War College. Because no replacement was announced, Luce informed Mahan that until the latter heard otherwise from the department, it fell to him as senior officer present to pick up the administrative reigns. When Mahan reported for duty at Newport at the end of August 1886, therefore, no further word having been heard from Washington, he became the de facto president of the War College. The title was not nearly as grand as it sounded; Mahan received no boost in pay, and he and his family ended up being quartered in the college lecture hall.

The term opened on September 6, 1886, and ran until November 20.[91] Because his flagship was in port, Luce delivered the opening address—the science of history again—to the twenty-one officers (including two Marines) enrolled plus various spectators from his squadron. Over the next several weeks the commodore delivered three further presentations, all focused on naval tactics.[92] For reasons that remain unclear, "owing to a combination of circumstances," he later told Ashe, Mahan did not begin lecturing until the end of October.[93] The most likely explanations are either that Luce took his slots or that Mahan was absorbed with administrative duties. Midway through the term he dashed off a quick note to Ashe, mentioning that certain officers in Washington opposed to the War College (Luce's critics) were making his life difficult by choking off congressional appropriations.[94] When Mahan finally presented his lectures (probably six, though possibly eight), he was pleasantly taken aback by the favorable reception.[95] Those who heard him agreed he was a good instructor.[96]

For the next two years, teaching and scholarship remained a secondary occupation for Mahan as he became absorbed in his administrative duties and in lobbying Washington for funds to keep the fledging

War College operating. The handful of letters Mahan wrote to Ashe while serving as president (from September 1886 to November 1888) consist mainly of apologies for not having written sooner and complaints about being submerged in paperwork and politics.[97] The story of Mahan's battle to keep the War College from being closed, and how he threw himself body and soul into the task, has been told many times before and thus need not be repeated here.[98] Suffice it to say that ultimately Luce's enemies prevailed, and in 1889 the three different naval training establishments in Newport (each reporting to a different bureau) were consolidated into a single command. For his pains, Mahan was banished to the Pacific northwest to look at possible sites for a new naval base.

What none of these previous accounts mentions, it should be noted, is that Mahan proved to be an unexpectedly skillful bureaucratic warrior. Though he professed to loathe office politics and administrative legerdemain, the fact is that he played the weak hand he had been dealt very well. In the process of lobbying in Washington, face-to-face with senators and congressmen, he gained additional important insights into how the world worked and how Washington functioned—which of course are not quite the same thing.

THE INFLUENCE OF LUCE ON MAHAN?

Mahan always remained grateful to Luce for rescuing him from the *Wachusett*, but although he almost became one he was not his mentor's creature, and his ideas must be distinguished from Luce's. Mostly because he was initially overwhelmed by his task and uncertain how to begin, Mahan started down the path indicated by Luce, to study history through a combination of the "scientific method" and a "comparative approach" that took the "immutable principles" of tactics uncovered by Jomini's analysis of land warfare and applied them to sea warfare. Very quickly, however, Mahan began to query Luce's instructions as he found himself being pulled in quite a different direction by his insight into the influence of sea power on world history. As one Mahan scholar noticed, "[he] was not intellectually comfortable at the task of making tactics scientific. He knew that was a part of Luce's purpose from the beginning but he shied at the gate."[99] Mahan still agreed with Luce that "the chief object and end of a fleet" was battle and shared Luce's desire to achieve a codification of naval tactics. But in so agreeing, as we shall see, Mahan insisted one must never lose sight of the ultimate purpose of battle, which was determined by political goals.

Similarly, while Mahan incorporated some of his mentor's ideas into his own work, such as borrowing concepts and terminology from Jomini and subscribing to the notion of *a few* immutable "principles," he did so under pressure and never embraced them as Luce did or allowed them to shape his analysis to anything like the same degree.[100] Where Luce saw governing "laws," Mahan saw "patterns"; where Luce employed dogmatism to make his point, Mahan presented nuance and qualification. Moreover, whereas Luce pressed for the study of *how* a navy fought, Mahan wanted to explain *why* it fought; whereas Luce wanted to fathom the outcome and significance of battles, Mahan wanted to comprehend the outcome and significance of wars.

These major differences in outlook and intent notwithstanding, to outsiders Mahan loyally preached Luce's core message. In 1887, he stated officially that "the art of naval war has never received systematic treatment, and, so far as is known, amid all the immense activity now bestowed upon the development of the materiel of war, nowhere in the world is there an organized attempt being made to effect such treatment except at the Naval War College."[101] At the same time, however, Mahan made subtle but important changes to his predecessor's core curriculum. To meet complaints that it was insufficiently practical to be of much use to the Navy, he introduced new courses that touched on geopolitics and geostrategy, topics much more in line with his own views and interests than Luce's fixation on naval tactics. For instance, Mahan presented a short course of lectures on the strategic implications of an Isthmian Canal, in his own words "designed to familiarize the minds of officers with the great issues that are maturing in the waters of Central America; the importance of those regions from the point of view of military control, if not of war; and also incidentally to awaken intention of the close connection between the commercial and naval interest of a country."[102] The significance of this course, a consideration of commercial and economic factors blended with geostrategy over time, should not be underestimated. During the late 1880s, this was a most popular topic for discussion in public and political circles. Moreover, it was difficult to argue that the subject was not relevant or useful, especially considering that no one serving in the Navy Department had given this important question any thought at all. Indeed, even Luce was impressed with Mahan's new course, in March 1889 holding it up to the incoming Secretary of the Navy as the prime example of the useful work the Naval War College might perform.[103] Mahan's thoughts on Isthmian policy were ultimately published, six months after the appearance of *Influence*, and as will be shown in chapter 4 they gained attention and gathered much praise.

In his spare moments, Mahan honed the manuscript that would eventually become *Influence*. To be clear, what became the book was not simply a copy of his lectures, as has been so often asserted, but rather a separate manuscript written in parallel, at the same time, and drawing on the same notes harvested from the same sources. As we shall see in later chapters, the book employed a distinctly different core thread from that used in the lectures. On September 4, 1888, believing his manuscript finished, he submitted it to Charles Scribner's Sons, who five years before had published *Gulf and Inland Waters*. The covering letter presented the manuscript as analzying "the bearing of naval power upon the general course of History in Western Europe and America between the years 1660 and 1783." Mahan further explained that "it carries along a general thread of the history of the times, with a view to eliciting the effect of naval and commercial power on events; the treatment of naval affairs proper being not an exhaustive account of all that happened, but rather a selection of such campaigns and battles as have a tactical or strategic value, and so afford an opportunity for pointing a lesson."[104] Note the joint emphasis on commercial as well as naval power. Scribner's took less than two weeks, however, to reject Mahan's manuscript as too technical. Over the course of the next twelve months, Mahan approached numerous other publishers but received the same negative response.

Although Luce thought Mahan's manuscript an impressive piece of work and publicly said so, he saw it as a mere prelude to the main event. "This is a laborious work and, for our navy, a very important one," the admiral explained to Lt. John F. Meigs, a leading gunnery expert who two years before had lectured at the War College on gunnery matters and was now serving at the Bureau of Ordnance in Washington.[105]

> If carried out, it will place us at once in the front rank of the Navies of the world in the Science of Naval Warfare. The *practice* of the art, is, of course, another matter. Captain Mahan's lectures, as well as his constant study, is leading up to that great end. If his lectures on "The Influence of Naval Power on the Growth of Nations," can be published, that subject will be disposed of, and he will be enabled to "unload" an immense mass of material, dismiss that branch of the subject from his mind, and start with those branches which cover modern implements of Naval Warfare. In this way he will come to the study and solution of the problem of Steam Tactics. That is the task, as you know, we had set ourselves to accomplish.

Luce, in other words, seems to have seen *Influence* as no more than a foundation on which to build something more important—a workable system of steam tactics. What is more, he evidently (and erroneously) believed that Mahan's purpose in writing *Influence* was in line with this overarching goal.[106] Luce made exactly the same point in another letter to J. S. Barnes, a former naval officer turned railway financier and a keen amateur naval historian. "It is desirable now that he [Mahan] should 'unload' as it were this large amount of ms [manuscript] to enable him to relieve his mind of its care &c &c that he may continue this very valuable work and bring his history down to the present time. For you must understand that this is but part of his work. He and his collaborators are yet to develop from the lessons of the past the Science of Modern Naval Warfare."[107] One cannot help but wonder whether this was how Mahan sold his work to Luce or how Luce rationalized Mahan's deviations from his orders.

In March 1889, Luce wrote the Navy Secretary that he and his followers remained committed to finishing their self-appointed task "to apply modern scientific methods to the study and raise naval warfare from the empirical stage to the dignity of a science."[108] This may have been true of Luce and most of his band, but Mahan was now proceeding along very different lines. Let us turn now to examine what the captain actually wrote.

CHAPTER 3

INFLUENCE

(1889–90)

The definite object proposed in this work is an examination of the general history of Europe and America with particular reference to the effect of sea power upon the course of that history. Historians generally have been unfamiliar with the conditions of the sea, having as to it neither special interest nor special knowledge; and the profound determining influence of maritime strength upon great issues has consequently been overlooked.

—ALFRED THAYER MAHAN, PREFACE TO *INFLUENCE*[1]

AFTER SCRIBNER'S DECLINED "The Influence of Naval Power on the Growth of Nations" in September 1888, Mahan spent more than a year hawking the manuscript to various U.S. publishers. His son later estimated that his father's renowned book was rejected another "eight or ten" times.[2] Twelve months later, Mahan was in despair and on the verge of giving up.[3] The chief criticism from publishers was that his manuscript was too technical; there was not a large enough market for a treatise aimed predominantly at a professional naval audience. Taking the point, Mahan made changes. At the end of September 1889, Mahan offered the revised manuscript to Little, Brown and Company of Boston.[4] Carrying a letter of introduction from James Soley, the Naval War College's lecturer in international law and also a published author, Mahan traveled up to Massachusetts and personally delivered the manuscript to James B. Brown, the senior partner.[5]

"By Soley's advice," Mahan afterward recounted to Luce, "I dwelt upon the fact that it was *popular* and *critical*; both of which are very true. In the historical treatment I had the probable knowledge of officers before my eyes and aimed above all at simplicity and coherence; while in recasting I have remembered the public, and endeavored to make nautical maneuvers clear by the avoidance of technical terms."[6] The meeting went well, and evidentially the changes he made proved sufficient. On October 16, Mahan jubilantly informed Luce that "Messrs. Little, Brown & Co have undertaken to publish the book."[7] Set in print early the following year, it was released for sale during the first week of May 1890, published under the title *The Influence of Sea Power upon History, 1660–1783.*

Mahan's last-minute revisions to his book were the cause of considerable confusion as to the main arguments within. What these were is obvious enough: to make his story appear more relevant to contemporary readers, Mahan peppered the historical narrative with analogies and allusions to the problems then facing the United States. These presentist asides are scattered throughout the book but are particularly visible in the first and last chapters. Though they helped Mahan sell his manuscript, their effect was to create interpretive challenges for readers of and a distraction to his explication of sea power.

For instance, Mahan used his book as a vehicle to intervene in the ongoing debate over future U.S. Navy force structure. As we saw in previous chapters, contrary to the conventional naval narrative, the 1880s had not put the Navy well on its way toward the promised land of plentiful battleships organized for decisive battle. Within Congress, a consensus had developed on the need for new warships but not yet on what types or how many should be built, let alone how much money should be provided. By the end of the decade, two principal schools of thought had emerged. One group, probably the larger, proposed simply modernizing the existing cruiser navy, albeit supplemented with sufficient small armor-clad ships to overmatch the South American navies in battle. The other, led by Adm. Luce, called for the armor-clad warships to be built as "true" battleships and constructed in sufficient numbers to give pause to any major European power contemplating encroachment into the Western Hemisphere. Needless to say, this was a far more costly proposition.

At meeting of the Naval Institute during the summer of 1889, Mahan sided openly with Luce by asserting to those assembled that cruiser navies were practically useless against navies supported by battleships and insisting that a *guerre de course* strategy would provide little actual deterrent. He affirmed that "It is much to be hoped that the whole question of dependence upon swift cruisers and commerce destroying, as a principal mode of warfare, may be more seriously considered than it has been by the navy. If I am right in my opinion, which I understand to be that of Admiral Luce as well, then a war against an enemy's commerce is an utterly *insufficient* instrument, regarded as the main operation of war, though doubtless valuable as a secondary operation, the United States and its people are committed to an erroneous and disastrous policy."[8] By policy, of course, he meant strategy.

Mahan deployed the same theme and phraseology in *Influence*—the suggestion that attacks against enemy commerce were "a most important secondary operation" recurs throughout the book. But nowhere is it explained clearly, leaving room for alternative interpretations of what exactly he meant. As we shall see a bit later in this chapter, by attempting to superimpose a contemporary theme atop a historical narrative—simultaneously trying to explain the importance of naval power generally and the unsuitability of *guerre de course* for present-day American strategic needs specifically—Mahan contradicted himself in some places and in others bent his treatment of the past out of shape. In direct consequence, his analysis of commerce warfare is one of the most confusing and least understood aspects of his book.

Equally distorting was Mahan's desire to raise the profile of the U.S. Navy in the eyes of an American public accustomed to thinking of war as the provenance of armies. His analysis of the American Revolutionary War, for instance, is blurred by his likely correct but insufficiently supported assertions that independence had less do with combat performance of the Continental Army and almost everything to do with French naval support. "The ultimate crushing of the Americans," he averred, "not by direct military effort but by exhaustion, was probable, if England were left unmolested to strangle their commerce and industries with her overwhelming naval strength."[9] At the time of writing, this was a both novel and radical argument. Mahan made several other similarly jarring and unsupported assertions, such as his claim that Jeffersonian myopia nearly led to disaster in the War of 1812, and that the U.S. (Union) Navy made a decisive contribution to the defeat of the Confederacy in the Civil War—again both probably true, but unsupported with evidence and poorly integrated into his general thesis. The overall effect of such editorial intrusions muddied rather than clarified his historical analysis.

Exacerbating the opacity of his text was Mahan's inexperience as a writer. *Influence* was not Mahan's first book, of course, but it was the first book in which he attempted to paint on so broad a canvas: *Gulf and Inland Waters* represented a miniature compared to *Influence*'s large portrait. He did not make the transition with complete success. *Influence* was a first stab at an extremely complex topic that he had identified but not fully mapped in his own mind. As a result, he often buried in the chapters important points that deserved to be up front either in the introduction or chapter 1 because they clearly informed his analysis beyond the immediate context in which he situated them. The truth is that in many respects the book was a mess, and it is a mistake to pretend this messiness away. Bearing these caveats about his editorial intrusions and inexperience in mind, however, it is still possible to discern Mahan's main arguments in *Influence*.

At the most basic level, *Influence* was a book about power; more specifically, the acquisition, development, and employment by the state of power on the sea. The title indicated this central proposition, and the preface boldly stated it: historians had completely overlooked the importance of sea power as a factor in world history.[10] Mahan acknowledged this was an elusive subject, for two reasons. First, "[It] acts on an element [i.e., the sea] strange to most writers, as its members have been from time immemorial a strange race apart, without prophets of their own, neither themselves nor their calling understood, its immense determining influence upon the history of that era, and consequently upon the history of the world, has been overlooked."[11] Mainstream historians, he observed with a touch of asperity, had no conception of the sea as a domain distinct and separate from the land, viewing it as merely an extension of the land or as a subsidiary thereof. Meanwhile, specialist naval historians were just too parochial in their outlook, "limiting themselves generally to the duty of simple chroniclers of naval occurrences."[12]

The second reason for the elusiveness of the subject was that sea power was a complex and subtle force that defied easy definition. Mahan allowed that "It is easy to say in a general way, that the use and control of the sea is and has been a great factor in the history of the world; it is more troublesome to seek out and show its exact bearing at a particular juncture. Yet, unless this be done, the acknowledgment of general importance remains vague and unsubstantial; not resting, as it should, upon a collection of special instances in which the precise effect has been made clear, by an analysis of the conditions at the given moments."[13] This is what he set out to supply.

Although Mahan was the first to coin the term "sea power," naval historians ever since have complained that "he neglected to define it to any degree of precision."[14] But he did, just not in the way that his critics thought it should be defined. Mahan conceptualized sea power and framed his arguments in terms of geopolitics, geoeconomics, and national or "grand" strategy, not in terms of naval operations and steam tactics. Further, his concept was—and had to be—an elastic concept because its precise form and character varied over time and space. That is to say, he believed that although it was possible to identify the chief ingredients that made up sea power, the exact formula depended on circumstances and context.

The impossibility of defining the concept with precision notwithstanding, Mahan regarded the importance of sea power as manifest and the mechanics of how it worked to be almost self-evident. For Mahan, sea power was rather like a conjuring trick—baffling to the audience until the trick was explained, whereon its working became obvious. He embedded these points within the opening pages of his manuscript and, as will be shown, he took pains to remind his readers of them throughout the book.

In the preface, introduction, and opening to chapter 1 of *Influence*, Mahan explained the object, purpose, and significance of sea power primarily in terms of economic interest.[15] His main argument posited a dynamic interrelationship between sea commerce, wealth generation and state power; or, if one prefers, the correlation between levels of international trade, economic prosperity, and national strength relative to other powers. In the pages that followed, Mahan also developed a number of related subsidiary arguments. For instance, he insisted that sea power operated in peace as well as in war, railing constantly in his book against those writers who buried themselves in the minutiae of naval operations. But the main theme was the trifecta of Commerce, Wealth, and Power, which runs continually through the book from first page to last.

Mahan believed that state power was primarily (though not entirely) a function of a society's wealth, and more particularly the generation of new wealth—a dynamic and recurring process—thorough commercial activity. The more intense the pace of economic activity, the faster society generated new wealth. The state could tap this pool of wealth either by imposing taxes on its society (mainly in the form of excise duties) or by issuing bonds (in effect, borrowing from the wealthier merchant classes within society). The state could then spend its revenues from taxes or loans in a variety of ways to develop and expand its power, be it by military or naval conquest, the purchase of territory, the sponsorship of colonies, subsidizing of allies, or the reinvestment in the domestic economy to further encourage economic development in order to generate yet more wealth that could be taxed. States never simply hoarded their treasure: in a sense they invested it.

From his reading of history, Mahan deduced that international trade was the greatest wealth-generation machine in modern times.

Almost any form of economic activity would create wealth, but international trade yielded the greatest returns both directly and indirectly by fostering ancillary commercial activity, which in turn stimulated further trade. Crudely put, the pursuit of overseas trade put in motion a virtuous circle of wealth generation. By contrast, he explained, "the way in which the Spaniards and their kindred nation, the Portuguese, sought wealth" though expropriation of Aztec treasure "not only brought a blot upon the national character, but was also fatal to the growth of a healthy commerce; and so to the industries upon which commerce lives, and ultimately to that national wealth which was sought by mistaken paths."[16] What Mahan was suggesting here, in other words, was that the Iberian approach led to consumption more than investment, and consequently the Iberian powers failed to set in motion the process whereby commerce begat more commerce and thus more wealth.

Through commerce and trade, Mahan argued, any nation might develop sufficient wealth to permit the development of a strong navy and international power. This rule held true, he argued, even for a territorially weak state. During the seventeenth century, for instance, Dutch traders had enjoyed a practical monopoly over the Far East spice trade, which allowed their commerce to flourish and the Low Countries to become for a period the most developed provinces in Europe.[17] The state associated with this region,

> whose political name was the United Provinces, had now reached the summit of its influence and power,—a power based, as has already been explained, wholly upon the sea, and upon the use of that element made by the great maritime and commercial genius of the Dutch people. A recent French author thus describes the commercial and colonial conditions, at the accession of Louis XIV [1643], of this people, which beyond any other in modern times, save only England, has shown how the harvest of the sea can lift up to wealth and power a country intrinsically weak and without resources.[18]

However, while international trade was necessary to attain sea power, it was not sufficient. Indeed, for the Dutch, "the decline of the Republic and the nation was to be more striking and rapid than the rise."[19] Mahan buried his clearest explanation of why international trade was insufficient, and what else was needed, in chapter 5 of the book, covering the War of the Spanish Succession (1701–14). He wrote,

> The sea power of England therefore was not merely in the great navy, with which we too commonly and exclusively associate it; France had had such a navy in 1688, and it shriveled away like a leaf in the fire. Neither was it in a prosperous commerce alone; a few years after the date at which we have arrived, the commerce of France took on fair proportions, but the first blast of war swept it off the seas as the navy of Cromwell had once swept that of Holland. It was in the union of the two, carefully fostered, that England made the gain of sea power over and beyond all other States.[20]

Thus, for Mahan, international commerce joined a large navy and a committed government as the tripod on which sea power rested.

Mahan's belief in the importance of sea commerce rested on three axioms, the first two of which he helpfully articulated in the introduction, while the third he unhelpfully buried deep in the main text. The first is that competition for wealth inevitably leads to conflict between states. "The history of sea power," Mahan insisted in the first line of the first paragraph of the introduction, is largely "a narrative of contests between nations, of mutual rivalries, of violence frequently culminating in war."[21] In the same opening paragraph, he went on to articulate explicitly this claim and connect it to his central argument concerning commerce, wealth, and power.

> The profound influence of sea commerce upon the wealth and strength of countries was clearly seen long before the true principles which governed its growth and prosperity were detected. To secure to one's own people a disproportionate share of such

benefits, every effort was made to exclude others, either by the peaceful legislative means of monopoly or prohibitory regulations, or, when these failed, by direct violence. The clash of interests, the angry feelings roused by conflicting attempts thus to appropriate the larger share, if not the whole, of the advantages of commerce, of distant unsettled commercial regions, led to wars.[22]

To protect the source of its nation's wealth, it followed, the state must invest in naval protection.

Mahan's second axiom about the importance of sea commerce was that "both travel and traffic by water have always been easier and cheaper than by land."[23] This was another way of saying that business profit was not simply a function of monopoly pricing but also of minimizing costs, especially transportation costs. He elaborated: "The commercial greatness of Holland was due not only to her shipping at sea, but also to the numerous tranquil water-ways which gave such cheap and easy access to her own interior and to that of Germany. This advantage of carriage by water over that by land was yet more marked in a period when roads were few and very bad, wars frequent and society unsettled, as was the case two hundred years ago."[24] Writing in 1889, Mahan allowed that the advent of the railway had changed the position somewhat. "In most civilized countries, now, the destruction or disappearance of the coasting trade would only be an inconvenience, although water transit is still the cheaper."[25] Nonetheless, although an enemy naval blockade could no longer physically prevent the movement of goods within a country, it would still make the transportation of goods more difficult and more costly. In Mahan's opinion, these increased expenses would multiply over time to become significant. "Under modern conditions," he noted, "home trade is but a part of the business of a country bordering on the sea."[26] What he was hinting at here, but did not spell out until several years later, was that national economic systems were now far more complex than those of the pre-industrial age and that the effective interdiction of an enemy's overseas trade, combined with the derangement of their local transportation networks, could seriously damage the enemy's economy.

These considerations led Mahan to propound what became one of his most famous and enduring ideas, the likening of the sea to a global "common" (the seven oceans being all connected comprised the sea). In the opening paragraph to chapter 1, Mahan set out his argument and identified what would become the bedrock on which he built his geopolitical model of how the world worked: "The first and most obvious light in which the sea presents itself from the political and social point of view is that of a great highway; or better, perhaps, of a wide common, over which men may pass in all directions, but on which some well-worn paths show that controlling reasons have led them to choose certain lines of travel rather than others. These lines of travel are called trade routes, and the reasons which have determined them are to be sought in the history of the world."[27] Those "controlling reasons," of course, hinged on commercial and economic interests. What may be less obvious, but is vital to appreciate, is that Mahan was explaining here the importance of access to the common, in times of both peace and war. It was *access* to the common, not *control* thereof, that he saw as the critical factor—at least for the United States—to prevent an enemy from denying the United States access to the common.

But there was another, more sophisticated and less understood aspect to the "common" thesis. At the end of chapter 2 in his book, Mahan pointed out, not only did the "common" serve as a portal to potential trading partners and thus the generation of wealth, but for an unprepared nation the "common" could also become a source of vulnerability and danger. In another wonderfully crafted passage, he explained that in wartime "It is not the taking of individual ships or convoys, be they few or many, that strikes down the money power of a nation; it is the possession of that overbearing power on the sea which drives the enemy's flag from it, or allows it to appear only as a fugitive; and which, by controlling the great common, closes the highways by which commerce moves to and from the enemy's shores."[28]As hinted at above and again alluded to here, Mahan indicated his awareness of the interconnectedness of national and international economic activity, as well as its fundamentally dynamic character. The operative part of the quote above is found in the final clause: a nation subject to denial of access to the common would find not merely itself cut off from trade and diplomacy with foreign nations, but its domestic economy also subject to severe dislocation. The object aimed at was to "strike down" the enemy's "money power" to continue the war.

The third axiom supporting Mahan's belief in the paramount importance of sea commerce for national economic activity was that to thrive and prosper, a nation must vigorously interact with the outside world both economically and intellectually. To be cut off from the outside world either voluntarily (through isolationism) or involuntarily (through blockade) was inevitably fatal. Mahan buried this precept at the end of chapter 4, covering the wars in Europe at the very end of the seventeenth century, though it articulates a worldview that clearly pervades the work as a whole. "A nation cannot subsist indefinitely off itself, however powerful in numbers and strong in internal resources," he reasoned.[29] Borrowing the language of evolutionary biology to serve as a metaphor, a technique he would develop and deploy much more effectively in his next book, Mahan compared a nation, and more specifically national economic activity, to a living organism. "Neither individual nations nor men can thrive when severed from natural intercourse with their kind; whatever the native vigor of constitution, it requires healthful surroundings, and freedom to draw to itself from near and from far all that is conducive to its growth and strength and general welfare. Not only must the internal organism work satisfactorily, the processes of decay and renewal, of movement and circulation, go on easily, but, from sources external to themselves, both mind and body must receive healthful and varied nourishment."[30] In this analogy, economic relationships embodied the circulatory system of human affairs and commerce represented the lifeblood of the both the individual and the state. What is most striking, however, is the emphasis on the dynamism of the system. To become economically and intellectually isolated, Mahan thus seemed to be arguing, either imposed or self-imposed, was to be sedentary, which must inevitably lead to what might be termed societal atherosclerosis.[31]

METHODOLOGY AND CONSTRUCTION OF THE BOOK

Influence is best understood as a long interpretive essay rather than a conventional research monograph. That is to say, Mahan based his book largely on the work of others but retold the story from a different perspective to produce a new analysis of international history for the period from 1660 to 1783. As he explained in his preface, his aim in so doing was to show "the profound determining influence of maritime strength upon great issues" and to provide "an estimate of the effect of sea power upon history and the prosperity of nations"; in sea power, he argued, "is to be found the key to much of the history, as well as of the policy, of nations bordering upon the sea."[32]

In keeping with Mahan's penchant for analogies, the construction of *Influence* may be compared to that of a rope. Each strand of the rope represents a particular aspect of international history, which he identified as the "wars, politics, social and economic conditions of countries."[33] In effect, what Mahan did was to unravel the rope that represented international history for the period from 1660 to 1783. After separating out the various strands, he then remade the rope by inserting at its core a new "sea power" strand; in effect, he retwisted the original strands around the new one to create a new and much stronger rope. By itself, the sea power strand was of little use: it needed to be supported by being interwoven within the broader context. Hence, as he stated in the preface, "the present work aims at putting maritime interests in the foreground, without divorcing them, however, from their surroundings of cause and effect in general history, but seeking to show how they modified the latter, and were modified by them."[34] In the conclusion section of chapter 1, Mahan repeated: "There will next be examined the general history of Europe and America, with particular reference to the effect exercised upon that history, *and upon the welfare of the people*, by sea power in its broadest sense."[35] Here again Mahan was emphasizing the analytical breadth of his concept, linking wealth and welfare, and including them within his explanation for relative power: naval, state, and commercial.

Mahan's commitment to broad context prevented his focus on sea power from making the book monocausal or reductionist. In the opening to chapter 2, which focused on the Anglo-Dutch Wars of the mid-seventeenth century, Mahan acknowledged that sea power was "but one factor in that general advance and decay of nations which is called their history; and if sight be lost of the other factors to which it is so closely related, a distorted view, either exaggerated or the reverse, of its importance will be formed. It is with the belief that this importance is vastly underrated, if not practically lost sight of . . . that this study has been undertaken."[36] This statement did not qualify his thesis as to the importance of sea power but rather described his methodological approach, which readers may recall he had articulated in similar terms to Luce back in 1886: "I have carefully followed up this [modern] period both in respect of naval history and the general struggles of Europe; for it has seemed to me, with reference to my subject, that the attempt to violently separate the naval history from that context will be something like, to capsize a proverb, Hamlet with all but the part of Hamlet left out."[37] Farther along in same chapter, Mahan again reminds readers that "as other states exercised a powerful influence upon the course of events, and our aim is not merely naval history but an appreciation of the effect of naval *and* commercial power upon the course of general history, it is necessary to state shortly the condition of the rest of Europe."[38] In chapter 5 he yet again pauses his analysis to reiterate that he intends "not a tactical or strategic discussion of certain naval problems divorced from their surroundings of cause and effect in general history, but an appreciation of the effect of sea power upon the general result of the war and upon the prosperity of nations."[39] In short, he sought continually to subordinate his analysis of naval campaigns and combat operations to his explanation of the outcomes of war and their impact on long-term national prosperity.

Mahan wove his core arguments into his narrative of events spanning 1660–1783, broken down chronologically into thirteen chapters. It should be noted, however, that the book skews heavily toward the period from 1775 to 1783, covering the American Revolutionary War—nearly 40 percent of the text is devoted to 4 percent of the chronology.[40] Within the body chapters, Mahan explored two principal themes. First, how sea power works—recalling that it works in both peacetime and wartime—and why it is often so hard to detect. Second, how sea power is applied in wartime—the operational methods. When grappling with the text, it is helpful to keep in mind these two disparate lines of argumentation.

Mahan's use of imprecise terminology does not make this easy. The words "strategy," "strategic," and "strategical" appear around 120 times in the text, mainly in the introduction, chapter 1, and the conclusion, but nowhere does Mahan ever explicitly and positively define the root word "strategy."[41] This is not to say that Mahan made no attempt to clarify his meaning. In the introduction, he drew a distinction between "tactics of the battlefield" and "those wider operations of war which are comprised under the name of strategy."[42] A page later he offered that "before hostile armies or fleets are brought into contact (a word which perhaps better than any other indicates the dividing line between tactics and strategy), there are a number of questions to be decided, covering the whole plan of operations throughout the theatre of war."[43] He thus identified for readers where he drew the boundary between tactics and strategy, and seems to have thought this would suffice for his purposes. His definition therefore was implicit rather than explicit, negative rather than positive, in that he defined the word "strategy" by what it was not. To say the least, this was an unorthodox way of defining any key term. Yet, to be fair, it must be remembered that when Mahan was writing, at the end of the nineteenth century, the word "strategy" conventionally applied to military rather than naval operations. He employed it because he found it useful and no equivalent word even existed in the naval lexicon. In so doing, however, he was aware that the word did not quite fit. Indeed, he highlighted the fact in his introduction, when explaining the inapplicability of Jomini's definition of the word in the naval context.[44] (Jomini, of course, was a land warfare theorist.)

The problem is that Mahan subsequently employed "strategy" to encompass everything other than battle tactics. He used the word in connection with decision making at the intersection of policy (the domain of politicians) and operations (the domain of admirals) and

at the intersection of operations and tactics.[45] He also used the term
in conjunction with discussions on the formulation of national policy,
the application of naval force, the conduct of diplomacy, and even
geography. In all instances, he expected his readers to infer his precise
meaning from the surrounding context. For Mahan, therefore, strategy encompassed the coordination by the state, in the interest of the
state, of all national assets and activity connected to the sea.[46] Accordingly, everything related to preparations and planning for the future
therefore became "strategical."

Mahan's interest in sea power at the policy and strategic levels
come through most strongly in the first half of the book, dealing with
various European wars; the second half of the book, dealing with
the American Revolutionary War, focuses at the operational level. In
the European chapters, Mahan treats naval operations as secondary
to the working of sea power on a grander scale. In dealing with the
Nine Years' War (aka the War of the League of Augsburg, 1688–97)
between France on the one side and most of Europe on the other, he
describes the Anglo-Dutch victory in the naval Battle of La Hogue
(1692) as unimportant and summarizes the rest of the war in terms of
sea power without battles:

> The five remaining years of the War of the League of Augsburg,
> in which all Europe was in arms against France, are marked by no
> great sea battles, nor any single maritime event of the first impor-
> tance. To appreciate the effect of the sea power of the allies, it is
> necessary to sum up and condense an account of the quiet, steady
> pressure which it brought to bear and maintained in all quarters
> against France. It is thus indeed that sea power usually acts, and
> just because so quiet in its working, it is the more likely to be
> unnoticed and must be somewhat carefully pointed out.[47]

Mahan detects the same quiet workings of sea power in his treatment
of the War of the Spanish Succession (1701–14). When the line of
royal succession for Spain failed and arrangements had to be made
for a new king with ramifications for the European balance of power,

"this balance of power was no longer understood in the narrow sense of continental possessions; the effect of the new arrangements upon commerce, shipping, and the control both of the ocean and the Mediterranean, was closely looked to."[48] Surveying both this war and the following decades, Mahan penned one of his finest, most evocative, passages that contain within a crib of his best thoughts.

> The noiseless, steady, exhausting pressure with which sea power acts, cutting off the resources of the enemy while maintaining its own, supporting war in scenes where it does not appear itself, or appears only in the background, and striking open blows at rare intervals, though lost to most, is emphasized to the careful reader by the events of this war and of the half-century that followed. The overwhelming sea power of England was the determining factor in European history during the period mentioned, maintaining war abroad while keeping its own people in prosperity at home, and building up the great empire which is now seen; but from its very greatness its action, by escaping opposition, escapes attention.[49]

Mahan does not insist on sea power as the monocausal explanation of national power, but he does emphasize its salience: "Is it meant, it may be asked, to attribute to sea power alone the greatness or wealth of any State? Certainly not. The dual use and control of the sea is but one link in the chain of exchange by which wealth accumulates; but it is the central link, which lays under contribution other nations for the benefit of the one holding it, and which, history seems to assert, most surely of all gathers to itself riches."[50] In his treatment of the Seven Years' War (1756–63), between England and Prussia on one side and France, Austria, Russia, and Sweden on the other, Mahan insisted that students seeking the significance of these events mistakenly focused on the war on land. However remarkable Frederick the Great's brilliant defense of little Prussia against the three continental Powers of Europe, from Mahan's perspective it seemed that in the long run events outside Europe proved far more important. In his judgment, "the great questions to be determined by [the war], concerning the world's history, were the dominion of the sea and the control of distant countries, the possession of colonies, and, dependent upon these, the increase of wealth."[51] In other words, the real significance of the war in international history was its effect on the ownership of so many components of international trade, the great wealth-generating machine. Echoing his assessment of the Nine Years' War and the War of the Spanish Succession, Mahan explained that "Sea power does not appear directly in its effects upon the struggle, but indirectly it was felt in two ways,—first, by the subsidies which the abundant wealth and credit of England enabled her to give Frederick, in whose thrifty and able hands they went far; and second, in the embarrassment caused to France by the attacks of England upon her colonies and her own sea-coast, in the destruction of her commerce."[52] In Mahan's telling, the British triumphed in the Seven Years' War through the ruthless application of sea power. By safeguarding their trade overseas, they maintained economic prosperity at home.[53] In turn, this made possible massive British subsidies to Frederick the Great that enabled Prussia to thwart French territorial and political ambitions on the continent. The Royal Navy, meanwhile, destroyed French commerce by capturing their colonies and merchant fleets, as well as by interdicting their coastal transportation system. The net effect of this sea campaign was to wreck the French economy and so to starve the French state of revenues. Britain negotiated a very favorable peace, having effectively reduced her enemies to various degrees of penury. Thus, for Mahan, the Seven Years' War illustrated the working of sea power and the controlling impact of money on the waging of war and of peace.

Mahan's stress on the importance in wartime of continuing to generate wealth in order to maintain the sinews of war—on economic factors, in other words—supported his overall emphasis on economic factors as components of sea power. In chapter 1, he offhandedly remarked that "sea power in the broad sense . . . includes not only the military strength afloat, that rules the sea or any part of it by force of arms, but also the peaceful commerce and shipping from which alone a military fleet naturally and healthfully springs, and on which it securely rests."[54] Seventy pages later, at the end of the chapter, he again stressed the importance of "peaceful commerce; upon which alone, it cannot be too often insisted, a thoroughly strong navy can be based."[55] The European chapters make clear that the correlation between international trade and national economic development lay at the heart of this sea power concept.

COMPETING APPROACHES TO THE
APPLICATION OF SEA POWER

Turning now from the general workings of sea power in both peace and war to its application in wartime through naval operations, we come to perhaps the most provocative part of our analysis. If Mahan is famous for one idea, it is for advocating always to prioritize control of the sea through decisive battle. Until command of the sea was secured, he deprecated the diversion of warships to attacks on enemy commerce—or so it is supposed. If this was what he argued, then it would seem to call into serious question the validity of the foregoing argument that Mahan understood sea power primarily in economic-commercial terms—because how could someone who regarded commerce as the lifeblood of sea power eschew a form of warfare that targeted it?

Closer reading of *Influence* shows that the contradictions within Mahan's text are more apparent than real, the product of poor writing, poor structure, and above all his efforts to improve the marketability of his book by his inserting frequent analogies between the past and the present. Put more simply, in trying simultaneously to play historian and contemporary analyst, he twisted himself into knots. In both the introduction and chapter 1 of *Influence*, Mahan was far from dismissive as to the importance of attacking enemy commerce and declared that one of the particular aims of his book was to explore "the military value of commerce-destroying as a decisive or a secondary operation of war."[56] To borrow modern terminology, he clearly envisioned the character of war more as a battle of attrition than of annihilation. He consistently maintained that in time of war, all other things being equal, relative economic and fiscal strength would prove decisive. Accordingly, in the long run, the surest way to bring about a favorable peace was to maintain one's own sea commerce while pre-venting the enemy's; decimating their maritime commerce would, in effect, destroy their wealth-generation machine, severing their "sin-ews of war" and thereby hamstringing their military capacity. Thus the conventional interpretation of Mahan's views on commerce in war gets him nearly backwards, though to be fair he was hardly a model of clarity.

Part of the confusion over Mahan's thoughts on commerce warfare stems from his failure to distinguish clearly and consistently between ends and means. This lack of distinction sometimes also obscures the fact that he regarded decisive battle—a clash between rival bat-tle fleets—not as an end unto itself but as a means to an end. As we saw above, he used the word "strategy" indiscriminately, sometimes to refer to political ends (which we would now call strategy) and other times to refer to military means (which we would now call operations). Only at the very end of his book did he attempt to distinguish between these two concepts, and even then he did so in a way that was unclear. Instead of using the language of ends versus means, or political versus military, he instead used the language of "object" (political ends) and "objective" (military means): "In a war undertaken for any object, even if that object be the possession of a particular territory or posi-tion, an attack directly upon the place coveted may not be, from the military point of view, the best means of obtaining it. The end upon which the military operations are directed may therefore be other than the object which the belligerent government wishes to obtain, and it has received a name of its own,—the objective."[57] He could scarcely have chosen two words less likely to convey the key conceptual dis-tinction that he was trying to draw, and in any case did not use those words or integrate the distinction consistently in his text. Ironically, in so doing he was borrowing the vocabulary of Jomini. It is interesting to find, moreover, that Mahan explained his meaning quite clearly in one of his original lectures written around the same time. There he wrote: "It may thus happen that the object of the war may not be the objective of the military plan. The object of the war, indeed, may not be the gain of territory at all, but of privileges or rights denied before;

or to put an end to wrongs done to the declarant. Even so, an attack upon some of the enemy's possessions will probably form part of the plan of operations."[58] Why in preparing *Influence* he opted to exclude this clarification can never be known.

Manifestly, contrary to the common view, Mahan did not regard attacking commerce and seeking sea control as conceptual opposites. From the operational standpoint, they may be opposites in that one targets the enemy's merchant fleet and the other their war fleet, but from the strategic standpoint they run parallel. Both approaches sought the same strategic (political) object, namely the inflicting of the significant economic pressure on the enemy (through commerce prevention) sufficient to induce them to consent to peace on terms favorable to oneself. Far from viewing the deliberate targeting of enemy oceanic commerce as a misallocation of naval resource, therefore, Mahan viewed *systematic* commerce warfare as the very foundation of wartime sea power. What he objected to was the *unsystematic* attack more commonly known as *guerre de course*. In promoting the pursuit of decisive battle, moreover, he never suggested ignoring attacks on enemy commerce until their fleet had been destroyed. It was a matter of priorities in the allocation of scarce resources.

By far the greatest source of confusion surrounding Mahan's views on commerce warfare was the result of his failure to draw and maintain clear and consistent distinctions between different types (or methods) of commercial warfare. In different places in *Influence*, and at different times in his subsequent work, he referred to "commerce prevention," "commerce destruction," and "commerce raiding," and it did not help that whoever indexed the book also failed to distinguish between them. Yet with hindsight, one may discern a pattern and hierarchy to his usage, albeit not a perfect one. In general, his usage was that commerce *prevention* was the proper and overarching goal of naval warfare. Stepping down to the strategic level, he discussed commerce *destruction* and commerce *raiding* as competing approaches to the destruction of enemy commerce. The key distinction between them was that whereas the former was systematic in approach, the latter was unsystematic. But Mahan was not always consistent. Sometimes he used *prevention* and *destruction* interchangeably rather than treating them as separate categories. Inconsistent usage and lack of definition hardly made for a clear message.

In the pages of *Influence*, Mahan argued that commerce prevention might be accomplished one of two ways: either by deploying warships directly against enemy merchantmen or indirectly by attaining "command of the sea" (sea control) in order to impose a blockade. It is important to note that in each case the ends were the same but the means were different—direct attack on the enemy's sea commerce versus indirect attack achieved through sea control in order to impose a blockade. In drawing this key distinction, Mahan made no secret of his marked preference for seeking sea control ahead of commerce destruction, and there can be no question of this. In a sense (and borrowing a Clausewitzian metaphor), he was espousing the importance of identifying the enemy's center of gravity and of concentrating force against it, but the center of gravity he had in mind was commercial rather than naval. The "true end" of the Navy, he insisted, was "to preponderate over the enemy's navy and so control the sea."[59] The first half of this statement has the focus on destruction of the enemy's battle fleet familiar from caricatures of Mahan. But the second half is unfamiliar: it makes the "end" of preponderance merely the means to the end of sea control—*not* an end unto itself.

Several pages later, Mahan reiterated more clearly that he saw sea control as merely the means to the end of strangling enemy commerce (while confusingly using the word "object" to describe both the political end and the military means): "If its object is to break up the enemy's power on the sea, cutting off his communications with the rest of his possessions, drying up the sources of his wealth in his commerce, and making possible a closure of his ports, then the object of attack must be his organized military forces afloat; in short, his navy."[60] Despite his double use of the word "object," this quotation makes clear that Mahan regarded the enemy's fleet as the military objective, but only as the *means* to achieve the overarching political *object*—the "break[ing] up [of] the enemy's power on the sea," the "cutting off [of] his communications," the "drying up the sources of his wealth," and the "closure of his ports."[61] Operationally, this last—the closure of ports through blockade—was the key to all the others, as he made clear in the closing pages of *Influence*: "[A country] . . . when its wealth is scattered in thousands of going and coming ships, when the roots of the system spread wide and far, and strike deep, it can stand many a cruel shock and lose many a goodly bough without the life being touched. Only by military command of the sea by prolonged control of the strategic centers of commerce, can such an attack be fatal; and such control can be wrung from a powerful navy only by fighting and overcoming it."[62] For Mahan, then, the advantage of sea control achieved through decisive battle was that it permitted effective blockade, which in turn enabled commerce prevention—the application of sea power in its most potent form.

Mahan further blurred the picture containing his thoughts on commerce warfare by sometimes referring to cruising warfare, privateering, and *guerre de course*, terms that again he neglected to define with consistency and precision. At the beginning and end of the book, he unequivocally equated *guerre de course* with a form of commerce destruction and used it as a synonym for commerce raiding and commerce destruction.[63] Elsewhere, however, he presented it as something quite different and to be avoided at all costs. In chapter 2, for instance, Mahan viewed *guerre de course* as fundamentally different: an unsystematic, almost haphazard, approach to commerce destruction, a form of insurgency (irregular) warfare and little more than licensed piracy. "This plan," he wrote (not wishing to dignify *guerre de course* as a strategy), and lacing his description with pejoratives, "which involves only the maintenance of a few swift cruisers and can be backed by the spirit of greed in a nation, fitting out privateers without direct expense to the State, possesses the specious attractions which economy always presents."[64] The most that *guerre de course* could do, he insisted, was to "embarrass" the enemy state (though not bankrupt it) and "distress" the enemy population (i.e., provoke social unrest though not on a scale to threaten political overthrow of the state).[65] Here was an implicit sense of a means–end relationship: naval-operational means had to achieve a political-economic end. Translated into modern language, Mahan was saying that *guerre de course* was unsystematic and thus could never be regarded as an effective form of commerce raiding, and because it could never inflict politically significant pressure on the enemy, it could never qualify as a legitimate method of commerce prevention.

Returning to Mahan's consistent preference for seeking command of the sea ahead of commerce destruction, or, if preferred, choosing the indirect ahead of the direct approach to commerce prevention, Mahan in fact acknowledged that both approaches were theoretically legitimate. In chapter 9, the pivot between the European and American halves of the book covering the period from 1756 to 1775, he stated that

> [the French] subordinated the control of the sea by the destruction of the enemy's fleets, of his organized naval forces, to the success of particular operations, the retention of particular points [i.e., ports], the carrying out of particular ulterior strategic [i.e., political] ends. It is not necessary to endeavor to force upon others the conviction of the present writer that such a policy, however applicable as an exception, is faulty as a rule; but it is most desirable that all persons responsible for the conduct of naval affairs should recognize that the two lines of policy, in direct contradiction to each other, do exist.[66]

In promoting sea control (indirect attack) over commerce destruction (direct attack) as the preferred operational approach, Mahan never claimed that the latter could not work: rather, he claimed that in the past it had never been made to work sufficiently well or quickly enough to generate decisive political pressure.[67] His objection, in other words, was historically qualified, not theoretically absolute. Indeed, he acknowledged that given adequate resources and favorable circumstances, direct attack on the enemy merchant marine might produce politically significant results. "Such a war, however, cannot stand alone; it must be *supported*, to use the military phrase; unsubstantial and evanescent in itself, it cannot reach far from its base. That base must be either home ports, or else some solid outpost of the national power, on the shore or the sea; a distant dependency or a powerful fleet. Failing such support, the cruiser can only dash out hurriedly a short distance from home."[68] In chapter 5, Mahan again admitted the legitimacy of commerce destruction if "based on powerful fleets or neighboring seaports."[69] Three pages later he amplified that "commerce-destroying warfare, to be destructive, must be seconded by a squadron warfare, and by divisions of ships-of-the-line; which, forcing the enemy to unite his forces, permit the cruisers to make fortunate attempts upon his trade."[70] Again, the implicit meaning here is that previous attempts to wage commerce destruction had failed mainly because they had been attempted unsystematically, and consequently attacks had been only sporadic.[71] Hence Mahan could not lay down an ironclad law against commerce destruction. Instead, he observed that "the attack and defense of commerce is still a living question."[72]

Writing at the end of the 1880s, Mahan had good reason to stay his hand in condemning commerce destruction. At the end of chapter 2, he alluded to the possibility that "modern developments" might render it difficult to maintain an effective blockade.[73] What modern developments? Throughout the 1880s, French naval theorists of the so-called *Jeune Ecole* (whose work Mahan had read) claimed that new naval technology in the form of mines and torpedoes now made blockade practically impossible.[74] Much more serious, he thought, were recent developments in international law. Directly after uttering his famous pronouncement that "it is not the taking of individual ships or convoys, be they few or many, that strikes down the money power of a nation" (see note 27), Mahan wondered if "effective blockade" might be exercised "less efficiently now than in the days when the neutral flag had not its present immunity."[75]

Mahan was referring here to the 1856 Paris Declaration respecting Maritime Law, which many read as tightening up on the laws of blockade as well as providing merchantmen flying neutral flags with protection from seizure by belligerents.[76] In reality, ambiguities and potential loopholes riddled both the declaration and international law generally, leading Mahan to predict that all sorts of friction and misunderstandings would ensue in wartime. "It is not unlikely," he went on to forecast in the same chapter, that in the next war "between maritime nations, an attempt may be made by the one having a great sea power and wishing to break down its enemy's commerce, to interpret the phrase 'effective blockade' in the manner that best suits its interests at the time; to assert that the speed and disposal of its ships make the blockade effective at much greater distances and with fewer ships than formerly. The determination of such a question will depend, not upon the weaker belligerent, but upon neutral powers; it will raise the issue between belligerent and neutral rights."[77] If the state of international law rendered indirect commerce destruction through effective blockade impossible, it followed that direct commerce destruction through attacks on the enemy merchant fleet might be the only option.

Notwithstanding Mahan's concessions in these early chapters of *Influence,* that in the future direct commerce destruction might work better and blockades prove less effective than in the past, in his later chapters he adopted a strikingly different stance. Indeed, when discussing the subject in connection with the American Revolutionary War, he went out of his way to denigrate commerce destruction—often employing tendentious reasoning and convoluted argument—though he stopped short of actually condemning it as fundamentally wrong.[78] Most of Mahan's readers and reviewers did not have to grapple with this inconsistency because they typically ignored his argument in the first half of the book in favor of that given in the second half. Focusing on the latter produced the widespread yet mistaken belief that Mahan was vehemently opposed to seeing warships deployed directly against enemy merchantmen, when the argument in the first half of the book qualifies this reading in important ways.

Mahan's desire to influence contemporary U.S. political debate on the direction of naval policy warped his analysis of commerce destruction in the chapters most likely to appeal to his American readers—those on the American Revolutionary War. In chapter 1, while explaining the structure of his book, Mahan heavy-handedly interposed that "public opinion in the United States has great faith in war directed against an enemy's commerce; but it must be remembered that the [American] Republic has no ports very near the great centers of trade abroad. Her geographical position is therefore singularly disadvantageous for carrying on successful commerce-destroying, unless she finds bases in the ports of an ally."[79] In the immediately following chapters chronicling various European wars, Mahan indicated his marked preference for following a sea control strategy ahead of a commerce destruction strategy. He nevertheless qualified his objections to the latter and grudgingly admitted it was a legitimate application of sea power, but which for various reasons had never been made to work. In the chapters on the American Revolutionary War, however, when covering the same topic, Mahan expressed his views with more vigor and less qualification. In the conclusion of *Influence* he was positively doctrinaire on the subject: "The harassment and distress caused to a country by serious interference with its commerce will be conceded by all. It is doubtless a most important secondary operation of naval war, and is not likely to be abandoned till war itself shall cease; but regarded as a primary and fundamental measure, sufficient in itself to crush an enemy, it is probably a delusion, and a most dangerous delusion, when presented in the fascinating garb of cheapness to the representatives of a people."[80] "Representatives of a people"? Transparently, he was not providing his readers here with a summing up of French naval policy at the end of the eighteenth century at the time of Louis XVI, but leaving his fellow citizens at the end of the nineteenth century with a positive affirmation that could not be misunderstood.

More to the point, given his earlier comments, how could Mahan so sweepingly dismiss attacks made on enemy trade as of only secondary importance? How can this statement be reconciled with his insistence, a couple of pages earlier, that the war ended in 1783 "due to the financial embarrassment of France, not to her naval humiliation"?[81] Though temperamentally loath to admit any misjudgment, scholarly or otherwise, Mahan likely came to regret his choice of words in the closing pages. This throwaway remark, probably inserted to make his manuscript appear more relevant to contemporary readers, not only contradicted his arguments made earlier in the book but sat uneasily with the overarching theme of his book, that the accumulation and exercise of power was largely (though not solely) a function of wealth and that the single most important source of wealth generation derived from the profits of international trade and the resultant commerce. The most likely explanation is Mahan intended his "secondary" remark to apply only in the narrowly naval sense: "a most important secondary *operation* of *naval* war," as distinct from a primary strategic object. This interpretation would be more consistent with his subsequent work.

Furthermore, from Mahan's perspective, it was just as important for Americans to grasp that they were more vulnerable to enemy sea control than they appreciated as it was for them to understand that they were less capable of engaging in commerce destruction than generally believed. At the junction of chapters 2 and 3, Mahan reversed his emphasis on the commercial importance of sea control by discussing its impact from the perspective of a state on the receiving end. "It is with the belief that importance is vastly underrated, if not practically lost sight of, by people unconnected with the sea, and particularly by the people of the United States in our own day, that this study has been undertaken," he wrote.[82] The American people had to realize that thanks to the growth of the international economy, the United States was not insulated from and thus immune to the trepidations of European naval powers. Neither geography nor international law would supply sufficient protection.

For this, the United States needed a proper navy. "The profound humiliation of France, which reached its depths between 1760 and 1763," he pleaded, "has an instructive lesson for the United States in this our period [1880s] of commercial and naval decadence."[83] Mahan warned that the present-day United States was much more vulnerable than it had been in the past to the economic disruption resulting from the application of sea power:

> It is true that neutral ships can then enter other ports of the United States than those [which they usually enter]; but what a dislocation of the carrying trade of the country, what failure of supplies

at times, what inadequate means of transport by rail or water, of dockage, of lighterage, of warehousing, will be involved in such an enforced change of the port of entry! Will there be no money loss, no suffering, consequent upon this? And when with much pain and expense these evils have been partially remedied, the enemy may be led to stop the new inlets as he did the old. The people of the United States will certainly not starve, but they may suffer grievously.[84]

Similarly, on the next page:

Without asserting a narrow parallelism between the United States and either [Britain or France], it may safely be said that it is essential to the welfare of the whole country that the conditions of trade and commerce should remain, as far as possible, unaffected by an external war. In order to do this, the enemy must be kept not only out of our ports, but far away from our coasts.[85]

Here, Mahan was advocating two things. First, and most obviously, he wanted a larger U.S. Navy. Second, and more significantly, he advocated a redefinition of national security to encompass U.S. control over the entire Western Hemisphere. Both of these remedies stemmed from his belief that the United States was vulnerable to foreign sea power, far more so than was generally realized.

In sum, Mahan mixed his message on the issue of commerce destruction by trying to pursue two incompatible objectives. On the one hand, as a historian and more particularly as the inventor of "sea power," he saw that attacking commerce flowed logically from his central proposition that the principal political object of sea power, the primary raison d'être of a navy, was to protect one's own trade while attacking the enemy's. While he could condemn *guerre de course* as unsound in practice, he could not simply denounce commerce destruction without risk of undermining his main argument of what a navy was for. Additionally, he could not rule out that direct commerce destruction might work if implemented correctly.

On the other hand, Mahan was writing as a naval officer/pundit with a political agenda seeking contemporary relevance, aiming to persuade the American voting public of 1889 that a navy built solely around cruisers could never be a substitute for one also containing a nucleus of battleships. The vehemence with which he denounced eighteenth-century ideas on *guerre de course* and privateers reflected his professional abhorrence for their late nineteenth-century equivalents, auxiliary cruisers manned by naval militia. As will be shown in the next chapter, when Mahan produced his book there was serious talk in the United States of building a naval force comprised of converted merchant ships manned by state militias. It is difficult to escape the conclusion that contemporary issues surrounding U.S. naval and fiscal policy drove his unwillingness to admit the legitimacy of commerce destruction in any form, which was farther than he really intended to go.

The Influence of Sea Power upon History is a famous and remarkable book, but it is not a great book. It advanced several novel propositions of lasting significance and contained some marvelous historical analysis; it made connections and offered insights that professional historians had never before supplied. It also was a truly original work. As Theodore Roosevelt, an avid reader of history, publicly remarked several years after the first publication of *Influence*, "It seems almost incredible, when we think of the immense part played by naval power in history, that no historian should ever yet have treated it at length from the philosophic standpoint; yet this is literally the case."[86] Roosevelt was correct. This was indeed Mahan's achievement and deserves to be recognized as such.

By the standards of the day, moreover, it was a creditable piece of scholarship, albeit one that bears the hallmarks—the strengths and weaknesses—of a first monograph. Mahan demonstrated his mastery of the available literature. He mentally processed massive quantities of conflicting data relating to technically complex subject matter, distilled its essence, and ultimately presented it in reasonably coherent form. This should not be understated: it is not easy to produce a monograph. This is especially true when one considers that he was working in a poorly mapped field of study, and much of what had been mapped was of questionable reliability. (Bad history makes the task of serious scholars much more difficult.) On the whole, Mahan was judicious in choosing his sources. Granted, when viewed as a historical monograph his tome may be criticized for not incorporating more primary sources, but considering his personal circumstances, his intended audience, and the fact that he was practically pioneering a new field, not to mention that the "archives" of the day were largely uncataloged and may have been unavailable to him, such criticism seems a trifle harsh—especially since no professional historian had previously tried to engage with this material.

What disqualifies *Influence* from being classed as a truly great book are its structural flaws. *Influence* is very much a book of two halves—115 years of European history followed by the 7 years spanning the American Revolutionary War. In the first half, moreover, the emphasis is on the interplay between politics, economics, and national strategy, whereas the second half is much more conventionally "naval history" with operations very much to the fore. Readers who have focused on different halves can easily come away with different impressions of what Mahan was trying to say.

More seriously still, the lack of definitions and conflation of terminology, particularly the failure to distinguish clearly between policy, strategy, and operations, or between commerce prevention, commerce destruction, and commerce raiding, make for much ambiguity, as does the excessive qualification and haphazard scattering of arguments. Mahan asked a great deal of his readers by pursuing multiple objectives simultaneously. His effort to explain the complex working of sea power through his analysis of strategic policy in many ways conflicted with his simultaneous desire to teach lessons about naval operations— the art and science of naval command. The almost random insertion into the text of various other subsidiary points, together with his crude policy agenda intrusions, confuse more than illuminate. Many of his editorial intrusions in the name of contemporary relevance serve as often to perplex as to clarify.

These defects notwithstanding, Mahan's main argument was both original and important. Not only was sea power more significant than ever appreciated, and its mechanics never seriously analyzed, it was also far more potent—and historically influential—than anyone had realized. In this context, the most important and extraordinary feature of *Influence* was its emphasis on the symbiotic connection between naval power and economics and between international commerce and national prosperity. True, not all of Mahan's ideas were fully developed, but the point he was driving at was visible. Participation in international trade was a critical necessity of national economic life, and consequently access to the common was essential. The potency of sea power impressed and yet at the same time frightened him. *Influence* was written from the perspective not of Britain, as is so often supposed, but from that of her most persistent unsuccessful challenger: France. As a U.S. naval officer writing in the late 1880s, Mahan was less interested in the benefits of naval strength than in the reciprocal implications: the consequences of naval unpreparedness. From this point of view, the ocean was no longer a barrier protecting the United States from prospective antagonists in the Old World, but now, in the age of steam, a highway that might carry them rapidly to the republic's front door.

For Mahan, the most important lesson was this: the nation that allowed the Royal Navy to impose an effective blockade of its ports—to place a noose around its economic neck—would find it very difficult to escape. The consequences, he warned, were stark; what is more, the British would not be distracted from tightening the knot by any spasmodic harassment of their sea commerce. Mahan was not arguing that the United States needed to build a navy as great as Britain's, something far too expensive—both fiscally and politically—to contemplate at the time, but he did suggest that the United States might build a medium-sized navy sufficient against even the mighty Royal Navy to keep open the nation's access to the common.[87] Accordingly, Mahan did not write *Influence* as a playbook for national greatness but rather as one for the protection of national prosperity in a dangerous world. Nor was it his final statement on these subjects.

PART II

CHAPTER 4

BENJAMIN TRACY AND THE QUESTION OF INFLUENCE

(1889–90)

The prosperity of the whole interior depends upon the uninterrupted supply of the demands of a foreign market. If, when war comes, we are not in a position to protect the transportation of our food products, the foreign market will be closed. By the blockade of such great outlets as Galveston, New Orleans, and Mobile in the Gulf, and the Chesapeake and Delaware and New York on the Atlantic, the great industry of the interior will be paralyzed.

—BENJAMIN FRANKLIN TRACY, 1891[1]

THE PUBLICATION OF *Influence* unquestionably transformed Mahan's life, though not as quickly or precisely in the ways that are often supposed. Contrary to popular belief, his book was not instantly acclaimed as a classic. Within the Navy, Mahan was still seen as (now-retired) Rear Adm. Stephen Luce's creature. By contrast, in political circles the publication of *Influence* commanded greater respect and led to a blossoming of his friendships with several leading politicians. Through them, Mahan was introduced to the editors of leading periodicals who were impressed by his book and intrigued by the novelty of several arguments within the opening chapters.

There exists considerable misunderstanding about the effect of *Influence* on U.S. naval policy. In most accounts, Mahan's book is interpreted in the context of a triumphalist narrative about the transformation of the Navy from a cruiser force built for coastal defense and *guerre de course* to an oceangoing fleet of battleships built for sea control. In so doing, they have often paired it with the famous 1889 annual report by Secretary of the Navy Benjamin Tracy, published six months before *Influence*, depicting Tracy's report and Mahan's book as pivotal in this apparent transformation.

The close association traditionally seen between the Tracy report and Mahan's book justifies, or rather demands, scrutiny of the former alongside the latter. In particular, the tendency to separate the study of the U.S. Navy from analysis of the U.S. political economy, discussed in chapter 1 of this book, has caused previous writers to overemphasize purely naval considerations and disregard the domestic political factors driving the Tracy report. Furthermore, their commitment to the triumphalist story of naval transformation has led them to neglect parts of the Tracy report that do not fit the story and to exaggerate the speed and extent of this transformation, if transformation there was. In order to arrive at a proper appreciation of what Mahan wrote and why it mattered, therefore, it is necessary to explore the Tracy report in detail.

Although the conventional view is that Mahan influenced Tracy, there is no evidence of this, and in truth Mahan got more out of Tracy. Shortly after the publication of *Influence*, Mahan did catch the Secretary's eye. Tracy went out of his way to help Mahan, most importantly by giving him time to write and by unofficially bringing him into the Navy Department, which afforded Mahan new insight into the policymaking process.

In the presidential election of 1888, the Republican Party regained control of the White House with Benjamin Harrison's victory. Harrison won on a platform of economic nationalism, promising to safeguard the home market for domestic producers by maintaining a high tariff on imports, while at the same time pledging to find outlets for surplus American products in overseas markets.[2] The contradictory thrusts of these two policies—tariffs on foreign imports on the one hand while seeking markets in these for American produce on the other, which would give foreign nations the grounds for retaliatory taxation—apparently did not worry the electors. Promising all things to everyone, the Republican Party achieved a landslide victory and gained working majorities in both houses of Congress for the first time since 1875. Their majority in the House was due mainly to large gains in western agricultural districts, the significance of which was explained at the end of chapter 1.

After his inauguration in March 1889, Harrison forged ahead with his economic agenda to expand overseas markets, appointing powerful, like-minded individuals to his cabinet.[3] Most notably, and despite strong misgivings, he brought back the maverick, arch-expansionist James Blaine as secretary of state, thus signaling his determination to adopt an assertive foreign policy. Blaine, it will be recalled, aspired to the imposition of U.S. commercial dominance of the Western Hemisphere—a new empire.[4] Although the president and the secretary possessed slightly different ideas on what exactly this would entail, one point on which they agreed was that a larger U.S. Navy would strengthen their hand. With the issue of fleet expansion related so closely to both foreign policy and tariff policy, it should not be surprising that Harrison regarded the post of Navy Secretary "as one of the most important in my Cabinet."[5]

For this office the new president selected Benjamin Franklin Tracy, a politically prominent judge and a close friend of New York City's "boss" Tom Platt. At the time, it was common knowledge that Tracy in fact owed his selection to James Blaine and to Harrison's need to satisfy the claims of the New York political machine for an appropriate share of executive spoils.[6] Tracy, or "General" Tracy as he preferred to be addressed (having been elevated to the honorific rank of general of volunteers as a political reward), formally assumed responsibility for the Navy Department on March 6, 1889. Tracy had no previous connection whatsoever with the Navy and was as surprised as anyone at being given the job. He was expecting to be made attorney general.[7]

On assuming office, Tracy announced his policy goals with suitable vagueness. "We need a navy, a better navy," he told a group of journalists.[8] He did not elaborate. Since the week before President Harrison had issued a similar statement in his inaugural address, and throughout the election campaign the need for naval expansion had figured prominently (though ambiguously) in many of Harrison's speeches, Tracy knew that he stood on politically uncontroversial ground. In any case, Tracy's correspondence shows also that he was a firm supporter of Blaine's vigorous foreign policy, and on joining the Cabinet he immediately sided with those pressing for an aggressive stance in a dispute then ongoing with Germany and Britain over naval basing rights in Samoa.[9] He was equally assertive in pressing for the establishment of coaling stations in the Caribbean and the Pacific, and he took a dim view of those small countries that declined to lease the necessary land to the U.S. Navy.

Tracy approached the thorny issue of fleet structure with extreme caution. His first move was to organize the chiefs of the five department bureaus responsible for naval materiel into a "Board on Construction" and invite them to send him their thoughts on future force structure. Next, he solicited the opinion of fleet officers and charged Commo. William P. McCann to form a team and submit their recommendations.[10] Tracy also courted the leading members of the House and Senate navy committees.[11] After six months, Tracy had talked to practically everyone connected to or known to have strong opinions about the Navy. At this stage, however, contrary to suppositions made by several writers, there is no evidence that he had yet talked to Capt. Mahan—in fact it is most unlikely—let alone recruited him into his inner circle of advisors.

Naturally, Tracy's ignorance of the Navy and his determination to consult widely gave rise to considerable lobbying. In essence, the various contending factions presented Tracy with two principal options. One was to maintain the current direction and build a mostly cruiser navy supplemented by a number of small armor-clad ships (like the *Texas*) to guarantee the upper hand in a war against one of the South American navies. Advocates of this approach, like (the now retired) Adm. Robert Shufeldt, imagined that in the event of war with a major European power, the United States would simply tuck away these pocket armored ships while relying on its cruisers (plus auxiliary cruisers) to wage *guerre de course* against the enemy's foreign trade. This was the traditional strategy, of course.

The leading alternative, advocated by Adm. Luce, entailed more or less the same overarching strategic conception—a *guerre de course*—but called for the armored vessels to be built more capable (thus more expensive) and in sufficient numbers to form a squadron.[12] To be clear, these were to be in addition to the cruisers, not as an alternative to them. Luce was not proposing a switchover. It was a quality issue: he wanted the "battle-ships" able not merely to crush any South American upstart but powerful enough even to give pause for thought to any European navy considering encroachment into the Western Hemisphere. Even then, Luce seems to have envisioned this battle squadron not as an offensive unit tasked with seeking out and destroying the enemy's fleet in order to establish local sea control but rather as a defensive force to prevent the enemy from establishing local control and imposing a blockade of U.S. commercial centers. At this stage, there was no question of the United States building a battle fleet sufficient to guarantee regional or hemispheric sea control against the first-class naval powers (Britain and France); before 1916, this was an unknown concept.

Tracy's willingness to consult notwithstanding, in the informed opinion of Benjamin Cooling, Tracy's biographer, who also cataloged the Tracy Papers for the Library of Congress, Tracy remained "independent both in mind and action." He listened, he learned, but he formed his own opinions as to the direction to be taken.[13] With this judgment, it is hard to disagree, as Admiral of the Navy David Dixon Porter soon discovered to his irritation. Having boasted to Luce in early March 1889 that his "strong friend" President Harrison would "express to the Secretary his wishes that he shall consult me," Porter quickly found that consultation was all he got.[14] After their first meeting, Porter was disabused yet "much impressed with the profound knowledge he [Tracy] possesses of naval affairs which I think must have been born in him!"[15] This was sarcasm: Porter in fact considered Tracy pompous and opinionated. Manifestly, Tracy was determined to be his own Navy Secretary.

During his first six months in office, Tracy held his cards close. Not until August 1889, while touring the Portsmouth Navy Yard, did he issue his first public statement on the subject of fleet expansion, yet the crumbs of information he dropped that day proved misleading in light of what followed. "If Congress will give us the money to put into a plant we will immediately begin to build steel cruisers at this yard and at all the others," he vouchsafed to the attending journalists"; he added that contracts for five new cruisers would shortly be let.[16] From his remarks and actions, Tracy appeared content with the broad direction of naval policy, to maintain and update the existing cruising navy. Notably, issuing his statement while visiting a navy yard carried an implied threat that if private builders did not moderate their prices, the government would build warships itself. Sure enough, the following month Tracy awarded contracts for two of the five cruisers to the Norfolk and Brooklyn Navy Yards—much to the fury of Senator Eugene Hale, chairman of the Senate Navy Committee, whose state included the Bath Iron Works. "The ships will cost more money, take more time to build, and will not be so good in the end," Hale fumed.[17]

Given Tracy's passivity thus far, it therefore came as something of a surprise when, at the end of November 1889, he revealed in the Secretary's annual report to Congress that he was not at all happy with the current direction of naval policy. Historians of all stripes have long recognized Tracy's 1889 annual report as a very important policy document. Harold and Margaret Sprout labeled it "one of the most forceful documents in the entire history of American naval policy"; Walter LaFeber agreed it was "epochal."[18] At the time of publication it was greeted with almost unanimous approval. "Secretary Tracy states the principles of a national policy with the clearness and force of a business proposition," declared the *New York Times*.[19] Cdr. French Chadwick, a rising star within the Navy, viewed it as "the best state paper which has ever been issued from the Navy Department. And I know of none from any Department of late years, certainly, which can compare with it in clearness of statement and in stating succinctly a policy. It is indeed the first which I have ever known which has given definitely a real policy of any sort."[20] The report ran to fifty printed pages and said a good deal about the state of the Navy and the need for reform. Even today it makes impressive reading. But what was the essential policy recommended therein?

THE TRACY REPORT

In most history books, Secretary Tracy's report of 1889 is generally represented as a clarion call for the U.S. Navy to graduate from a cruiser (or frigate) navy into a battleship navy committed to decisive battle with the enemy. To an extent, this interpretation is understandable. The report proposed a U.S. Navy consisting of 20 battleships, 60 cruisers, and 20 upgraded monitors for coastal defense.[21] Charles Boutelle, the chairman of the House Naval Committee, tongue-in-cheek dubbed this "the ultimate naval force."[22] These were certainly eye-catching numbers, yet they were no greater than those put forward by Adm. Rodgers eight years before. The difference was that whereas previously the call for battleships had been repudiated by the legislature (and also by Secretary Hunt), this time it was swiftly answered. Six months later, in June 1890, Congress authorized the construction of three *Indiana*-class battleships.

Conventionally, the construction of these battleships is seen as a watershed moment for the U.S. Navy. "By 1890 a new outlook had definitely established itself in the minds of those who guided American naval policy," George Davis declared; for instance, "broadside battleships took the place of cruisers and monitors as the main source of our naval power." [23] Even scholars of the caliber of George Baer have insisted that "around 1890 the U.S. Navy *transformed itself* according to a role and structure expressed by the protean concept of sea power as an offensive battle fleet employed by a competitive maritime nation."[24] To the extent that Congress plays any role in this transformation, its willingness to increase the Navy is explained as a response to European encroachments in South America.

Furthermore, because historians have inferred a similarity between the messages contained in Tracy's report and Mahan's book, they have assumed that Mahan's influence on Tracy was immediate and considerable. Published within months of each other, the Tracy report and Mahan's *Influence* seem like twin stars pointing the way to a new navy. The Sprouts unequivocally declared that Mahan was behind the Tracy report. The only problem was that *Influence* appeared six months *after* Tracy published his report. Undaunted by this chronological inconvenience, they nevertheless insisted that Mahan's forthcoming book "provided an ideological basis which made Secretary Tracy's annual report for that year one of the most forceful documents in the entire history of American naval policy. Whether Mahan drafted certain passages, whether Tracy had access to Mahan's manuscript, or whether he merely consulted him, it is difficult to say, but the ideas were indubitably Mahan's."[25]

In making these assertions, however, the Sprouts provided no evidence. Neither Mahan's nor Tracy's private correspondence gives even a hint of a meeting between them. The day after the Secretary's report appeared, moreover, Mahan wrote to Luce intimating that he had no connection to it, remarking only that "his [Tracy's] report, so far as reported in our paper, the *N.Y. Times*, is gratifying not merely by the solidity of his opinions, but by the decisive manner in which they are expressed."[26] If Mahan had been consulting with Tracy, it would have been uncharacteristic of him not to have confided the fact in Luce; he certainly did so on subsequent occasions. This evidentiary hole notwithstanding, many have continued to parrot the presumption that Tracy must have seen Mahan's manuscript before it appeared in print. Accordingly, they have allowed this unsupported assertion to frame their analysis of naval policy of the period, and they have interpreted Tracy's policy recommendations alongside what they take to be Mahan's.[27]

There are a number of problems with this approach, even beyond the lack of evidence of a Mahan–Tracy connection. For one thing, read carefully, the Tracy report has more contradictions and less consistency than hindsight has imbued it with. Once again, historians have achieved a narrative coherence only by omitting a great deal of material that does not fit into the standard triumphalist narrative. Even what seems obvious or clear in fact is not. Though Tracy unquestionably advocated the construction of battleships, for instance, what he meant by the term "battle-ship" (its characteristics and intended role) cannot be safely assumed. The words and warship categories used in 1889—including "battleship"—lacked the clear and stable meanings they later acquired. In his report, Tracy referred to the projected large cruiser *New York* also as a "battleship"—which begs the question of what, in his mind, were the respective functions of cruisers and battleships.[28] This was no slip of the pen, nor was the elision of battleships and armored cruisers unique to Tracy. In a letter written four weeks later to the chairman of the House Naval Committee, Adm. Luce agreed that an armored cruiser "will probably be equal to a battleship" and advised that they be counted as equivalents.[29]

Adding further to confusion, several pages later in the same report Tracy announced the redesignation of the two 'armor-clad' warships authorized two years earlier as "second-class battleships." These British-designed but American-built warships had been ordered by Congress (over the objections of the Navy Department) in response to concerns expressed by members of the House Naval Committee over the recent Brazilian purchase from Britain of two armored warships more powerful than anything in the U.S. fleet, and rumors that Argentina and Chile were in the process of acquiring similar vessels.[30] The two were commissioned as the *Texas* and the *Maine*. Neither was remotely fit to lie in a first-class European line-of-battle; they were at best "pocket-battleships," to employ a familiar albeit anachronistic term, designed to fight but too powerful to be classed as mere cruisers yet no match for a first-class battleship. This is not splitting hairs. If the transition to a battleship navy—as understood in the modern sense—is to be regarded as an epochal change, then it matters a great deal what proponents envisioned when they spoke of battleships. A warship's nomenclature cannot be taken as a reliable indication of its intended mission.

In substance as well as nomenclature, Tracy's clarity of vision was more apparent than real. His report was predicated on the assessment that, as presently constituted, the U.S. Navy was pretty much useless for achieving the goals of national policy, or rather the Republican expansionists' vision of what that policy should be. Contemporaries agreed that it was as much a politically inspired foreign policy pronouncement as it was an Olympian statement on naval policy; the *New York Times* printed its analysis of the report under the banner of "Uncle Sam's Little Navy."[31] "Secretary Tracy," the editors explained to their readers, "shows that our present navy, with all its reinforcements, actual and provided for, would make but a poor showing against much weaker powers. When all the ships now authorized are completed we shall have an effective force of only 42 vessels—11 armored and 31 unarmored—and only 3 of the former are designed for fighting at sea."[32] The editors quoted Tracy's assessment that "we are absolutely at the mercy of states having less than one-tenth of our population, one thirtieth of our wealth, and one-hundredth of our area."[33]

What did Tracy see as wrong with the naval force he had inherited? He framed his explanation in unmistakably expansionist language: "So far the increase has been mainly in the direction of unarmored cruisers. These vessels, while useful in deterring commercial states from aggression and as an auxiliary to secure celerity and efficiency in larger operations, do not constitute a fighting force, even when it is intended exclusively for defense. To meet the attack of ironclads, ironclads are indispensable."[34]

Basically, Tracy's pitch was that Congress must pay for what he termed a naval "fighting force."[35] Echoing Luce's arguments published several months earlier in the *North American Review*, the Secretary explained that their role would not be limited to the defense of ports nor even to the continental United States. "We cannot be indifferent to events taking place in close proximity to its own coasts, threatening the freedom of its commerce and the security of its seaport cities. The questions that have arisen and that will continue to arise in the Gulf of Mexico and the Pacific concern the prosperity and development of the United States too closely to be further ignored, and our interests in these localities are too important to be left longer unprotected."[36]

Tracy justified the necessity for such powerful, oceangoing, and above all expensive warships in economic terms. "It is a practical business question of insuring our property and our trade, in which the commercial cities of the coast, the ports of our lake frontier, and the centers of production in the interior are alike interested," he maintained.[37] And a page later: "It is the premium paid by the United States for the insurance of its acquired wealth and its growing industries. Compared with the interests that are secured, the rate is low. It is a cheap price to pay for safety. We collect in duties in six months at a single port a greater sum than we could spend in building a new navy in six years."[38]

The real difficulty in treating the Tracy report as "epochal," and consequently accepting the conclusion that henceforth the U.S. Navy became a battleship navy aiming at sea control, is that Tracy remained firmly wedded to *guerre de course* as the basis of U.S. naval strategy. The evidence for this is incontrovertible—and, incidentally, it puts a gaping hole in the theory that Mahan ghostwrote much of the report. Moreover, further illustrating that Tracy was very much his own man, the Navy Secretary was also flirting—more than flirting, in fact—with the idea of developing an auxiliary navy and supportive of state-level initiatives to form naval militias, a positive heresy so far as Mahan and most naval officers was concerned.[39] Not only were militia-manned auxiliary cruisers the very antithesis of professionalism, but they also represented potential competition for funds allocated by Congress to the naval defense of the United States.

Acknowledging that the U.S. Navy possessed insufficient cruisers to mount a serious attack on enemy seaborne commerce, the Secretary proposed that "Our deficiency should be supplied either by a line of fast merchantmen, constructed with special reference to use in time of war, which will enable the Government to avail itself of their services at critical moments, or we should build a fleet of at least five first-class cruisers of the very highest rate of speed, certainly not less than 22 knots."[40]

Although the U.S. Navy would soon become reasonably confident it could build a cruiser of such speed, in 1889 such a warship lay beyond the outer edge of the technologically possible, especially if built in the United States. Accordingly, in 1889 and in the years immediately following, Tracy opted for the safer option of establishing an auxiliary navy comprised of merchantmen designed with an eye to rapid conversion into armed merchant cruisers. This was not only the simplest and surest way of expanding the cruiser fleet, but also the most politically appealing for a Republican administration. Sponsoring the construction of armed merchant cruisers offered a vehicle for providing U.S. shipbuilders and shipowners with the subsidies from the government they had long sought. The possibility also appealed to some Democrats for ideological reasons, on the grounds that a naval militia was less threatening than a large professional standing navy.[41]

The question of government subsidies to shipbuilders had a long and fraught history in U.S. politics. Almost since the founding of the republic and until the outbreak of the Civil War, the U.S. Merchant Marine (USMM) had been second only to the British in both number and technological sophistication of its vessels, with all others a long way behind. During the Civil War, however, U.S. merchantmen had suffered severely at the hands of Confederate raiders and many of the remainder had abandoned the American registry. After the war, Congress barred any from returning. By 1890, the USMM had shriveled into insignificance.[42] Barely 10 percent of U.S. oceanic trade was carried in U.S. bottoms. The reasons were various and complicated, but perhaps the most important was that U.S. law required U.S. registered ships to be built by U.S. shipbuilders. In the age of sail this was not a problem; American shipbuilders were among the finest in the world. But as sail and wood were replaced by steam and iron, the same shipbuilders struggled. After the war, British (and German) merchant ships not only cost less but also were cheaper to run, owing to a combination of superior British hulls and engines and generally lower labor costs. Quite simply, in being forced to buy American, U.S. shipping lines could not compete.[43]

Unable to get the prohibition on purchasing foreign-built ships lifted, shipowners resorted to claiming that they were the victims of "unfair" foreign competition and thus required subsidies to level the playing field. This self-serving intervention in the domestic political economy sought to distribute revenues from the Republican tariff to Republican shipyards in the Northeast. Unsurprisingly, it gained little traction in the South or West, or among Democrats.[44] For a brief period beginning in 1872, Congress was persuaded to issue generous "mail contracts" (in effect, subsidies); but two years later the scheme collapsed in a blizzard of corruption and scandal.[45] For the next fifteen years, both parties saw that proposing subsidies for merchant ships risked losing more votes than it would gain because it so clearly benefited the notoriously corrupt urban East Coast districts.

Accordingly, advocates of subsidies developed a new line of argument to exploit growing public interest in the Navy: subsidies were a matter of national defense. American shipowners and shipbuilders joined hands to form the appropriately named American Shipping and Industrial League and renewed their demands for the Treasury Department to provide subventions for the construction of fast merchantmen and, separately, to pay owners of the new vessels a subsidy per mile sailed.[46] To be eligible for this bounty, shipbuilders had to build vessels that were not only faster than was economically practicable (because faster ships were more expensive to run) but also "constructed under the supervision of the Navy Department, with particular reference to prompt and economical conversion into auxiliary cruisers, of sufficient strength and stability to carry and sustain at least four effective rifled cannon."[47]

In 1889, the Republican Party was sufficiently interested in the Shipping League to put the idea to the American public. It was President Harrison, not Secretary Tracy, who seems to have been the real driving force behind this initiative; and Blaine, who hailed from Maine, heartily approved.[48] In his inaugural address of March 4, 1889,

Harrison connected the desirability of expanding the U.S. Navy to the desirability of a similar expansion in the merchant marine. "The construction of a sufficient number of modern war ships and of their necessary armament should progress as rapidly as is consistent with care and perfection in plans and workmanship. . . . We should encourage the establishment of American steamship lines. The exchanges of commerce demand stated, reliable, and rapid means of communication, and until these are provided the development of our trade with the States lying south of us is impossible."

Six months later, in October 1889, Harrison publicly floated the idea of subsidies for the building of mail steamers or fast merchant-men.[49] Six weeks after that, in his First Annual Message (delivered a few days after Tracy's report to Congress), Harrison called for "such appropriations be made for ocean mail service in American steamships between our ports and those of Central and South America, China, Japan, and the important islands in both of the great oceans as will be liberally remunerative for the service rendered and as will encourage the establishment and in some fair degree equalize the chances of American steamship lines in the competitions which they must meet."[50]

The point to note in all this is that Harrison (and Tracy) were connecting the expansion of the U.S. Navy to the growth of the USMM. The president was quite explicit on this point, going on to propose that "we should also make provision for a naval reserve to consist of such merchant ships of American construction and of a specified tonnage and speed as the owners will consent to place at the use of the Government in case of need as armed cruisers."[51] Though Harrison thus presented this subsidy scheme as one of lofty national interest, the Democratic-leaning, anti-tariff *New York Times* sniffed base political motives and quickly denounced it as fraudulent. Commenting on the speech the following morning, the editor flatly stated that "it is nonsense to talk about subsidies and liberal compensation for mail service as a means of building up American shipping."[52] Over the next several days, newspaper staff systematically demolished the arguments in favor of subsidies put forward by President Harrison, Secretary

Tracy, and Senator Hale.[53] Yes, these journalistic criticisms contained more than a trace of partisanship, but the core objection happened to be true.

As time passed and further details emerged, it became glaringly apparent that the Harrison administration was trying to force a particularly rancid piece of pork down taxpayer throats. Beginning on January 22, 1890, the House of Representatives debated a bill put forward by John Farquar, chairman of the newly created House Commission on Merchant Marine and Fisheries.[54] According to the *New York Times*, which kept a close watch the bill's progress through Congress, at that time it seemed likely to pass despite the noxious whiff of corruption surrounding it. Somehow, Farquar had managed to forge a workable cross-party consensus. As the *Times* subsequently reported on March 17, "the House is divided on the question without regard to Party. Some of the Democrats are known to entertain the opinion that a subsidy will encourage capital to invest in ships. A good many Republicans will support subsidies because the party is committed to that policy."[55]

Then suddenly, for reasons that are unclear, the bill stalled. Southern Democrats withdrew their support en bloc.[56] Over the course of the next six months or so it became increasingly apparent that the proposed subsidies had been structured to benefit a handful of (northern) interests.[57] Worse, the costs entailed were opaque, to say the least. "No man can tell what would be the expense of passing the subsidy bill," the *Times* remarked.[58] As support ebbed, the generosity of the proposed subsidies was increasingly watered down and the bill slipped farther and farther down the order of business.[59] A much more modest bill was finally passed into law at the end of 1891, which the *New York Times* labeled as a blatant fraud: "It seems to be a policy of idiocy, but it has method in it. It helps to keep up the outrageous tariff, and adds to the interests which get profit from the government, and which helps to keep in power the party that is responsible for the policy."[60] Subsequently, from 1892, Tracy quietly shifted his auxiliary cruisers idea to the back burner in favor of building fast warships that were purposely designed for commerce raiding.[61] Meanwhile, the idea of state naval militias developed a momentum of its own, but that is another story.

Politics also pervaded Tracy's thinking on battleships. In his 1889 report, Tracy requested from Congress an appropriation to construct eight battleships of a design to be determined. How much of this was politics and how much was wishful thinking cannot be said. Yet it seems pertinent to note that, for want of key components, chiefly steel, armor, and ordnance, the Navy was struggling to build the two "second-class battleships" already on the stocks, and it had not even begun some of the warships authorized under the previous administration.[62] Given the limitations in warship construction capacity, Admiral Luce thought Tracy's request for eight more battleships ridiculously optimistic, doubting that more than two could be built simultaneously.[63]

Charles Boutelle agreed that Tracy's request was unrealistic. A former naval officer who had commanded a gunboat in David Farragut's squadron during the famous attack on Mobile Bay, Boutelle not only favored naval expansion but agreed with the necessity of "building some powerful, heavily armored coast line-of-battle ships, with enough coal endurance to operate on the Isthmus &c and strong enough to break any blockade and protect our harbors and coast. These vessels could be made more powerful than ships calculated to carry the heaviest batteries into remote foreign waters."[64] Yet in so doing, he clearly envisioned them being employed primarily as a defensive force whose wartime role would be to keep open the approaches to East Coast ports. Furthermore, as he told Luce, "I think the country has looked somewhat askance at the programme of building great fleets of ponderous ironclad ships to send abroad and it seemed to me that the first duty would be to protect our cities and provide for raising a blockade of our ports—or rather preventing it."[65] As to the number required, however, Boutelle remained nervous of political and public opinion. The nation was by no means sold on the idea of a new navy, and "while the country is well disposed toward a reasonably liberal increase of the Navy, we don't want to scare them off the nest."[66]

It defies belief to think that Tracy was so naive as to expect that Congress would permit the Navy to construct eight battleships at once. He must have known there was insufficient support for fleet expansion at such breakneck speed and that he must cut the Navy's coat to the available length of political cloth. His commitment to the force structure he proposed in his 1889 report should not be exaggerated, nor should his achievement in securing funding for the three battleships. The following year, Tracy quietly reduced the size of his ideal battleship fleet from twenty to twelve.[67] For the remainder of his term as Secretary, he obtained for the Navy only one more battleship and two more cruisers, plus a few gunboats.[68]

To sum up: Setting Tracy's 1889 report in its proper context, alongside Harrison's contemporaneous State of the Union speech, reveals the shortcomings of conventional interpretations of the report. The Tracy report did not outline an autonomous naval policy independent of a static political background, as it is often portrayed. Rather, changing domestic politics and national goals were driving the naval policy laid out therein. The strategic concept was not to build a fleet capable of exerting and exercising sea control but rather to build an adequate defensive force—the same basic goal since 1865—and to rely on a *guerre de course* to apply pressure. The creation of an "auxiliary navy" was undeniably a key plank in Tracy's vision of how a *guerre de course* would be waged; also undeniably, the building of the auxiliary navy depended on subsidies to shipbuilders and shipowners, the provision of which was in turn bound up with the tariff issue. The evidence suggests, on balance, that the needs of the Navy were not the driving consideration here.

THE INFLUENCE OF MAHAN ON TRACY

So how and where does Mahan fit into the naval policy picture of the early 1890s? Did he enjoy any influence over Tracy's naval policy, and if he did, then what was the nature of that influence?[69] Most importantly, what, if any, was the significance of the relationship between the two for the development of Mahan's thinking on sea power? For want of evidence, we do not know in any detail what Mahan made of the actual report when he finally read the full text. We may speculate that he must have been pleased by the request for the construction of a small battle fleet, yet surely he must have been unhappy with the Secretary's clear, continuing adherence to a commerce-raiding strategy and his openness to armed merchant cruisers and the encouragement of a naval militia.

Tracy, for his part, certainly was aware of Capt. Mahan when he wrote his report. On assuming office, both Luce and David Dixon Porter urged the secretary to find him employment, but nothing came of it.[70] In September 1889, Mahan became effectively unemployed. Uncertain of his next assignment and unwilling (or unable) to continue renting in Newport, Mahan took his family to live with his mother in New Jersey.[71] Over the next ten months, the Bureau of Navigation struggled to find him an assignment in order that he might qualify at least for shore pay. During this period he was shuttled from pillar to post, performing a variety of odd jobs—"making a strategic study of the North-West Coast at the request of the [naval] Intelligence Office for their files," serving on various court-martial boards, lecturing at the Newport Torpedo Station (which had temporarily been amalgamated into the Naval War College), and overseeing the construction of a new building on Coasters Island at Newport (the site of the present Naval War College).[72] The only consolation was that this allowed him ample spare time to put the finishing touches on his book manuscript, which became *Influence*.[73]

Toward the end of the first week of May 1890, the first copies of *Influence* became available, and Mahan at once began sending out complimentary copies, including one to Secretary Tracy.[74] This is the first tangible evidence of a direct connection between the two, six months after the publication of the "epochal" Tracy report. There is no hint in Mahan's covering letter to Tracy of any prior acquaintance, let alone any previous communication between them on the subject of the book. There is no question, however, that very soon afterward Tracy and Mahan became not only acquainted but forged a close working relationship. In his memoirs, Mahan suggested that after *Influence* was published, the Navy Department more or less left him to his own devices and in effect allowed him a two-year paid sabbatical. He wrote,

In 1890 and 1891 there was no session of the [War] College. During this period of suspended animation its activities were limited to my own preparations for continuing the historical course through the wars of the French Revolution and Empire, with a view to the resumption of teaching. I was kept on this duty; and I think no one else was busy in direct connection with the institution, though the former lecturers were for the most part available. It is evident how particularly fortunate such circumstances were to an author. For the two years that they lasted I had no cares beyond writing; was unvexed by either pecuniary anxieties or interference from my superiors.[75]

The reality was more complex. Around July 1890, Tracy approached Mahan and tasked him secretly to help the ONI in drawing up contingency plans in the event of war with Great Britain.[76] At that time, there was no "special relationship"—indeed, many Americans still saw Britain as their hereditary enemy—and war between the two nations seemed by no means unlikely. In any case, the work was to be performed under the direction of the newly appointed assistant Secretary of the Navy, James Soley, who was an old friend of Mahan's.[77] At the same time, Tracy transferred administrative responsibility for the ONI to Soley's office from the Bureau of Navigation.[78] To be clear, Mahan's position was entirely unofficial, and he possessed no executive powers or status. Officially, he was assigned to "special duty"—an ambiguous status intended to conceal what he was really doing. Perhaps more to the point, he was able to work mainly from home and also had plenty of time to read and write.

At exactly the same time that Mahan was working with the ONI on contemporary war plans, looking at modern trade networks, and trying to work out where British commerce was most vulnerable to attack, he was examining precisely the same subject from one hundred years before.[79] Even before *Influence* was published, Mahan had already began work on its sequel, covering the period from the beginning of the French Revolution to the close of the Napoleonic Wars. His various letters to Luce during the spring of 1890 indicate a shifting and sharpening of focus: the economic factors submerged within extended accounts of combat operations in *Influence* now received, as we shall see, his full attention. He concentrated his research on piecing together the economic history of the period in order to gauge the impact and effectiveness of the Royal Navy's blockade on the French economy, and of Napoleon's continental embargo against Britain. By October 1890, Mahan was, quite literally, up to his neck in a century's worth of British trade statistics.[80]

As was his wont, Mahan drew parallels between the present and the past. In other words, his study of the Napoleonic Wars informed his thoughts on contemporary problems, and vice versa: there was cross-fertilization of analysis. A passage from Mahan's autobiography hints at this. Writing of his work in the early 1890s, Mahan observed,

> we had then certain accepted maxims, dating mainly from 1812, which were as thoroughly current in the country—and I fear in the navy, too—as the "dollar of the daddies" [a silver dollar] was not long after. One was that commerce destroying was the great efficient weapon of naval warfare. Everybody—the navy as well— believed we had beaten Great Britain in 1812, brought her to her knees, by the destruction of her commerce through the system observed by us of single cruisers; naval or privateers. From that erroneous premise was deduced the conclusion of a navy of cruisers, and small cruisers at that; no battleships nor fleets. Then we wanted a navy for coast defense only, no aggressive action in our pious souls; an amusing instance being that our first battle-ships were styled "coast defense" battleships, a nomenclature which probably facilitated the appropriations. They were that; but they were capable of better things, as the event has proved. But the very fact that such talk passed unchallenged as that about commerce-destroying by scattered cruisers, and war by mere defense— known to all military students as utterly futile and ruinous—shows the need then existent of a comprehensive survey of the contemporary condition of the world, and of the stage which naval material had reached.[81]

In this passage, Mahan's determined hostility to *guerre de course* comes across loud and clear, which is not surprising. Far more interesting is his insinuation that U.S. thinking about war with Britain in 1890 was built on a misunderstanding of the War of 1812. What he was saying here is that employing bad (or faulty) history can have real-world consequences. In so doing, Mahan took pains to stress that he was not opposed to warships attacking enemy commerce per se. On the contrary: "This is not the place for a discussion of commerce-destroying as a method of war; but having myself given, as I believe, historical demonstration that as a sole or principal resource, *maintained by scattered cruisers only*, it is insufficient, I wish to warn public opinion against the reaction, the return swing of the pendulum, seen by me with dismay, which would make it of no use at all, and under the plea of immunity to 'private property' so called, would exempt from attack the maritime commerce of belligerents."[82]

Mahan was both aware of and afraid that his scholarship was being used in some quarters to argue that because commerce destruction was ineffective, there should be no objection to attacks on merchantmen being outlawed by international treaty. He of course believed the exact opposite: that *systematic* commerce destruction was in wartime the very foundation of naval strategy. What he objected to was *unsystematic* attacks, more commonly known as *guerre de course*.

The few who have examined Mahan's early war plans for the ONI have more or less dismissed them as impracticable rubbish.[83] His recommendation was to concentrate the fleet—such as it was—at New York in an effort to keep open the port to commercial traffic while the Army attempted to invade Canada. Incidentally, this matched exactly with what he had intimated the year before in *Influence*—that the problem confronting the U.S. Navy in a war against Britain would be to prevent an effective blockade of U.S. seaports.[84] Certainly, in light of subsequent efforts they appear simplistic. But what other options were open to the United States, given the very limited warfighting capabilities of the Navy at this time? No fool, Mahan himself was far from enthusiastic about these plans and viewed the prospects of success as dim. He possessed little faith in the ability of the U.S. Army to quickly subdue the entirety of Canada—as a student of history, he recalled the United States had failed twice before—and if the Army did manage to occupy the majority of lower Canada, he doubted whether this would prove sufficient leverage over Britain in peace talks. The British Empire, Mahan opined in the fall of 1890, was in a position to inflict greater (economic) damage on the United States, with greater speed and certainty, than the United States could inflict in return. In other words, the United States would probably lose. As he put it,

> It is upon our Atlantic seaboard that the mistress [i.e., Great Britain] of Halifax, of Bermuda, and of Jamaica will now defend Vancouver and the Canadian Pacific. In the present state of our seaboard defense she can do so absolutely. What is all Canada compared with our exposed great cities? Even were the coast fortified, she could still do so, if our navy be no stronger than is as yet designed. *What harm can we do Canada proportionate to the injury we should suffer by the interruption of our coasting trade, and by a blockade of Boston, New York, the Delaware, and the Chesapeake?* Such a blockade Great Britain certainly could make technically efficient, under the somewhat loose definitions of international law. Neutrals would accept it as such.[85]

Here again we see Mahan making clear the importance he attached to sea trade and access to the common. Manifestly, his aim was to awaken the Navy to the real nature of the threat faced: loss of access to the "great common" would unleash natural economic forces leading to derangement and dislocation, resulting in the devastation of the U.S. economy.

Mahan's contribution to the 1890 war plans (as well as the plans themselves) remains unclear. We know that those in authority who read them, including the Secretary, found them satisfactory, but we know little about their purpose or effect.[86] "Mr. Tracy kept matters in his own hands, consulted when he wished to consult and acted without consultation as he chose," Mahan recalled in a letter to Luce several years later, "Nor do I remember that I was ever directed to consult anyone else in the Dept.; certainly very rarely, if ever. At times, I saw War Dept. officials by the secretary's direction, for a special purpose. Mr. Tracy consulted others as he did me—Ramsey, Folger, I know, & doubtless others."[87] The real significance lies elsewhere: quite simply, Mahan's appointment to write the war plans gave him direct access to the Navy Secretary, and he frequently met with Tracy face-to-face. At the same time, relatively unburdened with administrative duties, Mahan had the leisure he needed to expand his reading horizons, to refine and revise his ideas, and to complete his second book. In effect, he enjoyed an almost uninterrupted two-year sabbatical from naval service while continuing to collect the salary of a U.S. Navy captain, albeit without benefits and allowances. In presenting to Tracy a copy of his new book, *The Influence of Sea Power upon the French Revolution and Empire, 1793–1812,* Mahan acknowledged his debt to the Secretary; "that I have been able to complete it is due wholly to your support—I may say even to your protection."[88]

That Tracy valued Mahan's counsel seems equally beyond doubt. So happy was Tracy with Mahan's work for him that he invited Mahan to pick his next assignment.[89] Aware that it soon would be his turn for sea duty, the captain initially toyed with the idea of accepting command of a cruiser in home waters but finally summoned the nerve to confess to Tracy that "If the law remains as now, I purpose to retire at the end of my forty years—in 1896, believing that I can achieve greater success personally, with my pen, than by continuing on the active list . . . with my retirement only three years off, I do not wish to go to sea, as that would necessarily interrupt my present studies, and break threads which, at my age, I may not be able again to unite. In fact my whole aim maybe frustrated. I wish, therefore to continue employed as I have been through your administration."[90]

Mahan's honesty with Tracy paid off; the Secretary reappointed him as the president of the reconstituted Naval War College, along with a promise to keep him there for as long as possible.[91] Many within the department disapproved of Mahan being given what they regarded as special treatment.[92]

Yet Tracy's satisfaction with Mahan's work should not be taken as translating into significant influence by the latter over the former. Possessed of an independent mind and believing strongly in civilian, not military, control over policy, Tracy never would have allowed himself to be taken by the hand by a naval officer, certainly not consciously.[93] What is more, in one important area of naval policy, Tracy consistently refused to follow the captain's advice: throughout his administration Tracy remained wedded to the *guerre de course* as the foundation of U.S. Navy strategy in wartime. Furthermore, his support for large-scale battleship construction was at best equivocal.

In the annual report of the Secretary of the Navy published at the end of November 1890, for instance, several months after he brought Mahan within his circle of advisors, Tracy pronounced the *New York* (now a cruiser) as "in many respects one of the most important vessels of the new Navy."[94] In his 1891 report, he again extolled the virtues of the latest designed U.S. cruisers, highlighting their qualities as commerce raiders.[95] In his (final) 1892 report, Tracy lauded the qualities of the *New York*–class cruisers, suggesting that "four such ships" could virtually annihilate British commerce—a suggestion that Mahan would have rejected as preposterous—and concluding that "nothing can be a more effective argument for continued peace than such a vessel as this, especially when considered by a nation having a large commerce afloat."[96] What are we to make of such consistently expressed statements that contradict the standard depiction of Tracy as a card-carrying battleship man?

It seems likely that Tracy was hedging his bets. Better than anyone else, he understood the problems the Navy faced in constructing modern battleships and the risks entailed. For a time it was touch and go whether Andrew Carnegie's steel company would be able to produce the high-quality steel needed for modern warships, and the quantity, at the agreed price. It was not beyond the realm of possibility that if the true magnitude of the Navy Department's problems with the manufacturers of armor became known, the resulting scandal would have produced a violent backlash against the Navy in Congress, as had occurred in recent years.[97] In other words, during the early

1890s, the future of the U.S. Navy as a first-class power and player on the world stage was by no means certain. The risk that the battleship program might fail—for reasons technological, political, or fiscal—was very real. It was therefore wise of Tracy to keep in hand a second string for his policy bow. He pushed ahead as far as he was able rather than as far as he wished, obliged to steer a meandering course around various administrative, technological, and industrial obstacles.

The first Secretary of the Navy truly to accept Mahan's views on *guerre de course*, and to say so publicly, was Tracy's successor, Hilary Herbert of Alabama, who was appointed in March 1893 in the second Grover Cleveland administration.[98] What persuaded him to renounce the traditional operational stance, or so he said, was Mahan's second monograph, *The Influence of Sea Power upon the French Revolution and Empire, 1793–1812*.[99]

CHAPTER 5

REVISED INFLUENCE
Economics and War (1890–92)

*It was from the first evident that Great Britain, having in the three
kingdoms but fifteen million inhabitants, could not invade the territory
of France with its population of over twenty-five millions. This was
the more true because the demands of her navy, of her great mercantile
shipping, and of a manufacturing and industrial system not only vast
but complex, so that interference with parts would seriously derange
the whole, left for recruiting the British armies a fraction, insignificant
when compared with the resources in men of France.*

—ALFRED THAYER MAHAN, MAY 1892[1]

IN PREVIOUS CHAPTERS WE SAW how current domestic political
debate strongly affected Mahan's explication of his concept of sea
power. Just as much as his extensive reading and historical research,
his understanding of how the world worked, in both the present and
the past, was shaped by his views on contemporary events and no less
importantly by his desire to have an effect on them. Mahan's worldview was unusually dynamic: each shift in his perspective on some
contemporary issue caused an incremental modification to his concept
of sea power and how it worked, and through a feedback loop each
modification to his ideas caused a shift in his understanding of the
events happening around him. Mahan freely admitted that he framed

Influence at least in part as a response to contemporary political issues that touched on naval policy and the future of the U.S. Navy more generally. "My object has been to follow, as far as I could, in the footsteps of military historians," he told U.S. senator Henry Cabot Lodge (a history PhD from Harvard), "endeavoring to make the experience of the past influence the opinions and shape the policy of the future."[2]

Yet it was also shown in chapter 3 that Mahan's attempt to present his ideas on sea power and on contemporary events side by side under the same cover met with limited success. That is to say, his drawing of parallels between present and past confused rather more than they enlightened. Happily, soon after the publication of *Influence*, Mahan was given the opportunity to voice his thoughts on contemporary events untethered from historical analysis. Around July 1890, Horace Scudder, the editor of the *Atlantic* (the premier magazine read by U.S. elites), invited the captain to expand on some of the ideas he had touched on in his recent book. How he came to Scudder's attention is unknown, though most likely it was thanks to Theodore Roosevelt.[3]

By mid-September 1890, Mahan had sketched a draft that contained propositions that ran counter to declared policy of the U.S. government. Wary of the imputation of impropriety of such an act by a serving naval officer, Mahan sought the advice of his mentor, Adm. Stephen B. Luce.[4] Was it appropriate, he enquired, for a serving officer to publish their thoughts on "questions which enter into present politics"? He added: "my doubts are mainly as to my exordium, on the first three pages."[5] Luce evidently told Mahan not to worry, and the following week he formally submitted his paper to Scudder.[6] Mahan completed the final proofs the following month.[7] The article appeared in the December 1890 issue under the title of "The United States Looking Outward" (Mahan thought "The United States Asleep" would have been a more apt title), and it received much attention.

Mahan's first major article merits closer attention than it usually is given, for it sheds considerable light on the development of his ideas, how his mind worked, and how he made mental connections. Biographer Robert Seager, though acknowledging the piece was "widely read," dismissed it bag and baggage as an "imperialist epistle" and a naked piece of navalist propaganda.[8] "The article," he thought, "called boldly for vigorous American competition for world trade and for the penetration of overseas markets to solve the dilemma of domestic industrial overproduction. Further, it drew attention to the nation's need to defend its existing strategic and commercial interests in Samoa, Hawaii, and at the Isthmus of Panama. It also pointed to the existence of an increasingly competitive European state system, the jungle nature of which could only endanger the security of an unarmed America. Mahan therefore demanded the building of a large and mobile combat navy."[9]

Seager's précis, while not exactly wrong as to the details, is incorrect as to the main thrust of his argument and its central message. His error was in ignoring the first three pages of the article—which clearly supplies the context for what follows—perhaps because what Mahan wrote did not relate directly to navies. These pages, the "exordium" that had particularly worried Mahan, relate to U.S. tariff policy, and more specifically to the enactment of the infamous (1890) McKinley tariff. To understand why Mahan felt such trepidation at stepping on political toes, some background is necessary.

The tariff was an important and complex subject. During the 1888 general election and for most of the term of the Harrison administration (1889–93), it was generally acknowledged as the leading political issue of the day.[10] Today, scholars generally agree that it represented much more than an economic policy designed to protect nascent American industries from technologically more advanced European competition, often to the detriment of U.S. consumers (who had to pay more for inferior homemade goods) and certainly to the disadvantage of U.S. agricultural interests. It also yielded enormous revenues that allowed the U.S. Treasury to pay off the national debt at an extraordinary rate, and to spend in other directions too. Political scientist Richard Bensel has shown that tariff protection "was the primary pillar for the Republican party in popular politics."[11] In other words, "the tariff was not essential to American industrialization in its own right but it was absolutely indispensable as the ground on which the Republican developmental coalition was constructed."[12] Stated plainly, the ruling Republican Party used tariff revenues to forge the coalition of interest groups on which it depended for political power.

Besides the East Coast industrialists and their employees (who benefited from the higher wages enabled by the tariff), this coalition of interest groups also included Louisiana sugar growers and Western sheep farmers thanks to otherwise anomalous tariffs on sugar and wool. The Republican Party also used tariff revenues to purchase support from veterans of the Union Army (over the course of which more than two million men enlisted) by providing generous pensions and not scrutinizing applications too closely. During the Harrison administration, payments to veterans practically doubled.[13] By 1893, the Treasury was *annually* paying out $156.7 million to veterans. To put this number in perspective (and to illustrate the administration's priorities), total Army expenditures that year were just $51.9 million, while expenditures on the Navy (including construction) ran to a mere $22.5 million.[14] Quite simply, the tariff was *the* pivotal political issue of the day because it touched everything else. Monetary reform, railroad regulation, the building of the Isthmian Canal, the revival of the merchant marine, and of course U.S. naval policy—none of these issues could be settled without consideration of tariff policy. The complex political aspects aside, tariff revenues represented the government's single largest source of income.[15]

While the tariff held together the Republican coalition, it alienated those involved in the most important sector of the U.S. economy: agriculture. Although the 1890s was a period of rapid industrial growth for the United States, the agriculture sector remained the largest employer and the greatest source of export revenues. Throughout this decade, agriculture (mainly cotton exports) still accounted for nearly 80 percent (by value) of U.S. foreign trade.[16] Yet despite its economic importance, agriculture was also the sector of the U.S. economy hurting the most during the Harrison administration.

During the winter of 1889, Secretary of Agriculture Jeremiah Rusk, perhaps the most powerful figure in the Harrison administration, implored the president to do something to alleviate worsening distress in the agricultural West, if only to prevent what was called "an agricultural uprising" leading to Republican decimation in the upcoming midterms.[17] Except for a small uptick during the winter of 1890, the price of wheat and other farm products remained depressed through the fall of 1896, a situation for which the tariff bore substantial blame. The chief cause of depressed prices at home was higher European tariffs, which constricted U.S. farm exports and thereby caused a glut of produce at home. As Harrison knew perfectly well, European tariffs against U.S. farm produce had been imposed largely in retaliation for U.S. tariffs against European-manufactured goods. Meanwhile, farm bankruptcies in the United States continued to rise, and in the western states there was much unhappiness over the government's failure to alleviate the situation.

Hoping to slide the tariff to the back burner, Harrison delegated responsibility for the review of tariff policy to a party stalwart, William McKinley of Ohio, appointing him chairman of a committee to put forward specific recommendations.[18] McKinley completed this task in May 1890. The result was the so-called McKinley tariff, which jacked up the duties on imported goods to almost 50 percent.[19] Harrison and his principal lieutenants—Joseph Blaine, Jerimiah Rusk, Whitelaw Reid, and Benjamin Tracy—were all appalled at the magnitude of increase and fearful of the impact on voters, especially in the grain-producing West.[20] Some years later, Theodore Roosevelt reminded Tracy of a conversation they had shortly after the election in which Tracy had expressed deep concern that "we might key the duties up too high, in a spirit of ultra-protection, and thereby run the risk of a great rebuff at the polls."[21] Blaine's last-minute insertion of a "reciprocity clause" into the bill, designed to give him leverage in negotiating bilateral trade deals with various South American countries, amounted to very little.[22] Among the various interest groups that made up the Republican Party there was insufficient interest in surrendering their privileges to be able to carve out the space needed to negotiate any major trade treaties. The McKinley tariff passed into law on October 1, 1890. In the midterms held the following month, the Republics lost twenty-nine of the forty-four districts they had held in the agricultural West, and along with them their majority in the House.[23]

This, then, was the prevailing political landscape when Mahan composed his intervention published as "The United States Looking Outward."[24] It opened with lines squarely and unmistakably addressed to the tariff debate:

Indications are not wanting of an approaching change in the thoughts and policy of Americans as to their relations with the world outside their own borders. For the past quarter of a century, the predominant idea, which has successfully asserted itself at the polls and shaped the course of the government, has been to preserve the home market for the home industries. The employer and the workman have alike been taught to look at the various economical measures proposed from this point of view, to regard with hostility any step favoring the intrusion of the foreign producer upon their own domain, and rather to demand increasingly rigorous measures of exclusion than to acquiesce in any loosening of the chain that binds the consumer to them. The inevitable consequence has followed, as in all cases when the mind or the eye is exclusively fixed in one direction, that the danger of loss or the prospect of advantage in another quarter has been overlooked; and although the abounding resources of the country have maintained the exports at a high figure, this flattering result has been due more to the super-abundant bounty of Nature than to the demand of other nations for our protected manufactures.[25]

In the pages that followed, Mahan went on to make clear that he regarded "the recent tariff legislation" as both politically and economically myopic, if not downright stupid, comparing U.S. protectionism to Napoleon's enactment in 1806 of the notorious Continental System—an equally ill-judged economic policy which, as we shall see in chapter 8, Mahan believed had fatally undermined the Napoleonic Empire.

A fortnight before the article was published, Mahan highlighted for Horace Scudder what he intended to be the central message of his article: "If my belief, that the United States is about to be forced out of her policy of isolation, is well founded, the age needs prophets to arouse the people."[26] To be clear, the isolation he had in mind was more economic than political. In recent years, he argued, the economic world had changed profoundly, and this global change compelled the United States to shift its stance on the world stage. Whereas in the past a policy of high tariffs made sense, the advantages were becoming less and less obvious. Mahan predicted that the potential growth of the domestic market would be far less than the predicted growth of the international market. This prediction, it should be noted, aligned perfectly with his belief, expressed in *Influence*, that the international trading system was the greatest wealth-generation machine in history. In order to participate in the next surge in international trade, which Mahan insisted was just around the corner, the United States must move away from protection toward free trade; the gains in so doing would far outweigh the loss that would result from opening the home market to foreign competition. Basically, Mahan argued that maintaining national prosperity meant abandoning protectionism. In so doing he was thus taking a political stand.

It was only after denouncing the McKinley tariff—a domestic political-economic issue—as a policy wrong turn that Mahan turned to lay out his overseas navalist agenda. Mahan's arguments on this score flowed from his belief, also laid out clearly in *Influence*, that competition for international trade led to conflict as sure as night followed day. Or as he put it in his article, the quest for foreign trade contained "dangerous germs of quarrel, against which it is at least prudent to be prepared." Mahan went on to draw attention to the "restlessness in the world at large which is deeply significant, if not ominous."[27] Not only were European powers staking out territorial claims across the globe, but these powers—Germany in particular—exhibited a willingness to fight for global markets. He foresaw particular trouble when the Isthmian Canal was finished: "In a general way, it is evident enough that this canal, by modifying the direction of trade routes, will induce a great increase of commercial activity and carrying trade throughout the Caribbean Sea; and that this now comparatively deserted nook of the ocean will, like the Red Sea, become a great thoroughfare of shipping, and attract, as never before in our day, the interest and ambition of maritime nations. Every position in that sea will have enhanced commercial and military value, and the canal itself will become a strategic centre of the most vital importance."[28]

Mahan felt that "militarily speaking, the piercing of the Isthmus is nothing but a disaster to the United States, in the present state of her military and naval preparation" because "the United States is woefully unready, not only in fact, but in purpose, to assert in the Caribbean and Central America a weight of influence proportioned to the extent of her interests. We have not the navy, and, what is worse, we are not willing to have the navy, that will weigh seriously in any disputes with those nations whose interests will there conflict with our own."

In thus pointing out the relative weakness of the U.S. Navy, Mahan took the opportunity to put across another major argument buried within the pages of *Influence*, namely the blindness of Americans to the vulnerability of the United States to a hostile sea power. Alluding to his secret work with the Office of Naval Intelligence on developing naval war plans, Mahan rejected arguments that the United States had nothing to fear from Great Britain because in the event of war the former would simply invade Canada. As already mentioned, he worried that the British could inflict far more pain on the United States by imposing a blockade of the East Coast, and in so doing generate far more pressure than a U.S. occupation of Canada would accomplish. Mahan was arguing that the United States was not nearly so strong militarily, or economically, as was believed. When one understood how sea power worked, he reasoned, then the national vulnerability became clear.

In summary, therefore, Mahan's "The United States Looking Outward" was certainly punditry but much more than crude navalist propaganda. Besides (correctly) anticipating a major shift in U.S. public opinion, what he had accomplished was to sketch out the consequences likely to follow from the ongoing transformation in the world economic system. Mahan perceived massive changes in the world; he tried to make sense of what was happening and identify the salient characteristics, and he tried to discern the strategic implications of these changes. In these respects he was a pioneer. It is true that as yet he only dimly made out the precise shape and form of that transformation—another ten years would pass before he would describe what he discerned in a way that clearly could be recognized as a description of "globalization." Nevertheless, already he had identified the growth in the volume and importance of global trade as a critical factor in international relations and perceived its implications for U.S. politics and policy. As he concluded in his article, "Whether they will or no, Americans must now begin to look outward. The growing production of the country demands it. An increasing volume of public sentiment demands it. The position of the United States, between the two Old Worlds and the two great oceans, makes the same claim."

FRENCH REVOLUTIONARY WAR

The increasing importance Mahan now attached to understanding economic issues, and more especially the dynamics of economic processes, is apparent also in his second monograph, which carried the story of sea power forward to 1814 with the fall of Napoleon. Mahan began work on the sequel before *Influence* was published. Very early on in his research, his focus began to shift toward understanding the economic history of the period. Requesting help with locating sources on April 4, 1890, Mahan explained to Luce that "I have been trying for some time latterly to gather information as to the effect upon commerce of the wars between 1793 and 1805; not only in the matter of prizes taken and state papers in the shape of decrees, orders in council, and so forth but also the modifications in the routes followed by trade in consequence of the ebb and flow of military control, especially in the sea."[29]

Mahan unhappily admitted that "so far I have had little success. I do not mean to imply that I have not met hints and straws of information . . . but what I want is to find the work, to some extent at least, done to my hand, the information garnered and systematized."[30] Five days later, Mahan wrote again to Luce, this time crabbing on his difficulty in finding anything useful on French economic history. "I fancy I shall nowhere find just what I want, which emphasizes the

necessity of its being done by me," he sighed.[31] More importantly,
Mahan issued an explicit statement on the increasing importance he
attached to the economic component of sea power. The subject "is
not strategy nor tactics," he admitted to a probably skeptical Luce,
"yet from my point of view essential to a full presentation of the maritime history of any epoch."[32]

Subsequent letters from Mahan to Luce illustrate how the relationship between economics and war came steadily into ever sharper
focus. The deeper he dug, the more he realized that this aspect of the
French wars of revolution and empire—the Napoleonic era—had not
before been systematically studied and yet was central to the understanding of it. "There have been statements made which seem to me
only half-truths as to the prosperity of Great Britain during the Napoleonic Wars," he remarked to Luce a few months later, "and as far as
my own imperfect information goes I think many of the speakers have
but a partial knowledge of the matter, and overlooked many factors of
importance."[33] In another letter he elaborated that "I have collected a
great many facts, and have had to study the subject very carefully, for
want of any systematic treatise."[34] Providing yet more evidence of the
importance he attached to understanding the economics of warfare,
Mahan wrote,

> I propose to bring it in [the subject of economics and war], in a
> chapter (or lecture) on Commerce Destroying, to which it belongs;
> but the subject demands a book, and I am surprised if none has
> been produced, except that, as one man said, everyone connected
> with or affected by it would be glad to forget that it ever existed. In
> its far reaching ramifications, its multiplicity of incidents, its effects
> on the populations, and on the course of events, it affords a field
> for a powerful and interesting work. But to produce it requires
> time and opportunities out of my reach.[35]

At the end of December 1890, Mahan began writing up his notes
on "the Commerce Destroying of the Wars 1793–1815." [36] It took
him eighteen months or so to finish these and the rest of his new

book. Recalling this period of his life in his autobiography, Mahan explicitly identified the French historian Henri Martin as his inspiration. He elaborated: "Colbert, as expounded by Martin, sent me in later days to the study of trade statistics; as indicative of naval or political conditions deflecting commercial interchange, and influencing national prosperity. The strong interest such searches had for me may show a natural bent, and certainly conduced to the understanding of sea power in its broadest sense."[37]

Published in December 1892, *The Influence of Sea Power upon the French Revolution and Empire, 1793–1812* appeared in two volumes (to distinguish it from Mahan's first book, it will be referenced hereafter simply as *French Revolution and Empire*). As its full title implied, Mahan conceived of the work as a chronological continuation of *Influence*, his first monograph. In the preface, Mahan declared—once again—that his primary aim was to demonstrate the importance of sea power as a factor in "shaping the destinies of nations and of the world."[38] In building his case he employed the same analytical scaffolding as he had in *Influence*, retelling the history of Western Europe and the Americas around his idea of sea power. Again, the interrelationship between trade, wealth, and power formed the heart of his analysis, premised on the fact that carriage by water was always "easier and ampler than by land."[39] He further pronounced that the sea was "the mother of all prosperity" and "the greatest of all sources of renewing vitality."[40]

Pursuant to this theme, Mahan put forward a novel thesis in *French Revolution and Empire*. At that time, most core histories of the French revolutionary wars—often, though inaccurately, referred to simply as the Napoleonic Wars—identified the key events of the conflict as having occurred on land between the continental powers, treating the actions of the British Royal Navy as merely incidental and secondary to the outcome. Mahan strongly disagreed. On the very first page he nailed his colors to the mast by declaring that from beginning to end, British sea power had been *the* determining factor.[41] He lambasted previous scholars—especially British historians—for failing to take proper account of the maritime dimension of the conflict, taking particular aim at Thomas Macaulay's five-volume *History of England*.[42]

Mahan's new monograph was far more readable than his previous effort; indeed, it was the most accessible piece of scholarship he ever produced. Although the subject matter he dealt with was often exceedingly complex and his treatment of it highly detailed, his narrative was not at all convoluted. His writing was coherent, smooth, and cut no corners. No matter how complicated the topic, he supplied his readers with clear and comprehensive analysis of every aspect of his subject, great and small. Mahan also achieved greater authoritativeness, incorporating a broader range of state papers and original documents. Best of all, Mahan made far fewer editorial intrusions than he had in *Influence*, and where he did draw analogies between historical and current events his touch was deft and the effect illuminating.[43] The effect was to sweep readers forward through the new book on a wave of coherent narrative detail.

In his anxiety to improve the readability of his tomes, however—and perhaps a reluctance to admit any previous error too openly—Mahan eschewed laying out all of his main arguments in his introduction, preferring instead to scatter them throughout the 791 pages of the main text. More awkwardly still, he deliberately chose to make his points implicitly rather than explicitly, expecting his readers to divine his meaning through consideration of surrounding narrative context. "My utterances are generally made passively," he admitted to a friend, and "although I attempt no controversy, I have fled the necessity of supporting my case all through, and consequently a certain amount of argument underlies the current of my story—though it does not, I hope, rise too obtrusively to the surface."[44] It did not.

Mahan's second book both continued and modified arguments made in his first. Many of the themes identified in the previous analysis of *Influence*—the operation of sea power in peace as well as war, international trade's catalyzing effects on ancillary domestic economic activity, the complexity of economic systems, the futility of unsystematic commerce raiding, and the role of international law in maritime war—appear again in *French Revolution and Empire*. But as compared to *Influence*, the second book develops these broader themes much more robustly. What is more, there is no tension, as there was in *Influence*, between a European half focused on the economic character of naval warfare and an American half focused on combat operations, nor are there any crude denunciations of commerce destruction transparently intended to intervene in contemporary debate rather than to summarize historical conclusions. The result is that *French Revolution and Empire* conveys far more clearly Mahan's conviction that sea power was fundamentally political-economic in character and that the ultimate end of naval force was to strangle enemy commerce, not to destroy an enemy battle fleet. Put differently, while *Influence* supplies evidence, thanks to Mahan's ambiguity, to support the conventional caricature of him as obsessed with destruction of the enemy battle fleet, *French Revolution and Empire* renders that caricature unsupportable.

Further, the order in which Mahan wrote the chapters of *French Revolution and Empire* underscores the greater importance he attached to economics and at the same time helps to explain why the book's focus on economics was so much more consistent than *Influence*'s. From his letters, we know that Mahan wrote *French Revolution and Empire* backwards. That is, the first chapters he composed appear at the end of the second volume, as chapters 17 and 18 (with chapter 19 as the summary and conclusion).[45] We also know that he saw these chapters as the real heart of his book. "Taken together," he recalled in his autobiography with surprising frankness, "these three chapters, final but first written, contain the main argument of the book."[46] Furthermore, they contained no combat operations, just a close analysis of the impact of the war on international and national commercial systems. In conception, construction, and function, therefore, the preceding sixteen chapters (including the entire first volume) were but preamble and prelude.

In these closing chapters, Mahan reexamined the mechanics of commerce destruction much more closely than before, as well as its reciprocal (so to speak), the process of wealth generation. This led him to look more closely at the linkages *between* trade, wealth, and power, to scrutinize the importance of the relationship between oceanic trade and broader commercial activity and to reconsider the disruptive effects on these economic processes caused by the application of naval force. This shift in analytical focus produced a change in narrative emphasis away from the operational application of naval force toward its impact on general commercial activity and state finances. Put crudely, Mahan's book—or rather his conception of sea power—became less naval and more economic.[47]

On the first page of the chapter 1, for instance, Mahan bluntly stated that Great Britain's "relentless purpose and mighty wealth were to exert the deceive influence upon the result of the war."[48] Several chapters later he explicitly subordinated the naval to the economic by declaring that "the policy of Great Britain was to control the sea for the protection of commerce, and to sustain on shore the continental powers in a war against France—*chiefly* by money, but *also* by naval cooperation when feasible."[49] Note the words in italics. Both commercial and naval were necessary, but clearly one was primary and one was secondary. Unquestionably, the most obvious manifestation of Mahan's greater economic focus was his text. The pages of *French Revolution and Empire*, particularly the first volume, still contained plenty on combat operations, analyzed in exhaustive detail. Yet for every page Mahan wrote describing naval combat or detailing the course of a naval campaign, he provided twenty discussing aspects of trade policy or the economic consequences of naval attack on maritime trade. At the beginning of chapter 17 he bluntly stated that "The annals of the times are consequently filled, not with naval battles, but with notes of vessels taken and retaken; of convoys, stealing along the coast of France, chased, harassed and driven ashore, by the omnipresent cruisers of the enemy. Nor was it commerce alone that was thus injured. The supplying of the naval ports, even with French products, chiefly depended upon the coasting vessels; and embarrassment, amounting often to disability, was constantly entailed by the unflagging industry of the hostile ships."[50]

The centrality of economics is visible in other ways, too. For instance, the chief protagonist of *French Revolution and Empire* was not an admiral, nor even a member of the Board of Admiralty, but rather William Pitt (the younger)—who from 1783 to 1801, and again from May 1804 until his death in January 1806, served simultaneously as Prime Minister and Chancellor of the Exchequer of Great Britain. Mahan lauded Pitt as a "strategic genius" and the architect of the grand strategy that produced victory after more than twenty expensive years of nearly continuous war. Under Pitt's leadership and at his direction, Mahan explained, the United Kingdom became "the storehouse of the world's commerce. The more thriving that commerce, the better for her, if it could be concentrated in her own borders. Thus France and the whole world should become tributary to a wealth and to a power by which, not Great Britain only, but the world should be saved. It [Pitt's strategy] was a great conception . . . it was radically sound and in the end victorious, for upon Great Britain and upon commerce hung the destinies of the world."[51]

Mahan's emphasis on economics similarly came through in his warm approval of various British expeditions to capture French sugar islands, at odds with his reputation as a proponent of always focusing on the enemy fleet. "Among the leading objects contemplated by the British ministry in this war was the control of the East and West Indies, particularly of the latter," he explained, "as among the most important sources as well as markets of British trade."[52] Mahan argued that the economic benefits of capturing them were tremendous and far outweighed the military loss they represented to France, which used them as bases of operation for corsairs.[53] As the war continued, British merchants increasingly became the sole purveyors of what were known as "tropical goods" to the world and thus were able to charge monopoly prices.

Already by the late eighteenth century, coffee and especially sugar had become necessities of life for upper- and middle-income European families, and even for wealthier artisan families as well.[54] The profits earned were enormous. The British government collected a hefty percentage of these profits through the imposition of excise duties—in 1802, 25 percent of all excise revenues came from Caribbean trade. Pitt's policy of capturing sugar islands thus buttressed the

British financial stability and boosted the creditworthiness of the government, making possible the state's borrowing of astronomical (for the day) sums of money to maintain an enormous navy and to finance the field armies of its allies.[55]

What Mahan was suggesting here, in effect, was that although combat might seem to be the essence of war, its character—certainly when fought at sea—was fundamentally economic. It was a sort of naval variation on Carl von Clausewitz's famous metaphor about land warfare: its grammar was combat, but its logic was political. In his concluding chapter, Mahan tried to drive this point home by employing the language of evolutionary biology as a metaphor to articulate his thoughts on the almost symbiotic relationship in wartime between sea power and international economics. Reaffirming his belief that sea power had been the most important factor in determining the outcome of the war, Mahan reflected,

> The circumstances of the times had placed this force wholly in the hands of Great Britain. She wielded it as absolute mistress. Its action, like that of all the other forces in the strife, depended in part upon the direction given it by the British leaders for the purposes of war. From this point of view, its structure appears to be simple and rudimentary; the related movements of a few principal parts are open to inspection and susceptible of criticism. But from another point of view, in its course and influence, this wonderful and mysterious power is seen to be a complex organism, endued with a life of its own, receiving and imparting countless impulses, moving in a thousand currents which twine in and around one another in infinite flexibility, not quite defying the investigation which they provoke, but rendering it exceedingly laborious. This Power feels and is moved by many interests; it has a great history in the past, it is making a great and yet more wonderful history in the present. Grown to the size of a colossus, which overshadows the earth without a second,—unless it be the new rival rising in the Western hemisphere,—it is now assailed with a fury and virulence never before displayed. Attacked in every quarter and by every

means, sought to be cut off alike from the sources and from the issues of its enterprise, it adapts itself with the readiness of instinct to every change. It yields here, it pushes there; it gives ground in one quarter, it advances in another; it bears heavy burdens, it receives heavy blows; but throughout all it lives and it grows. It does not grow because of the war, but it does grow in spite of the war. The war impedes and checks, but does not stop, its progress.[56]

Sea power, this "wonderful and mysterious power," was clearly far more than the Royal Navy: it was a "complex organism" responsive to "many interests." On the next page, Mahan reaffirmed his conviction that its character was fundamentally commercial-economic:

Whatever the fluctuation of its fortunes or the mistakes of govern-ments in the past, the sea power of Great Britain had at the open-ing of the French Revolution attained proportions, and shown a tenacity of life, which carried the promise of the vast expansion of our own day. Painfully harassed during the American Revolution, and suffering from the combined attacks of France, Spain, and Holland, seeing then large portions of its carrying trade pass into the hands of neutrals, and bereft by the event of war of its most powerful colonies, it had not only survived these strains, but by the immediate and sustained reaction of the peace had, in 1793, more than regained its pre-eminence. Once more it stood ready, not only to protect its own country, but to sustain, with its well proved vitality, the demands of the continental war; where the armies of her allies, long untouched by the fires which breathed in France and England, were but a part of the machinery through which the maritime power of the latter energized.[57]

"Carrying trade" and "colonies" were two of the "currents" that fed into sea power, which in turn "energized" not only navies but also armies. Here one is again reminded of Clausewitz, and particularly of Alan Beyerchen's brilliant analysis of the complex relationship between war and policy in Clausewitz.[58] Just as Clausewitz detected feedback between land war and politics, so Mahan detected feedback between sea power and national political economy. Economics fed into sea power, and sea power fed back into economics, and so on, ad infinitum, "receiving and imparting countless impulses, moving in a thousand currents which twine in and around one another in infinite flexibility."[59]

In the years that followed, whenever Mahan discussed the French Revolutionary Wars in one of his articles, he attributed British victory primarily to British *economic* strength—made possible or enabled by the Royal Navy's control of the common, the shorthand for which was "command of the sea." In an 1894 article, for instance, Mahan wrote that "Great Britain's navy, in the French Wars, not only protected her own commerce, but also annihilated that of the enemy; and both conditions—not one alone—were essential to her triumph."[60] Three years later, in a piece for *Harper's Magazine*, he explained that "during the wars of the French Revolution . . . the life of Great Britain, and consequently the issue of the strife, depended upon the vigor of British commerce."[61] In the same piece he further observed that "centers of commercial interest are automatically centers of political interest and thus of military interest because they represent nodes of communications."[62] The chain of causality is the key to Mahan's argument—commercial importance creates political interest and *thus* military interest. Thus commerce, not combat, lay at the forefront of his concept of sea power.

REVIEW OF THE COMMERCIAL WAR

Mahan did not content himself with abstractions about sea power and economics: the pages of *French Revolution and Empire* also contained an exhaustive reexamination of the mechanics of commerce warfare.[63] Mahan's analysis was predicated on his recognition that for a variety of reasons, geography being the most obvious, neither France nor Britain was in a position to inflict a mortal blow on the other, except by attacking the economic foundations of their state (and society). "As in the case of an impregnable fortress, the only alternative for either of these contestants was to reduce the other by starvation," he

wrote, meaning fiscal and economic starvation.[64] In Mahan's estimation, from 1795 the French abandoned all attempts to challenge the
Royal Navy for command of the sea, instead adopting a strategy of
commerce destruction that aimed "to force the English to a shameful
bankruptcy."[65] Over the next twenty-odd years of conflict, he calculated, French maritime forces captured a staggering 11,000 British
merchantmen.

> It is the great and conspicuous instance of commerce-destroying,
> carried on over a long series of years, with a vigor and thorough-
> ness never surpassed, and supported, moreover, by an unparalleled
> closure of the continental markets of Great Britain. The Directory
> first, and Napoleon afterwards, abandoned all attempts to contest
> the control of the sea, and threw themselves, as Louis XIV had done
> before them, wholly upon a cruising war against commerce. It will
> be well in this day, when the same tendency so extensively prevails,
> to examine somewhat carefully what this accepted loss [i.e., the
> loss of merchantmen accepted by the British] really meant, how it
> was felt by the British people at the time, and what expectation can
> reasonably be deduced from it that, by abandoning military con-
> trol of the sea, and depending exclusively upon scattered cruisers,
> a country dependent as Great Britain is upon external commerce
> can be brought to terms.[66]

Mahan cautioned his readers not to be overly impressed by this apparently large number of merchantmen lost. It was necessary to con-
textualize the number of captures; that is to say, it was necessary to
understand what this number really meant. By most metrics it was a
large number, but was it a significant number? Mahan found it was
not. Over the same twenty-year period in which Britain lost 11,000
merchantmen, the value of total British overseas commerce (reflected
in customs receipts) more than doubled. Furthermore, whereas British ships could obtain war risk insurance at 5 percent, owners of neutral ships were obliged to pay premiums on the order of 20 to 30
percent on the value of their cargoes.[67] After exhausting all sources

of evidence available to him, Mahan estimated that these 11,000 captures represented, at most, a 2.5 percent loss to British trade.[68] Yes, there were periods when British losses had been heavier or insurance had cost more, such as in 1810. But at no time, he thought, did France come close to achieving their aim of "bankrupting" the British state. Accordingly, Mahan reiterated his belief that while commerce-raiding strategies were, from a political standpoint, rational strategic-policy choice selections, militarily they were impractical to implement and achieve.[69]

The British campaign against French commerce, of course, followed the opposite strategy of sea control and relentless blockade, and enjoyed far greater success. Mahan observed that "While the scattered cruisers of France were thus worrying, by a petty and inconclusive warfare, the commerce of Great Britain and its neutral carriers, the great British fleets, being left in quiet possession of the seas by the avowed purpose of the Directory to limit its efforts to the *guerre de course*, swept from the ocean every merchant ship wearing a hostile flag, and imposed upon the neutral trade with France the extreme limitations of maritime international law, as held by the British courts."[70]

Mahan was particularly impressed by the fact—admitted by several contemporary French writers—that in 1798 not a single French flagged merchant ship put to sea.[71] In effect, French trade had been annihilated. But what impressed him even more were the knock-on effects on broader French commercial and economic activity.[72] Mahan noted that ordinarily, overseas trade played a key role in multiplying local (domestic) commercial activity. Explained simply, profits earned by merchants engaged in overseas trade fed into their local economies, generating more commerce and raising local incomes (and thus additional demand for overseas produce): in effect, trade created a virtuous economic circle.

The British destruction of French overseas trade hurt not only the shipowners and merchants whose cargoes had been taken, therefore, but also their clients and customers—every butcher, baker, and candlestick maker in their town. In sum, British naval action thus generated in France a vicious economic circle. There were two crucial points

in this analysis. First, Mahan obviously understood economic activity
to be fundamentally a dynamic and interconnected process, not static
and broken up into semiautarkic blocs. Second, he understood that
maritime "commerce war" was not simply an affair of attacks on merchantmen at sea. In other words, Mahan's focus was not directed at
the attacks by warships on enemy trade per se, but on the knock-on
effects of such attacks on the wider enemy economy when conducted
in a sustained and systematic manner.

These economic blows struck both the French state and French
society, creating both fiscal and political problems. The reduction
in French commercial activity meant a double reduction in revenues, both directly from the loss of revenues from taxes on trade and
indirectly from the decrease in the state's ability to borrow, contingent on tax revenues. Even more impressive to Mahan was how the
derangement of the French economy caused by the British blockade
undermined French social stability, creating for the French government not just fiscal but also political problems.[73] He explained the
process this way:

> In the general distrust and perplexity individuals and communities
> took to hoarding both money and food, moved by the dangers of
> transit and by fear of the scarcity which they saw to be impend-
> ing. This stagnation of internal circulation was accompanied by the
> entire destruction of maritime commerce, due to the pressure of
> the British navy and to the insane decree of Nivose 29 (January 19,
> 1798). Both concurred to paralyze the energies of the people, to
> foster indolence and penury, and by sheer want to induce a state of
> violence with which the executive was unable to cope.[74]

It was the effect of British sea power on *the sociopolitical stability of
France* to which Mahan was alluding when he spoke of "that noiseless
pressure upon the vitals of France, that compulsion, whose silence,
when once noted, becomes to the observer the most striking and
awful mark of the working of Sea Power."[75] He went on to argue that
British application of sea power forced the French government into

a series of arbitrary expedients to solve immediate fiscal or political problems, usually involving the confiscation by the State of someone's private property.[76] These attacks on private property rights simultaneously inflamed and unnerved public opinion not only in France but throughout the European continent, undermining the legitimacy of the state and fostering dissent, in so doing sowing the seeds of counterrevolution.[77] As Mahan elaborated, "Underlying the other contentions, affecting them all with the unheeded, quiet, but persistent action which ordinarily characterizes the exertions of sea power, fermenting continually in the hearts of the people, was the commercial warfare, the absence of that maritime peace for which the nations sighed."[78]

In short, Mahan contended that the working of sea power pushed Napoleon into taking countervailing actions that were ultimately counterproductive, and in so doing unleashed within the French Empire socioeconomic forces that proved beyond the ability of the state to control.[79] He thus argued that France was defeated through sea power, in consequence of economic isolation from without and economic disorder within.[80]

This analysis of the mechanics by which the operational application of sea power achieved political ends marked an important advance from *Influence*. Certainly, one can find gestures in *Influence* to the elements of Mahan's argument in *French Revolution and Empire* about the workings of sea power. But what had been mere gestures in his first book became a precise and concrete explanation in his second of the linkages between deliberate naval interference with international trade on the one hand and the fiscal, economic, and sociopolitical impact of that interference on the other.

THE NATURE OF WAR

In viewing the character of war at sea as fundamentally economic, Mahan was not dismissing the importance of combat (operations) in war; he was simply drawing a distinction between war and combat, encouraging his audience not to conflate them with the aim of stimulating more careful analysis of the relationship between them.[81] Mahan began thinking of war as an essentially "political" act sometime around

1890. In forming this conception, it is possible that he had been influenced indirectly by the writings of Clausewitz—both his father and Luce were students of the Prussian general.[82] More likely, however, it was a case of independent discovery. The argument that it was the latter seems stronger when one recognizes the differences between the Mahanian and Clausewitzian views on the nature of war, most especially the central importance attached by the former to the role of economic rivalry and economics generally. If Clausewitz regarded war as an essentially political act, then Mahan regarded it as an essentially political-economic act. He did so, moreover, in a dual sense: sea power worked through economics both to destabilize an enemy's politics and to achieve one's own (economic) policy goals.

Well ahead of their time and intrinsically difficult for many of his readers to grasp, Mahan's concepts consequently often went unheeded. It might be said that readers discarded his conclusions but took the research and insights they had been based on and drew their own. In particular, his notion that war was defined as much if not more by economics than by combat flew in the face of established wisdom and apparent common sense. Of course, as has been conceded already, Mahan did a poor job selling his ideas, preferring to advance them implicitly rather than explicitly, and failing to define or consistently apply his terms. It did not help either that some of the ideas contained in his second book appeared to contradict what he had written in his first. Even today, it is popularly held that Mahan preached above all else that the enemy's fleet, not its trade, should always be the naval focus of attention, an indefensible interpretation of his arguments in *French Revolution and Empire*. Before we address this mistaken belief, it will be useful to recall what Mahan actually *had* argued, and in so doing show that although he had made some changes to his argument, the significance of these modifications was more apparent than real.

As demonstrated in the previous chapter, Mahan explained in the first half of *Influence* that states maintained naval forces primarily to ensure their nation unfettered access to the global common; this was because sea trade was so critical to the nation's commerce and general prosperity. In time of war, competing maritime powers would vie with each other for "command of the sea" in order to safeguard their own trade (and with it economic prosperity and their tax base), and as far as possible to damage the sea trade of their enemies in an effort to sever their economic sinews and hamstring their war effort. Mahan allowed that in theory, a systematic attack on the enemy's commerce *could* bring an enemy to terms, but assessed the practical obstacles as too great to make this a realistic strategy. Far better and more certain, he argued, was to focus one's naval effort *first* on winning command of the sea, *then* on blockading the enemy coast in order to cut off enemy access to the "common" while simultaneously (and at low risk) interdicting the enemy's coastal and riverine water traffic in order to intensify the derangement of their economy. It was on this chain of logic that he concluded, "only by military command of the sea by prolonged control of the strategic centers of commerce, can such an attack be fatal; and such control can be wrung from a powerful navy only by fighting and overcoming it."[83] Decisive battle was a means to the end of commerce prevention, not an end unto itself.

Attentive contemporary readers noticed this logic chain. Theodore Roosevelt, for instance, in his review of *French Revolution and Empire*, remarked that "Captain Mahan's second work is in some ways even more interesting than his first," then added, "he [Mahan] has not, of course, the chance to develop a new idea of first-rate importance, for this idea has already been developed in his first volume."[84] For Roosevelt, then, the main argument developed in both books was the same: "One of the strongest features of Mahan's book is the way in which he shows that mere commerce-destroying is not of decisive weight in the result of a great war. It may greatly irritate and annoy an enemy, but it can only seriously cripple him if the commerce-destroying is carried on with the help of great fighting fleets. This is a lesson that we in America especially need to learn."[85]

Thus Roosevelt clearly (and rightly) read Mahan as saying that commerce destruction, when backed by a fleet, *could* cripple an enemy. Others, however, were either not so attentive to detail or perhaps subconsciously rejected Mahan's notion of the centrality of economics in war. The lengthy review of *Influence* by the British naval

historian John Knox Laughton, for instance, saw only the military side
of sea power, the economic dimensions of the thesis passing far above
his head. Revealing more about the narrowness of his own worldview than about the book ostensibly under review, Laughton failed to
note Mahan's critical distinction between *guerre de course* and commerce destruction.[86] Laughton was being not merely misleading but
flat wrong in saying that "Captain Mahan maintains—we think most
rightly maintains—that the only true policy of a naval force is to fight
whenever opportunity offers; to seek for the advantage and use it to
the utmost in crushing, in destroying the enemy's fleet." [87] In charac-
terizing Mahan's argument this way, he fueled public misperceptions.

Another subtle though very important difference between *Influence* and *French Revolution and Empire* was in Mahan's use of the
term "strategy." Readers will recall from previous chapters that at
this time, in naval circles at least, the term was not commonplace and
had no agreed definition or generally accepted meaning. In *Influence*,
Mahan had early on defined strategy as relating to everything above
the level of tactics and had gone on to employ the word with little
discrimination.[88] As Jon Sumida noted, "for Mahan, naval strategy
in war was concerned with the functions of navies, their objectives
and deployments, logistics, communications, and in particular the
form and priority of commerce raiding."[89] This was certainly true of
the original *Influence*. In *French Revolution and Empire,* however, a
more exact pattern of usage emerges. Henceforth, when discussing
warfare, instead of employing one line of separation he used three.
In addition to a line between tactics and everything else, he drew
another line separating policy from everything else and yet another
between strategy and combat operations. Expressed as a hierarchy,
therefore, there was policy, strategy, combat operations, and tactics.
(It is important to note that Mahan's understanding of combat operations was similar to though not quite the same as today's understanding of the term "operational level" of war as defined in current
textbooks and manuals.)

For Mahan to classify an action as strategic, it had to relate or con-
form to some clearly defined policy object. Actions not so linked were

relegated to mere combat operations (i.e., *combat for the sake of combat*)—military activities that Mahan saw as foolish. It is illustrative that Mahan made himself most unpopular in certain quarters by dismissing the early frigate actions during the Anglo-American War of 1812 as mere duels and "lustrous examples" of "the sterile glory of fighting battles merely to win them."[90] More to the point, readers will also notice that by thus reserving the use of "strategy" to action relating directly to policy, he further reinforced his distinction between war and combat. Before leaving this subject, a final word on the suggestion that "Mahan's strategic argument was consistently based upon the principle of concentration of force and consideration of logistical context."[91] Again, though technically correct, this statement requires clarification. Concentration of *effort* rather than concentration of *force* better captures Mahan's meaning; the word "force" is often taken to imply "warships," whereas "effort" more clearly relates to "task" or "mission." At the risk of seeming pedantic, to be yet more precise, Mahan believed in the concentration of strategic effort, but also in the concentration of tactical force.

BLOCKADE AND LAW

Mahan's developing thoughts on the nature of strategy found their clearest expression in *French Revolution and Empire* in his treatment of commerce destroying and its impact on neutrals. This was an important (and complex) topic in its own right and will be treated more fully in chapter 8. For the present, however, we shall touch on the subject only insofar as it relates to the development of Mahan's strategic thought during the 1890s.

In all wars, attempts by a belligerent to regulate their enemy's use of the common has prompted friction with neutral powers and often led to recriminations and conflict. Commerce in wartime had been (and remains) a bitterly controversial subject. In essence, neutrals resent interference with their use of the sea for commerce, while belligerents resent neutrals providing aid and comfort to their enemies, especially if doing so prolongs the conflict. The root of the problem is that wars create scarcity and, for the merchant, scarcity translates into higher prices and thus profits. Put more simply, neutral merchants have powerful incentives to trade with belligerents (preferably with both sides).

Over the centuries, nations have striven to establish treaties between themselves designed to define the respective commercial rights of belligerents and neutrals in wartime, thereby reducing friction and the probability of wider conflict. Gradually, there emerged from these various bilateral agreements certain "principles" that came to form the basis of what became known as international maritime law. In the nineteenth century, however, these "principles" were poorly and inconsistently defined. What is more, there existed no international court to arbitrate different interpretations, let alone one with appellate jurisdiction over sovereign states possessing the means to enforce compliance with its rulings.

Moreover, there were severe practical drawbacks to the legal method of reducing friction in war. First, neutral merchants still had powerful incentives (in the form of supernormal profits) to exploit gray areas or even to disregard the provisions of the law. Second, and more seriously, international law was predicated on an outdated model of how the commercial world actually worked. From the late nineteenth century onward, as the world became smaller and smaller thanks to revolutions in agriculture and industry, as well as the invention of myriad new technologies, especially in global communications, day-to-day business practices had changed beyond recognition, rendering much established law and the supposed principles on which it was based inapplicable or even irrelevant. Third, no state on earth possessed the administrative machinery necessary to regulate their own international commerce to ensure their merchants' compliance. Fourth, the application of the law depended on the circumstances of each case, which were often unique and difficult to establish. In other words, it proved impossible to agree on a legal regime that could provide for all contingencies, and indeed there were good reasons why parties did not want one.

In *French Revolution and Empire*, Mahan dealt at some length with the question of international law, since it purported to govern the maritime commerce that Mahan saw as the determining issue of the war between the British and French Empires.[92] The effectiveness of the British blockade hinged on their ability to regulate neutral commerce, especially the merchant marine belonging to their former colonies in the United States. Defying all previous American writers on the subject (and apparently most since), Mahan presented the British measures against U.S. trade as rational, proportionate, and legitimate.

Mahan reached this novel (and noxious) conclusion by seeking to understand the essential dynamics of the commercial war rather than isolated incidents. Realizing that parts could be mistaken for the whole and that statistics could be manipulated to prove almost any argument, he thus urged readers not to lose sight of the forest for the trees:[93]

> In so broad and complicated a subject, a probable conclusion can only be reached by disregarding the mass of details, of statistics, with which the disputants have rather obscured than elucidated the subject, and by seeking the underlying principle which guided, or should have guided, either government. It is possible to form a very strong argument, for or against either, by fastening upon the inevitable inconveniences entailed upon each nation by the measures of its adversary and by its own course. It is by impressions received from these incidents—or accidents—the accompaniments rather than the essentials of the two systems, that the debates of Parliament and the conclusions of historians have been colored.[94]

The "essentials" involved two unavoidable realities. First, neutral trade sustained conflict. Second, the positions and perspectives of belligerents and neutrals were fundamentally at odds. In other words, they were "antinomious." An antinomy is a contradiction between two beliefs or conclusions that are in themselves reasonable. The word is akin to, but different from, a paradox.

Though Mahan did not employ this precise word, he discussed the concept of antinomy at length in his treatment of the neutral-international law problem, and in later years treated the subject yet more broadly.[95] Basically, Mahan possessed no confidence in the international legal system to cope with antimony or defuse friction over the long term. To his way of thinking, from a strategic standpoint, debating the rights and wrongs of British, French, or neutral behavior during the war was unproductive and indeed a complete waste of time. "Opinions," he saw,

> will probably always differ, according to the authority attributed by individuals to the *dicta* of International Law. It may be admitted at once that neither Napoleon's decrees nor the British orders can be justified at that bar, except by the simple plea of self-preservation,—the first law of states even more of men; for no government is empowered to assent to that last sacrifice, which the individual may make for the noblest motives. The beneficent influence of International Law is indisputable, nor should its authority be lightly undermined; but it cannot prevent the interests of belligerents and neutrals from clashing nor speak with perfect clearness in all cases where they do.[96]

He then supplied a textbook definition of antinomious conflict to explain why international law could neither prevent nor resolve clashes of interest: "It is evident that these two lines of argument [the perspectives of the belligerent and neutral] do not fairly meet each other; they resemble rather opposite and equal weights in a balance, which will quickly be overturned when passion or interest, combined with power, is thrown in upon either side. Starting from such fundamentally different premises, interested parties might argue on indefinitely in parallel lines, without ever approaching a point of contact."[97]

For Mahan, "antinomy" was the essence of being able to think strategically: the ability to act while holding simultaneously in one's head multiple contradictory positions, each resting on an equally valid set of principles, or inferences drawn from those principles, yet at the same time fundamentally unresolvable.

Mahan gradually developed his notion of antinomy and gave it more general application. For him, accepting antinomy meant accepting complexity and thus grappling with the reality of the situation rather than a simplified abstraction of it. He explicitly articulated this concept in a letter he wrote some four months after *French Revolution and Empire* appeared in print. He noted,

> There are two sides to most questions; and, indeed, I feel without the least shame, that a careful reader will find me contradicting myself from time to time, simply because I look now on one side, now on the other. The dangerous man in war is he who gets hold of one side of the truth and thinks himself then equipped with a pass key to unlock all problems. To my mind the solution to the difficulties of war, (and for that matter of most problems in *practical* life), is not to attempt to strike a mean between the two opposite sides of a truth, but to hold them both, and under the influence of both to decide a particular case.[98]

In other words, to choose or privilege one side of the argument in making strategy is to create an abstraction of the problem to be solved. The strategist must hold in their head at the same time multiple conflicting positions, yet at the same time be able to act.

<hr />

By the end of 1892, Mahan was mentally exhausted from researching and writing *French Revolution and Empire* and consequently disinclined to begin another historical monograph.[99] "Thank God! It is done," he exclaimed directly after finishing. "I don't think I shall ever again tackle such a task."[100] Six months later, he summarily rejected a suggestion from his publisher to produce a naval history of the American Civil War on the grounds that it would take too long to research and that "it will, in my judgement, involve work much in excess of remuneration."[101] A year later he felt sufficiently refreshed to undergo a partial change of heart—a book on the Anglo-American War of 1812. "My present intention," he told his publishers in June

1893, "is to close my book-making with 1812 and turn my atten-tion in future to the magazines."[102] Mahan envisioned that the book could be completed quickly and would act as the capstone of his sea power series.[103] But on picking up the subject he very quickly put it down again. He would not complete his last monograph for another twelve years. Instead, he turned his hand to naval biographies. The first, a rather sketchy effort written and researched in the space of twelve months, dealt with David Glasgow Farragut and was an abject failure; the second, a rather more substantial work, detailing the life of Horatio Nelson, proved to be a highly profitable though intellec-tually unsatisfying venture. Though important as expositions of his ideas on naval leadership, neither biography really advanced his con-cept of sea power and thus will not be examined in the present work. Mahan's articles are something else, however, and to them we turn in the next chapter.

CHAPTER 6

PROPHET IN EXILE

(1892–97)

Human society is a complete living organism, with circulation, heart, and members. The heart lies at the set of international commercial exchanges, the circulation flows through the arteries of trade, and the members usually show more or less vitality in proportion to their direct relations with the heart. Moreover, this organism, like all others, is never perfectly quiescent, but ceaselessly contracts or expands.

—BROOKS ADAMS, "THE DECAY OF ENGLAND"[1]

OUT OF LOVE WITH THE SEA, exasperated with the pettifogging naval bureaucracy, and dreading the thought of having to live in the cramped accommodations found in modern steel warships—far worse than those provided on old-fashioned sailing vessels—Mahan dreamed of retiring from the Navy on completion of forty years' service. "It is a nuisance, and I think worse, a mistake, for a man to go to sea again at fifty, after five years on terra firma," he remarked to another naval officer in May 1891. "I talk about retiring when our law allows, five years hence—the decision, however, will turn upon family interests which have yet to take shape."[2] What held Mahan back from retirement was a concern over money: the naval pension of a captain, $3,275 per annum, was insufficient to support his family comfortably in the New York metropolis where they wished to live, and he also had three children to educate.

With the publication of "The United States Looking Outward" for the *Atlantic* at the end of 1890, however, Mahan gained a footing in the world of paid publishing. As previously mentioned, writing then was considerably more lucrative than it is today, and newspaper byliners could earn a respectable income. Mahan's unique blend of geopolitics, domestic politics, international economics, and history proved successful with his readers, and the editor of the *Atlantic*, Horace Scudder, invited him to produce more such commentaries. Mahan was naturally delighted. "I entirely adopt your views as to the direction of my future efforts," he told Scudder, "and, were I assured of freedom of course, would ask your suggestions now as [to] more particular details of reading and thought upon public matters connected with my own line of thought."[3]

In addition, Scudder agreed to take from Mahan some "historical" pieces, at $125 apiece, beginning with four biographical essays of famous naval leaders, obviously spun off from his books on sea power. Mahan often referred to these derivative pieces as "potboilers," written unashamedly to make money.[4] Yet not all of Mahan's articles were potboilers. Several were written to clarify key elements of his sea power thesis; others developed previously stray thoughts found in his books; and a number were simply exercises in polemics dressed in history, whose objective was to influence policy makers in favor of a particular course of action. In order to develop a full picture of Mahan's ideas, it is necessary to venture beyond his monographs and his best-known articles.

Mahan was not slow to see that his goal of retirement might be brought closer if he could supplement his pension by becoming a professional pundit. Writing four or five articles a year, which seemed eminently feasible, would more than bridge the $500-odd drop in income that would result from retirement. At the end of 1892, he told Scudder that this was now his goal. "If circumstances would permit my withdrawal from active service, I should gladly and by preference undertake to make a specialty of them [magazine articles]. I am persuaded that the navy—and I may even say the country—needs a voice to speak constantly of our external matters generally. Except myself,

I know no one in the navy disposed to identify himself with such a career."[5]

On February 1, 1893, Mahan stepped deeper into the world of punditry with the publication of a letter to the editor of the *New York Times* commenting on the recent upheavals in Hawaii. A fortnight earlier, U.S. sailors and marines had unofficially facilitated a coup in the islands; the new provisional government of wealthy American sugar planters at once petitioned Washington for the islands to be annexed to the United States. The matter generated much controversy. Mahan's signal contribution was to suggest that the decision whether or not to approve annexation should not be limited to political and constitutional questions but should also be considered from a national strategic perspective. He further ventured that this question needed to be considered from an Asian as well as a European context.

Mahan's comments were original and attracted the notice of Walter Hines Page, editor of the *Forum,* who invited the captain to expand on his topic in the pages of his magazine.[6] At this time, Page was very much the coming man in the publishing world, and indeed four years later he would succeed Scudder at the *Atlantic*; thus he was an important connection for Mahan to make. The two remained on friendly terms thereafter.[7] Incidentally, this was the same Walter Page who would serve as U.S. ambassador to Great Britain during World War I. Burton J. Hendrick, a three-time winner of the Pulitzer Prize who worked for Page at this time, recalled that his boss was not an easy man to impress and had aspirations beyond the merely reportorial:[8]

> [His] system of "making up" the magazine at first somewhat astounded his associates. A month or two in advance of publication day he would draw up his table of contents. This, in its preliminary stage, amounted to nothing except a list of the main subjects which he aspired to handle in that number. . . . Page would then fix upon the inevitable men who could write most readably and most authoritatively upon these topics, and "go after" them. Sometimes he would write one of his matchless editorial letters; at other times

he would make a personal visit; if necessary he would use any available friends in a wire-pulling campaign.[9]

Mahan required no such additional encouragement and produced the requested commentary inside of a week. It appeared in the March 1893 issue of the *Forum* under the title "Hawaii and Our Future Sea Power," at the height of the debate in Washington over whether or not to annex.

In this article, Mahan rehearsed themes familiar from his first two books while developing their contemporary implications for the United States. Echoing *Influence*, he wrote of the "broad sea common along which, and along which alone, in all the ages prosperity has moved. Land carriage, always restricted and therefore always slow, toils enviously but hopelessly behind, vainly seeking to replace and supplant the royal highway of nature's own making."[10] On the next page he presented his conception more strongly: "Let us start from the fundamental truth, warranted by history, that the control of the seas, and especially along the great lines drawn by national interest or national commerce, is the chief among the merely material elements in the power and prosperity of nations. It is so because the sea is the world's greatest medium of circulation."[11]

Next, after laying out his conception of the world, Mahan drew for his readers a rudimentary geostrategic map of the Pacific Ocean. Having thus dressed his foundations, Mahan proceeded to argue that the Hawaiian Islands lay at the strategic as well as the geographic epicenter of the Pacific Ocean. All steam-powered ships traversing the ocean—merchantmen and warships—had to call at these islands, simply because they were the only practical coaling station for thousands of miles in any direction. Similarly, if and when they were laid, any transpacific undersea cables must pass through the islands. From a strategic point of view, moreover, the establishment of a foreign naval base (or coaling station) in Hawaii would represent a danger to the U.S. West Coast, whereas a U.S. base there would act as a bulwark against serious overseas attack from across the Pacific. Mahan thus presented the annexation of Hawaii as a vital long-term investment in the protection of the country. Though he did not say so explicitly, it did not take much imagination to see that a U.S.-controlled Hawaii would serve also as a bridgehead into Asia.[12]

As soon as he was finished, Mahan turned to work on a similar piece for the *Atlantic*, this time dealing with the strategic implications of the Isthmian Canal. Herein, Mahan boldly asserted that "the surest prosperity of nations" is to be found in oceanic trade.[13] He then proceeded to serve up a cocktail of economics and geopolitics, supplemented with a generous slug of the political history of Central America. He followed this with an explanation of the strategic benefits that accrued from occupation or ownership of key strategic positions within the region—in this instance the Isthmian Canal: "Their tenure, like the key of a military position, exerts a vital effect upon the course of trade, and so upon the struggle, not only for bare existence, but for that increase of wealth, of prosperity, and of general consideration, which affect both the happiness and the dignity of nations."[14] In short, looking to the future, possession or control of the Isthmian Canal by the United States would yield major long-term economic and strategic benefits; conversely, if another power obtained control, the United States would suffer economically and strategically.

In conception and construction, the articles on Hawaii and the canal were very similar. In both, Mahan employed the same core thread found in *Influence* and *French Revolution and Empire*; namely, that international trade was the greatest wealth-generating machine in modern history; that commerce made the world go around; and that history showed that economic rivalry often led conflict. In each of the articles, Mahan supplied his readers with a summary of his theory of the "common" serving as the principal conduit for global commerce. Thus, Mahan's concept of sea power served as the conceptual scaffolding for his analysis of contemporary events, just as his perception of contemporary events informed the construction of his sea power thesis, as we saw in previous chapters. For Mahan, they were two sides of the same coin.

Students of Mahan have tended to dwell on the accuracy and prescience—or lack thereof—of the captain's analysis in this pair of articles. That is the wrong focus. The important aspect of the articles, in terms of Mahan's intellectual trajectory and their contribution to public debate, was not the answers he supplied but the questions he asked. These were intelligent, original, and complex. Others, as we shall soon see, were attempting to think through the relationship between international trade, the domestic political economy, and U.S. foreign policy, but Mahan was the only analyst trying to consider those subjects alongside naval power and geostrategy. In effect, he was inventing the conceptual category we now call geopolitics.

METAMORPHOSIS IN EXILE

By the spring of 1893, Mahan's success in publishing articles seemed to put him well on the way to gaining his financial freedom from naval service. The only potential cloud on his horizon was that it was seven years since his last tour of sea duty.[15] Since 1891, Navy Secretary Benjamin Tracy had permitted Mahan to defer taking his turn. But with the defeat of Benjamin Harrison and the Republicans in the 1892 elections, and the return to power of Grover Cleveland and the Democrats, Tracy was no longer in charge at the Navy Department and thus no longer in a position to protect Mahan. Nevertheless, before Tracy had departed, Mahan had pulled all the political wires he could to ensure he might remain on "special duty" until permitted to retire, such as doing odd jobs for the Secretary and lecturing at the War College while continuing to write.[16] And he might have succeeded, had he not just trodden on some powerful political toes by writing the aforementioned article for the *Forum*, which had unequivocally supported the Republican calls for the annexation of Hawaii.

The new Secretary of the Navy, Hilary Herbert—who had yet to read Mahan's work—took a dim view of naval officers on the active list interfering in politics and promptly banished Mahan to sea.[17] On April 18, 1893, the Navy Department ordered Mahan to prepare for sea service, and on May 11 he formally took command of the cruiser *Chicago*—the C of the ABCD ships.[18] Though the biggest warship in the fleet, this was far from a plum assignment. She was an uncomfortable vessel and plagued with innumerable defects that required constant attention. Her propulsion system was so unreliable that the Board of Inspection had recommended she remain in home waters. Instead, however, the Department decided to kill two birds with one stone by making *Chicago* the flagship of Rear Adm. Henry Erben, a notoriously irascible old sea dog assigned to command the Navy's European squadron—which consisted of the *Chicago* alone.[19] Not only was Mahan being sent away, therefore, but to add insult to injury he also had to share his quarters with a senior officer inclined to meddle. He knew he was being punished for his outspokenness: several friends in high places told him so.[20] Mahan found it hard to conceal his bitterness. He resented having to be careful about what he now wrote, "owing to the way our government looks on the expression of political opinions, however general, by officers—particularly if diametrically opposed to the traditions of the party in office."[21]

At first, Mahan hoped to find enough time on board the *Chicago* to continue writing his next big book, *Life of Nelson*, plus the odd magazine article to keep him in funds.[22] "I have become exceedingly interested in professional literary work," he told his old friend Sam Ashe, optimistically adding, "and have now a fair promise of success at it."[23] But command absorbed more time than he had anticipated, and Mahan found it impossible to establish a good writing routine.[24] "I despair of ever doing any good work unless fully at leisure to allow my mind to sleep on the subject," he shared with his wife, Ellen: "I cannot take it up and lay it down."[25] After six months he had squeezed out barely a hundred mediocre pages of *Life of Nelson*. Mahan's anxiety over the pace and quality of his work was compounded by the dread that the opportunity to make a financial windfall was slipping through his figures. His publishers encouraged him to believe that *Life of Nelson* could be an international best seller and earn him thousands.[26] In addition, he craved making a name for himself as a serious man of letters. "I intend to make the life of Nelson the *great* work of my own life," he told his daughter.[27]

After nine months together on board the *Chicago*, Mahan's relations with the interfering Adm. Erben broke down. Worried about the impact of a recent poor fitness report on his reputation and unable to write effectively, in July 1894 Mahan packed away his scholar's pen.[28] Family finances, however, compelled him to continue cranking out potboilers, none of which were ambitious in scope or impressive in substance, but they satisfied his clients and helped pay the bills. By now, Mahan was receiving so many requests that he was obliged to turn business away.[29] "I have now propositions for magazine articles which would bring me in $500 but I can't write a line," he despaired in June 1894.[30] Five months later and another thousand dollars had escaped him.[31] "I promise myself, if I can ever get rid of my naval shackles, to take up that line of life—advocating one true policy by article writing."[32] His frustration shows clearly in the letter he wrote to his wife on November 1, 1894: "I have now so many requests for articles it is tantalizing to be unable to comply—but I seem smitten with lethargy or paralysis after my morning's work. I can't think it is either indolence or fancy—in view of the steadiness of my brain work under better conditions."[33]

Banishment to Europe had its compensations, however, and many years later Mahan would look back on his tour of duty in Europe as a tremendous stroke of good fortune.[34] An assignment to Europe meant visits to England. Beginning with an invitation to dine with Queen Victoria, British society greeted the American captain with open arms.[35] His next appointment was lunch in London with the prime minister. For the next six weeks, Mahan met the great and the good and impressed all whom he met. He reveled in the attention. Through the social connections he made, moreover, Mahan gained privileged access to Horatio Nelson's papers. There was another, even more tangible reward: The visit to England considerably boosted sales of his books on both sides of the Atlantic, thus alleviating some of his financial worries; during his two years away from home, the royalties on his books alone yielded an impressive $3,700, plus another $1,000 earned from articles—more than the salary of a U.S. Navy captain in command of a deployed warship. His annual income had doubled.

Mahan's success in England rebounded across the Atlantic and raised his profile and his standing at home. In September 1893, he learned from Cdr. Bowman McCalla that Secretary Herbert had recently devoured his two-volume *French Revolution and Empire* and had been deeply impressed. "He [Herbert] said," Mahan gleefully reported to his wife, that "the books repaid all the money hitherto expended on the College" and had converted him to the value of the War College.[36] The following month, the Secretary wrote him directly to praise his scholarship and signal that his star at home was again in the ascendance. "In my opinion, you deserve all the encomiums of the British and American press for this great work," Herbert enthused, calling it "by far the ablest history I have ever read of the epoch." More gratifyingly still, the Secretary added, "I am particularly struck with your citations from history of the comparatively little effect of commerce destroyers in bringing war to a successful conclusion, and expect to use in my forthcoming report the information you have therein set forth in my arguments for the building of battleships."[37] It is with this 1893 report, not with Tracy's better-known 1889 report, that we might unequivocally state that Mahan was now influencing naval policy. True to his word, six weeks later Herbert pronounced in his 1893 annual report that "The military value of a commerce-destroying fleet is easily overrated. Cruisers directed against an enemy's wealth afloat are capable of doing great damage. They create consternation among merchants and worry the people against whose property there are directed, but unsupported by ships of the line their operations are perhaps never decisive of a war."[38] In February 1894 Herbert wrote Mahan again, promising him that on completing his tour of duty he would be allowed to see out his final years of service in relative peace and comfort back at the Naval War College.[39]

As captain of the *Chicago*, although Mahan lacked the time and the mental energy to work on new material, he found enough of both to reflect on what he had already written. During 1894, he produced an article that clarified some key arguments he had made in his sea power books and another in which he amplified his thoughts on the formulation of strategy. In an essay requested by the *North American Review* to consider the "Possibilities of an Anglo-American Reunion," Mahan took the opportunity to recast his argument laid out in "The United States Looking Outward" in much stronger economic terms.[40]

He lamented that "it is impossible that one who sees in the sea—in the function which it discharges towards the world at large—the potent factor in national prosperity and in the course of history, should not desire a change in the mental attitude of our [American] countrymen towards maritime affairs."[41] Several pages later, Mahan inserted an important elucidation of his position on war and commerce. Passing serenely over the possibility that his own inconsistent terminology might bear some blame, he chided another writer for misrepresenting his arguments by failing to see "the difference between the *guerre-de-course*, which is inconclusive, and commerce-destroying (or commerce prevention) through strategic control of the sea by powerful navies. Some nations more than others, but all maritime nations more or less, depend for their prosperity upon maritime commerce, and probably upon it more than upon any other single factor."[42] In the closing paragraph, Mahan restated his position more plainly still, insisting that "it is *only* when effort is frittered away in the feeble dissemination of the *guerre-de-course*, instead of being concentrated in a great combination to control the sea, that commerce-destroying justly incurs the reproach of misdirected effort."[43] These sentences conveyed clearly the argument that Mahan had muddled in *Influence*.

Similarly, in the spring of 1894, the Royal United Services Institute (RUSI) on Whitehall invited Mahan to present a paper in London titled "Blockade in Relation to Naval Strategy," which was later published in RUSI's *Journal* and also in the U.S. Naval Institute's *Proceedings*.[44] This was a curious piece of work. For the most part it dealt with the narrowly technical subject as suggested by the title—the practicability of blockade in the age of steam and torpedoes.[45] Of far greater interest, however, were some prefatory remarks made on the importance of considering the psychological dimensions to warfare. Here, Mahan observed that "experiments upon war, in time of peace, have little advantage over a game, unless the effects of danger and of doubt, in inducing caution and precaution, can be represented to an extent that they now rarely are."[46] Expressed more simply, "men will not in war undertake, with a light heart, adventures which in summer maneuvers entail no more grievous burden of care than a boy's game of hide and seek. Valuable as are the lessons of mimic warfare, there cannot in it be adequately reproduced the element arising from the sense of imminent danger."[47]

The point Mahan was driving at here was that doubt, uncertainty, and the crushing burden of responsibility were key elements in the practical application of naval force, and that these psychological factors absolutely must be taken into consideration when formulating strategy. "Failure to achieve great results is more often due to anxiety about one's own dangers than to over-confidence and rashness," he postulated, and the "tendency to see all the difficulties on our own side and the advantages on the other."[48] He went on to argue that the art of strategy was akin to risk management:

> There are few, if any, characteristics of the utterances which I from time to time hear, or read, on the subject of actual warfare, which impress me more strongly than the constantly recurring tendency to reject any solution of a problem which does not wholly eliminate the element of doubt, or uncertainty, or risk. Instead of frankly recognizing that almost all warlike undertakings present at best but a choice of difficulties—that absolute certainty is unattainable—that the "art" of war consists not in stacking the cards, but, as Napoleon phrased it, in getting the most of the chances on your side—that some risk, not merely of death but of failure, must be undergone—instead of this, people wish so to arrange their programme as to have a perfectly sure thing of it.[49]

To Mahan's way of thinking, therefore, the aim of the strategist was to devise a plan of action "which in the great majority of cases will reward a right line action, consistently followed through the ups and downs of good and evil fortune."[50] Choosing a "right line of action," of course, was to some degree a function of applying strategic "principles" derived from the "patient study" of history.[51] But this was far from the be-all and end-all of the subject, and also it was not a mechanical process. Context was all important: "When we have correctly stated the principles, it by no means necessarily follows that the application of them will be the same, or superficially even much like those of previous generations."[52] So much for Mahan being rigid and doctrinaire in his thinking.

BACK ON SHORE

Another year would pass before Mahan finally returned home. One week after arriving back in New York, on March 31, 1895, the *Chicago* was put into dock to be completely rebuilt. A couple of weeks later, with the paperwork finally complete, Mahan was at last free. He returned to New York a celebrated man.[53] He was now widely regarded as the premier expert on naval and international affairs, and his published thoughts were widely cited. On February 8, 1895, for instance, Democratic senator John Tyler Morgan of Alabama, a former Confederate general and a key figure in the Foreign Relations Committee, held aloft his copy of *Influence* on the floor of the Senate and proceeded to demonstrate that he (or maybe an aide) had read the book very carefully.[54] His speech merits quoting at length to demonstrate that his contemporary audience—including people who mattered from Alabama—correctly divined its message.

Rather than caricature Mahan as a simplistic proponent of decisive fleet battles, Morgan astutely described Mahan's idea of sea power "as a proposition of universal political economy. I cannot call it anything else."[55] What is more, Morgan delivered this speech not in the context of a naval spending bill but during a debate on whether the federal government should pay for the laying of a cable from San Francisco to Hawaii, and it was in this context that Morgan used Mahan's work. Capt. Mahan "has recently produced a book that has given him a splendid reputation, a well-deserved reputation in all of the civilized world," Morgan explained to the Senate,

> He saw around him upon the oceans of the earth the vast commercial interchange going on from place to place of the productions of various countries. He had spread out before him in history the panorama of the naval engagements that had taken place; and he had the sagacity (which appears now to be a very simple thing as

we look back upon it and read the book), to connect the prosperity of the different nations with the sea power that they had developed. He established beyond any denial the fact that the sea power of the greatest of these nations (dependent in some degree, of course, upon their productions and the numbers, extent, and character of the population), has been the source from which they have derived their principal wealth and progress.[56]

Morgan demonstrated further insight into Mahan's work when, after remarking that "we are obliged to have a Navy or else have no profit from commerce," he recognized that sea power was not simply a synonym for naval power.[57]

Meanwhile, at home, Mahan spent the early summer of 1895 finishing a couple of potboilers promised to *Century* magazine. In June 1895, he told one British naval officer friend (Bouverie Clark) that he looked forward "within a month to begin serious and consecutive work on my Life of Nelson."[58] Twelve months later, the end of his manuscript, as well as his naval career, was in sight at last.[59] Owing to the Venezuelan boundary dispute, which in 1896 nearly prompted war between Britain and the United States, he did not finally separate from the service until November 17, 1896, after the crisis had subsided. It is a measure of his desperation to retire that by this date he was practically at the top of the captain's list and thus within mere months for automatic promotion to the rank of commodore and an increase in pay.[60] Despite the entreaties of several friends to postpone sending in his papers, Mahan remained resolved. As he explained afterward to Sam Ashe, he simply did not trust the naval leadership. Retirement "frees me from the possibility of interruption by the Dept. I lose future promotion and increases in pay, and have taken the chance that I may more than make good the loss by writing. Like all other moves there is a risk of failure, but I think the chances are good . . . [but] I cannot for a year or two know just how I stand to win or lose."[61]

As 1897 began, retired Capt. Mahan was putting the finishing touches on his Nelson manuscript while developing his contacts in the publishing world. Very quickly he landed a contract with Scribner's (which in addition to publishing books also put out a leading popular monthly magazine) to produce four essays on naval battles at $400 apiece, clearly spun off from his recently completed Nelson biography. Looking to the future, Mahan was keen to revert to publishing serious analytical commentaries on current affairs, both international and domestic—the sort or pieces he had begun to write five years earlier. As he mused to a British army officer he had befriended in England, who was himself something of a pundit, "I am at times troubled with doubts as to whether I should not write and think upon contemporary events more than I do. Many thoughts throng through my mind, and for a moment cry for utterance, and the question sometimes arises 'ought you not to give these, which die in the utterance, but in dying perhaps give life to the future, to take precedence over work such as you are now doing, from which you hope your own increase of reputation, but which may add little to the general welfare.'"[62] Yet Mahan's desire to influence public opinion and policy makers was counterbalanced by his wariness to not again offend the political administration and thus risk punishment by pressing his arguments too forcibly. Even for retired officers, criticizing current government policy was a dangerous game.

Accordingly, during the first half of 1897, Mahan produced a trio of uninspired articles for *Harper's Magazine*, "Preparedness for Naval War," "A Twentieth Century Outlook," and "The Strategic Features of the Caribbean Sea and the Gulf of Mexico." Each touched on (though obliquely) one or more of the leading issues of the day, including the Venezuelan boundary dispute; the Anglo-American Olney-Pauncefote arbitration treaty, which passed the House in January but was rejected by the Senate in May 1897; the Isthmian Canal; the U.S. response to growing European colonial interest in Central America; and the Cuban revolution (1895–98). In each, Mahan gently reminded the bellicose elements within the Cleveland administration that the U.S. Navy was no match for the Royal Navy, even in their own backyard. None of the articles have withstood the test of time, and they are barely comprehensible to modern readers unfamiliar with the issues of the 1890s and their background contexts. Though each contains one or two interesting observations, all lacked originality. Of the three, "The Strategic Features of the Caribbean Sea" was probably the best. Yet even here Mahan had done no more than employ the same formula as his 1893 isthmus paper for the *Atlantic*, supplying readers with a lesson in geopolitical strategy prefaced by a brief exposition of sea power, pointing out—carefully this time—the strategic advantages that would accrue from possession of Cuba. This was nothing new.

ECONOMIC TURMOIL IN THE UNITED STATES: THE PANIC OF 1893 TO THE ELECTION OF 1896

Judging from his published work immediately after his retirement from the Navy, readers would be forgiven for thinking that Mahan's ideas had stagnated. Outwardly, it seemed that he was merely revisiting his research notes, recycling his arguments, and repackaging his thoughts in order to make as much money as possible. In mid-1897 he even persuaded Little, Brown and Company to publish in book form an anthology of his previously published magazine articles.[63] Though perhaps surprising to modern readers, during the 1890s this was standard practice in the publishing world as a way of reaching a wider audience.

Beneath the surface, however, Mahan's private correspondence reveals another story. Enough fragments from this period have survived to reveal his increasingly rich social and intellectual life, and his assimilation into a network of thinkers and policy makers centered on New York City. Mahan's new fame gave him his entrée into East Coast society, where his acquaintance with many leading figures in England, combined with his bonhomie, modesty, and quiet dignity, made him a welcome dinner companion or house guest. After moving into a renovated brownstone on the Upper West Side of New York City, he pursued a much more active social life centered on the University and Century Clubs. He also was a member of several dining societies. On Mahan's retirement, former Secretary of the Navy William Whitney hosted a farewell banquet in New York on his behalf, attended by eighty leading men of the day, including not just politicians and lawyers but also bankers and businessmen.[64] Hitherto,

Mahan's understanding of the world was shaped by what he saw and what he read; henceforth it was supplemented by what he gleaned from talks with leading figures in all walks of life. Over time, the latter source became increasingly important.

As we have seen in previous chapters, Mahan always paid close attention to—and indeed was fascinated by—domestic politics, and especially economic issues. Previously, it was possible to glean Mahan's innermost thoughts on such subjects from his correspondence with Sam Ashe. Unfortunately, between November 1893 and November 1896 the two did not communicate; the former was too busy commanding the *Chicago* while the latter was preoccupied salvaging his family fortune, which suffered badly during the Panic of 1893.[65] This lacuna notwithstanding, Mahan's other correspondence shows that he still kept a watchful eye on domestic events.

In August 1893, for instance, Mahan wrote to his wife from England to discuss family finances. "I want you to have about $400 at the beginning of a month in the Bank," he told her, and "the rest could go to Savings Bank only hesitate to put all in one bank."[66] The next day he asked her to open a new account with a Boston- rather than New York–based bank, "so as not to have all the eggs in one basket."[67] These letters, apparently showing Mahan micromanaging his wife's household spending, in fact show him paying close attention to the financial panic back home and being alert, before most Americans, to the danger of banks becoming insolvent: Mahan was instructing his wife to divide up their savings in order to spread their risk. He was right to be cautious about where he kept their nest egg: over the next couple of years more than five hundred banks closed their doors. Other letters to his wife from the period show Mahan worrying that the spiraling panic might induce Congress to cut naval pay and pensions (which perhaps spurred him to write potboilers). Fortunately, this awful possibility did not materialize. Instead, Congress opted to scale back pensions for Civil War veterans.

More interestingly still, Mahan's correspondence reveals that he knew many of the leading economists of the day living in the environs of New York City and even attended lectures on economic subjects.[68]

He was well acquainted, for instance, with Henry W. Farnam, a professor of political economy at Yale University and owner/editor of the
Yale Review; Mahan and his wife stayed with Farnam for three days
when they visited New Haven at the end of June 1897 to receive his
honorary doctorate.[69] In fact, the Mahans and Farnams seem to have
known each other for some time, well enough for Ellen Mahan to
write Henry Farnam asking for tickets to the sold-out Yale–Harvard
baseball game and to remember her to his wife.[70] It was probably Farnam who introduced Mahan to his protégé, Arthur T. Hadley, who
was also on the faculty at Yale and then the most celebrated American
economist of the day (it likely was Hadley who educated Mahan on
the workings of railway transportation systems).[71] Although the earliest surviving correspondence, from Mahan to Hadley, dates from
1905, the content and tone demonstrate an old friendship and that
the two met frequently; in all the surviving letters, Mahan addressed
the economist as "my dear Dr. Hadley," a familiar he reserved for his
older and closest friends.[72] The same April 1905 letter also reveals
that Mahan sent Hadley the page proofs for his latest book and asked
him for comments: authors do not send their page proofs to mere
acquaintances. Both were members of the Century Club and several
learned societies.[73]

A much clearer window into Mahan's innermost thoughts opened,
or rather reopened, in November 1896. The presidential election that
month, which historians regard as one of the most significant in U.S.
history, prompted Mahan to renew his correspondence with Sam
Ashe. "To my mind," the captain wrote four days after the hustings
closed, "this has been the most important—even critical—election the
country has ever passed through in my time; I don't except the war."[74]
What makes this assessment particularly striking is that the election
was almost entirely fought over the woeful state of the domestic economy and worry over deepening divisions within U.S. society. The
"paramount issue of the hour," as William Jennings Bryan stated in
his celebrated "Cross of Gold" speech that effectively won him the
Democratic nomination, was monetary policy. Foreign policy issues
had little or no impact on the election result.

Led by Bryan, the Democrats ran on a platform of "free silver." In practical terms, this translated into minting silver into coins and allowing debtors to use them to repay loans. There were some disagreements over the exact quantity of silver to be turned into money, but these were mere details. In actuality, the free-silver debate was really about gold (hence Bryan's allusion to the crucifixion of ordinary Americans on a cross of gold), specifically the abandonment by the United States of the gold standard.[75] The reasons behind Bryan's advocacy of moving away from gold have been explained elsewhere many times.[76] For Mahan, by far the more important aspect of the subject was the likely consequence of such a departure from international norms. Most experts (then and now) agree that switching from a gold to a silver standard would have been punished by the market. At best, it would have led to inflation of prices at home and a devaluation of the dollar overseas—good for debtors and exporters (especially farmers who qualified on both counts) but bad for creditors and especially bankers. At worst, which was most likely, it would have resulted in apocalyptic disruption to the American capital markets and banking system, and might even have capsized the entire U.S. economy.[77]

Mahan sided firmly with those who viewed "free silver" with alarm. "I believe the [Democratic] platform to have been in the main wrong and even revolutionary," he protested to Ashe, "and I confess I have not found in the *speeches* of Mr. Bryan the proof that he is both intelligent and honest. He may be the one or the other, I can't find it in his speeches that he is both."[78] Writing again on the subject a couple of months later, Mahan acknowledged to Ashe that he struggled to understand all of the financial ins and outs: "It is over late in life for me to turn political economist, or to affect anything more than a belief in the broad proposition I advance—just as, on the tariff, I don't pretend any mastery of detail."[79] He was too modest. In venting to his friend his disapproval of "free silver," Mahan showed a sound grasp of the essentials, just as he had twenty years before.[80] And as Richard Bensel makes clear, moreover, at its root the silver issue was not all that complicated—it was only the contorted variants of the free-silver scheme that made it seem complicated.

Several months before the election, when it seemed that Bryan stood a real chance of winning, Mahan again demonstrated his basic fluency in monetary matters by asking his publisher if the royalties on his British book sales (denominated in sterling) could be paid to him in gold. "We are all, I imagine, getting our umbrellas ready to put up, if Bryan is elected," he explained to his editor. "As a salaried government officer I shall be among the hardest hit [by the resulting inflation], if the change comes, and I want to secure myself on the foreign sales—the gold sales."[81] His reasoning was clear and correct: "A book now which sells here at $4.00 may be in England 18 s[hillings]; but I suppose if we get on a silver basis, the prices abroad would remain as it now is, but you could scarcely raise your price here in proportion to the depreciation of the currency."[82]

Underlying the centrality of monetary policy in the election of 1896 was the Panic of 1893 and the ensuing depression. As touched on in previous chapters, William Appleman Williams and Walter LaFeber demonstrated that many if not most contemporary Americans believed that domestic overproduction had led to the Depression, and that the best way out of their economic mess was to find new overseas markets. In essence, the theory of overproduction was a popular explanation for the economic malaise that plagued the U.S. economy in the decades that followed the Civil War, which sprouted during the early 1880s and reached fruition during the mid-1890s. It offered an answer to what traditional economic theory could not explain, namely why the U.S. economy seemed trapped in an unending boom-bust cycle. Although in aggregate the economy expanded tremendously during the thirty years following the war, the years of unquestioned prosperity were few and far between, resulting in spasmodic growth and employment. With each cyclical downswing, moreover, public unhappiness ratcheted higher. The historians of the Wisconsin School show that the concept of overproduction filled the American journals of the 1880s and 1890s and permeated the correspondence of most leading men of the day. It might be added that the frequency with which the concept was cited is analogous to the popularity of economic ideas put forward by William Philips in the late 1950s, Milton Friedman in the

1970s, Arthur Laffer in the 1980s, and the recreant economists who preached modern monetary theory in the 2010s and 2020s.

Acute social turmoil lent urgency to this quest for overseas markets. In Williams' words, "Because of its dramatic and extensive nature, the Crisis of the 1890s raised in many sections of American society the specter of chaos and revolution. Faced with growing militancy, conservatives and reformers came to share the same conviction that something drastic had to be done, not only to solve the immediate problem, but to prevent the recurrence of such crises. That an expansionist foreign policy would provide such relief and prevention rapidly became an integral and vital part of all but an infinitesimal segment of the response to the general crisis."[83]

The work of the Wisconsin School is important for showing that the mainspring for the new American assertiveness overseas, including naval expansion, was rooted not in external diplomatic factors but rather in internal economic factors. While hostile critics have grossly mischaracterized its proponents as "economic determinists" or "Marxists," in fact their scholarship was based on intensive archival research and a still unrivaled charting of popular perceptions and the intellectual currents of period. Their work thus remains crucial in understanding Mahan's intellectual milieu.

Far more than Williams, Walter LaFeber read Mahan closely and was impressed by his "tightly knit justification of why and how his country could expand beyond its continental limits."[84] The naval side of the story did not interest him, however. Though LaFeber acknowledged that naval expansion was an important factor in American politics during this period, to explain its growth during the 1890s he was content to follow the standard general narrative supplied by Harold and Margaret Sprout.[85] Instead, he focused on Mahan's connection to a powerful clique of American intellectuals, including politicians, businessmen, and economists, who were grappling with the socioeconomic problems confronting the United States at that time, something the Sprouts had completely ignored.

From his scrutiny of contemporary journals and periodicals, LaFeber identified Mahan, along with the eccentric Brooks Adams (brother-in-law to Henry Cabot Lodge and also related to Stephen Luce), the Reverend Josiah Strong, and Frederick Jackson Turner as four of the leading theoreticians of the day. Their writings, he argued, "typified the expansive tendencies of their generation" and "exemplified certain beliefs which determined the nature of American foreign policy."[86] "It is, of course, impossible to estimate the number of Americans who accepted the arguments of these four men," LaFeber acknowledged, but "What cannot be controverted is that the writings of these men typified and in some specific instances directly influenced the thought of American policy makers who created the new empire."[87] In Republican circles inhabited by the likes of Henry Cabot Lodge, Theodore Roosevelt, William McKinley, Elihu Root, William Rockhill, and John Hay, the writings of Mahan, Adams, and Turner attracted particular interest.[88]

Reading Mahan's later work alongside that of Turner and especially Adams reveals much overlap and cross-fertilization, which is not surprising considering that all three knew each other well and often referenced or otherwise drew inspiration from each other's work (Mahan and Strong were also acquainted).[89] Turner, of course, was a historian and the author of the famous "frontier thesis" that explained America's long history of relative prosperity as a function of the nation's ability to expand westward across the continent, a viewpoint that encouraged American businessmen to look for markets beyond the national territorial frontiers and to view foreign nations that stood in the way with a jaundiced eye.[90]

Adams' work in particular helps to illustrate the backdrop to Mahan's own writings and helps to explain the forces that impelled the latter to look ever closer at international economics. Also a proponent of the concept of overproduction, like Mahan, Adams viewed the world through predominantly economic eyes and from a global rather than national (or continental) perspective.[91] He painted pictures of the future with a broad brush on a large canvas.[92] His signature theory was that since the fall of Rome, the world had moved through identifiable cycles and "phases of civilization."[93] For Adams, the dynamic economic forces unleashed by the Industrial Revolution dominated the course of the late nineteenth century.[94] Intensifying economic rivalry, and more especially the exploitation of industrial economies of scale, explained much. Mahan and Adams had their differences—the former believed that maritime systems yielded greater relative advantages, whereas the latter thought that "Continental" systems had the edge—yet their essentially economic outlooks on how the world worked were more similar than dissimilar.[95]

Economics was also central to the worldview of another important figure in Mahan's social and intellectual circles, Charles A. Conant.[96] A well-respected, New York–based financial journalist, Conant was an economist with a reputation as a popularizer of complex economic ideas.[97] In the preface to his 1896 book *Modern Banks of Issue*, Conant modestly told his readers that his aim was "to bring together, in compact form, the leading facts regarding the banks of the world." In fact, Conant's analysis of the history of financial panics was both original and important.[98] There is no question that Conant read Mahan, Adams, and Turner. As the Wisconsin School authors Carl Parrini and Martin Sklar have shown, moreover, Conant, along with two other leading economists of the day—Arthur Hadley (professor of economics at Yale) and Jeramiah Jenks (professor of economics at Cornell)—were tied in to the same New York Republican circles that Mahan moved in. Conant, Hadley, and Jenks all received important official appointments in the McKinley and Roosevelt administrations. Mahan demonstrably was friends with Hadley, probably knew Conant through Teddy Roosevelt, and possibly knew Jenks as well. Adams and Conant certainly knew and admired each other's work.[99]

To help understand Mahan's worldview, it is useful to examine the writings of Conant, who offered a fascinatingly novel take on overproduction theory, one much more palatable to members of the Republican Party.[100] (Readers who find political economic argument less than exciting might wish to skip over the next few paragraphs to the end of the chapter.) Conant explained his theory in "The Economic Basis of 'Imperialism,'" an article published in September 1898 by the *North American Review*, the journal founded by Henry Cabot Lodge and to which Mahan also contributed. In his opening paragraph, Conant alluded unmistakably to the ideas of Mahan, Turner, and Adams:

> The United States today seems about to enter upon a path marked out for them as the children of the Anglo-Saxon race, not yet traversed because there has been so much to do at home. Almost as if by magic, the importance of naval power as the advanced agent of commercial supremacy has flashed upon the mind of the country. The irresistible tendency to expansion, which drove the Goths, the Vandals, and finally our Saxon ancestors in successive and irresistible waves over the decadent provinces of Rome, seems again in operation, demanding new outlets for American capital and new opportunities for American enterprise. [101]

For Conant, overproduction (and the attendant unemployment) was only the symptom of an underlying disease, which he termed "surplus capital"—excess savings. This resulted from industrialization and corporatization (the consolidation of numerous smaller firms into fewer larger ones) disrupting traditional patterns of economic activity.[102] Industrialization and especially corporatization were unavoidable if business was to take full advantage of economies of scale and division of labor, and so lower costs.[103] But the rational pursuit of these benefits came with unavoidable costs: "It is the excess of saving, with the resulting accumulation of unconsumed goods, in the great industrial countries, which is one of the world maladies of the economic situation of today. It lies at the root of a large share of industrial discontent."[104] Time was the root of the problem. When the economy was prospering and prices rising, businesses install new plants; large factories not only required considerable investment but took time to build. By the time the new factory had been completed, economic conditions had invariably changed. In such cases, with their capital sunk, investors invariably cut the prices of their wares and hoped for better times.[105]

Rejecting populist explanations, Conant argued that surplus capital was not the result of irrational behavior or disequilibrium within the market but rather of fundamental changes in the economic system resulting from industrialization.[106] Conant nevertheless concluded that people were right to be concerned about surplus capital. "It is proposed to point out in this article how great this excess is at the present time, how profoundly it is disturbing economic conditions in the older countries, and how necessary to the salvation of these countries is an outlet for their surplus savings, if the entire fabric of the present economic order is not to be shaken by a social revolution."[107]

But whereas populists wanted to break up concentrations of wealth in corporations and trusts—the Republicans' political base— Conant wanted to leave them intact and solve the problem another way: he advocated the government stepping in to save capitalism and staving off left-wing calls for the redistribution of wealth by regulating corporations and finding new markets abroad.[108] This form of redistribution, so to speak, of goods and capital abroad through exports would forestall the need for activist redistribution at home. If the populist solution was what the historian Charles Beard famously termed the "open door" at home (a strong central government redistributing wealth from business elites to the common man), then the Republican solution offered by Conant was the "open door" abroad (the central government working on behalf of business elites to open overseas markets). Accordingly, Conant concluded that "the United States cannot afford to adhere to a policy of isolation when other nations are reaching out for the command of these [Latin American and Chinese] new markets."[109] By placing banking and business at the center of overproduction and by offering a solution that did not threaten Republican interests, Conant thus rendered overproduction theory much more palatable to the bankers, magnates, and corporate lawyers of the Metropolitan elite—and to the Republican leadership.

The purpose of the foregoing analysis is not to compare and contrast Mahan's ideas with those of Adams, Turner, Conant, and others, but rather to show how closely in step his thoughts were with the leading intellectuals of the day and to illustrate the centrality of economics to the nature of the contemporary problems he was trying to understand and write about. Indeed, one might go further and say that it is impossible to understand Mahan's writing unless one first understands the political-economic aspects of his subjects. As time went by, moreover, he became ever more economically focused and, with the help of the likes of Hadley, Farnam, Adams, and likely also Conant, ever sharper in his analysis. Mahan's published articles and his private correspondence demonstrate that he was observing the changes in the world around him, trying to order and make sense of them, to discern what was and was not important, and, to the extent possible, to create a workable model that could be used to generate insights for the future. As such, Mahan was a pioneer and the furthest thing from a narrow navalist, the point being that he paid close attention to domestic issues like tariff reform, monetary policy, and social unrest (albeit from a military-strategic perspective), as well as to international issues like the changing size and structure of the global economy and the spread of European colonialism. All were components and contexts of sea power.

In an article published by *Harper's Magazine* in June 1898 but actually written the previous January, Mahan provided a summary of his new and much broader concept of sea power. It contained also his latest thoughts on the nature of the relationship between commerce and war, the distinction between commerce raiding and commerce destruction, and the centrality of economic factors in wartime and in achieving a successful peace. He wrote,

> In the summary of points to be dealt with has been included the opinion that offensive action by a navy may be limited to merely preying upon the enemy's commerce—that being considered not only a real injury, but one great enough to bring him to peace. Concerning this, it will suffice here to say that national maritime commerce does not consist in a number of ships sprinkled, as by a pepper-pot, over the surface of the ocean. Rightly viewed, it

constitutes a great system, with the strength and weakness of such. Its strength is that possessed by all organized power, namely, that it can undergo a good deal of local injury, such as scattered cruisers may inflict, causing inconvenience and suffering, without receiving vital harm. A strong man cannot be made to quit his work by sticking pins in him, or by bruising his shins or blacking his eyes; he must be hit in a vital part, or have a bone broken, to be laid up. The weaknesses of commerce—the fatally vulnerable parts of its system—are the commercial routes over which ships pass. They are the bones, the skeleton, the framework of the organism. Hold them, break them, and commerce falls with a crash, even though no ship is taken, but all locked up in safe ports. But to effect this is not the work of dispersed cruisers picking up ships here and there, as birds pick up crumbs, but of vessels massed into powerful fleets, holding the sea, or at the least making the highways too dangerous for use. A navy so planned is for defense indeed, in the true sense that the best defense is to crush your enemy by depriving him of the use of the sea.[110]

The point that Mahan was making here was that destruction of an enemy's commercial system would eventually compel them to sue for peace. The operative word here was "system"—Mahan recognized economic activity as modular and systematic, and argued that "the weaknesses of commerce—the fatally vulnerable parts of its system— are the commercial routes over which ships pass." In other words, sea transportation was at the same time the most vital and most vulnerable cog in the economic machine.

In January 1899, another journal invited Mahan to comment on the recent U.S. acquisition of the Philippines. He wrote: "I have been asked to contribute to the discussion of this matter something from my own usual point of view; which is, of course, the bearing of sea power upon the security and the progress of nations. Well, one great element of sea power, which, it will be remembered, *is commercial before it is military*, is that there be territorial bases of action in the regions important to its commerce."[111]

Sea power "is commercial before it is military." He could not have been more explicit. The object of sea power was to exert pressure on enemies by exerting control over access to the global trading system. To extend the metaphor of Brooks Adams at the beginning of this chapter, trade routes represented the arteries of the world economic system. Oceanic trade represented the lifeblood that fed the component parts of the body, the world composed of nation-states. Those parts of the body that were well fed with the "blood" of trade prospered; those that were not atrophied.

CHAPTER 7

RETURN TO DUTY

The Spanish War (1898–99)

The brilliant, but vague, excitement and glory of war, in its more stirring phases, touches readily the popular imagination, as does intense action of every description. It has all the charm of the dramatic, heightened by the splendor of the heroic. But where there is no appeal beyond the imagination to the intellect, such impressions lack distinctness, and leave no really useful results.

—ALFRED THAYER MAHAN, DECEMBER 1898[1]

MAHAN SELDOM TALKED ABOUT his recall to service during the Spanish-American War. In his autobiography, published just ten years after the event, he did not even mention that during the war, between May and August of 1898, he had been a member of the Naval War Board within the Office of the Secretary of the Navy. Though from time to time he mentioned the subject in articles, he always understated his personal contribution and downplayed the importance of the Naval War Board within the decision-making machinery of the Navy Department.[2] Even in the confidential history of the Naval War Board he prepared in 1906 for Adm. George Dewey, then-president of the General Board of the Navy, Mahan bent over backward to stress that it had been nothing more than an extemporized ad hoc advisory body that just sat and talked.[3] He insisted that "no definitive orders were given to those who thus met as a Board," stressing that "it possessed neither original nor executive powers."[4]

This was all technically true. Mahan's story also was consistent with the (repeated) assurances already given by the Navy Department to Congress that the board existed merely "to advise the Secretary in regard to the Department's strategic policy, and to this end it prepared for his consideration and signature orders affecting this policy."[5] When reading such statements, however, it is important to understand that for anyone in the Navy Department to have even hinted that the Naval War Board did anything more would have courted serious political trouble. It should also be noted that when writing the 1906 confidential history, Mahan knew that Dewey wanted it tailored for a particular purpose: to persuade Congress to permit the creation within the department of a naval staff system.[6] This was a goal that Mahan (and Luce) had long shared but that many congressmen viewed with deep suspicion, for it raised numerous concerns over the proper relationship between state and society and civilian control over the military. In other words, Mahan produced his report with a clear political purpose in immediate view—to demonstrate the necessity for administrative reform, not to chronicle the accomplishments of a previous improvised committee. More simply, he had good reasons for telling only half the story.

Mahan's discretion has caused historians some irritation and no little confusion. Even David Trask, author of *The War with Spain in 1898*, far and away the best book on the subject, grumbled over Mahan's "perverse tendency" to understate the role of the Naval War Board.[7] (Remarkable as it may seem, there still is no good history detailing the naval side of the war.) In his narrative, Trask opined that the Naval War Board "simply served as an advisory body" and "did not decide the movement of any forces at sea," yet on the very next page he credited the same board with having exercised "considerable influence on naval operations in the Caribbean," and elsewhere in his text suggested that the board "influenced events notably."[8] Alas, Trask neither elucidated nor elaborated. But given that he was a historian of the Army rather than the Navy, and thus perhaps disinclined to probe arcane naval matters too deeply, and given also the operational focus of his analysis, such inconsistencies do not detract from the overall accomplishment of his book.[9] In fact, however, the Naval War Board in general and Mahan in particular played a far greater role during the Spanish-American War and participated more actively in the decision-making process than was admitted at the time or recognized since.

Not only did the Naval War Board wield more power within the Department than previously allowed, but its members attended high-level war policy meetings chaired by President William McKinley. With regard to the latter, Mahan was still more discreet, feeling himself bound by "a general obligation of silence as to what occurs in such meetings."[10] Proving the extent of Mahan's contributions at these meetings, or the level of his influence on the formulation of policy, is of course nearly impossible, though it may be mentioned in passing that historians have struggled to "prove" the level of anyone else's influence. What is beyond question, nevertheless, is that Mahan was one of only a handful of men present in the rooms where key decisions were made. He was thus, at the very least, an eyewitness to the practical and above all political difficulties attending the formulation and execution of strategic policy during the Spanish-American War.

Separately, Mahan also served as the Navy's liaison with the State Department pertaining to all matters relating to the blockade of Cuba. His experience here caused him to pay much closer attention to the subject of commerce warfare, and in particular to the belligerent right of capture at sea, leading him to revise drastically his thoughts on the subject. At the end of the war Mahan was involved in the peace negotiations, though his exact role remains unclear. As we shall see below and in the next chapter, the insights he gleaned from his unique access to high-level decision making led to important changes in his understanding of war and caused him further to modify his concept of sea power.

To set the scene, let us return to the beginning of 1897, shortly after the inauguration of Republican William McKinley as the twenty-fifth president of the United States. For the post of Secretary of the Navy, McKinley selected John D. Long, a former governor of Massachusetts and congressman, who was reputably given the post solely on the strength of his longtime friendship with the president.[11] As Navy Secretary, Long proved to be a reasonably efficient though unenergetic administrator, in part because his health was fragile but also because he came to the post unburdened with ambition or expertise. It is indicative that Long was the first executive in more than twenty years not to attempt a cleansing of the Augean stables that was the Navy Department bureaucracy. This is not to say that "Governor" Long, as he liked to be addressed, was lazy, uninterested, or incompetent. His diary suggests a man who took a philosophical and laid-back approach to life. He delighted in boasting that he was "a civilian who does not know the stem from the stern of a ship."[12] He possessed a dry sense of humor. In his autobiography, he confessed that it amused him to watch those around him living their lives and to reflect on the "frictions, foibles and faults which are a part of all human nature."[13]

In June 1897, as relations between the United States and Spain over Cuba began to simmer, Governor Long authorized a meeting of naval officers to discuss the general scheme of operations to be followed in the event that Spain and the United States came to blows.[14] By the standards of the day this was an unusual step. Exactly who suggested the meeting to Long remains unclear. In any case, those present at this "strategy meeting" included the new commander in chief of the North Atlantic Squadron, the "scrupulous and slow" Rear Adm. Montgomery Sicard, along with the senior bureau chiefs plus the junior yet highly regarded Cdr. Casper Goodrich, then-president of the Naval War College.[15] The result was a singularly unimpressive three-page report exhibiting a distinct lack of realism as to what was logistically possible, an apparent assumption that Spanish naval and ground forces would remain entirely passive, and a disconcerting unwillingness to choose between the competing operational proposals necessary to forge a coherent strategy.[16] Basically, Sicard favored doing everything and rejecting nothing. To be fair, however, it must be said that Long provided no political guidance to assist the Navy in narrowing the options. Over the following six months, discussion of the subject continued spasmodically as the prospect of war grew, though few if any concrete preparations were made. Trask is essentially correct in summarizing that "the navy had no really settled conception of what it might undertake in the event of war with Spain."[17]

In December 1897, President McKinley devoted considerable space to the interminable Cuban crisis in his State of the Union address, publicly expressing his desire that the chaos in Cuba would soon end.[18] Through diplomatic channels, the administration was much more forceful in pressing its wishes. On January 24, 1898, McKinley ordered the battleship *Maine* to the Cuban capital of Havana, ostensibly on a goodwill visit but in fact to signal his administration's impatience with the Spanish failure to quell the ongoing insurrection. For Theodore Roosevelt, the rambunctious assistant Secretary of the Navy, it seemed that additional steps should be taken. On the evening of January 13, Roosevelt alerted Long that the U.S. Navy was far from ready to fight a war: its few modern warships were scattered across the globe and most were short of everything from ammunition to crew. "Certain things should be done at once if there is any reasonable chance of trouble with Spain during the next six months," Roosevelt implored; "the disposition of the fleet on foreign stations should be radically altered, and altered without delay."[19] Long, however, displayed no enthusiasm for such changes. After their tête-à-tête, he confided in his diary that "He [Roosevelt] bores me with plans of naval and military movements, and the necessity of having some scheme of attack arranged for instant execution in case of an emergency. By tomorrow morning he will have got half a dozen heads of bureaus together and have spoiled twenty pages of good writing paper."[20]

In the weeks that followed, as the situation in Cuba deteriorated, the tone of the press coverage became increasingly shrill, and American diplomacy grew more belligerent, the necessity for active preparations by the Navy became increasingly pressing. Thanks to Roosevelt's incessant prodding, the Department had at last stirred from its slumber, though Secretary Long remained determined "to leave all such matters to the bureaus to which they belong, and rely upon my bureau chiefs or other officers at naval stations or on board ship, limiting myself to the general direction of affairs."[21] This was all well and good, but Long himself was hardly a font of energetic direction. The bureaus were administrative rather than planning or policy bodies and, what is more, none of their chiefs at that time were regarded as highfliers or had reputations for any strategic sagacity.

With reluctance, and perhaps because he was unwell, several weeks later Long ended up delegating to Roosevelt the task of coordinating the day-to-day departmental action and the drafting of orders, while reserving the final say to himself. Some initiatives he approved but many others he canceled, in so doing leaving Roosevelt with an impression of arbitrariness.[22] Long, of course, saw the position differently. In his diary he confided that he was nervous at placing so much responsibility in Roosevelt's hands: "He is so enthusiastic and loyal that he is, in certain respects, invaluable, yet I lack confidence in his good judgement and discretion. He goes off very impulsively."[23] Roosevelt was perfectly aware of what Long thought about him and, what is more, knew that the Secretary's concerns were widely shared. He unhappily confessed to retired Adm. Luce that "the Secretary is continually warned against me as being an innovator, a bit of an incendiary etc., and even his great kindness to me cannot make him always feel that I am not over-hasty in these matters."[24] Roosevelt suspected (or knew) that Long was holding back from him certain information concerning the government's intentions. "You have been Secretary of the Navy," Teddy archly wrote to former Navy Secretary Benjamin Tracy, "and you know that the assistant is necessarily and properly ignorant of the larger policies and purposes of the administration. All I can do with the light I have is to advise, and I have advised about [accelerating] building the battleships and torpedo boats."[25]

On February 15, 1898, the *Maine* blew up and sank at her mooring inside Havana harbor. As is well known, public opinion in the

United States blamed the Spaniards for sabotage and howled for
revenge.[26] It was, Mahan noted, "an anxious time."[27] Though retired,
he remained in correspondence with a great number of still-active officers, many of whom had served under him in previous years.[28] No one
knew what would happen next. What were McKinley's intentions at
this stage? Did he believe that the United States could not afford to
go to war for fear of damaging the sputtering national economy? Or
did he believe that the United States could not afford not to go to war
because the ongoing insurrection in Cuba was threatening to damage
the U.S. economic recovery? Historians remain divided.[29]

In any case, on March 9, 1898, the president asked Congress to
pass a $50 million emergency appropriation bill for national defense.
Suddenly flush with funds, the Navy Department mobilized the fleet:
warships were recommissioned and others hurriedly purchased "off
the shelf" from foreign yards, and merchantmen of all shapes and sizes
leased for service as auxiliary cruisers and supply ships.[30] With the possibility of actual conflict looming ever larger, yet lacking the aptitude,
expertise, or inclination to take charge, Long expanded Roosevelt's
authority and allowed him to organize and chair a new committee to
"coordinate the work of the department and the fleet, and to keep
a general surveillance over the larger strategical and technical questions which could not be dealt with by the commanders-in-chief of the
several squadrons."[31] Besides Roosevelt, the members (initially) were
Rear Adm. Arent Crowninshield (BuNAV), Capt. Albert S. Barker
(former captain of the battleship *Oregon*, serving as aide to the Secretary while awaiting orders), and Cdr. Richardson Clover (ONI).[32]
This committee was known at the time by several names but ultimately became called the Naval War Board. It oversaw arrangements
for mobilizing the fleet (including the purchase of new ships from
various European builders) and forming their crews from available
personnel supplemented by various state naval militias.[33]

According to Mahan's 1906 report, for which he buttressed his
recollections using recent interviews with other surviving members,
the "Board" was never formally appointed but rather emerged ad hoc
from various meetings held within the Navy Department to try and

bring order to the mounting chaos consequent on the decision to mobilize.[34] There was a shortage of office space and an even greater shortage of staff. Because of the great rush of work, squabbles broke out over the use of clerical staff—in particular, which office should enjoy the services of a Miss Lamb, who normally worked in the library.[35] Mahan further recorded that at these early meetings "other officers also were at times present, officially yet informally, and afterwards dropped out, with equal informality." These gatherings, moreover, tended to be periodic rather than scheduled, "simply a meeting of the officers whose other particular duties indicated them to be the proper persons for fruitful conversations, and for coordination of the many and speedy steps which had to be taken, outside and above Bureau action, in the pressing preparation for war."[36] Decision making, in other words, was conducted by committee.

As is well known, in addition to coordinating departmental action for mobilization, Roosevelt also took the lead in formulating naval strategy, a task much complicated by the general lack of consensus in the Navy as to what could be done, let alone would be done— plus innumerable unhelpful outside suggestions as to what should be done.[37] Former Navy Secretary (now Senator) William Chandler, for instance, pressed Long for the fleet to be deployed forward. "Shouldn't our Asiatic squadron be strengthened by adding a battleship, if the squadron is to remain there? With a battleship it could take Manila; without it, it can do little and might as well come home. But I should not favor its return. Our Pacific coast hasn't many harbors like the Atlantic; and besides, a Spanish fleet [of reinforcements] is not likely to appear there."[38]

Demands by other senior politicians for warships to stay at home and guard their home states compounded the pressure to scatter the fleet hither and thither. Long found it amusing that the loudest jingoes for war also tended to be the loudest in demanding naval protection for their hometowns—simultaneously clamoring for the fleet be deployed both offensively and defensively—and he singled out Senators Chandler and William P. Frye (both from far distant Maine) as the worst offenders.[39] "If you know anything about the coast of Maine,"

Mahan snorted in a letter to one friend, the place was already "absolutely protected by its own military insignificance."[40]

Since becoming Assistant Secretary of the Navy, Roosevelt had
stayed in close touch with Mahan, encouraging him to write him and
"throw out ideas for consideration."[41] It was no surprise, therefore,
that on March 10, just one day after Congress passed the emergency
appropriation bill, Roosevelt turned to Mahan for advice.[42] "I ear-
nestly wish that my chief [Long] would get you on here to consult
in the present crisis," he flattered.[43] Over the next fortnight the two
discussed the Navy's options in the event of war. Sadly, only fragments of their correspondence have survived, and then only letters
from Roosevelt to Mahan. Nonetheless, it is possible to infer something of the advice Mahan gave from Roosevelt's replies to his letters, to references therein to certain surviving documents, and from
their later correspondence recalling this time.[44] It seems likely, for
instance, that Mahan dissuaded Roosevelt from supporting proposals
to send a detachment across the Atlantic to raid the Spanish north
coast, to deploy first-line warships for the defense of coastal cities, or
to launch any premature attacks on Puerto Rico before control of
Cuba was established.[45] But these were hardly profound suggestions,
and anyway the options were limited. The U.S. Navy possessed barely
sufficient warships to impose a partial blockade of Cuba, let alone
anything more.[46]

On March 14, Roosevelt wrote Mahan, telling him that "I further
agree with you with all my heart about local coast defense. I shall urge,
and have urged, the President and the Secretary to pay absolutely
no heed to the outcries for protection from Spanish raids. Take the
worst—a bombardment of New York. It would amount to absolutely
nothing, as affecting the course of a war, or damaging permanently
the prosperity of the country."[47] Several days later, Mahan sent Roosevelt some comments on the Department's latest plan of campaign,
for which the latter thanked him profusely. "There is no question that
you stand head and shoulders above the rest of us! You have given us
just the suggestions we want, I am going to show your letter to the
Secretary first, and then get some members of the Board to go over it.

. . . You probably don't know how much your letter has really helped me clearly to formulate certain things which I had only vaguely in mind. I think I have studied your books to pretty good purpose."[48]

A couple of days later, the Navy Department couriered a memorandum prepared by Roosevelt and countersigned by Long to Rear Adm. William Sampson, commanding the main fleet assembling at Key West, outlining the strategic deliberations in Washington and forwarding the semblance of a plan.[49] Roosevelt thought Mahan's letters to him so valuable that he sent them along in the same bundle.[50] Apparently, they were never returned.

On March 26, 1898, informed by Roosevelt that war now seemed less likely, Mahan proceeded to Europe for a long-planned six-month family vacation.[51] Nevertheless, before he left, Teddy assured him that "your address will be kept, and I can assure you we will communicate with you at once in the event of need."[52] On April 9, 1898, Mahan and his family disembarked in Naples. While the Mahans meandered northward through Italy, at home public demands for action over Cuba became irresistible. On April 11, McKinley asked Congress for the authority to send American troops to Cuba. With war increasingly likely, Long invited Rear Adm. Montgomery Sicard to join his personal staff and promptly appointed him to the Naval War Board. The Secretary's reasons for doing so are not entirely clear, for the admiral possessed no particular reputation for strategy or administration. Long's diary entry seems to imply he was motivated more by pity than conviction of the admiral's abilities. "This is rather a sad case," he wrote; "[Sicard] was in command of the fighting fleet, closing his naval service with what seemed to be an opportunity for the highest distinction in command. His health broke down, and I was compelled to retire him, after medical survey. He has been very manly about it and recognizes the propriety of my action, the evidence of which I see at once in the appearance of broken health which he manifests."[53]

The following week, Adm. Sicard along with the Capt. Crowninshield (both members of the Naval War Board) accompanied the Navy Secretary to a strategy conference with President McKinley and representatives of the Army. Long left the White House meeting unimpressed by what he had heard. He afterwards wrote in his diary that it "reminds me of what must have been a similar scene in the early days of our civil war when President Lincoln was surrounded by military advisors who were all at sixes and sevens."[54]

On April 25, Congress finally declared war on Spain. That same day, Roosevelt gave Long notice of his intention to resign and join one of the volunteer cavalry regiments being raised for the duration. The Secretary was more than a little annoyed at the loss of his industrious deputy, perhaps belatedly realizing that he was losing the mainspring that had been driving the mobilization of the fleet. He sighed to himself that "My assistant secretary, Roosevelt, has determined upon resigning, in order to go into the army and take part in the war. He has been of great use; a man of unbounded energy and force, and thoroughly honest, which is the main thing. He has lost his head to the unutterable folly of deserting the post where he is of the most service and running off to ride a horse, and probably, brush mosquitoes from his neck in the Florida sands."[55]

Yet Roosevelt did not say goodbye to the Navy Department until May 6 and did not actually depart the Washington to join his outfit— the fabled Rough Riders—until May 10.[56] This meant that Roosevelt almost certainly met with Mahan and briefed him on recent events.[57] But this is to get ahead of the story.

For most of April, Mahan of course had been in Italy. But as soon as war had been declared, the Navy Department tracked him to a hotel in Rome and telegraphed orders to report at once to Washington. Leaving his family to continue their vacation, Mahan rushed back home (via ship and train) as quickly as he could. Mahan cryptically admitted in his 1906 report that "having reason to infer I was to be a member [of the Naval War Board], in passing through Paris I telegraphed to the Navy Department certain opinions of my own," as if to say that he had been promised the appointment the previous month.[58] Capt. William Puleston, Mahan's biographer, had no doubt that this was in fact the case and that it had been Roosevelt who had issued the promise.[59] Mahan reached New York on Friday, May 7, and after stopping by his house to fish his uniforms out of mothballs, the next morning he took a train to Washington. For the next three and a half months, until the end of the war, he resided at Theodore Roosevelt's house, just off Dupont Circle.

MAHAN'S WAR SERVICE

On May 9, 1898, Capt. Alfred Thayer Mahan reported for duty at the sprawling State, War and Navy Building on Pennsylvania Avenue in Washington. Secretary Long, who apparently had not met him before, greeted him with bemusement. In his diary that day he wrote that "Captain Mahan, on the retired list, returns under orders from abroad for duty on the War Board. He has achieved great distinction as a writer of naval history, and has made a very thorough study of naval strategy. No naval officer stands higher today. Yet, I doubt very much whether he will be of much value practically. He may be, or he may not. That remains to be seen."[60]

One thing seems quite clear from this entry: Long had not been responsible for Mahan's recall, but neither did he send him away. A clerk found space for the captain to pitch a desk in a musty top-floor garret at the back of the east wing that was used to store old books and papers. Sharing this glorified closet was Rear Adm. Sicard, who, after Roosevelt's departure, found himself elevated to president of the Naval War Board.[61]

Mahan's first act the following morning was to hand Secretary Long a typed memorandum calling for "the 'Board of War' [sic] to be abolished, and that in place of it, to perform the functions with which it is now entrusted, there be appointed a single officer, to be known by such title as may seem convenient to designate his duties."[62] Not surprisingly, Long was taken aback by Mahan's request—in effect to make himself redundant. "I ask him what he wants, and he says he wants some one man appointed Chief of Staff, to take the whole responsibility of the Naval War Board; to advise with others, but to have the determination of things in his own hands," a bemused Long complained to his diary. "I ask him if this won't require just as much discussion, and he says—yes; just as much exhaustion of brain power, and he says—yes."[63] Long replied that he could not see the point. For some

historians, that Mahan should have put forward such a suggestion at
this time reflected dogmatism and a lack of judgment.[64] The beginning
of a war, they scoff, was neither the time nor the place to upend the
naval bureaucracy and reorganize the distribution of business.

Yet before leaving this subject, it is worth considering a question
that few historians have bothered to ask: namely, who was the officer
Mahan had in mind for the position? Though some have suggested
that he thought of himself as the ideal candidate, Mahan did not in
fact want the job and was intelligent enough to see that he lacked the
stature within the service to be given it if he asked. "I conceive my
well established reputation to be that of a writer," he told one friend,
the week after submitting his memorandum, "and have no ambition
to be considered a great general officer, or man of action, for I know
I am not either."[65] So who, then? It beggars belief that Mahan did not
have someone in mind.

It transpires that in naval circles at this time there was a considerable body of opinion that thought the war offered the perfect opportunity to break congressional resistance to much-needed reform of the
Navy Department. Retired Adm. Stephen B. Luce certainly thought
so. Writing in mid-May to Senator Henry Cabot Lodge, he complained (apparently not for the first time) that "our Navy Department
is not organized for a state of war; you will search in vain for any office
or officer in it specially charged with duties connected with the operations of war."[66] Banging loudly on the drum of reform, Luce pleaded:
"let Congress now give what the Navy has been wanting for during the
past fifty-six years: a Navy Department organized for war."[67] Lodge's
reply speaks for itself: "I quite agree with you that there ought to be
a chief of staff in the Navy Department and I have thought so for
many years."[68] But the key part of Luce's letter to Lodge is found in
the scrawled postscript: Luce here added, "for chief of General Staff
probably Rear Admiral [John] Walker would inspire more confidence
among the officers of the fleet than anyone else of his rank."[69]

Roosevelt was another calling for the recall of Walker to become
the navy's first de facto chief of naval operations.[70] So too was Capt.
French Chadwick, commanding the *New York* and chief of staff to

Rear Adm. William T. Sampson, the fleet commander in chief. Indeed, the week before Mahan returned to Washington, Chadwick wrote directly to Secretary Long and urged him to appoint Walker because "there is no possible question from a military point of view (which is the only view to take at the moment) that the person nearest you should be a military man of ability and force, and at once having the complete confidence of the service."[71] Though he had served a term as chief of the Bureau of Equipment and thus was a Navy insider, Chadwick also favored a restructuring of the Navy Department, and indeed four years earlier had published an article in *Proceedings* suggesting "the creation of a general staff to oversee naval operations and to formulate war plans."[72]

It seems like no mere coincidence, then, that a couple of days after reading Mahan's memo, Long invited Rear Adm. John Walker to his office for a chat—or was it an unofficial interview? Long recorded the details of their conversation in his diary. Though undoubtedly the most accomplished officer of his generation, Walker had retired due to age (at sixty-two years) the previous year. Undoubtedly he was a superlative manager and widely respected for his many abilities; he was also arrogant and opinionated. Afraid that recalling yet another officer out of retirement would provoke an outcry from senior officers keen to be given opportunities to excel, Long concluded he would find Walker too difficult to work with.[73] As far as Long was concerned, this was the end of the matter and the subject of administrative reorganization was dropped. Mahan accepted the decision and settled down to work.

But what work? Answering this straightforward question is no easy task; it is necessary to review the evidence methodically. To begin with, by this date—mid-May 1898—the Naval War Board had been whittled down to Sicard, Mahan, and Crowninshield. While Sicard possessed the authority that came with his rank and seniority, and Mahan had the ideas and the contacts, Crowninshield was the only one who indisputably wielded real power within the department (and possessed a proper office of his own in the main suite). As chief of the Bureau of Navigation, Crowninshield sat like a spider at the center of the naval bureaucratic web. Since the Tracy administrative reforms of 1889, the correspondence from all other bureaus was routed through Navigation, leading the bureau to regard itself very much as the first among equals. In June 1898, Crowninshield had occasion to remind Secretary Long that "In one sense, Navigation is not a Bureau, but a part of the Secretary's office. It keeps the records of the fleet and its personnel, and prepares orders concerning the same for you to sign, a duty performed by no other bureau; it has under it no supplies; in other words, Navigation is the Adjutant General's Office of the Navy Department."[74]

What Crowninshield was saying here, in effect, was that his Bureau of Navigation acted as gatekeeper to the Secretary's office. His staff drafted all orders requiring formal approval and sifted and forwarded what they thought the Secretary needed to see. Long acknowledged the truth of this testimony. After the war, in a letter to a newspaper editor asking who was responsible for drafting the wartime orders sent to then-Commo. George Dewey in the Philippines, he recalled that "In the routine of department work, while every dispatch or letter is important, yet usually the subordinate, in whose line it comes, writes it and his superior (Crowninshield in this case) passes on it, and if it comes to me as Secretary for my signature, as it did in this case, I pass on it and sign it. It then becomes mine in responsibility though it may not have been mine in composition."[75]

Of course, there were occasions when another bureau chief sometimes waylaid the Secretary in a corridor, explained his problem, and obtained from him verbal permission to act. In June 1898, for instance, Rear Adm. Royal Bradford, chief of equipment, remonstrated to Long that he could not be held responsible for supplying the fleet with sufficient coal unless he was allowed to direct the movements of fleet colliers. Long evidently was persuaded and approved his request. Upon learning of this change in arrangements, Crowninshield at once confronted Long and insisted "that your verbal orders concerning colliers be revoked, and that the colliers be placed on exactly the same basis as any other naval vessel."[76] Crowninshield won his case and control of the colliers reverted to his office.

This is not to suggest that Crowninshield was the real power within the Navy Department, or that the Naval War Board was merely an extension of his bureau, or that Mahan was de facto his subordinate. On the contrary. By repute, Crowninshield was a singularly unimaginative officer, who lacked initiative and was a stickler for the rigid application of rules. In previous assignments he had never shone, and his career had been unexceptional even by the standards of the day. He been appointed chief of the Bureau of Navigation the year before, only after the high-flying Henry Clay Taylor (then a junior captain) had declined the post.[77] No one had a good word to say about him in the various published postwar memoirs, and indeed most said nothing about him at all.[78] The significant exception was George Dewey (of Manila fame), who assailed Crowninshield as "a pronounced bureaucrat, with whose temperament and methods I had little more sympathy than had the majority of the officers of the navy at that time."[79] Which may have been so. But Long evidently appreciated his qualities (whatever they were), for in 1901 he reappointed him to a second term as chief of the Bureau of Navigation. Beyond this, little else is known of this officer.[80]

By mid-May 1898, the main line of the Navy's strategy had been pretty much agreed on. Following Mahan's recommendations submitted in March and endorsed by Roosevelt, the plan was for Sampson's fleet "to establish a strict blockade, particularly of the eastern half of the island, and of the [northern] ports of Havana and Matanzas [connected by rail to Havana]."[81] The intent was to starve the Spanish garrisons into submission.[82] This was to be the mechanism of pressure and the primary instrument of coercion.[83] As Mahan made very clear in his account written immediately after the war, the objective aimed at was not to sink the Spanish fleet; no one in Washington anticipated the Spanish admiralty would be so incompetent as to deliver up its fleet piecemeal for execution, as more or less would happen in the weeks ahead.

Upon returning to duty, Mahan was shocked at the level of "ignorant clamor and contagious panic" among the general public and no less disconcerted by how much public opinion was impeding the prosecution of the war.[84] Instead of allowing the Navy to deploy in full force against Cuba and focus on the blockade, the administration had insisted on scattering a significant portion up and down the East Coast to protect against the chimera of marauding Spanish corsairs. In particular, on March 17 President McKinley had directed the Navy Department to retain at home a "Flying Squadron" at Hampton Roads (comprising approximately one quarter of available modern warships) to act as a kind of fire brigade for the protection of the East Coast.[85] Additional, albeit obsolescent, craft were assigned for the direct protection of unimportant though politically well-represented East Coast cites. These precautions were demanded because the United States could not locate a squadron of four (reasonably) modern cruisers under the command of the Spanish admiral Pascual Cervera.

Mahan regarded the dispersion of the U.S. fleet to allay political fears as utterly foolish. "I believe we should accept whatever damage it can thereafter, or ever do, rather than loosen our grip on Havana or Cienfuegos," he railed to his Naval War Board colleagues on May 19, warning that "if the Spanish division [Cervera's squadron] can play on our fears like a musician on a piano, [then] goodbye success."[86] "The public is an honest and in the main well-meaning fellow, but in current questions of the day a good deal of a fool," a clearly irritated Mahan remarked to a friend several days later, taking care to convey nothing of his opinion of his political masters.[87] Theodore Roosevelt shared Mahan's exasperation at the diversion of warships from the main fleet operating off Cuba. "You are entirely right," Roosevelt agreed. "The flying squad[ron] was looked upon with hysterical anxiety by the North east and its representatives in Congress. If you can get in to see me, or motor over to take lunch with me at Oyster Bay, I should really like to tell you about some the requests made to me for ships to protect Portland, . . . Maine Narragansett Pier, and other points of like vast strategic importance!"[88]

In the realm of strategy, therefore, Mahan's principal contribution was to throw his considerable weight behind those who wanted to concentrate effort on the principal task—the naval and commercial blockade of Cuba—and to prepare for the secondary task of convoying the transports carrying the U.S. Army invasion force when it was finally ready to move. Holding this line proved to be something of a challenge, for there were endless calls from various quarters for the detachment of warships for various wildcat missions (there was always somebody with a "good" idea). As Mahan wryly observed a few years later in the pages of his book on the War of 1812, "There is, however, in the human mind an inveterate tendency to dispersion of effort, due apparently to the wish to do at once as many things as may be; a disposition also to take as many chances as possible in an apparent lottery, with the more hope [*sic*] that some one of them will come up successful. Not an aggregate big result, and one only, whether hit or miss, but a division of resources and powers which shall insure possible compensation in one direction for what is not gained, or may even be lost, in another."[89]

During the Spanish-American War, in other words, Mahan's contribution was to keep everyone focused on blockading Cuba.[90] As he later wrote (in December 1898), the "principle of concentration of effort upon the single purpose—the blockade—forbade, *a priori*, any attempts at bombardment by which our armored ships should be brought within range of disablement by heavy guns on shore."[91]

While Mahan and his colleagues played no formal role in the planning or execution of operations, in practice they occasionally intervened. Although wireless telegraphy had not yet been invented and consequently warships at sea remained oblivious to events beyond their horizons, the world was now connected by undersea telegraph cables. Very soon, the Navy Department found itself the unexpected beneficiary of information received from across the globe, containing some useful snippets.[92] It fell to the Naval War Board, as the only organized body available, to act as the clearinghouse for this surprisingly bountiful source of intelligence. This was not the limit of the board's duties, however. In his 1906 report, Mahan casually recalled that "there were periods long enough to be of importance at such an instant, in which he [Sampson] was out of touch of the situation; whereas the Department, stationary at Washington, could and did receive conditional information, and could take necessary steps."[93] Mahan further let slip that there were other occasions when the Naval War Board acted on its superior intelligence and moved warships—meaning it did play an active role, however small, in fleet operations.

More than one historian who has studied the extant primary documents has reasoned that the Naval War Board acted as "the primary (but not the entire) decision-making body for the overall strategic plans of the Spanish-American War and most assuredly for all naval plans and orders," suggesting that "The most striking proof of the Board's paramount influence are memoranda, and there were myriads of them, drawn up by the Naval War Board on its official stationery for Secretary Long. These suggestions were issued without alteration as orders under Long's name. They cover a wide spectrum—from minutiæ, such as sending a collier to re-coal a ship, to a major operational plan."[94]

Long unquestionably did endorse the majority of the Naval War Board's written recommendations, most of which related to technical naval matters—indeed, how could any civilian head have done otherwise? But we know from other sources that Long sometimes composed and issued orders off his own bat, though it is impossible to say how many times he did so or even identify precisely which ones he penned.[95] As a consequence, the board's memoranda cannot in and of themselves be regarded as sufficient proof of that body's authority, but they certainly represent a powerful indication that it did in fact exercise considerable influence.

The most important work by the Naval War Board in fact lay outside of the Navy Department, by helping to coordinate U.S. naval, military, and foreign policy actions. Mahan and Sicard regularly, but Crowninshield only occasionally, accompanied the Secretary to meetings at the White House to decide the conduct of the war. Afterward, Mahan always remained discreet about what had transpired at these meetings. He never alluded to them in any of his published work, not even years after the event. Only occasionally, to close friends, did he let slip that "I have had occasion to see the President somewhat from the inside, in the occasional consultations on Army and Navy matters, and have been very favorably impressed with his force and firmness, which I had been inclined to doubt."[96]

For accounts of what transpired at these White House meetings we must rely on Secretary Long. On May 26, for instance, Long recorded in his diary that

> [t]he President called together the Secretary of War, General Miles, myself, and the Naval War Board. We met at the White House and went with the President over the whole situation, from the Philippines to Porto Rico [*sic*]. Secretary [for War Russell A.] Alger who, at the last Cabinet meeting, announced that he had 75,000 men ready to put into Cuba, now says that they are not prepared and will not be for some two or three weeks. Alger is an enthusiastic, patriotic, and spirited man, but does not seem to have things in hand. There is friction between him and his officers, from which the Navy is entirely free. He is apt to promise a great deal more than he can execute, simply because he is not thoroughly informed as to his own resources and preparations.[97]

On June 19, Long wrote his wife an apology for missing an engagement, explaining that "I was detained at the White House yesterday afternoon at a meeting of the Secretary of War, General Alger, and my Naval War Board, making arrangements for further military activities."[98] Long mentioned that "the President is very desirous to make an attack upon P[uerto] R[ico], but I am inclined to think we [would] better dispose of Santiago [de Cuba] first"—which, of course, was Mahan's recommendation.[99]

In another letter sent his wife, dated July 14, Long describes a three-hour conference that had taken place the previous day, discussing how best to break the deadlock at Santiago. This problem had arisen from the reluctance of Gen. William Shafter, commanding the U.S. expeditionary force in Cuba, to mount a frontal assault against the Spanish fortifications defending the heights above the city, and the blunt refusal by Admiral Sampson (backed by Long and the Naval War Board) to provide a distraction by emulating Farragut at Mobile Bay and "damning the torpedoes" guarding the narrow entrance to the port.

This important meeting was attended by the majority of McKinley's cabinet, who arrived in ones and twos and joined in the discussion. In his diary, Long reveals that Mahan not only attended this critical policy meeting, but was allowed to participate actively in the discussions:

> There was a very pretty scrimmage between Captain Mahan and Secretary Alger. Alger began his usual complaint about the Navy. We have furnished him transports to carry his men, on account of his own neglect in making provision for transportation. We have landed them; have helped him in every way we can; and have destroyed the Spanish fleet. Now he is constantly grumbling because we don't run the risk of blowing up our ships by going over the mines at the entrance of Santiago harbor and capturing the city, which he ought to capture himself, having some 20,000 troops against perhaps 5,000 or 6,000. . . . Mahan, at last, lost his patience and sailed into Alger; told him he didn't know anything about the use or purpose of the Navy, and that he did not propose to sit by and hear the navy attacked. It rather pleased the President, who, I think, was glad of the rebuke.[100]

Besides laying into the Secretary of War during a cabinet meeting, Mahan later claimed (and Long confirmed) that it was he who offered the compromise ultimately adopted, whereby instead of assaulting Santiago, the United States simply walked in after agreeing to ferry the Spanish garrison and all its equipment back across the Atlantic in U.S. government chartered ships.[101]

For most of his three-month stint in Washington during the summer of 1898, Mahan wore a second hat, arguably more important than the one he wore for the Naval War Board. In addition to residing in Roosevelt's townhouse, Mahan dined frequently with Teddy's closest political friend, Senator Henry Cabot Lodge.[102] Often these were working dinners. For instance, during the third week of June, Secretary of State "Judge" William Day was present and the conversation turned to the spoils of war and the territorial concessions the United States wanted to wring from Spain.[103] After one such meeting, Lodge relayed to Roosevelt (the two remained in close contact throughout the war) that "Day tells me there is no longer any question in any one's mind that we must have Port Rico [*sic*]; that he said to me some time ago was a matter of course. He dined with me the other night and Mahan and I talked over the Philippines with him for two hours. He said at the end that he thought we could not escape our destiny there. The feeling of the country is overwhelming against giving the Philippines back to Spain."[104]

Mahan also played an important, albeit indirect, role in framing the war aims and the terms of peace presented to Spain. These took the form of a report to Congress, issued by the Naval War Board but actually written by Mahan, providing a list of Spanish-owned islands that should be annexed to become the nucleus for an American global network of coaling stations, as well as the strategic rationale behind each choice.[105]

Though Mahan may have met Secretary Day only a couple of times (it is impossible to say how often), he frequently strolled across the building to the State Department wing to see the assistant Secretary, John Bassett Moore, to discuss matters pertaining to contraband law and the blockade.[106] The State Department was housed in the southern wing of the State, War and Navy Building, and the Navy Department in the eastern wing. Very quickly, Mahan and Moore became friends. Writing of Day and Moore in August 1898, Mahan intimated that it was Moore who was really running the show: "his chief [Day] only consented to take office on condition of his [Moore's] acceptance, and that he [Moore] only accepted on condition that his term was temporary—till the war was over."[107] In any case, directly after the peace was signed, true to his word Bassett Moore returned to his chair in international law at Columbia University. Mahan, meanwhile, returned to his home in New York, just down the road. In the years that followed, the professor tutored the retired naval captain on the history of international law (a subject in which Mahan became very interested in later life).

More than forty years after the close of the Spanish-American War, while attending a memorial service for his long-dead friend,

Moore disclosed that back in 1898 Mahan had been the conduit for many back-channel communications between Washington and various European capitals. "While he [Mahan] held this post, our conferences became more and more frequent, not only because of our official positions but also because of our common intellectual interests. Moreover, while serving as a member of the Board of Strategy [*sic*], Mahan by reason of his worldwide renown, naturally received many communications from important personages abroad, not only in relation to the conduct of the war but also in relation to the terms of peace."[108]

Secretary Long was not only aware of but approved of Mahan's outside liaisons.[109] Indeed, Long also dined with Lodge, possibly at the same time.[110] The fact that the senior senator from his home state so clearly trusted Mahan may have encouraged the Secretary to give the retired scholar-captain another look. Whatever the reason, by midsummer Secretary Long became noticeably friendlier toward Mahan, allowing him to bypass Sicard and to write him directly with his ideas.[111] By the end of the war the two had become friendly, if not actually friends, and afterward they continued their correspondence.

AFTERWARD

After the war, Mahan remained tight-lipped not only about his own activities but about what he thought of the general conduct of the war. Though he occasionally dropped hints of his disapproval, he never elaborated on his dissatisfaction in public. His reticence may be explained by two factors. First, he was loyal to the service; he did not wish to tarnish the reputation of the Navy and so risk smothering the newfound support in Congress for yet greater naval appropriations. Here it is well to consider his anger at the damage done to the service by the distasteful squabble over the laurels for the victory at Santiago between Admirals Sampson and Schley. Second, and probably even more important, Mahan had no wish to cause any embarrassment to Secretary Long, especially after he quietly prevented the court-martial of Mahan's younger brother (who had followed Alfred into the service and would rise to become an admiral), also helping to cover up a still unknown background incident.[112] Mahan was always loyal to his friends and to those who helped him.

Privately, however, Mahan was scathing about what he had observed inside the Navy Department—though, it must be stressed, he was always careful to exempt Long from his criticism. One of the first letters he wrote on the subject after returning home at the end of August 1898 was to his old mentor, Stephen Luce. In it, Mahan lambasted the internal organization and very ethos of the Navy Department. Dripping with sarcasm, he recounted that on returning to Washington in May, he found the Naval War Board housed

> under the eaves of the Dept Building in room with one window, which theretofore had been used as a lumber room for books no longer needed for the Library. As the Board was supposed to furnish the Dept with brains for the trivial & secondary purpose of carrying on the operations of the war, the high eligibility of this pasture for broken down books "turned out to grass" was considerately clear, and the forcing process of a Washington summer and in such conditions upon our mental faculties was evident also. However, war being actually on, and a wholesome fear of the enemy existent, it was conceded that possibly a naval organization existed for some other purpose than to administer, and we recd. regard enough at last to give us two rooms from the Library. The incident, [sic] nevertheless aptly shows the place preparations for war occupies in the mind of the Dep't and, after all we must recognize that like Popes and Czars, Secretaries pass away; but the Papacy, & the Czardom, & the Navy Dep't remains. It is with an institution, not a person, chiefly, that we have to deal.[113]

Mahan's letter makes for amusing reading, and probably for this reason has been often quoted. Anyone who has spent a hot and humid summer in Washington will surely empathize with his distress at having to work in a poorly ventilated top-floor room. Yet in and of itself, Mahan's complaint was neither original nor particularly significant. He was not the first reform-minded naval officer—and certainly not the last—to give vent to his frustration with the byzantine bureau-cracy that was the Navy Department, and there was nothing special or unique about the substance of his complaints. To understand what he was really driving at here, it is necessary to read the letter from Luce to Mahan that prompted it.

Mahan's comments quoted above were in fact a response to an appeal by Luce to reopen the hoary issue of naval administrative reform.[114] "The argument in favor of a permanent Naval War Board under what name so-ever one may please to call it, whether General Staff, or any other title, are too familiar to you to need recapitula-tion," Luce declared.[115] He urged Mahan to exploit his prestige and his influence to submit a formal recommendation along these lines to Secretary Long. Better understanding how to play the administrative game, Mahan recognized that such an approach would not work. "I do not wholly refuse to do what you suggest," he tactfully replied to his old mentor, "but I own to a certain hopelessness which is not conducive to doing."[116] What Mahan was saying here was that Navy Secretaries came and went, and in the greater scheme of things they did not matter very much: "it is with an institution, not a person, chiefly, that we have to deal." Instead, Mahan offered to broadcast the problem to the nation, suggesting that the "series of articles for a magazine I am just beginning will afford a better lever to move public opinion, & naval opinion than a letter to the Secy."[117]

From the beginning of the Spanish-American War, Mahan's opin-ion had been in much demand by newspaper editors, and although he declined to give any interviews or produce anything while the conflict raged, he signaled his willingness to write about his impressions on its conclusion. Within two weeks of returning to Washington in May, he had received three offers to present his thoughts and observations to the public. "You come second in order of application to me," Mahan replied to the editor of *Century Magazine* on May 17, "of course I am forced to know now a good deal of what goes on, and am mak-ing my mental comments on the operations, as illustrative of the the-ory & practice of war."[118] By conflict's end just three months later, Mahan found himself awash with requests and in a position to name

his terms. He ultimately signed with *McClure's Magazine* (an illustrated monthly) for a series of five articles that netted him $2,500, the
first of these appearing in December 1898.[119] In addition, Mahan was
allowed to reserve his copyright. A year later, he arranged for these
five articles to be republished in a single volume with a new preface,
which earned him another $1,000. But it was not simply about the
money. As was often the case with Mahan's writings, there were wheels
within wheels.

Mahan's book of articles, *Lessons of the War with Spain*, was not
particularly good history. He began writing the original articles
directly after the war, and they were more or less complete before
the end of 1898. In consequence, Mahan was unable to make use of
various Spanish sources, in particular Spanish admiral Pascual Cervera's letters and memoirs, which became available only the following
year.[120] These would have broadened Mahan's perspective on the Spanish Navy's crippling limitations, all prefigured before the war, which
Mahan barely touched on in his *Lessons*. Similarly, Mahan made no
direct reference to the importance of Britain's benevolent neutrality.[121]
In the Far East, for instance, Commo. George Dewey was allowed to
refit his squadron at the Royal Navy's dockyard in Hong Kong, to use
British cables to communicate with Washington, and even to replenish
his coal bunkers. In the Caribbean, by contrast, the local British commander in chief (the legendary Vice Adm. Sir John "Jacky" Fisher)
denied Spanish cruisers access to local British coaling and communications facilities and warned them to be very careful in interfering with
British flagged merchantmen. The denial of coal combined with the
threat of retaliation made it all but impossible for Cervera to attack
American trade at sea. From his position in the Navy Department and
his contacts in the State Department, Mahan better than anyone else
would have known about (and understood) all of this.

Yet Mahan never intended his book to be a faithful history of the
war just concluded. His eyes were on the future, and he crafted his
book accordingly. The goal was to mold American public opinion.
In the preface, indeed, he explicitly stated that his aim was to provide
readers with more than just a narrative summary of operations in the

Spanish-American conflict or to "elicit some of the lessons derivable from the war." Rather, he hoped to counteract the sort of strategically counterproductive demands, for instance for the naval protection of coastal cities, that had exasperated him during the war, through educating public opinion. In his words, he aspired to teach his readers "in a form as little technical and as much popular as is consistent with seriousness of treatment, some of the elementary conceptions of warfare in general and of naval warfare in particular. The importance of popular understanding is twofold. It promotes interest and induces intelligent pressure upon the representatives of the people . . . and . . . it also tends to avert the unintelligent pressure which, when war exists, is apt to assume the form of unreasoning and unreasonable panic."[122]

Within the pages of *Lessons of the War with Spain,* Mahan provided his readers with the clearest exposition yet of his ideas on the use and importance of history, both for professional officers and laymen interested in naval affairs. More importantly still, Mahan presented a modified version of his concept of sea power, emphasizing its economic character, by explaining the importance of defending one's own vital economic interests and of attacking the enemy's economy as the surest way to generate significant pressure and to bring the war to a successful close.

Mahan's central message was that the Navy went into the war with Spain intending to achieve victory—defined as the attainment of U.S. political goals—through a blockade of Cuba. This strategy was fully consistent with the teachings of history. In the event, however, and quite unexpectedly, victory had been achieved through the decimation of the Spanish fleet. There is of course deep irony in the fact that the supposed champion of decisive battle depicted it as accidental, and economic pressure as the real mechanism of coercion. In stressing that the original strategic intent had been to seek victory through a blockade, Mahan intimated that the victory achieved was largely a function of Spanish incompetence more than American prowess in combat. He observed that "All is well that ends well—so far at least as the wholly past is concerned; but for the instruction of the future it is necessary not to cast the past entirely behind our backs before its teachings have been pondered and assimilated. We cannot expect ever again to have an enemy so entirely inapt as Spain showed herself to be."[123]

Looking to the future, Mahan was anxious that Americans should better understand how navies operated. As mentioned, on returning to the United States in May 1898, he had been shocked by the level of public panic and the degree to which it was hindering the Navy's attempt to prosecute the war through a blockade of Cuba. Though scornful of public opinion, Mahan was thus respectful of its power, and he remained so ever after. It is instructive to note that six years later, in his confidential history written for Dewey, Mahan implored the General Board of the Navy never to forget that fleet deployment in wartime—and thus strategy—must inevitably be constrained by political considerations. "In a popular government, it is of no avail to try and calm people's fears by rational military considerations," he stressed; "they clamor to be visibly defended."[124]

Yet for all of Mahan's annoyance at the diversion of naval resources away from the blockade force, he acknowledged that that during the war the United States had left vital interests at home dangerously exposed. Public opinion had grounds for concern, in other words—it just had the wrong concerns. The threat lay not in isolated bombardments of cities, which were somewhat akin to the scattered attacks of *guerre de course*, but in interference with the U.S. coastal trade, which represented a commercial center of gravity capable of disrupting the entire U.S. economy. In his first article on the conduct of the Spanish-American War, penned in late October 1898, Mahan pointed out that "Protected from any serious attempt at invasion by our isolated position, and by our vast intrinsic strength, we are nevertheless vulnerable in an extensive seaboard, greater, relatively to our population and wealth—great as they are—than that of any other state. Upon this, moreover, rests an immense coasting trade, the importance of which to our internal commercial system is now scarcely realized, but will be keenly felt if we ever are unable to insure its freedom of movement."[125]

Subsequently, he elaborated that U.S. coastal trade "was, and remains, an extremely vulnerable interest, one the protection of which will make heavy demands upon us in any maritime war. Nor can it be urged that that interest alone will suffer by its own interruption. The bulky cargoes carried by it cannot be transferred to the coastwise railroads without overtaxing the capacities of the latter; all of which means, ultimately, increase of cost and consequent suffering to the consumer, together with serious injury to all related industries dependent upon this traffic."[126] Mahan's point here was that national economic systems were fundamentally dynamic in nature and fragile in character, and that second- and third-order consequences would cause widespread economic derangement. How many naval officers or other government officials ever thought to consider the implications of disruption to the coastal trade for the national rail network? Then again, how many naval officers were friends with Henry Farnam and Arthur Hadley, two of the leading experts on the U.S. railway system?

In his third article, completed toward the end of November 1898, Mahan reordered his arguments and placed even greater emphasis on the importance of considering the economic dimensions of the war.[127] He now argued that the scale of American panic and the diversion of so many warships from Adm. Sampson's main fleet mattered because it had undermined the offensive potential of the U.S. Navy to attack the enemy's commercial system.[128] Not only had the United States failed to defend itself adequately against the possibility of attacks on its own commerce, in other words, it had also failed to strike adequately at the enemy's commerce. The Navy's primary mission, he insisted, should always be to exploit de facto command of the sea to blockade the enemy and destroy its commerce. After reviewing the technical methods of capturing enemy property on the sea and concisely explaining all the legal ins and outs of contraband law versus blockade law (reflecting his many talks on the subject with John Bassett Moore), Mahan averred that commerce destruction and economic attack lay at the heart of sea power.[129]

> Blockade, however, is but one form of the unbloody pressure brought to bear upon an enemy by interruption of his commerce. The stoppage of commerce, in whole or in part, exhausts without fighting. It compels peace without sacrificing life. It is the most

scientific warfare, because the least sanguinary, and because, like the highest strategy, it is directed against the communications,— the resources,—not the persons, of the enemy. It has been the glory of sea-power that its ends are attained by draining men of their dollars instead of their blood. Eliminate the attack upon an enemy's sea-borne commerce from the conditions of naval war,—in which heretofore it has been always a most important factor,—and the sacrifice of life will be proportionately increased, for two reasons: First, the whole decision of the contest will rest upon actual conflict; and, second, failing decisive results in battle, the war will be prolonged, because by retaining his trade uninjured the enemy retains all his money power to keep up his armed forces.[130]

In this and the articles that followed, Mahan contended that the Navy should have and could have applied the blockade of Cuba tighter and sooner despite the shortage of suitable craft to carry out interdictions.[131] He further insisted that "the establishment and maintenance of the blockade therefore was, in the judgement of the present writer, not only the first step in order, but also the first, by far, in importance, open to the Government of the United States."[132] The commercial blockade of Cuba, he thus intimated, represented the foundation of American strategy throughout the war.

Mahan's claims for the importance of the blockade during the Spanish conflict were corroborated by French Chadwick in his own history of the war published twelve years later. Chadwick, it will be recalled, had been flag captain and chief of staff to Adm. Sampson and thus in a good position to know.[133] Although his account mentions the frequent receipt of "pressing telegrams" from Washington to make the blockade effective, and provides much detail on individual actions, it contains almost no analysis.[134] More naval historians, fixated on combat operations, seldom even mention the blockade of Cuba let alone discuss its wider significance. Army historian David Trask acknowledged it was likely a major factor in undermining the Spanish willingness to fight but adds nothing more.[135] The truth is that, except for a chapter in the French Chadwick's old history, we know little about the blockade from U.S. sources other than it happened. From Spanish (and British) sources, we may glean rather more—that, in fact, the U.S. Navy lacked the resources to enforce the blockade of Cienfuegos and many other ports and harbors; plenty of matériel and supplies reached Cuba from Jamaica, Mexico, and Colombia, but for want of money, organization, and time, not enough to affect the final outcome.

THE IMMUNITY DEBATE

Mahan was spurred to emphasize the importance of blockade in war by a movement then afoot within the United States calling for "the freedom from seizure on the sea of private property in time of war."[136] Some background is necessary. The day after declaring war, the United States issued a proclamation announcing its intention to conduct commercial warfare against Spanish trade according to the rules laid down under the 1856 Treaty of Paris, even though technically neither the United States nor Spain were signatories. In practical terms, this meant that the United States meant to exercise the right of capture and confiscation of Spanish-owned merchantmen and their cargoes. Within the business community, this conjured up painful memories of the depredations by Raphael Semmes and the *Alabama* during the Civil War.[137] A few days later, accordingly, a group of Massachusetts businessmen started a petition calling on the U.S. government to repudiate the belligerent's right to confiscate Spanish-owned property caught by U.S. warships (clearly hoping the Spanish would reciprocate and not confiscate any of their property, if captured). This of course directly contradicted the Navy's strategy. The department became aware of the petition after Henry Lee Higginson, senior partner of the eponymous Boston bankers, alerted Secretary Long that it was circulating and asked him if he wished it to be encouraged. "I shall not sign it unless you like to have it signed; otherwise, if you like to have it signed, I can get plenty of signatures of the best kind," Higginson told Long.[138] Long's reply has not survived, thought it was probably in the negative. In any case, the petition was forgotten for the duration.

However, directly after the formal end of the war, on November 4, 1898, Charles H. Butler, a New York–based international lawyer, revived the idea of immunity from capture of private property at sea— referred to hereafter simply as "immunity"—in the form of a petition addressed to President McKinley.[139] Over the next several weeks, Butler summoned business organizations throughout the country to endorse his "memorial," as the petition was termed. On the morning of November 15, Mahan awoke to the news that the editors of the *New York Times* supported Butler's enlightened initiative and had expressed their hope that the city's chamber of commerce would do likewise.[140] Mahan thought the proposal was a terrible idea, and the same morning he sat down to write a detailed explanation why. His letter was published on November 17, ten days before he had finished his third article for *McClure's Magazine* on the Spanish-American War, quoted at length above.[141] Once again, contemporary issues intruded on and interacted with his treatment of historical events.

Contra the proponents of "immunity," Mahan argued that naval warfare was not at all analogous to land warfare. He ridiculed the memorial's suggestion that soldiers in combat zones were punctilious in respecting theoretical property rights (he had known Gen. William T. Sherman very well, having met him during the Civil War at the end of his march through Georgia). In this assessment he received public support from Cdr. Charles Stockton, the Navy's leading expert on war and law, who further pointed out that during the recent Franco-Prussian War (1870–71), the invading German army had requisitioned over 600 million francs of property for which the owners were never compensated.[142] Stockton was even more direct in suggesting, albeit politely, that Butler and his supporters were spouting nonsense.

But the real target of Mahan's riposte lay elsewhere. Commercial activity, he argued, especially when derived from international trade, represented the basis of national life and thus represented a legitimate object of attack. As he had shown in his books, the taxes on commercial activity generated the revenues for the state necessary to wage war; such revenues could be spent either directly on war making or set aside as collateral to underpin the borrowing of even larger sums by the state with which to prosecute a war. In Mahan's own words: "The exchange of goods, commerce, is the financial life of a nation, and it is now a commonplace that money is the sinews of war. Commerce, therefore, and especially maritime commerce, bears to the military life of a nation at large just the relation that the communications of an army in campaign bear to the efficiency of that army . . . destroy the commerce of a nation, and its military life is so far sapped as to reduce its powers of resistance, and so to hasten peace."[143]

Warming to his theme, Mahan pointed out that in view of the economic dependencies between nations—one of the key characteristics of what is known today as globalization—any disruption to part of the system was certain to disrupt the wider global economic system and consequently exacerbate financial losses for commercial interests. Anticipating Ivan Bloch and Norman Angell, long celebrated as the authors of the idea that globalization and economic interdependence made future wars unthinkable, Mahan suggested that such economic disruption should be a powerful deterrent to nation-states contemplating war. In his own words: "It is to the increase and extension of commercial bonds, and their intricate blendings, whereby so many communities are affected financially by an outbreak of war, that we owe, more than to any other one influence, the comparative rarity of war now." By contrast, he continued, to "assure the nations, and the general community, that their financial interests will suffer no more than the additional tax for maintaining active hostilities . . . and you will have removed one of the most efficient preventives of war."[144] With an eye fixed firmly on the future, Mahan pointed out that as a growing naval power (though with a negligible merchant marine), the United States would soon be well placed to wield the weapon of sea power.

For many—perhaps most—readers of the *New York Times* (then and now), Mahan's emphasis on the importance of economic factors ahead of naval combat may have come as a surprise. His reputation, after all, was built on his supposed advocacy of battleships and the paramount importance of victory in battle. Yet his more nuanced line of argument would have been recognizable to anyone who had kept abreast of his writings, especially to those who had read his 1894 article "Anglo-American Reunion." Written while commanding the *Chicago*, Mahan had observed that "Blows at commerce are blows at the communications of the state; they intercept its nourishment, they starve its life, they cut the roots of its power, the sinews of war. While war remains a factor, a sad but inevitable factor of our history, it is a fond hope that commerce can be exempt from its operations, because in very truth blows against it are the most deadly that can be struck."[145]

During the closing week of November 1898, readers of the *New York Times* were treated to a verbal joust between the various interested parties, each refusing to charge directly toward each other.[146] Reading these letters, one is instantly reminded of Mahan's comment in *French Revolution and Empire* when discussing perspectives at the beginning of the nineteenth century on exactly the same basic issue: "starting from such fundamentally different premises, interested parties might argue on indefinitely in parallel lines, without ever approaching a point of contact."[147] Mahan wrote from the perspective of belligerent rights, while his opponents wrote from the perspective of neutral rights—and never the twain did meet.

At the beginning of December 1898, the immunity lobby won high-level endorsement. Butler's memorial had gathered sufficient public support that McKinley felt obliged to mention the subject in his State of the Union address, telling Congress,

> The experiences of the last year bring forcibly home to us a sense of the burdens and the waste of war. We desire, in common with most civilized nations, to reduce to the lowest possible point the damage sustained in time of war by peaceable trade and commerce. It is true we may suffer in such cases less than other communities, but all nations are damaged more or less by the state of uneasiness and apprehension into which an outbreak of hostilities throws the entire commercial world. It should be our object, therefore, to minimize, so far as practicable, this inevitable loss and disturbance. This purpose can probably best be accomplished by an international

agreement to regard all private property at sea as exempt from capture or destruction by the forces of belligerent powers.[148]

The editors of the *New York Times* congratulated themselves, smugly
reporting that President McKinley "adopts in his message substantially and almost exactly the arguments for that policy embodied in the
memorial presented to him."[149] But the real credit (or discredit) for
McKinley's move lay elsewhere.

Already in August 1898, Tsar Nicholas II of Russia had proposed
an international conference to discuss "ideas in the furtherance of
national economy and international peace in the interests of human-
ity," what became known at the First Hague peace or disarmament
conference. Of course, the tsar was not motivated by humanitarian
considerations. The reality was that the Russians did not currently possess the financial wherewithal to modernize their army (as Germany
and Austria-Hungary were in the process of doing) and at the same
time modernize their navy (as Britain and France were doing), and
thus were cynically hoping to buy themselves some financial breathing
space by encouraging the other powers to pause their rearmament.
However, such was the power of the international peace movement
among Western nations (particularly strong in the United States) that
McKinley could not afford to spurn such an invitation.[150] In contemporary parlance, the optics would have been poor. As one Republican
Party official close to McKinley admitted after talking over the subject
with him, "no one here expects that the conference will have great
practical results," yet the president felt that his administration "should
for political reasons take part in the conference most elaborately and
conspicuously. It will be a very good thing to talk about on the stump
next year, and will help to sweeten the rather bitter pill of warfare and
war taxation."[151]

To lead the U.S. delegation, President McKinley and State Department secretary John Hay picked Andrew Dickson White—historian,
politician, diplomat, and then-ambassador to Germany—known to be
sympathetic to the aspirations of the peace movement. White, however, was mistrustful of the proffered chalice, privately admitting to

his friends that "I had hoped to evade the Hague business, but the appointment came in such a way that I had no choice but to take it."[152] At Secretary of State John Hay's urging, the president also appointed Capt. Mahan, regarding him not only as an authority on the naval aspects of the issue but also hoping to exploit his celebrity to raise the profile of the U.S. delegation.[153] That it was Hay who nominated Mahan is consistent with the claim by Hay's first biographer that "Mahan was seeing Secretary of State John Hay rather frequently during the period" and enjoyed his confidence.[154]

It falls outside the scope of this work to recount all the work of the first peace conference convened at The Hague over the summer of 1899. For Mahan, only the immunity issue really mattered. Much to the annoyance of the *New York Times,* the U.S. delegation made only a half-hearted attempt to get the subject added to the existing conference agenda.[155] Besides, as the private correspondence between White and Secretary Hay makes clear, the focus of U.S. effort lay elsewhere, in securing arbitration treaties.[156] Nevertheless, there were some informal discussions of the subject of immunity. Mahan, however, declined to participate in any of these unofficial discussions and along with the British naval delegate, Vice Adm. "Jacky" Fisher, made plain to all his disapproval of the whole idea. In his diary, or at least in the version of it that appeared eighteen years later in his published memoirs, White recalled

a long meeting of the American delegation, which elaborated the final draft of our communication . . . on the immunity of private property on the high seas. Various passages were stricken out, some of them—and, indeed, one of the best—in deference to the ideas of Captain Mahan, who, though he is willing, under instructions from the government, to join in presenting the memorial, does not wish to sign anything which can possibly be regarded as indicating a personal belief in the establishment of such immunity. His is the natural view of a sailor; but the argument with which he supports it does not at all convince me. It is that during war we should do everything possible to weaken and worry the adversary, in order that he may be the sooner ready for peace; but this argument proves too much, since it would oblige us, if logically carried out, to go back to the marauding and atrocities of the Thirty Years War.[157]

Though this entry was not authentic in that it does not appear in the original diary, the recollection was accurate enough in representing Mahan's position and thus is instructive. White's correspondence makes clear that he regarded Mahan as a nuisance and found his worldview morally repugnant. Worse still, the captain was annoyingly competent. Grudgingly, White admitted that it was Mahan's simple naval mind, not the learned jurists, that discerned the pitfalls in the case his colleagues were trying to build—which, had they been put forward, would certainly have been repudiated back home and caused the United States much diplomatic embarrassment.[158]

Nevertheless, writing to Secretary Hay after the conference ended, White poured scorn on the "the gallant captain" and his views on immunity. He condescendingly advised that "It seems to me that a lawyer's view rather than that of the most eminent naval authority may well be taken of the subject as a whole."[159] In the years ahead, Mahan would encounter this haughty attitude many more times when presenting his contrary opinion on the subject. It irked him no end that international lawyers arrogated to themselves a special authority to dictate on the subject of law and war when they had no conception of the latter, or, more often, simply ignored this element in the equation. What is more, as we shall see in the next chapters, Mahan said so publicly.

PART III

CHAPTER 8

THE RECASTING OF
SEA POWER

(1899–1905)

*The Bar Association of the United States has manifestly cast aside
the Sword of Liberty. Justice and Law have ignored the significance of
the Great Seal of the United States, with its emblematic olive branch
and thirteen arrows, "all proper," and now claim that, without force,
Law and moral suasion have carried us through one hundred years
of history . . . a stranger would have inferred that at last the lawyers
of America had discovered the sovereign panacea of a Government
without force, either visible or in reserve. I was in hopes the Civil War
had dispelled this dangerous illusion, but it seems not.*

—WILLIAM T. SHERMAN, FEBRUARY 5, 1890[1]

BY THE TIME MAHAN HAD completed his service at the first Hague
Peace Conference, he had become a household name in the United
States. On August 13, 1899, the *New York Times* informed its readers
that "Captain Mahan" had boarded a liner in Liverpool sailing for
New York.[2] For the next seven or eight years, his movements would
regularly be reported in the social pages and his opinions sought
and commented on in newspaper editorials. Editors on both sides
of the Atlantic fell over themselves with offers to publish his words,

promising top dollar. Mahan was at the height of his intellectual powers and influence, and his views commanded near-universal respect.

While still in Europe, as the peace conference was winding down,
Mahan had contemplated picking up where he had left off and completing some unfinished projects. Declining an offer from a British
publisher to write on the strategic implications of Russian expansionism in the Far East, very much a topic du jour, Mahan expressed his
desire to scale back his writing on contemporary events in order to
free up more time for his scholarship. "Since my *Life of Nelson* was
completed, near two and a half years ago," he explained in a letter to
the prominent naval journalist James Thursfield, "I have been entirely
stopped from serious book work by occasional articles, and the necessity of limiting myself very strictly in that direction has been more
and more forced upon my mind. I have two books which I have been
intending to write for two years, and I must not postpone them farther than my return home."[3] These books were *Lessons of the War
with Spain, and Other Articles*, an omnibus of Mahan's articles on the
subject first published by *McClure's Magazine*; and *Sea Power in Its
Relations to the War of 1812*, the third and final installment of his sea
power trilogy, a manuscript he had been working at sporadically for
practically a decade.[4]

A fortnight after sending this letter, however, Mahan changed his
mind and opted for a different direction. He informed his publisher
that now, after finishing *Lessons of the War with Spain*, he intended to
write a textbook for use in British schools.[5] Sampson Low, Marston,
Searle, & Rivington, the publisher who had approached him with the
suggestion, advised that there was a considerable market for such a
volume, and by implication considerable money to be made. Refocus-
ing on the textbook necessarily meant returning his book on the War
of 1812 to the back burner. Mahan's decision was not simply a function of his desire to earn money, though it was certainly a consideration. The real reason was that he still could not see how to frame the
structure of the book—to create an analytic skeleton around which to
organize the myriad facts he had accumulated and the complex arguments he wished to present.

At the same time, to his dismay, Mahan grasped that many of his readers seemed confused by what he had already written, evidenced by some of the reactions to his published thoughts during the recent debate over the immunity from capture of private property at sea. Increasingly seeing the subject as important, he was anxious to correct these misconceptions—which were not entirely the fault of his readers, for since the publication of his last major monograph, eight years previously, his views on the workings of sea power had undergone considerable modification, especially his views on the importance and role of commerce destroying. Entwined with his desire to clarify his concept of sea power, Mahan wished also to demonstrate to everyone that his model based on historical studies was applicable to the future as well. To this end, he redoubled his effort to understand the precise workings of the international trading system in order to be able to see more clearly the processes and mechanisms of rigorously applied naval pressure against commerce and so to better explain to his skeptics the true potency of sea power.

Mahan faced several obstacles, however. As he had found when writing *The Influence of Sea Power upon the French Revolution and Empire*, there simply were no good economic histories of the period, nor indeed on war and economics generally. Although Henry Adams' nine-volume *History of the United States of America* contained some useful material, it was too generalized for his purposes.[6] Except for Adam Smith's *The Wealth of Nations*, which Mahan read closely, major treatises written in English dealing with the relationship between economics and war were few.[7] These deficiencies in the secondary literature obliged Mahan to expend considerable time and effort to do the necessary primary-source research himself. "My present reading for *1812* has forced me to cover much of our own history, not only since the Revolution, but also economical data prior to the Revolution," he reported to John Brown in May 1901, adding that "I have now a pretty fair understanding of the *War of 1812* and a very miserable showing it is for our people."[8]

Moreover, in order to demonstrate the continuing relevance of sea power theory, Mahan was compelled to study not only the economic system as it existed nearly one hundred years before but also the modern system. He needed to determine if, and if so how, the points and mechanisms of pressure on the economic system had shifted. That required him to come to grips with the post-1870 transformation of global trade, known to scholars today as the first period of globalization.[9] Not until around 1902 had the insights he had gained from his recent research finished percolating through his brain and emboldened him to publish his preliminary thoughts on the strategic implications of globalization. These we will examine below.

Mahan thus had intellectual as well as pecuniary reasons for wanting to defer the completion of his next monograph in favor of writing the textbook. Indeed, he seems to have seen the latter and a necessary precursor to the former. It offered him an opportunity to iron out some of the wrinkles in his overarching concept of sea power, and to correct some of the misperceptions of what he had previously argued on the subject. In a sense, Mahan seems to have envisioned his proposed textbook as an abridgement and an update of his previous *Influence* books. In December 1900, he explained to the naval historian John Laughton that

> I have at last settled down—at least I hope so—to a re-presentation and condensation of my two books on Sea Power; but while the argument—main—remains the same, I rather propose a considerable difference of treatment, and in order to the completeness of my idea must strike its roots a little further back, and carry the argument a little further forward; all which requires more reading and *you* know how that sort of thing widens on you. Luckily, I am immensely interested, even absorbed, so though protracted the task is not tedious.[10]

In the spring of 1901, however, Samson Low canceled the textbook project and upset Mahan's plans. Undaunted, the captain returned to his American publisher and floated the idea of repackaging the material already gathered into a textbook for the American market.[11] Although initially interested, by the end of 1901 Little, Brown too rejected the proposal.[12] In light of the later confusion surrounding his work, it is a shame that Mahan never completed the consolidation of his ideas on sea power in an easy-to-digest form.

But these developments lay in the future. On his return from The Hague in the fall of 1899, instead of reducing his output of magazine articles in order to make more time for his scholarly writing, Mahan increased his writings on contemporary geopolitical affairs. Within a matter of weeks, he contracted with *Harper's Magazine* to produce three articles commenting on developments in Asia. These appeared between December 1899 and May 1900 and were later republished under a single cover, along with a couple of others, under the title *The Problem of Asia and Its Effect upon International Policies*. He also wrote several stand-alone pieces. In April 1900, despite promising his publisher he would resume work on his book projects, he accepted yet another lucrative commission from the *Century Magazine*.[13] Between 1900 and 1902, Mahan published a staggering twenty-four articles that appeared across a broad range of periodicals. He had more work than he could reasonably manage and began to miss deadlines. What is more, "I get awfully tired at times of ransacking my brains, and working up what little they yield into readable form," he confessed to his old friend Bouverie Clark in early 1902. "To wake in the morning and feel I need to do nothing, not even get up if I don't choose, seems the height of bliss," he sighed.[14] "You can understand that, being well along in years, I look longingly to what may, if realized, simplify somewhat my problems of life," he told Leo Maxse, the editor of the British *National Review*.[15] So why could he not simply say no?

The answer is simple: Mahan had achieved a standard of living that he did not want to lose. For the first time in his life, he found himself living in comfort. He and his family enjoyed a large modern house located in a fashionable neighborhood in Manhattan. He belonged to several prestigious New York clubs, where he usually spent his afternoons, allowing him to keep abreast of contemporary events with access not just to all of the leading British and U.S. periodicals, but also to the leading men of the day.[16] Yet although Mahan was well off, he was by no means financially independent. Worries over the financial security of his immediate and extended family gnawed at him. Mahan's pecuniary anxieties in refusing magazine editors were compounded by their irresistible habit of raising the money offered whenever he exhibited any unwillingness to write. In late 1901, for instance, Leo Maxse offered him a staggering $3,000 for a string of six articles. Mahan just could not pass up so much easy money. "You should be under bonds as a disturber of the peace—my peace—by advancing such propositions as in your letter of 6th," Mahan replied to Maxse in jocular, albeit sardonic manner.[17]

To modern eyes, it may seem extraordinary that Mahan's prolix writing commanded such respect and high prices. Though he had made his name and reputation through his sea power books, editors on both sides of the Atlantic regarded "Captain Mahan" (his nom de plume) as much more than a simple naval historian. Not only was he an internationally recognized expert on contemporary geopolitics, but he always delivered good copy. Though his style was undeniably long-winded, he was nevertheless an effective writer, skilled at painting a geopolitical landscape with rapid and broad strokes of the brush. He could be depended on to provide readers with a coherent summary of the problem under discussion, and to identify the various disparate threads and show how they all connected. He also managed to advance his opinions unencumbered, with little political bias. Maxse admitted to Mahan that he was prepared to pay top dollar for his articles because they always attracted much interest.[18]

In the field of international affairs, editors saw Mahan as possessing an unusually well-informed opinion. It was no secret that he knew and was consulted by many leading political, business, and intellectual figures of the day. They, in turn, paid close attention to what he wrote.[19] "For Heaven's sake, my dear Captain, do not talk about your activities ending," the new vice president—and soon president—Theodore Roosevelt wrote Mahan in March 1901, after the latter revealed his despondency at the apparent lack of public interest in a recent article: "We must rely upon you as one of the foremost educators of public thought, and I trust for many years to come."[20]

Across the Atlantic, senior statesmen held Mahan in equally high regard.[21] In September 1902, Prime Minister Arthur James Balfour nominated Mahan to succeed Lord Acton as the Regius Professorship of Modern History at Cambridge University.[22] Balfour, probably the most intellectually gifted statesman of his day and a scholar in his own right, first met the captain back in 1893 when the *Chicago* visited England, and they had stayed in touch ever since.[23] Like Mahan, Balfour also tended to view international affairs through an economic lens. He too was fascinated by recent global economic developments. He not only admired Mahan's books but regarded them as major works of scholarship. "As histories, they seem to me quite unequalled for vivid interest and grasp," Balfour congratulated Mahan, "and an Englishman will learn from them more of the external history of his country than he could collect from all the tomes referring to the same subject by which they have been preceded."[24]

In putting forward Mahan's name for the Regius Professorship, Balfour acknowledged that appointing an American to one of the premier academic positions in Britain would excite public comment, while the selection of a naval officer ahead of a career scholar would very likely prove deeply unpopular with professional academics.[25] (It did—on both scores!) But Balfour was willing to fight to get Mahan: when King Edward VII disapproved of the nomination, Balfour pushed back. After consulting with the Duke of Devonshire, another leading British statesman and the chairman of the Cabinet Defence Committee, Balfour implored the king to reconsider: "I think is a mistake to suppose that Mahan is a merely *naval* historian in any narrow or technical sense. He is in truth *a historian of the British Empire from a military point of view*, and I do not think that a man who has done so much to bring home to our countrymen the nature of the process by which the Empire . . . has been built up, should be considered merely in the light of a professional historian, interested only in professional matters."[26] The Duke of Devonshire, it is worth noting, held Mahan's scholarship in equally high esteem.

WRITING ON CONTEMPORARY AFFAIRS

To understand why Mahan's opinion was in such demand is not difficult to see. At the turn of the century, there was a worldwide explosion
of interest in geopolitical affairs. For better or for worse, the Spanish-American War marked a watershed in the United States' foreign
relations with the outside world. The ease with which the republic
defeated a European colonial power—even one as decrepit as Spain—
generated a sense of national triumph. President William McKinley's
postwar decisions to annex Hawaii and retain the Philippines provoked far less (though by no means negligible) hue and cry than many
in government had feared. Domestic support for a more expansionist
foreign policy had taken root within the literate and politically energetic electorate. But to what end, and where would it end?

As will be recalled from earlier chapters, American expansion
stemmed substantially though not solely from a desire for sociopolitical stability through escape from the seemingly endless cycle of
economic boom and bust. The turmoil consequent to the Panic of
1893 in particular had generated a level of unhappiness within the
country that amounted to nothing less than a crisis in American capitalism. Commentators and politicians of all stripes worried openly
about social disorder. Around 1896, the U.S. economy appeared to
be turning the corner, but expansionism remained at the forefront of
public consciousness. Broad economic recovery in Europe, combined
with a series of calamitous Russian harvests, created a new surge in
foreign demand for U.S. wheat, propelling exports to record heights
and stimulated an upswing in domestic prosperity.[27] "That good times
are coming is now beyond doubt," a relieved Teddy Roosevelt told
Massachusetts senator Henry Cabot Lodge in August 1897. "Wheat
and Gold together, and the fact that the tariff is out of the way, and
the uneasiness abroad, all help."[28]

The years that followed saw considerable debate over how the
upswing could best be sustained and social stability at home safe-
guarded. One popular solution, pushed by farmers, was comprehensive reform of the home market, entailing greater government
intervention into the market and the redistribution of wealth, which

opponents derided as tantamount to socialism. The leading alternative, besides embarking on a war of conquest, was to "look outward" and adopt a policy of imperialism.[29] To Brooks Adams writing in 1898, these seemed the only practical solutions to the perennial problem of "over-production." "America has been irresistibly impelled to produce a large industrial surplus—a surplus, should no change occur, which will be larger in a few years than anything ever before known. Upon the existence of this surplus hinges the future, for the United States must provide sure and adequate outlets for her products, or be in danger of gluts more dangerous to her society than many panics such as 1873 and 1893."[30]

In the 1900 elections, President McKinley and the Republican Party ran on an explicit platform of expansion, decisively defeating the Democratic challenger, William Jennings Bryan. Throughout the election campaign, an intense national debate had gone on in newspapers and journals over the direction and degree to which the republic should assert itself in the world.

Mahan, though somewhat doubtful over the Philippines, was a longtime exponent of "looking outward" and cheered this shift in foreign policy, both privately and publicly. "We have a long row to hoe yet," he remarked to Senator Lodge in February 1899. Nevertheless, "the country is now fairly embarked on a career which will be beneficent to the world and honorable to ourselves in the community of nations."[31] Mahan contributed to this debate by presenting the case for expansion in terms of safeguarding the United States' long-term economic security, with a strategic twist. The author of *The Influence of Sea Power upon History*, who habitually viewed the world through his economics-tinted lens, had long maintained that all states viewed international commerce as the ultimate "prize" in the global power stakes. The competition for foreign markets therefore was certain to be fierce and might even lead to conflict. Writing for *Harper's Magazine* in the early spring of 1899, Mahan explained that "it has come to pass, in this closing year of a century, that the commerce of the world—which implies as a main incident the utilization of the sea, the chief medium of commerce—has become the prize for which all the great states of the world are in competition. Some, possibly, do not expect ever to be losers; but all either wish a greater share than they now have, or at the least to preserve their present proportion."[32]

In the introduction to *Lessons of the War with Spain*, published later the same year, Mahan pointed at Asia and warned of the clash of Western interests in China, observing that "it is evidentially a matter of economical—and therefore of political—importance to civilized nations to prevent the too preponderant control there of any one of their number, lest the energies of their own citizens be debarred from a fair opportunity to share in these advantages."[33]

A couple of years later, in 1902, Mahan extended this line of thought by explicitly linking international trade and geopolitical rivalry, and in a way designed to illustrate the continued applicability of his concept of sea power.

> The provision of markets for the production of an ever-increasing number of inhabitants is a leading political problem of the day, the solution for which is sought by methods commercial and methods political, so essentially combinative . . . that direct military action would be only a development of them, a direct consequent; not a breach of continuity in spirit, however it might be in form. As the interaction of commerce and finance shows a unity in the modern civilized world, so does the struggle for new markets, and for predominance in old, reveal the unsubdued diversity. Here every state is for itself; and in every great state the look for the desired object is outward.[34]

In endorsing expansion while warning of potential conflict, furthermore, Mahan cautioned his fellow citizens to view foreign rivals with greater respect and less complacency. Another recurring theme in Mahan's writings from this time was the necessity for Americans to act promptly to secure the economic security of their grandchildren—in other words, to look fifty years into the future. In his judgment, economic opportunities existed at present but they were rapidly vanishing.[35]

By the end of the 1890s, most Americans came to see overseas expansion as the panacea for their domestic economic problems, eyeing especially "the China market as the solution to the closed frontier and the industrial glut at home."[36] American businessmen proclaimed that given a fair field and no favor, they could outcompete the rest of the world.[37] In his classic monograph *China Market: America's Quest for Informal Empire, 1893–1901*, historian Thomas J. McCormick charted the shift in American China policy away from the traditional laissez-faire approach of Grover Cleveland toward the more assertive "Open Door" policy advocated by Secretary of State John Hay during the McKinley presidency. McCormick noted that "1899 produced a bumper crop of written and spoken words in behalf of some dramatic effort to gain universal support for the open door in China."[38]

In January 1898, however, Germany seized the Port of Kiachaow on the Shangdong Peninsula, and a couple of months later wrung a ninety-nine-year lease from the Chinese government for some five hundred square miles of Chinese territory. The German action started a scramble by the other industrial powers to establish their own treaty ports, and talk of apportioning the Celestial Kingdom into exclusive economic zones of influence followed in its wake. Americans worried that in the ensuing territorial scramble for China, the United States would be left empty handed, or rather that the prize of China market might be snatched from the United States' rightful grasp by the Old World empires.

In Mahan's judgment, the Russian Empire posed the greatest threat to Chinese integrity and thus to American long-term economic interests.[39] Possessing a contiguous border with China, the Russians possessed an enormous advantage relative to the Western powers. "The problem of Asia is looming largely, if vaguely, upon the future and may be precipitated at a moment," Mahan predicted darkly in April 1900.[40] Several months later he wrote directly to President McKinley, imploring him to place no stock in Russian promises of economic cooperation in China. In Mahan's view, as demonstrated at the recent Hague Peace Conference, the tsar habitually said one thing while doing another and therefore was not to be trusted.[41]

Mahan was not the first to suggest that Russian expansionism
threatened to block the United States' place in the China market.[42]
One of the first to connect the dots between Russia, China, and American prosperity was Charles Conant, the New York–based economist
whose pioneering work on business cycles we have already discussed
and whose signature idea was the concept of surplus capital, a more
sophisticated exposition of the popular theory of overproduction.[43]
Conant, readers will recall, moved in the same circles as Mahan and
wrote for the same journals; he had a gift for explaining the economic
issues of the day in plain language.[44]

In February 1899, several months before the appearance of Mahan's thoughts on the same subject in *Harper's Magazine*, Conant published a piece in the *North American Review* drawing attention to the
implications of Russia's systematic program of economic moderniza-
tion and monetary reforms. "Russia is organizing the machinery of
her economic system in a manner to make her the early and dangerous
rival of the great industrial nations," Conant warned.[45] At its present
rate of growth, he predicted, "Russia promises in another generation
to be the great competitor of the Anglo-Saxon race for the commercial and military supremacy of the world." So rich was the Russian
Empire in natural resources, and so focused her national leadership,
he feared, Russia might become "almost irresistible."[46] In an article
for the *Forum* published several months later—a few weeks after Mahan's article came out in *Harper's Magazine*—Conant expanded on his
theme and joined it to his surplus capital theory. Again, his conclusion
was basically the same as Mahan's, that "the civilized nations of the
world are entering a contest for financial and commercial supremacy
upon a grander scale than any in the past."[47]

A year later, in another piece for the *Forum*, Conant again endorsed
Mahan's map of the geo-strategic landscape in Asia and echoed his
concern that economic rivalry in China might spill over into conflict:
"The time has come when the intensity of the struggle for new markets and for opportunities for investment has forced the great commercial nations, by the instinct of self-preservation, to demand that the
field of competition be kept open, even by the exercise, if necessary,

of paramount military forces. In supporting this demand the United States will obey the motive of enlightened self-interest which actuates other producing nations. She cannot take any other course without condemning herself to industrial stagnation at home."[48] In the same piece, anticipating the famous "heartland thesis" of British geographer Halford Mackinder, Conant foresaw that "intrenched [sic] in Central Asia, Russia, with her railways system completed, would be in a strategic position which would endanger not only all China, but also the English possessions in India."[49]

Articles like these, by Conant and others, were useful to Mahan not only because they broadly corroborated his judgments but also because they obviated the necessity for him to spell out to his readers the importance of the China market to future U.S. prosperity. He merely needed to allude to this earlier work, knowing that he was addressing a well-educated and well-read contemporary audience. In part III of *The Problem of Asia*, for instance, "The argument of these papers rests upon the assumption, now quite generally accepted, that in the wide movement of expansion which has characterized the last quarter of the closing century, the Pacific Ocean in general and eastern Asia in particular are indicated as the predominant objects of interest, common to all nations, both in the near and in the remote future."[50] His reliance on this sort of shorthand reference has tended to conceal from later readers, unfamiliar with then-current debates, just how much stress he laid on economic security and how much he relied on the work of others to help get the message across. It should never be forgotten than Mahan was writing for his contemporaries, not posterity.

In the years that followed, Mahan remained transfixed by the Russian threat, constantly urging the McKinley administration that the best way to guarantee Chinese integrity and thus U.S. access to foreign markets was to maintain a firm foreign policy backed by a powerful navy. So great was his concern about Russia, however, that at times he had doubts that this would be sufficient. "I feel," he warned Theodore Roosevelt in March 1901, "that neither we nor Great Britain, separate or combined, can adequately check Russia by main force in Northern China; and that therefore naval power always at hand &

available in the Yangtze valley—the heart of China in every sense of
the word—is the true counter-check."[51] It is important to understand
that Mahan was talking here about the importance of sea power to
achieve economic influence in peacetime, not a military edge in wartime. The Yangtze was the economic heart of China. A year later,
writing to the Germanophobic British editor of the *National Review*,
"Russia I believe far more dangerous to you [Britain] than Germany,
& the latter has ever Russia on her back, I am reading diversely and
desultorily on the whole question & its cognates, fleet distribution,
European politics, colonial statistics etc., my mind being more and
more impressed with a certain solidarity of the whole. I trust this will
facilitate and better my treatment of the whole."[52]

Over the course of 1902, Mahan produced three major articles for
this journal detailing the threat to British interests posed by Russian
expansionism in various regions.[53] But Mahan's preoccupation with
Russia did not exist in a vacuum: like Conant's, it developed alongside
a close interest in the contemporary global economy.

In the previous chapters we have seen how as time passed, Mahan
looked more deeply into the workings of economic systems, recognizing that the effective application of sea power (and naval force)
necessitated a detailed understanding of how the global economy
functioned on a day-to-day level. More importantly still, between late
1899 and early 1902, Mahan came to the realization that economic
systems—old and modern—were fundamentally dynamic in nature.
Already aware of the economic interdependencies between nations,
over the same period he also came to appreciate just what this meant
and the strategic implications thereof. As the economic dimension
became ever more central to his concept of sea power, he increasingly
explained the primary purpose of navies in such terms.

Mahan's improved understanding of economic systems enhanced
his awareness of their inherent fragility. Back in 1895 he had expressed

his concern that workers in modern societies—industrialized, urbanized, and democratic—would be far less willing than their grandfathers to tolerate lower standards of living in wartime due to economic derangement. To use his term, the "moral stamina" of modern societies appeared much weaker.[54] But at that time he did not really develop this idea. After 1899 Mahan gave this insight much closer attention, realizing that it had major implications for his sea power thesis. Very simply, if society's tolerance of disruption and hardship had declined, then it followed that the effects of sea power (through systematic commerce destruction) would be felt more acutely and be more likely to generate significant political pressure more rapidly.

Here, of course, Mahan was doing no more than amplifying the (at the time) well-known ideas of Ivan Bloch, the Polish railway tycoon and financier–turned–military theorist. Predicated on the supposition that industrial-urban societies were fragile and that protracted war between the Great Powers risked socioeconomic collapse, Bloch prophesied that "the future of war [is] not fighting, but famine, not the slaying of men, but the bankruptcy of nations and the break-up of the whole social organization."[55] Bloch, it should be noted, also attended the 1899 Hague Peace Conference, and each delegate was presented with a copy of his work printed in French, which of course Mahan read fluently.[56] Even if Mahan had not troubled to wade through this multivolume treatise while at the conference, he would certainly have been exposed to Bloch's ideas (which were much discussed), and it is inconceivable that the two did not meet.

To be clear, Mahan's mental picture of how the international economy worked remained far from complete. It was analogous to catching sight of a large ship in a fog: through the haze, one may discern the outline and scale of the vessel. Some parts of the superstructure could be seen quite clearly, others only approximately and fleetingly, and some remained obscured. Because of this, and also because the concepts with which he was engaging were so new and so complex, and often the appropriate terminology did not yet exist, Mahan invariably employed metaphor to describe the parts he could see and the parts he could only glimpse.

Mahan acquired these new understandings not through any flash of insight but gradually over a period of years. In the second install-ment of *The Problem of Asia*, published in *Harper's Magazine* in March 1900, Mahan provided a crude approximation of his vision:

> The concrete expression of this singular importance of the sea is the merchandise in transit, the increment from which constitutes the material prosperity of nations. Surrender control of that, and the empire of the sea is like unto Samson shorn of his hair. . . . The body does not—cannot—live off itself; it simply assimilates and distributes that which it receives from outside, and this indispens-able external nutriment corresponds to external commerce in the body political and economical, drawing support to the state from outside sources. From these sources, maritime commerce is the great channel of communication; hence its supreme importance to the support of war. To interrupt internal trade produces derange-ment of functional processes, which may conduce to the end of a war, or may not. . . . As to the stoppage of external commerce, by capturing the so-called "private" property embarked, there can be no doubt about the effect. It conduces directly to the ends of war by producing a bloodless exhaustion, compelling submission, and that at the least expense of life and suffering.[57]

In the third installment, published two months later, he clarified why international trade was so important to nations, and accordingly why disruption to that trade could be so damaging:

> Communications dominate war; broadly considered, they are the most important single element in strategy, political or military. . . . For reasons previously explained, transit in large quantities and for great distances is decisively more easy and copious by water than by land. The sea, therefore, is the great medium of communications—of commerce. The very sound, "commerce," brings with it a sug-gestion of the sea, for it is maritime commerce that has in all ages been the most fruitful of wealth; and wealth is but the concrete

expression of a nation's life, material and mental. The power, therefore to insure these communications to one's self, and to interrupt
them for an adversary, affects the very root of a nation's vigor.[58]

Clearly what Mahan was trying to do here was describe the nature of
economic systems and how the effects of (naval) commerce destruction
were felt not just by maritime industries but throughout the national
economy. The potency of sea power, accordingly, was measured by the
extent to which the enemy's entire economy became deranged in consequence of naval action; the greater this derangement, moreover, the
greater would be the impact felt by the enemy's society and therefore
the greater the level of pressure on their political leaders to negotiate
an end to the war.

In a July 1902 article for the *National Review*, Mahan made
another attempt to weave these threads together to create for his
readers a broad picture of the global system.[59] The article opens with
a brief summary of why sea power was important, combined with
his reasoning why this concept seemed applicable to the future. "It
seems demonstrable, therefore, that as commerce is the engrossing
and predominant interest of the world today, so, in consequence of its
acquired expansion, oversea commerce, oversea political acquisition,
and maritime commercial routes are now the primary objects of external policy among nations. The instrument for the maintenance of policy directed upon these objects is the Navy."[60] Mahan then proceeded
to describe the global system and how it worked, eloquently capturing
its fundamentally dynamic character and why it was so important to
understand this. Read carefully, his finely nuanced argument in the
lengthy passage that follows need no interpretation:

> As regards the commercial factor, never before in the history of
> the world has it been so inextricably commingled with politics.
> The interdependency of nations for the necessities and luxuries of
> life have been marvelously increased by the growth of population
> and the habits of comfort contracted by the peoples of Europe and
> America. . . . The unmolested course of commerce, reacting upon

itself, has contributed also to its own rapid development, a result furthered by the prevalence of a purely economical conception of national greatness during the larger part of the century. This, with the vast increase in the rapidity of communications, has multiplied and strengthened the bonds knitting the interests of nations to one another, till the whole now forms an articulated system, not only of prodigious size and activity, but of an excessive sensitiveness, unequalled in former ages. National nerves are exasperated by the delicacy of financial situations and national resistance to hardship is sapped by generations that have known war only by the battlefield, not in the prolonged endurance of privation and strictness extending through years and reaching every class of the community.

The preservation of commercial and financial interests constitutes now a political consideration of the first importance, making for peace and deterring from war; a fact well worthy of observation by those who would exempt maritime commercial intercourse from the operations of naval war, under the illusory plea of protecting private property at sea.

Ships and cargoes in transit upon the sea are private property in only one point of view, and that the narrowest. Internationally considered, they are national wealth engaged in reproducing and multiplying itself, to the intensification of the national power, and that by the most effective process; for it relieves the nation from feeding upon itself, and makes the whole outer world contribute to its support. It is therefore a most proper object of attack; more humane and more conducive to the objects of war, than the slaughter of men. A great check on war would be removed by assuring immunity to a nation's sea-borne trade, the life blood of its power, the assurer of its credit, the purveyor of its comfort.[61]

For Mahan, the grand-strategic geopolitician, the ultimate use of naval force meant the ability either to impose or deflect a blockade, an action that he believed posed a serious threat to a national economy.[62] Writing for *Collier's Weekly*, Mahan expanded that: "The object of a blockade proper is to embarrass the finances of a country by shutting its ports to foreign commerce, thus deranging one main feature of its general markets, and thereby bring confusion into the whole."[63]

Looking past his metaphors, one can see that Mahan's conceptualization of how the world worked and thus how sea power worked had matured considerably from his basic "common" analogy found in his earlier *Influence* books, now more than ten years old. Better yet from his point of view, the new model resonated far better with modern economic conditions and therefore better demonstrated the continuing relevance and validity of his underlying sea power theory. What is more, Mahan was explaining sea power unmistakably in economic terms, insisting on the centrality of national economic activity to a nation's warfighting potential. Remarkably, he now argued that "in the general scheme its [the Navy's] office is essentially defensive. It protects the economical processes which sustain national endurance, and thus secures the foundation on which the vigor of war rests."[64]

Mahan articulated these interconnections, and their importance relative to each other, in a subsequent article for *Collier's Weekly*, which appeared in September 1902.[65] "War has ceased to be the natural, or even normal, consideration of nations, and *military considerations are simply accessory and subordinate to the other greater interests, economical and commercial*, which they assure and so subserve. In this article itself, turning as it does on military discussion, the starting point and foundation is the necessity to secure commerce . . . *this order is that of actual relative importance to the nation of the three elements—commercial, political, military*."[66]

The novelty and sophistication of Mahan's geostrategic analysis comes into sharper focus when it is contrasted with that of his British contemporary Halford Mackinder, the director of the London School of Economics. Mackinder unveiled his "formula," as he termed it, designed to be of "practical value as setting into perspective some of the competing forces in current international politics," in a paper to the Royal Geographic Society titled "The Geographical Pivot of History."[67] Delivered in January 1904 but not published until April, Mackinder's "heartland thesis," as it is sometimes called, owed a considerable intellectual debt, both in style and in substance, to both

Mahan and to Charles Conant (whose work had appeared in early 1899). In his text, Mackinder acknowledged his debt to "Captain Mahan" but did not mention Conant, who was far less well known in Britain.[68] It has not previously been appreciated that Mahan and Mackinder not only knew each other but were in direct correspondence, though alas none of their letters have survived.[69]

Like Mahan, Mackinder painted on a large canvas, and his chief subject was the problems for the Western maritime powers posed by Russian expansionism. He too thought that when calculating relative geopolitical power, in the long run economic potential weighed more heavily than present military might. Like Conant, Mackinder predicted that "the [twentieth] century will not be old before all Asia is covered with railways. The spaces within the Russian Empire and Mongolia are so vast, and their potentialities in population, wheat, cotton, fuel, and metals so incalculably great, that it is inevitable that a vast economic world more or less apart, will there develop inaccessible to oceanic commerce."[70] Put simply, Mackinder envisioned that in the not too distant future, central Asia, crisscrossed with railroads and rich in natural resources, with a population soon to be "numbered by the hundred million," would become economically autarkic—self-sufficient and independent of the maritime world.[71] What would happen, he wondered, when interests collided: would the continental or the maritime powers prevail? The looming competition between the bear and the whale worried Mahan also.[72]

When Mahan, the apostle of sea power, and Mackinder, the apostle of land power, are compared, as they frequently are, analysts typically judge the former less advanced than the latter: Mahan appears to them gripped by an anachronistic worship of the Royal Navy and Britain's insular power while Mackinder seems to have grasped that mass would crush them in the future. In fact, however, Mahan's worldview was no less modern but considerably more dynamic and inclusive. Mackinder displayed an essentially static and neo-mercantilistic conception of economic life, a world in which it was possible for an empire to wall itself off from the global system just at the time when the forces of globalization were making nations more, not less, dependent on each other. Mahan's worldview, by contrast, with the interdependent international trading system at its heart, was unmistakably dynamic. Where Mackinder saw stocks (of raw materials, people, railroads), Mahan saw flows (of ships, goods, money).

Mahan's different and superior understanding of contemporary economic processes comes through in his response to Mackinder, which has gone largely unnoticed. Though Mahan very much liked Mackinder's "The Geographical Pivot of History" and sent copies to important friends and acquaintances (including U.S. Secretary of State John Hay), he thought that Mackinder had made a serious error in his calculations. Maritime powers would always enjoy a major economic advantage: a lower cost of transportation, one of the central arguments in *Influence* and all of his subsequent books. "As a highway, a railroad competes in vain with a river—the greater speed cannot compensate for the smaller carriage. Because more facile and more copious, water traffic is for equal distances much cheaper; and, because cheaper, more useful in general. These distinctions are not accidental or temporary; they are of the nature of things, and permanent."[73] Further, "It is necessary to insist upon these facts; for the far greater speed of the railroad gives a very different impression to the average mind, which is prone to forget the limitations in capacity. Traffic, or exchange of goods, depends in aggregate result not upon speed only but upon the amounts that can be steadily delivered in long equal periods of time."[74]

Mahan was correct, and his objection—based on economic, not naval or military considerations—went to the heart of the difference between him and Mackinder. Mackinder, like most geostrategic thinkers, had not studied economic systems as carefully as Mahan. Mackinder's static, quasi-autarkic geoeconomic model certainly did not capture the realities of the globalized contemporary world, and as Mahan was about to argue, it did not even work well for the more mercantilist world a century earlier.

THE WAR OF 1812

In December 1902, with the revisions to his model of sea power now more or less straight in his mind and his desk almost clear of other obligations, Mahan at last steeled himself to finish his book on the War of 1812. "I had expected to do this nearly ten years ago; but other issues turned up, and the immediate advantage of magazine writing has shunted me more to it than it ought," he told Bouverie Clark on December 19.[75] As previously mentioned, there had been other reasons as well why he struggled to complete the third book in his sea power trilogy. Most pressingly, Mahan encountered enormous difficulty in framing his book—devising a workable format for integrating his arguments and evidence—in order to produce something that was both a significant piece of scholarship and one that would appeal to general readers.

Back in 1897 Mahan had envisioned covering the naval aspects of the story in only minimal detail, largely ignoring the Anglo-American frigate duels, in order to address the wider strategic and political issues. "It was from the first my purpose to make *1812* largely a philosophical study of the causes, course and result of the war in its broader aspects," he wrote, "and only under pressure did I accept the idea of treating the single ship fights."[76] But his publisher and his friends persuaded him that writing a naval history without detailed consideration of naval combat was unthinkable; Mahan relented albeit with reluctance. "I cannot yet but grudge the time I have to spend on them," he admitted to Luce.[77]

Another reason why Mahan preferred not to incorporate combat analysis in his new book was that he was aware that, if treated honestly, the subject had potential to do him much harm at home. In a couple of articles written during the 1890s, Mahan had admitted his disinterest in the "admirable but unavailing frigate actions."[78] More provocatively still, he had expressed his opinion that "never was blood spilled more uselessly than in the frigate fights."[79] These and other statements came dangerously close to belittling what were (until 1942) the U.S. Navy's finest achievements. Mahan also had to be careful when telling his American readers that, in his judgment, the United States had lost the war. As it turns out, this was also the view of Admiral Luce. "It is my hope that you will dispose of the popular delusion that 'we whipped England' in the war of 1812," Luce wrote Mahan in early

1903, "it is time the people of this country should be told the truth about that war whether it is palatable or not." But, Luce cautioned him, "at the same time one should not go to the other extreme."[80] Downplaying the significance of the American frigate victories risked upsetting many people. Mahan took the point and promised he would "endeavor however to so word my comment as not to give offense such as you mention."[81] The necessity still irritated him. "I wanted to omit the single ship actions," he later confessed, "but found it impossible; and it is true that our successes in them, exaggerated as they were in popular appreciation, gave the navy its first lift."[82] In later years he was more scathing.[83]

To Mahan's mind, at its root, the War of 1812 was mainly a tale of transoceanic economic rivalry. As he explained it, "England was one extremity, and the several West India Islands the other, of a traffic then one of the richest in the world; while the tropical articles of this exchange, if not absolute necessaries of life, had become by long indulgence indispensable to the great part of civilized mankind."[84] Locked in mortal combat with Napoleon, Britain wished to control this trade to generate the huge revenues needed to fight the French emperor who controlled most of Europe. American merchants wanted a share of the profits. Mahan insisted that it was simply impossible to comprehend anything of the war, its causes or its course, or make sense of strategic decisions taken by both sides, without clearly understanding its economic ancestry. It drove, constrained, and touched everything, including the political objectives of both parties. In short, to tell the story of the War of 1812 in a way that was both accurate and coherent, it was necessary to incorporate a considerable amount of economic and political history.

The problem, he knew, was that most readers had a low tolerance for economic history. As Mahan aseptically remarked in his autobiography: "I had foreseen that the War of 1812, as a whole, must be flat in interest as well as laborious in execution; and, upon the provocation of other duty, I readily turned from it in distaste. Nine years elapsed before I took it up; and then rather under the compulsion of completing my sea power series, as first designed, than from any inclination to the theme . . . it is impossible to infuse charm where from the facts of the case it does not exist."[85] On January 3, 1903, Mahan reported to Luce that he had finally assembled a suitable skeleton.[86] "The main thesis of my War of 1812 must necessarily be the sufferings of the country through the inadequacy of the Navy as compared with the actual power of the country to have made better preparation."[87] This indeed became the central argument of his book, craftily attributing any shortcomings exhibited by the U.S. Navy to prewar political myopia and parsimony.[88] So confident was he that the final hurdle had been cleared, and that at last he could begin serious writing, that he signed a contract with *Scribner's Magazine* to supply a serialized edition of his book, the first chapter to be delivered just nine months hence.

Mahan's optimism that he was close to the end proved premature, however. A year later he was obliged to admit to his publisher, John Brown, that the final manuscript still had not taken shape.[89] Organizing his material proved more complicated than he had expected.[90] It did not help either that Mahan could not resist making hay while the sun shone by continuing to produce magazine articles.[91] Not until the end of 1904 was his book on the War of 1812 mostly finished.[92] On March 30, 1905, he at last completed a draft manuscript, though it took another four months to apply the finishing touches.[93]

Mahan was proud of his new monograph, which appeared in December 1905 under the title *Sea Power in Its Relations to the War of 1812.* "In my own estimation, it is the best piece of historical writing I have ever done, superior by far in research, in treatment and in style," he boasted to his publisher.[94] Therein, Mahan presented an interpretation of the conflict that differed significantly from all previous accounts, viewing it less as a military event than as a clash of interests between economic rivals. He wanted to explain the why of the war and the larger background forces in motion, not merely to chronicle the combat operations in greater detail than before. In a very real sense, he reconceptualized the War of 1812.

By the standards of the day, Mahan's research was both groundbreaking and impressive. Additionally, we know that while writing his new book he consulted with Arthur Hadley and John Bassett Moore, and that Mahan's analysis passed muster with both.[95] Writing in the 1920s, Eli Heckscher, the Swedish economist who studied the economic history of the Napoleonic Era and would become one of the foremost economic historians of the twentieth century, acknowledged that "the only writer who, so far as I know, has embarked on a deeper analysis is the foremost naval historian of our time, the late Admiral Mahan of the United States Navy, who has undoubtedly cast much light on the history of the Continental System in his books."[96] Heckscher was not uncritical of Mahan's work. He thought Mahan too pro-British and believed he had overstated the effectiveness of Britain's blockade of France during the Napoleonic Wars, the consequence of his fixation on proving his concept of power. Nevertheless, Heckscher admitted the originality and value of Mahan's economic research, borrowing his statistics and several of his arguments.

Even today, Mahan's *1812* remains essential reading for naval and economic historians alike. Sometimes grudgingly but more often unwittingly, historians of the conflict continue to rely on many of his explanations and economic data.[97] His insights into and command of the strategic dimension of the war, as well as his explanations of the interconnections between the political, economic, and legal aspects of the conflict, remain unsurpassed. Even his treatment of the famous frigate actions (despite his lack of interest in the subject) proved models of exposition, displaying a masterly grasp of the technical intricacies of naval tactics and ship handling in sailing warships. Of course, his practitioner's experience of handling similar ships in wartime was an advantage. In order to concentrate on the central thread of Mahan's theory, we shall pass over several other important clarifications he made to his argument without comment.

Despite the superlative quality of Mahan's research and the enduring value of his analysis, *1812* is not a casual read.[98] As the naval historian William Dudley notes, "in reading Mahan's 1812, one realizes that he is not only re-writing the history of the war but also searching for justifications of his theories of sea power."[99] The complaint that it is really two books in one is valid, though in a slightly different way. Mahan's *1812* was designed as a history of the conflict viewed through the lens of sea power, and at the same time an elucidation of his concept of sea power. As mentioned, besides telling a coherent story, Mahan was anxious to provide his readers with a clearer exposition of his arguments, to correct several widespread misperceptions, and to demonstrate the continuing utility of his theories and their general applicability. Although in his recent articles he had clarified his meaning of key points, never before had he presented them as a coherent whole.

Mahan's *1812* was published in two volumes. The first four chapters reviewed the background contexts for the war in excruciating detail. His private correspondence indicates that he put more intellectual effort into these introductory chapters than any of the others.[100] In chapter 1, which extended to an exhausting 260 pages, he located the roots of the war in the squabbles between interest groups on either side of the Atlantic over the division of spoils from the lucrative West Indies trade. Chapter 2 contained lengthy expositions of the commercial system as it existed during his period of study, as well as a summary of contemporary perceptions of how wealth was generated, the importance thereto of overseas trade, and the division of the spoils. In so doing he repeatedly stressed the dynamic character of the international economy and of wealth generation generally, quietly criticizing previous historians for failing to go to the same trouble as he had. In chapters 3 and 4, Mahan looked more closely at the immediate antecedents to the war, analyzing the protagonists' respective policies and conflicting perspectives, and showing how and where each infringed on the interests of the other. Reading these first four chapters will leave readers in no doubt that Mahan built his concept of sea power on unmistakably economic foundations.

The heart of the book is found in chapter 5. Here, Mahan explained why commerce destruction was—and remained—central to the exercise of sea power and the prosecution of war.

It is desirable to explain here what was, *and is*, the particular specific utility of operations directed toward the destruction of an enemy's commerce; what its bearing upon [*sic*] the issues of war; and how, also, it affects the relative interests of antagonists, unequally paired in the matter of sea power. Without attempting to determine precisely the relative importance of internal and external commerce, which varies with each country, and admitting that the length of transportation entails a distinct element of increased cost upon the articles transported, it is nevertheless safe to say that, to nations having free access to the sea, the export and import trade is a very large factor in national prosperity and comfort. At the very least, it increases by so much the aggregate of commercial transactions, while the ease and copiousness of water carriage go far to compensate for the increase of distance. Furthermore, the public revenue of maritime states is largely derived from duties on imports. Hence arises, therefore, a large source of wealth, of money; and money— ready money or substantial credit—is proverbially the sinews of war, as the War of 1812 was amply to demonstrate.[101]

From this, Mahan concluded,

Produce [goods], is of little use, unless by freedom of exchange it can be converted into cash for governmental expenses. To this sea-commerce greatly contributes, and the extreme embarrassment under which the Unites States as a nation labored in 1814 was mainly due to commercial exclusion from the sea. To attack the commerce of the enemy is therefore to cripple him, in the measure of success achieved, in the particular factor which is vital to the maintenance of war. Moreover, in the complicated conditions of mercantile activity no one branch can be seriously injured without involving others.[102]

For Mahan, therefore, what really mattered in naval warfare was the knock-on "financial and political effect of 'commerce destroying,' as the modern phrase runs."[103] These lines were the immediate context for his observation, often quoted but seldom correctly presented or understood, that "Money, credit, is the life of war; lessen it, and vigor flags; destroy it, and resistance dies."[104] That is, his most famous aphorism was embedded in an expression of his conviction that sea power was essentially economic in character, and his insight that economic systems were fundamentally dynamic and interdependent, and the real effects were felt far downstream.

On the following page, he amplified that "in war, the primary object being immediate injury to the enemy's fighting power, it is not only legitimate in principle, but particularly effective, to seek the disorganization of his financial system, by a crushing attack upon one of its important factors, because effort thus is concentrated on a readily accessible, fundamental element of his general prosperity."[105]

After ramming home the distinction between "commerce raiding" and "commerce destruction," Mahan deployed the data he had gathered showing how the effects of "commerce destruction" at sea reverberated throughout the economy, causing widespread derangement.[106] In one typical example, he traced the knock-on effects of the Royal Navy's paralysis of the U.S. coastal trade south of New England (showing off his careful research in the process). The blockade caused that region to become "the distributing centre" of the United States, he explained.

> In consequence, the remainder of the country was practically drained of specie, which set to the northward and eastward. . . . It could not go far south, because the coasting trade was destroyed by the enemy's fleets, and the South could not send forward its produce by land to obtain money in return. The deposits in Massachusetts banks increased from $2,671,619, in 1810, to $8,875,589, in 1814; while in the same years the specie held was respectively $1,561,034 and $6,393,718.
>
> It was a day of small things, relatively to present gigantic commercial enterprises; but an accumulation of cash in one quarter, coinciding with penury in another, proves defect in circulation consequent upon embarrassed communications. That flour in Boston sold for $12.00 the barrel, while at Baltimore and Richmond it stood at $6.50 and $4.50, tells the same tale of congestion and deficiency, due to interruption of water communication.[107]

This passage is also a good illustration of why it is useful to read Mahan with knowledge of his context, in this case of the fact that he was a learned philosopher, as Suzanne Geissler has argued. The passage contains a biblical allusion—it was a "day of small things" references a passage in Zechariah 4:10—which further made Mahan's point.[108] In Zechariah, "small things" eventually lead to the construction of a large temple, just as small first-order consequences of naval pressure eventually lead to large higher-order consequences, like local financial disequilibrium and ultimately national commercial collapse.

Indeed, from his laboriously gathered statistical evidence, Mahan determined that the Royal Navy blockade so deranged the U.S. economy that it pushed the Madison administration to the brink of bankruptcy, compelling it to sue for peace without having achieved a single objective that had induced it to start the war two and half years before.[109] "After the winter of 1812–13 American commerce dwindled very rapidly, till in 1814 it was practically annihilated," Mahan found.[110] The British blockade, he elaborated, was "so severe as practically to annihilate the coasting trade, considered as a means of commercial exchange. It is not possible for deep-sea cruisers wholly to suppress the movement of small vessels, skirting the beaches from headland to headland; but their operations can be so much embarrassed as to reduce their usefulness to a bare alleviation of social necessities, inadequate to any scale of interchange deserving the name of commerce."[111] In short, the Royal Navy wrecked the U.S. economy, causing tax revenues to dry up and thus inhibiting the ability of the republic to continue the war.

After looking at the other side of the coin, by contrast, Mahan found that, contrary to popular myth, U.S. forces failed to generate anything like such pressure on the British. Ignoring Adm. Luce's warning that he was touching a nerve, Mahan casually dismissed the U.S. Navy's victories as "incidental" events that "had no effect upon the issue [the outcome of the war], except so far as they inspired moral enthusiasm and confidence."[112] Mahan was even less gentle in his assessment of the fabled effectiveness of American privateers. Certainly, he acknowledged, irregular forces made large captures and in so doing performed a valuable service. But the numbers had to be contextualized. What to American eyes were big numbers were to British ones comparatively small. The fact remained, Mahan showed, that "the sea was kept open to British commerce by the paramount power of the British navy. This could not prevent all mishaps; but it reduced them, by the annihilation of hostile navies, to such a small percentage of the whole shipping movement, that the British mercantile community found steady profit both in foreign and coasting trade, of which the United States at the same time was almost totally deprived."[113]

Put more plainly, "it must be remembered that such losses, however grievous in themselves, and productive of individual suffering, have by no means the decisive effect produced by the stoppage of commerce."[114] The operative word here is "decisive." "While the enemy [Britain] was losing a certain small proportion of vessels, the United States suffered practically an entire deprivation of external commerce; and her coasting trade was almost wholly suppressed."[115] "Such," Mahan concluded, "was the experience which sums up the forgotten bitter truth, concerning a war which has left in the United States a prevalent impression of distinguished success, because of a few brilliant naval actions and the closing battle of New Orleans."[116]

For Mahan then, the War of 1812 represented the prime exemplar of sea power—not America's, but Britain's. The conflict was settled not by combat but rather by what he famously termed "that noiseless pressure" of sea power.[117] Given the quality and quantity of his evidence, it is difficult to dispute this general argument. Even Harold and Margaret Sprout acknowledged that Mahan comprehensively demolished the "legend of victory" but, more sensitive to national feeling than Mahan, hastened to add that the U.S. Navy acquitted itself well. Their summary of the war leaves the reader with the impression that even if the United States lost the war, then at least the U.S. Navy won it![118] And from a narrowly naval institutionalist perspective, perhaps this was true: afterward, there was no more talk of abolishing the U.S. Navy. Most subsequent historians have hewed a similar line, focusing on the naval operations and paying only lip service to the economic aspects of the conflict. Few if any accurately summarize

Mahan's arguments, let alone engage with his economic judgments or his supporting evidence. The handful of naval historians who have disputed Mahan's portrayal of the British blockade as a mailed gauntlet clamped around America's economic throat, moreover, reply with nothing more than a patchwork of anecdotal evidence instead of gathering statistical data to refute Mahan's own price data, perhaps because Mahan's evidence cannot be refuted.[119]

All recent investigations by economic historians generally corroborate Mahan's main line of argument, though some have argued he slightly overstated his case.[120] In his short economic history of the United States, economist and Nobel laureate Douglass North summarized that "the British effectively ended our external trade and concluded an era of growth based on American neutrality in a world at war."[121] North concurred that "the blockade was complete except for the trickle of ships that could elude British frigates."[122] Similarly, Lance E. Davis and Stanley L. Engerman confirmed that by the end of the conflict, U.S. exports were down almost 90 percent.[123] One may quibble with a few percentage points here or there, but there is no getting around figures of this magnitude. Kevin O'Rourke, the leading economic historian of the period today, confirmed Mahan's findings that the British interdiction of U.S. coastal traffic caused huge price disparities in key commodities across the states, indicating shortages in some places and gluts in others. As he rather neatly put it, "price data do not lie: they faithfully reflect the conditions of relative abundance or scarcity within an economy."[124] The overwhelming balance of data shows unequivocally that the U.S. economy fared catastrophically at the hands of the Royal Navy, just as Mahan said it did.

In addition to downplaying the significance of the frigate actions and challenging the notion of American victory, Mahan courted further unpopularity at home by challenging several other conventional impressions of the war. One was the issue of impressment. In Mahan's opinion, the nature of the problem had been substantially misunderstood and the scale exaggerated.[125] He also delved deeply into the legal aspects of the conflict. He found the Madison administration's claims that Britain had violated American "rights" under the law of nations

to be tenuous and frequently tendentious, and he noted that its official stance by no means enjoyed universal support from contemporary
American jurists.[126] In so doing, Mahan used his book as a bridge to
reenter the simmering national debate over the immunity of private
property in time of war, a subject we will look at more closely in the
next chapter.[127] "The sea is the great scene of commerce," he spelled
out: "The property transported back and forth, circulating from state
to state in exchanges, is one of the greatest factors in national wealth.
The maritime nations have been, and are, the wealthy nations. To
prohibit such commerce to an enemy is, and historically has been, a
tremendous blow to his fighting power."[128]

It is important to remember that in formulating his conclusions
on such highly technical legal matters, Mahan consulted and enjoyed
the support of his friend John Basset Moore. Capt. William Puleston,
who in the course of researching his biography of Mahan met with
Moore and discussed Mahan, explained to his readers that "Moore,
who knew as much as any of his generation about the problems of
international law involved in the dispute, and whose career as Assistant
Secretary of State during the Spanish War gave him personal experience in dealing with problems of naval warfare, thought Mahan had
achieved the most impartial historical narrative ever written on that
conflict."[129] The point being that if Mahan's views on this subject
passed muster with an expert of Moore's unquestionable caliber, then
perhaps they merit greater respect than subsequent legal historians
(and professional international lawyers) have allowed.

The reading public greeted Mahan's *1812*, a very different kind of
naval history than they were used to, with confused and half-hearted
applause. It sold poorly and was not as widely reviewed as his previous
books. The first edition (six thousand copies) took thirty years to sell
and another thirty-five years passed before it was reprinted. Sales were
particularly poor in the home market.[130] As Admiral Luce had feared,

American readers did not appreciate having their history so disagreeably (however thoroughly) rewritten. Capt. Puleston concurred that "his general attitude was too judicious to satisfy some of his chauvinistic brother officers and superpatriotic citizens who thought he belittled American achievements."[131] The resentment has endured.

Others found Mahan's entire approach to the subject either discomfiting or perplexing. In the *American Historical Review*, for instance, Mahan was criticized for treating combat operations as almost irrelevant to the object and outcome of the war, the reviewer seemingly missing the point of the book that the conflict needed to be viewed less from the military and more from the political and economic perspectives.[132] There can be little doubt that others were similarly unhappy with Mahan's unconventional approach to the subject. After all, *1812* was marketed as a naval history book, and while it contained a fair amount of naval history, it did not read like a naval history book. "I was as disappointed as you with Mahan's War of 1812," President Theodore Roosevelt wrote after reading it the first time. "He is a curious fellow, for he cannot write in effective shape of the navy or of the fighting of his own country."[133] Roosevelt, it will be recalled, had produced his own book on the conflict, a stirring and intensely patriotic tome that, contra Mahan, saw the outcome of the war as a resounding victory for the United States and a humiliating defeat for Britain.[134] Among historians there is speculation that Roosevelt was nettled by Mahan's book, and this led to a cooling of relations between the two; "its effect was to contribute to Mahan's limited effectiveness in his dealings with Roosevelt during much of the latter's presidency."[135] Although there is some truth in this assessment, the cooling of relations in fact proved only temporary. What is more, the two had much more important matters to discuss, matters that related directly to the United States' ability to profit from sea power in the future.

CHAPTER 9

THE QUIXOTIC CRUSADE

(1905–7)

The loss of property weighs heavy with the most of mankind; heavier
often, than the sacrifices made on the field of battle. Death is popularly
considered the maximum punishment in war, but it is not; reduction
to poverty brings prayers for peace more surely and more quickly
than does the destruction of human life, as the selfishness of man has
demonstrated in more than one great conflict.

—PHILIP H. SHERIDAN, *THE PERSONAL MEMOIRS OF P. H. SHERIDAN*[1]

THIS CHAPTER DEALS WITH a crusade by Mahan that has attracted
little attention from scholars: his campaign against "immunity," that
is, the immunity of all private property at sea from capture (both personal and corporate) by a belligerent in wartime. Perhaps the subject
has seemed an esoteric issue of international law, unworthy of study;
perhaps, too, the conventional interpretation of Mahan as obsessed
with decisive battle fleet actions has rendered his interest in the subject
invisible. It is difficult, if not impossible, to make sense of his interest in immunity on the conventional combat-centric interpretation of
Mahan; yet his interest makes excellent sense when his concept of sea
power is viewed as fundamentally economic in nature, for the immunity question went to the heart of a naval power's ability to apply
economic pressure against an enemy in wartime.

Far from a narrow question of international law, the immunity issue had broad implications for diplomatic relations, the international political economy, and the interests of many powerful groups within the United States. As we saw at the end of chapter 7, Mahan's intervention in the subject was not welcomed. Chief among his antagonists was the peace movement bankrolled by Andrew Carnegie, the steel magnate–turned–philanthropist. Mahan's most vocal opponents, however, proved to be the growing community of international lawyers, based mainly in New York, who resented his interference in what they felt was their business. For reasons that will be explained below, Mahan disagreed fundamentally: the subject of immunity, he held, was far too important to the future of the United States to be left in the hands of the lawyers—who, he felt, did not understand the practical side of war nearly as well as they thought they did. His views on the subject were neatly encapsulated by his acerbic denouncement of President James Madison (a lawyer) during the War of 1812: "Like [President Thomas] Jefferson, he was wholly oblivious of the relevancy of Pompey's retort to a contention between two nations, each convinced of its own right: "Will you never have done with citing laws and privileges to men who wear swords"?[2] When discussing the intersection of law and war at sea, Mahan thought, the naval perspective merited at least equal weight to the legal perspective.

As shown, for Mahan, the interrelationship between trade, wealth, and power consistently represented the heart of his concept of sea power. "The history of Sea Power," Mahan had explicitly stated in the opening chapter of *The Influence of Sea Power upon History*, "is largely, though by no means solely, a narrative of contests between nations, or mutual rivalries, of violence frequently culminating in war," and in order "to secure to one's own people a disproportionate share of such benefits, every effort was made to exclude others, either by peaceful legislative methods or monopoly or prohibitory regulations, or, when these failed, by direct violence."[3] In other words, history showed that the most common cause of war was a clash of national interests over the spoils of international trade.

During the 1890s, as he came to better understand how the world worked, Mahan attached steadily more and more weight to economic considerations, both in his historical scholarship and in his geopolitical commentaries. As shown in chapter 7, he came to appreciate that the chief determinant of wealth and power was the *flow* of trade through the intrinsically dynamic global economic system. Trade flowed in both war and peace, and at all times the primary object of the navy was to ensure it did. That is to say, sea power was the precursor to safe flows of trade and exchange, which were the true generator of national wealth. In parallel, he progressively reconsidered his thoughts on commerce destruction in wartime, coming eventually to see it as the primary (political) *object* of sea power—as distinct from the military *objective* in naval warfare. By the same token, naval combat operations were merely the military means to the ultimate political end (i.e., systematic destruction of the enemy's commerce in order to generate discord within the enemy's society and internal pressure on their government).

In practical terms, Mahan judged the most effective and efficient form of commerce destruction to be a blockade of the enemy coast combined with, as much as possible, interdiction of navigable rivers and inland waterways. The intent here was to shut down the enemy's transportation system to prevent "exchange" and so to seriously derange their economy. By custom, formally establishing a blockade of the enemy coast allowed a belligerent to claim important benefits, most particularly the right to confiscate any neutral ship (and its cargo) caught trying to enter an enemy port. Since the 1856 Declaration of Paris, however, international opinion held that "Blockades, in order to be binding, must be effective, that is to say, maintained by a force sufficient really to prevent access to the coast of the enemy" (article 4). But exactly what constituted an "effective" blockade was a matter of considerable international disagreement. In any case, until the blockade was clearly effective, a process that could take many months, a navy's ability to regulate the trade between their enemy and neutrals rested on the even more problematic law of contraband, a term loosely defined as goods used directly by armed forces to prosecute war.

As previously related, from 1898, sparked by his experience during the Spanish-American War as the liaison officer between the Navy and State Departments on matters relating to blockade running, Mahan paid much closer attention to the "laws of nations" pertaining to maritime warfare. Tutored in the subject by John Bassett Moore, Mahan soon became reasonably expert in the subject and, as will be shown below, developed a distinctive, carefully reasoned perspective on the matter. Directly after the war, in the pages of the *New York Times*, Mahan challenged a campaign by peace activists to press the U.S. government into taking the lead in negotiating a new multilateral treaty guaranteeing the immunity (or exemption from capture) of private property at sea from interference in time of war. Their goal was to repeat the pioneering feat of the 1856 Declaration of Paris, which created new law, irrespective of custom, by international assent.[4] It is of course impossible to estimate the precise impact Mahan had on this subject at this time, but early in 1899 Mahan became the surprising choice of Secretary of State John Hay to join the delegation representing the United States at the first Hague Peace Conference.

Obeying Hay's instructions, Andrew White, the head of the U.S. delegation and himself an enthusiastic proponent of "immunity," tried to add to the conference agenda a discussion of the proposal that "The private property of all citizens or subjects of the signatory powers, with the exception of contraband of war, shall be exempt from capture or seizure on the high seas or elsewhere . . . but nothing herein contained shall extend exemption from seizure to vessels and their cargoes which may attempt to enter a port blockaded by the naval forces of any of the said powers."[5] This definition of "immunity" (and indeed the text of the motion proposed) was modeled on the so-called Marcy Amendment to the 1856 Declaration of Paris (after Secretary of State William L. Marcy) whereby the United States offered to sign the treaty outlawing privateering only if all private property at sea (except contraband) were made immune from capture, a condition that the major powers rejected.[6] To White's aggravation, however, Mahan openly proclaimed his skepticism of the whole idea and behind the scenes conducted a private guerrilla campaign. He planted sufficient seeds of doubt in the minds of other delegates that the conference organizers declined to add the subject to the 1899 agenda, though they assured White that it would be discussed at the next one.[7]

Consoled and even buoyed by this promise, in the years that followed the peace movement maintained steady pressure on the U.S. government, first the McKinley administration and then Roosevelt's, to advocate for "immunity."[8] Mahan, meanwhile, maintained his opposition. The first article he published on his return to New York from the first Hague Peace Conference was a piece for the *North American Review* disparaging the peace movement's one apparent tangible success at the recent conference, the establishment of the Permanent Court of Arbitration, insisting the whole conception was muddleheaded.[9] He had intended to follow this with another piece more directly explaining why the idea of "immunity" was a fallacy, but seemingly he never got around to finishing it.[10] He was probably too busy with other work. In other articles he wrote during the next couple of years, although he frequently touched on the question of immunity, he never tackled the subject head-on.

In April 1904, Mahan remained surprisingly silent after Congress passed a joint resolution imploring the president to "endeavor to bring about an understanding among the principal maritime powers with a view of incorporating into the permanent law of civilized nations the principle of the exemption of all private property at sea, not contraband, from capture or destruction by belligerents."[11] Because the subject went unreported by the *New York Times*, he perhaps missed this news. Nor did Mahan comment the following September when, in front of a delegation of peace activists visiting the White House, President Roosevelt undertook to call a second Hague Peace Conference. This earned the president much credit at home and was widely reported, especially in provincial newspapers.[12]

To a surprising degree—surprising given Roosevelt's supposed reputation as a blunt man who notoriously believed in direct action with a big stick—the concept of "peace" was an important plank in his 1904 reelection campaign.[13] As John Hay noted in his diary, the president "always speaks of the election as uncertain."[14] In the more cosmopolitan press, however, and especially abroad, Roosevelt's professed enthusiasm for the peace conference generated much cynical mirth. As the London correspondent for the *New York Times* archly noted, "the announcement is ignored in editorial comment by most of the London papers, and where discussed is not treated seriously, but rather as a bit of political play incident to the Presidential campaign."[15] The managing editor of the *New York Times* suspected the same.[16] In a dispatch to Berlin, the German ambassador in Washington claimed that Roosevelt had privately admitted to him that the journalistic suspicions were quite true.[17]

Even after Roosevelt unexpectedly followed through on his promise a couple of weeks later, authorizing Secretary Hay to invite all the leading powers to a second peace conference, his motives continued to be questioned.[18] The text of Hay's circular letter calling for a conference was released to the public on October 31, just four days before the general election.[19] Given that two of the principal naval powers, Russia and Japan, were presently at war with each other, and that two others, Britain and France, stood at that moment on the brink of joining in the fray, the idea of a peace conference early in 1905 seemed patently absurd to most serious commentators. If Mahan was following along, and he probably was, then from his perspective there seemed nothing much to worry about. Although Hay's circular had mentioned "immunity," it had done so only in passing when mentioning the recent joint resolution of Congress.[20] Moreover, elsewhere in his circular Hay acknowledged that it seemed "premature" to put forward concrete proposals, suggesting that at this stage participants should simply commit to "further codification of the universal ideas of right and justice which we call international law."[21]

On the morning of December 24, 1904, Capt. Mahan's eye was caught by a header in the *New York Times*: "Hague Conference Shelved." This must have seemed encouraging. The article below contained a summary of a just-released State Department communique formally announcing what everyone already knew, that although the international community favored the idea of a peace conference, it would be impossible to convene before the conclusion of the Russo-Japanese War. But then good news turned to bad. The communique continued with an assurance that the conference had been merely postponed, not canceled, and that the U.S. government remained committed to giving effect to the recent congressional joint resolution on "the important subject of the inviolability of private property in naval warfare."[22] The question of immunity had unexpectedly moved front and center. Mahan was spurred to act.

It is a measure of Mahan's unhappiness that he interrupted work on his *1812* manuscript to write directly to Roosevelt. Mahan's letter, penned on December 27, opened with an allusion to the *New York Times* article: "I have seen with concern that in issuing the invitations to a second Hague Conference, the United States puts in the foreground of subjects for consideration, the exemption from capture at sea of 'private property.'"[23] As a rising sea power, Mahan advised, this seemed a bad idea. "The question is one of expediency, and what was expedient to our weakness of a century ago is not expedient to our strength today," he stated. Instead of striving to weaken belligerent rights at sea, "we [the United States] need to fasten our grip on the sea."[24] Alluding to arguments contained in several of his recent articles, which he knew the president had read with approval, Mahan elaborated,

> The general situation of the United States, in the world policy of today, appears to me to make most impolitic this change. Circumstances almost irresistible are forcing us and Great Britain, not into alliance, but into a silent cooperation, dependent upon conditions probably irreversible in the next two generations. Our united naval strength can probably control the seas; but there is always a remaining chance of a combination in the East—the Western Pacific—which might approach an equilibrium. The future and policy of China remains uncertain. It may very well be that under such conditions the power to control commerce,—the lawful right international precedent now confers,—may be of immense, of decisive, importance.

To illustrate and support this, his main point, that "the power to control [sea] commerce . . . may be of immense, of decisive, importance," Mahan enclosed several draft chapters from his *1812* manuscript in which he identified the British destruction of American commerce as the critical factor of the war.

Mahan closed his letter with the rather incongruous insistence that his recommendation to the president to change course on the immunity "in no wise [*sic*] changes my known position about 'commerce destroying.' From the first, as now, I have held it 'a most important secondary operation, not likely to be abandoned till war itself shall cease'; but as a primary measure a delusion (*Sea Power*, p. 539)."[25] Here Mahan was engaging in verbal contortions: of course there was at least a tension, if not an outright contradiction, between his advice to Roosevelt on immunity and this remark about commerce destroying in *Influence* (which, as we saw in chapter 3, sat awkwardly alongside other remarks elsewhere in the same book that sea power was fundamentally about commerce).

More awkwardly still, Roosevelt, in his annual message to Congress the previous year, had "cordially renewed" his predecessor McKinley's support for immunity, and by way of support had alluded unmistakably to Mahan's own work in claiming "that as a practical matter it might be mentioned that while commerce destroying may cause serious loss and great annoyance, it can never be more than a subsidiary factor in bringing to terms a resolute foe. This was well recognized by all of our naval experts."[26] Thus, aside from Mahan's temperamental reluctance to admit any inconsistency, he had to contort himself to avoid suggesting that Roosevelt's generous and public endorsement of his scholarship had rested on a misreading.

Mahan had a further reason to tread carefully in his letter to Roosevelt. The subject of belligerent rights at sea was very much a live one. The Russo-Japanese War was raging and the Russians in particular had been pushing the boundaries of customary practice in ways that Roosevelt himself had labeled "preposterous."[27] Already the American business community was angry at the predations of the Russian Navy. With British encouragement, the United States had taken the international lead in pressuring Tsar Nicholas II to moderate his claims and restrain the zeal of Russian naval officers to sink and burn everything they encountered on the high seas.[28] At this time, in other words, it would have been politically awkward for Roosevelt to be seen as weak on neutral rights.

It is not surprising, therefore, that the president's reply to Mahan was guarded. "I am interested in your letter and the enclosure, and shall take them up with John Hay," he wrote Mahan on December 29, adding that "you open a big subject for discussion."[29] He evidently wasted no time because two days later Hay returned Mahan's letter, dismissing his plea out of hand as the opinion of a salty crank.[30] "It is, of course, the professional sailor's view of the question," Hay sniffed. "I do not think the considerations he brings to bear are weighty enough to cause us to reverse our traditional policy for the last century."[31] Quite probably Roosevelt and Hay discussed the matter at their weekly private meeting (the two usually met every Sunday directly after church), though if they did Hay did not think the matter important enough to mention in his diary.[32] Ever the politician, Roosevelt evidentially decided not to press the matter at this time; for what was the point? [33] He duly informed Mahan of his decision, though apparently in such a way as to not completely close the door, for over the next twenty-four months the captain peppered him with articles on the subject, trawled from various sources.[34] In the meantime, Mahan returned to his herculean task of completing *1812*. This he accomplished at the end of July 1905.[35]

With more time on his hands, Mahan returned to the fray. On September 9, 1905, he cautiously raised the subject of immunity again with Roosevelt, enclosing some clippings from recent newspapers as examples of "the extreme views that have been, and will be, advocated at the Peace Conference, believed to lie again in the near future."[36] During the intervening nine months much had happened. Most importantly the Russo-Japanese War was over. Just days before, on September 5, Roosevelt had successfully brokered the Treaty of Portsmouth bringing an end to the conflict, and in so doing earning himself a Nobel Peace Prize.[37] With the ink barely dry, already there was talk of convening the second Peace Conference early in the following year; indeed, on September 13, the Russian ambassador visited Roosevelt at his home in Oyster Bay to discuss the subject.[38] Two days after that, the tsar's government formally announced its willingness to participate.[39] Tactfully, Mahan did not mention another important change in context, the recent death (in July) of John Hay. But seeing as no date for the conference had yet been set, there was nothing to be gained in pressing the issue at that time. And besides, Mahan was exhausted after just finishing his monograph. At the end of month he sailed with his family to Europe for a nine-month rest cure, followed by an extended vacation in the South of France.[40]

By the beginning of 1906, Mahan had sufficiently recovered his energy to rejoin the battle over immunity. Writing from France at the end of January, he mentioned to John Knox Laughton that he was sifting reports on the Russo-Japanese War and was "particularly interested in the effect of commerce destruction, direct or indirect, regarded as contributive to the determination of war."[41] Mahan went on to disclose that he was interested in "immunity" and was lobbying Roosevelt on the subject, "but he [Roosevelt] is too busy to digest such a matter; & Hay's successor probably has not ever given thought to the matter."[42] Further clues as to the direction of Mahan's research and thinking at this time are provided in another letter (written the same day) to the naval correspondent for the *Times* of London. Belying his reputation as a man fixated on battles and battleships, Mahan confessed that he was not much interested in details on the Battle of Tsushima, the most decisive naval victory since Nelson's legendary triumph at Trafalgar. "I feel a greater interest," Mahan told him, in studying "the effects upon Japanese finance, shipping, & commerce, from the action of the Vladivostok squadron, while that had a comparatively free foot. The control of sea-bourne commerce is a factor in the policy of naval states which is receiving little attention, and what is given is marred by prepossession and imperfect consideration."[43]

Ten weeks later, in April 1906, Russia published the upcoming conference agenda, with "immunity" near the top of the list.[44] Distressed, Mahan wrote directly to Elihu Root, the new Secretary of

State, substantially reiterating what he had previously told Roosevelt and Hay, that the government had failed to think through all the implications of the proposed changes and that such a policy really was not in the nation's best long-term strategic interests.[45] Was "it too late to undertake a comprehensive examination of this subject in its civil, legal, and military aspects"? Had the General Board of the Navy been consulted?

In an enclosed five-page memorandum, Mahan elaborated his claim that immunity would be deleterious to U.S. interests.[46] In so doing, he incidentally explained how sea power really worked, and its true potency. "It is only in the broad light of effect upon the resources of war,—the sinews of war, to use a common expression,—that the propriety of interference with an enemy's commerce can be adequately weighed," Mahan insisted. In time of war, in other words, the significance of capturing enemy property at sea extended far beyond the mere capture of enemy-owned merchantmen and their cargoes: what really matter were the knock-on or downstream effects on the broader economy and its society. Pointing to U.S. policy during the Civil War, he rhetorically asked: "Why should the exchange of cotton against dry goods and various other articles, of notoriously innocent character so far as the maintenance of war is concerned, have been prevented by the United States, with the consent of the rest of the world, neither the sympathies nor the interests of which then went with the Union? Let the finances and general condition of the Southern Confederacy answer the question. To the downfall of the Confederacy, no single cause conduced more than did the entire destruction of its commerce." The point Mahan was making here is that the effects of the Union blockade on the South were not only direct (depriving the Confederacy of munitions) but also indirect (the derangement of the wider southern economy). The effectiveness of sea power was not generally appreciated, he explained, because so much of its impact on the enemy economy was invisible and intangible. In his own words,

> The destruction of the Confederacy's commerce was but one
> cause in the result, and it was indirect in action; but, like some

deep-seated local disease, it poisoned the springs of life, spreading with remorseless certainty through innumerable hidden channels into every part of the political frame, till the whole was faint unto death. [The effect of commerce destruction] is not immediately seen and therefore, to many, remains untraceable. Nevertheless the effect is clear and substantial, as should be immediately recognized by anyone who has even a casual opportunity to note the effect of fluctuations of trade upon the welfare of a community.

Comparing the working of sea power to that of a virus was a new and powerful analogy: an unseen and terrible agent that insidiously destroyed an enemy (and its economy) from within.

Root proved surprisingly receptive to Mahan's letter, replying that he had "already entertained and in private expressed serious doubts" about immunity. Alas, he went on, there was no possibility of removing the subject from the agenda because it had been the United States that had proposed it in the first place. Besides which, Root added, "the United States has advocated immunity of private property at sea so long and so positively that I cannot see how it is possible to make a volte face at The Hague."[47] Politicians hate being charged with inconsistency. Root nevertheless took the point that his predecessor had failed to give the subject the adequate consideration, and he acted on Mahan's suggestion to request that the Navy Department task the General Board to conduct a detailed study.[48]

Again, Root's covering letter to Secretary of the Navy was surprisingly yet unmistakably supportive: he highlighted Mahan's argument that maintaining the right of capture acted as a deterrent to war, adding his own view that "there is undoubtedly a question whether decreasing the danger to commerce would not also greatly decrease the reasons for peace, and whether the establishment of immunity might not result in sacrificing human life in order to save merchandise."[49] Assistant Secretary Truman Newberry directed the General Board to give its opinion.[50]

Four weeks later the General Board sent back a rambling and singularly unimpressive twenty-seven-page memorandum.[51] Although Adm.

George Dewey and his officers professed themselves to be in broad agreement with Capt. Mahan, their text made clear they had arrived at this conclusion via a different and much narrower path. Basically, or rather simplistically, Dewey argued that since the U.S. Merchant Marine had sunk into insignificance—in 1906 just eight U.S.-flagged merchantmen plied the Atlantic, and most of the fifty-one vessels in the Pacific were engaged in coastal trade up the West Coast—the United States was effectively immune to maritime pressure.[52] (This was an argument with which Mahan strongly disagreed.) By contrast, most of the republic's prospective enemies possessed significant merchant navies, which in time of war the U.S. Navy might prey on. The General Board hastened to add, however, that commerce raiding would not be U.S. strategy in a future war. Espousing orthodox "Mahanian" dogma (i.e., views incorrectly ascribed to Mahan), Dewey pontificated,

> The main dependence of any nation at sea will always be upon its fighting fleet, and the chief object for each belligerent to obtain will be for his fighting fleet to meet the enemy and by a decisive action settle the question of control of the sea, but such other operations of war as will injure the enemy must be considered, and as has been the case in the past so will it be in the future, that operations against the enemy's commerce, and the establishment of military and commercial blockades of his ports will have a very great effect in bringing a commercial nation to terms. The General Board does not consider, however, that commerce destroying will ever be more than an auxiliary operation of war.[53]

There is wonderful irony here—the senior admiral in the U.S. Navy preaching Mahanisms to Mahan!

The General Board's analysis, such as there was any, was strictly operational. It contained no discussion whatsoever of the broader economic considerations that underpinned Mahan's arguments.[54] It might even be said that the document illustrated the General Board's, and the Navy's, total failure to grasp the subject. But this was not the end of the matter. Several days later, Capt. William J. Barnette, a member of the General Board and, like Mahan, a member of the New York University Club and a disciple of Adm. Stephen Luce, covertly sent Mahan copies of the report and the accompanying correspondence. "I want to say to you privately that this paper was not entirely satisfactory to the majority of the board," Barnette revealed to Mahan, but the Board had been pressured to send Root something on paper before he sailed for Europe.[55] He asked Mahan to send suggestions for improving the report; alas he did not specify what he and others saw as its shortcomings. To add to the difficulty in working out what was going on here, it should be noted that Barnette regarded Admiral Dewey as incompetent and was at that time scheming to see him replaced as head of the Board, meaning that his motives in forwarding this confidential file cannot be safely assumed.

In any case, early in October 1906, the Navy Department forwarded Root a supplemental six-page report on the subject of immunity.[56] Though signed by Dewey, its message was pure Mahan. It opened with the extraordinary statement that "The General Board is of the opinion that out interests are now so closely bound up with Great Britain, that we should exert our diplomatic efforts to dissuade Great Britain from giving up the great advantage she now holds over Germany, due to her great navy and her excellent strategical position in regard to Germany's commerce. This great advantage would be lost to Great Britain should she join with the United States in its previously mistaken policy of urging an international agreement to exempt private property from seizure in time of war."

American and British interests parallel? Previous American policy mistaken? These were impolitic statements! Echoing Mahan's comments to Roosevelt back in December 1904, the memorandum went on to suggest that "the closing of the seas to German shipping would be a blow to Germany which she could not well withstand"—in other words, commerce destruction could produce strategically significant and potentially decisive results.[57]

The fact that Mahan sent the president a letter in mid-August 1906 making exactly the same points lends further credence to the suspicion that he had authored the addendum to the General Board's report. A fortnight earlier, at the end of July, Mahan had visited Roosevelt at his summer house at Oyster Bay and taken advantage of the opportunity to tackle him again face-to-face on the immunity issue.[58] Looking to the future and viewing the subject through a geopolitical lens, Mahan represented maritime capture as "the strongest hook in the jaws of Germany that the English speaking peoples have; a principal gauge for peace." Germany's "ambitions threaten us as well as Great Britain, and I cannot but think that final action on the question of so called private property at sea would be better deferred, and the question be thrown into the arena of discussion, that action when taken may be in full light."[59]

Mahan also used his visit to press Roosevelt to waive the "very proper and necessary regulation of the Navy" that forbade officers, even retired ones, from "discussing publicly matters of policy on which the Government is embarked."[60] Ever since the State Department had formally proposed immunity for the Hague Peace Conference—thereby embarking the government on the policy—this regulation had barred Mahan from publicly discussing the subject. Mahan wanted "to be free to write for publication concerning matters that might come before the approaching Hague Conference, notably the question of exemption of private property, so called, from maritime capture."[61]

This was necessary, Mahan argued, because the peace movement averred that public opinion was squarely behind immunity. Even though this sweeping claim was obviously rhetorical, for it could be neither proven nor quantified, Mahan was afraid that some within the administration might be swayed by the assertion. To the extent that there had been any public discussion of the subject, Mahan complained, only one side of the story had been told.[62] Perusal of various newspaper articles and editorials from the period substantiate the captain's complaint that advocates of immunity were presenting a grossly oversimplified explanation of an incredibly complex subject; inconvenient details—important details—were being glossed over if not actually suppressed. Further, the lawyers were claiming it was a matter for lawyers. To add insult to injury, Elihu Root, the Secretary of State, had at the beginning of 1906 done what Mahan could not do under Navy regulations and accepted the presidency of the American Society of International Lawyers, a professional society in the forefront of groups lobbying in favor of immunity!

Roosevelt pondered Mahan's letter for only a couple of days before acceding to his request to balance the scales. "Your position is a peculiar one, and without intending to treat this as a precedent, I desire you to have a free hand to discuss in any way you wish the so-called peace proposals," the president granted. "You have a deserved reputation as a specialist which makes this proper from the public standpoint. Indeed I think it important for you to write just what you think of the matter."[63] Roosevelt departed yet further from procedure by sending a copy of his permission letter to the Department of State with an instruction to keep it on file, thereby protecting Mahan from future prosecution or penalty.[64]

The president's uncommon action should not be taken as evidence that Mahan had successfully changed his mind on the immunity issue. At this time, it seems Roosevelt was neither convinced nor unconvinced.[65] Writing privately the week before to Whitelaw Reid, the U.S. ambassador to Britain, whose opinion he valued, Roosevelt mused that "it is eminently wise and proper that we should take real steps in advance toward the policy of minimizing the chances of war among civilized peoples." But at the same time he could see the contrary argument: "We must not grow sentimental and commit such [Thomas] Jefferson–[William Jennings] Bryan like pieces of idiotic folly" by placing the United States "at a hopeless disadvantage compared with military despotisms and military barbarians" such as Prussia and Russia.[66] Writing again to Reid several months later, Roosevelt stated his hot and cold position more succinctly still: "I hold to our traditional American view [on immunity], but in rather tepid fashion."[67]

Roosevelt's ambivalence aside, what really held him back from openly endorsing Mahan's viewpoint was his recognition that the issue was too politically charged (and Roosevelt too publicly committed) to even consider openly backtracking. The power of the peace

lobby aside, throughout 1906 and into 1907 Anglo-American relations were being complicated by a squabble over fishing rights on the
Newfoundland Grand Banks. The president could not be seen to be
giving ground to the British on any maritime-related issue at this time.
This explains his contradictory stance: on the one hand he permitted
his administration to promote immunity, while on the other he went
out of his way to remove obstacles preventing Mahan from lobbying
against it.[68] Unofficially, however, Roosevelt's sympathies seem to have
been steadily gravitating toward the captain's position. The following
month, in October, he wrote Mahan that he would be "commending
your 'War of 1812' for general reading" in his forthcoming Message
to Congress.[69] On December 3, the president delivered on his promise to publicize his work in a national forum, proclaiming before Congress that "nothing could be more instructive than a rational study of
the war of 1812, as it is told, for instance, by Captain Mahan."

Mahan was naturally delighted by all this. He wasted no time in
telling Leo Maxse, editor of the *National Review*, that "the difficulty
of which I once wrote you, in reference to my writing for publication
on topics likely to come before the Hague Conference, has been overcome."[70] Over the next several months, the two exchanged numerous
letters plotting how best to influence opinions.[71] "Our people have
hugged their delusion so long, a single paper cannot hope to stop
action at The Hague," Mahan worried at the end of 1906.[72] Ultimately,
Maxse agreed to pay for two articles (at $500 apiece). They also agreed
that timing was everything and that the *National Review* should not
publish them until the very eve of the conference in order to get in the
last word.[73] For this reason, Mahan passed up an opportunity (most
likely arranged by Root) to present his views in the inaugural (January 1907) issue of the *American Journal of International Law*.[74] The
journal turned instead to Rear Adm. Charles Stockton, who turned in
a solid though uninspiring historical summary of the subject.[75]

PREPARATIONS FOR THE HAGUE
Going back a bit, after becoming Secretary of State in July 1905,
Elihu Root wasted little time in making preparation for the impending

second Peace Conference. In January 1906, he selected the key pleni-potentiaries and held some preliminary meetings.[76] To head the U.S. delegation, Root chose Joseph H. Choate, one of the most prominent New York lawyers of his day, who had served as U.S. ambassador to the United Kingdom between 1899 and 1905.[77] Then seventy-five years old, Choate was a fanatic on the subject of immunity. The second member was Gen. Horace Porter, formerly personal secretary to Ulysses S. Grant, who afterward made his fortune as a railway robber baron and later served as U.S. ambassador to France from 1897 to 1905. Porter seems to have held no position on the subject. Judge Uriah Rose of Arkansas, the former head of the American Bar Association and the only one of the three fluent in French and German, was the third. Rose also favored immunity. In addition, two military officers were chosen to serve as expert advisers, though later they were upgraded to become plenipotentiaries. Brig. George B. Davis, the Army's Judge Advocate General, was an undisputed expert on the subject of law and war and had published a couple of well-regarded textbooks on the subject. Rear Adm. Charles Sperry, the president of the Naval War College from 1903 to 1906, was picked to represent the Navy.

Sperry's selection was a bit of a surprise: though he knew something of international law, his knowledge paled to that of Mahan's friend Rear Adm. Charles Stockton. Not only had Stockton lectured on the subject at the Naval War College for many years and authored the fleet's handbook on international law (*The* Naval War Code of the United States), but he was so well respected on the subject that on retiring from the service he was appointed professor of international law at George Washington University.[78] In 1906, when the American team for the Hague was being assembled, Stockton was still in uniform and available for duty, being currently assigned to miscellaneous duties in the Navy Department. The preference for Sperry ahead of Stockton is something of a mystery, especially considering that Stockton was subsequently recalled out of retirement for duty at the 1909 London Naval Conference on maritime law.

Sperry himself attributed his selection to the influence of his mentor, Rear Adm. George Converse, the chief of the Bureau of

Navigation, though he also cryptically acknowledged that other forces had been at work.[79] This may have had something to do with the fact that Stockton, his competitor, had served as U.S. naval attaché in London when Choate had been ambassador (had the two perhaps clashed?). Another possibility is that Stockton might have been suspected of bias. Not only was he a close friend of Mahan (so was Sperry, though much less so), but back in 1899 he had publicly supported Mahan's anti-immunity campaign with an article of his own in the *North American Review*.[80] Sperry's selection may even have had something to do with his marriage to the only grandchild of William Marcy—the same Marcy who proposed the unsuccessful amendment to the 1856 Declaration of Paris—and his status as the custodian of Marcy's private papers.[81] Or perhaps it was assumed that Sperry was more open-minded on the subject than Mahan or Stockton. If so, that assumption was quite incorrect. Sperry's correspondence with his son leaves no doubt that he was scornful of the government's naked political posturing over immunity "to please the popular fancy."[82] At the end of 1906, Sperry admitted to Deputy Secretary of State Robert Bacon that he was "in entire accord with the views of Captain Mahan and the General Board as to the immunity of private property on the high seas, which is the heart of the whole matter."[83]

After May 1906, the pace of State Department preparations for the upcoming conference slowed noticeably. Root, as he confessed to Mahan, now had doubts on the immunity question, agreeing with the captain that the subject had not been thought through and that immunity might not, in fact, be in the country's best interests. His subsequent action—or rather inaction—suggests his doubts were genuine. Writing to Ambassador Reid in London several months later, Root equivocated that "Of course it has been an almost traditional policy of the United States to favor immunity. I myself have grave doubts about it. I doubt very much whether the probabilities of war would not be greatly increased by relieving the commercial class in every great country from their apprehension to injury to their trade which always makes them advocates of peace."[84]

From October 1906 and for the next twelve months, Root declined to commit the U.S. government on the issue of immunity any further than it already had been. For instance, after Christmas 1906, when the newly appointed department solicitor (James Brown Scott) asked the veteran second assistant secretary of State Alvin Adee for advice on how to respond to a request from the Commerce Department for clarification of U.S. policy on the issue, he was advised not to ask. "The attitude of this govt is well known," Adee told him, "but . . . it may be that the govt might find it advisable to modify traditional policy."[85] Robert Bacon was only slightly more forthcoming when fielding a similar inquiry from his old friend Frank Taussig, head of the Department of Economics at Harvard College and author of the classic work on tariff policy. In a letter dated January 25, 1907, Bacon confided,

> The United States, as you know, have invariably stood for the immunity of private property from capture on the high seas. Some naval experts [i.e., Mahan], however, and others, feel that the circumstances have changed, and that the policy which formally commended itself for practical reasons, no longer commends itself. The government might feel it advisable either to change its policy or to modify its policy, in the light of the present state of things. It would, therefore, be embarrassing if a communication were made. . . . I regret very much that it does not seem wise for me to discuss the official views upon this subject just now.[86]

Similarly, when Rear Adm. Sperry asked the State Department for an outline of the government's position on immunity in order that he might prepare for the conference, he was told to wait.[87] Sperry cannot have been entirely surprised. The previous fortnight, Brigadier Davis had told him that Root appeared wracked with indecision on the immunity issue, his doubts fueled by none other than Robert Bacon, his deputy, and by Adee, the department's number three, who both, it transpires, were opposed to immunity.[88]

Root's doubts, though real, do not entirely explain his indecision over policy, however. The fact is that when it came to The Hague, his principal attention lay elsewhere. That is to say, Root was rather less interested in the immunity question than in sponsoring a different initiative at the peace conference. Passionate about the rule of law, he believed that arbitration was a much better way of settling national disputes between civilized powers than resorting to war.[89] He therefore proposed to build on one of the few achievements of the previous Hague Peace Conference, namely the establishment of the Permanent Court of Arbitration (sometimes called The Hague Tribunal, or simply the PCA) to adjudicate in international disputes not involving matters of sovereignty. Root, however, disliked the way in which the PCA had been constituted: in actuality it was little more than a roster of arbitrators detailed to join ad hoc committees, packed with retired diplomats who were predisposed to negotiate a diplomatic compromise instead of rigorously applying the rule of law. Root, the president of the American Society of International Lawyers, wanted the PCA converted to a "proper" international court staffed by international jurists.[90] The story has been well told already by other historians.[91] The legal scholar Frederic L. Kirgis convincingly suggests that Root's perspective on the subject throughout was in preventing future wars (i.e., through arbitration), not in regulating their conduct (i.e., through immunity).[92] This interpretation chimes with a remark Sperry made to a friend shortly after learning of his appointment to the U.S. team. "Judging from the conversations which took place when the delegation dined with the Secretary of State and again with the President [on March 1, 1906], no programme has been formulated on our part relating to questions of international maritime law, attention being concentrated on matters in other lines likely to be the subject of international arbitration."[93]

Not until April 20, 1907, just six weeks before the Hague Peace Conference was due to convene, did Root finally gather all parties to "formulate general attitudes on the principal questions."[94] The minutes of this meeting show unambiguously that he viewed "arbitration" as the primary topic and objective. When discussion finally turned to the question of immunity, Root admitted that he remained "not wholly clear as to the position that the government should take on this important question."[95] Remarkably, for it was already the eleventh hour, instead of announcing the U.S. policy, he proceeded to lay out what he saw as the pros and cons and then threw the question to the floor.

Adm. Sperry at once "deplored" immunity, proceeding to list the practical obstacles. So much of maritime international law was mired in controversy; so many established "principles" had been rendered inapplicable by technological advances; the divergence of opinion on so many issues and so many so-called principles was just too great.[96] More tellingly, Sperry warned that if immunity for innocent trade were incorporated into the law of nations, the result would be an expansion in the definition of contraband, and any such expansion would likely prove seriously detrimental to U.S. export interests.[97] Under current international rules, nations at war were perfectly entitled to define contraband however they wished. Sperry predicted that food—including the wheat exported by the midwestern and western farmers who constituted crucial swing votes in U.S. elections—would be the first item to be reclassified as contraband. No dilettante, for many months Sperry had been trying to warn the administration that the subject of immunity was "inseparably involved with the laws of contraband and blockade," and thus that it was a waste of time to seek international consensus to outlaw the right of capture without achieving simultaneous agreement over the definitions of contraband and blockade.[98]

During the meeting, at least, the only serious pushback to Sperry's arguments came from Choate, who implored Root that "we should not reduce the discussion to the level of national needs and interests" and demanded clear instructions to act in the interests of civilization.[99] As the meeting broke for lunch, Root appeared to signal an end to the debate by stating that "although he had great doubt on the question, he felt it his duty to instruct the delegation in favor of the immunity."[100] But after resumption, when Sperry again reminded him of the likelihood that food would become classified as contraband, Root promptly reversed himself, declaring that "in this whole matter we must consider the American interest and that the catalogue of contraband should be enlarged or limited according to this interest.

As a neutral and food producer we should be permitted to export necessities to either belligerent . . . if nations declare war it is natural that the American merchant should take advantage of the belligerent market."[101] Implicitly rejecting Choate's plea to act primarily in the interest of civilization, Root insisted that the position taken by the United States at The Hague, at least as regards contraband, must be governed by national interest: "we cannot afford to bargain the enlargement of the list of contraband for immunity or immune property. The neutral position of the United States must necessarily prevent any such concessions."[102] This was a positive statement and unequivocal. Root's commitment to the traditional policy of pushing for immunity, it transpires, was skin deep. Though he supported the motion—while admitting his reluctance—he was not prepared to see any expansion in the generally accepted list of contraband, seeing such as likely to be seriously detrimental to U.S. business interests. One can imagine Root thinking to himself that if the rest of the world rejected the United States' sage efforts to limit the conduct of the war, then all bets were off and the republic would act in its own best interests. Or it might be said that Root was even *more* attached to another traditional American policy, the freedom in any conflict to make money by selling to both sides. The meeting broke up with the matter unresolved.

Over the course of the next several weeks, as he packed for Europe, Choate pressed Root to get more fully behind immunity.[103] The former told his son that "The immunity of private property at sea will be the one important question" at the conference; Root, as we have seen, regarded arbitration as the key issue.[104] Writing to Root on May 7, Choate implored that his delegation "should be authorized to press it [immunity] with vigor to a vote upon its intrinsic merits, in the expectation that a majority of the nations represented will cordially support it."[105] Playing on Root's (and Roosevelt's) worry at being accused of hypocrisy, he averred that the United States was inescapably committed to the principle by statements made by administrations previous and current. Citing Andrew White, the head of the U.S. delegation to the first Hague Peace Conference in 1899, Choate further proclaimed (without evidence) that the majority of nations favored immunity and assuredly would vote in favor of the measure at the next conference. His private correspondence confirms that he was in contact with White as well as Carnegie and others in the peace party.[106]

Choate offered Root some thoughts for a "legal strategy" to present the U.S. case to the international community, by which he meant the advocating of U.S. self-interest in terms of legal principle. "I do not venture to suppose that you will adopt them, but I send them only in the hope that they may be of some slight service," he disingenuously remarked in the covering note.[107] The document read like a legal brief: lawyerly arguments on how to win an argument and persuade a jury. It also demonstrates that Choate possessed only a hazy understanding as to why naval powers might regard it as important to retain the right of capture—he really did not seem to care. He displayed no awareness whatsoever of the wider economic consequences attending the derangement of an enemy's maritime transportation systems.

Root withstood Choate's legalistic but emotionally charged exhortations, though whether from lack of conviction or continuing indecision is unclear. Regardless, either because he was too busy, insufficiently interested, or, most likely, did not want to have further dealings with Choate, Root delayed issuing the delegation's official instructions until after the delegation had sailed to Europe; they were sent by courier a week later.[108] These instructions, so platitudinous as to be clearly written with an eye for subsequent publication, gave Choate permission to plead at the conference for immunity but little else. He was permitted to lobby to gain support from other delegations but he was given no latitude to negotiate or authorized to make concessions in other areas in order to obtain such an agreement. This meant that he was required to refer back to Washington for further instructions. On the specific issue of immunity, Choate's instructions (item 6) read thus: "It will be appropriate for you to advocate the proposition formulated and presented by the American delegates to the First Conference as follows: The private property of all citizens or subjects of the signatory Powers, with the exception of contraband of war, shall be exempt from capture or seizure on the high seas, or elsewhere."[109] The secretary went on to command that "[y]ou should do all in your power to bring about an agreement upon what is to constitute contraband; and it is very desirable that the list should be limited as narrowly as possible."[110] The contrast in language on immunity versus contraband was striking; the priority seemed clear. Basically, Root attached greater weight to narrowing the definition of contraband than to obtaining consensus on immunity, yet in so doing chose to ignore Sperry's opinion that the two were inextricably linked.

MAHAN ON THE ATTACK

Understanding more of the background struggle to formulate U.S. policy going into the Hague Peace Conference, and the reasons for that struggle, we now return to Mahan's public campaign against immunity. From his correspondence with Leo Maxse, it is clear that Mahan's goal was to give the delegates attending pause by hurling a wrench into the works; he wanted to supply ammunition against the propaganda put out by the immunity lobby. He regarded his arguments as unanswerable and therefore bound to persuade all practically minded statesmen. "Very possibly the hard cold sense which I flatter myself I have put in my arguments will have a better chance when the effects of the fizz-stuff have evaporated," he told Maxse.[111]

Though Mahan was always careful to disclaim insider knowledge of the U.S. government's attitudes, he nevertheless felt confident that the administration (namely Roosevelt and Root) "would not be greatly disappointed to meet an insuperable objection."[112] "I believe that if this matter can be staved off this conference, it is very doubtful if it would be renewed by us at a future one," he revealed to Maxse.[113] Mahan wanted his articles published by the *National Review* at the last possible second in order to have the last word in the preconference public debate and so shape opinions going into the conference.

Mahan's scheme ran more or less according to plan, though Maxse unleashed Mahan's first broadside a little prematurely, while the majority of the U.S. delegation were still crossing the Atlantic. The main thrust of "The Practical Aspect of War," which appeared in the June issue of the *National Review*, was that the subject of immunity was not primarily a legal issue, as the peace movement and international lawyers were arguing, but a policy issue. Tackling the subject, furthermore, required a deep understanding of why nations went to war, of the character and nature of war, and most importantly of the relationship between trade and war.[114]

Advocates of immunity, Mahan declared, seemed implicitly to assume that war was simply a fight between the armed forces of each protagonist, a kind of gladiatorial contest quarantined from broad social, political, and economic forces. Nonsense! Instead, recapitulating his thesis in *Influence*, Mahan explained that most wars resulted from an irreconcilable clash of vital national interests, usually (though not always) economic and commercial. However elevated and laudable it might seem to settle disputes in a "civilized" manner by employing reason guided by laws instead of "uncivilized" and "barbaric" violence, the notion not only displayed a naive view of human nature but in fact was wholly impractical. Rather, the uncomfortable truth was war was the only *practical* way humans had found to settle their disputes. The fundamental condition of human existence was resource scarcity and an impulse embedded in all humans to improve their lot and thus competition for those scarce resources.[115] He wrote, "In putting forward these truths of material pressure with a bareness perhaps somewhat brutal, I must not be understood to justify, far less to advocate, the predominance of material considerations over moral. I simply look existing facts in the face, which is in strict accord with my proposed point of view—the Practical Aspect of War; the place of War in the economy of the world which now is."[116] Reiterating his argument in even blunter language, Mahan explained that history showed that when push came to shove, material considerations (i.e., economic considerations) almost always trumped moral ones.[117] "Between material and moral motives men and nations must commit themselves to a definite choice; one or the other—not both," he proclaimed. "Ye cannot serve God and Mammon."[118] To suggest otherwise was at best naive and at worst dishonest.

Mahan's other main argument against immunity was that the existing foundations for settling disputes through arbitration or law were far too shallow to bear the weight of any ruling in matters deemed of vital national interest. Except for the embryonic Court of Arbitration, the institutional apparatus to settle national differences simply did not exist, and even if it soon would the international court lacked both the authority and the means to enforce its rulings. Establishing such an apparatus, moreover, would not be as simple as the advocates of immunity breezily asserted. Yes, an international court with appellate powers had been proposed and might be established, but such a body would need "laid down for its guidance and governance certain established rules, or body of precedents, which by common agreement have reached the authority of law, and so may justly be styled law international; a code, to which appeal may be made, and upon which decision shall rest unchallengeable."[119] But, Mahan correctly pointed out, there was no universally accepted code of "law," or even a close approximation of one. Although the international community acknowledged the existence of certain legal principles and documented precedents, yet again none were clearly defined and several contradicted each other (as would be demonstrated almost daily during World War I). In drawing attention to these awkward facts, Mahan implicitly questioned the honesty of the peace movement and international lawyers, warning that "Where an antecedent body of accepted law is wanting, arbitration becomes a matter of personal beliefs or opinions on the part of the arbitrators; just as many so-called treatises on international law express the views of the writers, frequently discordant, as to what law ought to be, rather than a definition of what it is. Such a definition in fact is impossible, because there is not a law."[120] If there was no consensus on what the law was, or should be, and consequently the court's rulings were mere opinion, then why should a losing party respect them? "Why should I trust the crying needs of my children to the decisions of another than myself? Is it, indeed, moral to do so?" Mahan asked with a rhetorical flourish.[121]

The following month, the *National Review* unleashed Mahan's second broadside. In "The Question of Immunity" he approached the subject from a different angle.[122] As the title implied, it directly addressed the question of whether neutral merchantmen (and the cargoes they carried) should be immune from capture in time of war. Here, instead of scolding proponents of immunity for their ignorance of the nature and character of war, as he had done in his first broadside, he reprimanded them for their ignorance of how the real (economic) world actually worked. In so doing, he demonstrated how deeply their arguments were mired in economic misconception and misunderstanding. Far more than the first, moreover, his second article, one of the most impressive and tightest he ever wrote, was built directly on the concept of sea power. It contained perhaps his most concise articulation of the "mechanics" of sea power—that is to say, how it actually operated. It might be noted that after World War I, the British Admiralty held Mahan's main argument presented therein as authoritative, a digest of which was presented in a memorandum to the prime minister.[123]

Advocates of immunity, Mahan thundered, assumed that maritime commerce destruction played but a minor part in the outcome of wars. If commerce destruction was unimportant, they claimed, then such attacks were nothing more than acts of wanton barbarism (or simple theft) and inconsistent with the conduct of civilized nations. From Mahan's perspective this was completely wrong. To appreciate the importance of commerce destruction, he explained, one had to understand how economies functioned, especially to recognize that economic activity was a fundamentally dynamic process. As he had argued in his previous publications, most clearly in *War of 1812*, trade in goods and services represented money in circulation and fostered the commerce that led to wealth generation, which the state needed to tax to pay for the war it was fighting.

Once these connections were recognized and understood, Mahan thought, manifestly it was absurd "to exempt from the operations of war a financial feature [trade] so important to the war-waging ability of a belligerent [tax revenues], and at the same time so easily accessible to an enemy [i.e., vulnerable to attack]."[124] Accordingly, "The object aimed at, by the method of seizing vessels and cargoes at sea, is to stop the increase of the enemy's wealth by circulation, by stopping the transportation of his goods, of whatever character. This is the essence

of the matter."[125] In modern parlance, the primary object in applying naval force was to interdict the enemy's international trade—its
wealth-generation machine—in such a way as to apply significant and
hopefully decisive pressure so as to induce peace.

The effects of commerce destruction at sea extended beyond interdicting commercial and financial flows and preventing the generation
of wealth.[126] There was a second-order consequence: preventing the
circulation of wealth that set in motion other economic forces, the
cumulative effect of which was to derange the enemy's entire economy. In some parts of the enemy country there would be shortages,
in others there would be gluts: everywhere the relative prices of goods
would change, leading to general economic derangement. Over time,
economic chaos would generate a third-order consequence, which
Mahan termed the "dissolvent effect" on the entire society.[127] Put
simply, economic derangement would eventually lead to social turmoil. This argument, of course, was but a clearer restatement of Mahan's contention, made fifteen years before, that it had been British sea
power that had led to Napoleon's downfall: "The cessation of maritime
transportation deranged the entire financial system of France, largely
dependent upon foreign custom. She could neither raise revenue nor
borrow; both money and credit were wanting."[128] Mahan drove home
his point with a couple of more recent examples. One, of course, was
the War of 1812, during which the Royal Navy practically destroyed
the U.S. economy. The other was the American Civil War; Mahan
insisted that it really had been the Navy's blockade of the South that
broke the confederacy.[129]

But these were historical examples. In the more than forty years
since the American Civil War, the world economy had been visibly transformed. This transformation did not vitiate the historical
examples, however: on the contrary, it made them apply with even
greater force. Far from downplaying the magnitude of change, Mahan
emphasized it. He stressed the enormous growth in international
trade, highlighted the interdependencies and interconnectedness of
markets, and referenced recent societal changes. Characteristically,
much of this argument was implicit because he thought the linkages

and implications were sufficiently obvious. The bottom line, Mahan argued, was that twentieth-century nations were more—certainly not less—vulnerable to sea power. Globalization made the prospect of denying a nation access to the common, and thus the ability to participate in the international economy, even more potent:

> The very scale upon which commerce is now conducted, the facilities, conveniences, luxuries, which it has introduced into ordinary households, while swelling its volume, have made greater and more far-reaching the effects of any obstruction. The stoppage of a coasting-trade, the closing of a few principal ports of entry, would so congest the trunk lines [railways] of a national system that the influence would be felt instantly in every shop and household, and speedily in the national treasury. People also are now more luxurious, less hardened to bear, [sic] impatient over privations which their predecessors would hardly notice.[130]

Here again we see the reasoning underpinning Mahan's famous aphorism, often quoted but rarely understood, that "upon the maintenance of commerce the vitality of a state [depends]. Lessen it, and vigor flags; destroy it, and resistance dies."[131] The logic was that the power to attack sea commerce in wartime mattered a great deal.

IN THE AFTERMATH OF THE HAGUE

To review the events and the outcome of the second Hague Peace Conference, a subject that has long been shrouded in confusion and controversy, lies beyond the scope of the present study.[132] Not only were most participants clearly engaged in "lawfare"—the game of tailoring international law to suit one's own national interests—but the historical record as to who said what and why is not entirely reliable. The U.S. government's official history on the conference was compiled by James Brown Scott, who had been part of the U.S. delegation and was pro-immunity. It can be shown that Choate, staunchly pro-immunity, encouraged him to exclude the speeches of Sperry and Davis, the U.S. delegates who had voiced dissent.[133] How deep the manipulation of the historical record ran is impossible to say without much closer study, which probably is not worth the trouble. In any case, what transpired at the conference is of value to the present study only insofar as it sheds light on the development and exposition of Mahan's concept of sea power.

It can be shown that before the conference opened, Mahan's pair of articles was widely read and praised, including by those whose opinions mattered most, namely national policy makers and their plenipotentiaries in attendance. For instance, Sir Ernest Satow, the number two in the British delegation, recorded in his diary at the beginning of June that after lunch with his old friend Admiral Sir William Henderson, conversation turned to discussing "Mahan's article in the *National Review* and Julian Corbett's in the *XIX Century* for this month."[134] Several weeks later, Mahan was delighted to read in the papers that Satow had quoted directly from his paper in a speech to the conference.[135] Eyre Crowe, an up-and-coming diplomat who had been selected to run the British back office at The Hague, wrote Leo Maxse to say how impressed he was by Mahan's latest article: "As I have been a fairly attentive reader of his books and articles, his argument is familiar to me, but it is here restated with greater force and more definitely developed than I have seen in his previous writings."[136] Crowe mentioned that he had forwarded copies to each member of the British delegation.

Once the conference opened, Mahan was taken aback to see Choate pressing so vigorously for immunity. Midway through, he was afraid the motion might even pass. "I regret that our Gov't has persisted in presenting the project of immunity," he dolefully wrote Maxse on June 28, "but I know it has felt almost bound to do so."[137] To Admiral Luce he was more frank, his unhappiness with the Roosevelt administration more visible. "To me this is a day of shams; I think to have exposed one in 'private property.' I hope also to help demolish another by showing that the avoidance of war depends not upon pious 'resolutions,' or conferences, but upon a change of heart in mankind. Until that occurs War is inevitable, except by the 'practical' expedient of being ready for it."[138]

In fact, the position was not as bad as Mahan feared. Had he stayed in closer touch with his friends, he would have learned that his arguments had struck home and indeed given many a pause for thought. In June 1907, for instance, after meeting with the American conference delegates, Whitelaw Reid remarked to the president that "I am not yet quite so confident as Mr. Choate about either the support for immunity of private property at sea or the great advantage of it. Captain Mahan's arguments made some impression upon me; but as the matter wasn't in my field and I had enough to think of, I have never satisfactorily reasoned the case out in my own mind."[139]

A few weeks later, after a preconference meeting in London between the British and American teams, Reid was horrified at Choate's zealotry on the subject of immunity and his lack of tact. Secretary Root had explicitly charged Choate not to press discussion of the subject "to the point of irritation" and counseled that "after reasonable discussion, if no agreement is reached, it is better to lay the subject aside."[140] Reid clearly thought Choate had crossed the line when he informed Roosevelt that "The British, as I reported to Mr. Root before the Conference met, are extremely strong against the immunity of private property at sea—holding about the view which our Captain Mahan has so vigorously enforced. When Mr. Choate was here he seemed enthusiastic in favor of this doctrine and rather startled the Minister of Foreign Affairs by holding before him the prospect of a union of all nations against the British position."[141]

From Roosevelt's reply, it seems that Choate had indeed transgressed. He wrote back at once that he was "astounded at what you tell me Choate said," asking "is it worth my while to call the matter to the attention of either Root or Choate?"[142] In the event, the president seems to have stayed his hand, for in the weeks that followed Choate maintained his hectoring stance. Adm. Sperry seemed uncertain whether to be more embarrassed or relieved when he confided to his son that Choate's blathering was being ignored. "Nothing else counts for much, fortunately, as our vain, lazy and trifling friend the late ambassador to England [Choate], offends everyone and spoils whatever he touches: also he cannot even read French and is entirely ignorant of what is going on, knowing only enough to meddle."[143] The extent to which the other attendees recognized Choate as a buffoon is difficult to gauge without a great deal more research. Yet from the diary of Sir Ernest Satow it seems sufficiently clear that Choate was not popular with the British delegation.[144]

Regardless of Choate's effectiveness or otherwise, back in Washington neither Roosevelt nor Root were much interested in what happened at the conference. On several occasions in 1907, before the Hague Conference met, the president cautioned Andrew Carnegie that although "our representatives will go to the second peace conference at The Hague instructed to help in every practicable way to bring some steps nearer completion the great work which the first conference began," nevertheless "it is idle to expect that a task so tremendous can be settled by any one or two conferences, and those who demand the impossible from such a conference . . . prepare acute disappointment for themselves."[145] Privately, Roosevelt despised Carnegie for his interference in matters for which he was unfit and unqualified.[146] Carnegie probably suspected as much, and Roosevelt's letter was not well received.[147] Several days later, Root publicly reissued the administration's warning not to expect many results from The Hague.[148]

The historian Calvin Davis judges, correctly, that well before the conference convened Roosevelt had lost all interest in the subject.[149] A fortnight after the conference opened, Roosevelt freely admitted to his Secretary of State that "I have not followed things at The Hague" before going on to enquire "is there anything for me to do in this Hague Matter"?[150] All subsequent correspondence shows that he remained indifferent to the proceedings.[151] Elihu Root seemed no more energetic. The State Department files show he was slow to respond to Choate's telegrams, and his replies were usually evasive. "I am assiduously doing nothing," the Secretary admitted to Senator Lodge on July 2, 1907, "and discouraging communication from the Department by neglect of them."[152] It may be true, as Root's biographer argued, that his lethargy was the product of illness combined with depression brought on by his elder brother being terminally ill (Root's brother died on August 27). But the fact remains that he had never exhibited much interest in the codification of maritime law. His focus had always been fixed on the prevention of wars. Deliberately or not, Root's quiet inaction allowed immunity to wither on the vine.

//////////////////////////////

The world's press judged the second Hague Peace Conference a failure, but Choate insisted to Root that "on the contrary, as we can easily satisfy you it was a great success."[153] Scott, his aide, argued that in the field of maritime law, although the immediate results had been few, a watershed had been crossed and another conference (or two) would deliver more tangible results.[154] This assessment did not totally lack evidence. At the conference attendees had agreed to reorganize the Permanent Court of Arbitration along the lines Root proposed (staffed by lawyers rather than diplomats), the necessary preliminary step to creating the sort of "world court" peace advocates envisioned. Separately, the community of nations had agreed to establish a specialist International Prize Court to serve as an appellate court for cases involving capture at sea.[155] But, it must be stressed, nothing was yet up and running. Approval for these international courts had been granted only in principle, and there remained several major hurdles ahead. Choate had failed to obtain a consensus as to how judges for either court should be selected or agreement as to the principles that should govern the court's rulings. The differences in international opinion on this subject were as chasms.[156] Thus, from another perspective, the advance in the cause of international law was more apparent than real.

Mahan certainly thought so. Believing that the status quo had been maintained, he seemed jubilant that "The Hague Conference seems likely to adjourn having done less harm than might have been feared."[157] Even so, he recognized the second Hague Peace Conference as merely an opening round in an ongoing contest, and Roosevelt and Root agreed with this belief. No sooner did the second Peace Conference adjourn than the lobbying resumed in anticipation of the third, scheduled for 1915 but canceled because of World War

I. Writing in September 1907, Mahan revealed his intention to land the first blow by gathering together all the best arguments against immunity (including his two articles for the *National Review*) plus some more by other authors and publish them under a single cover.[158] Already he had secured permission to reproduce a piece by Julian Corbett.[159] "My object," Mahan explained to his friends and allies, is "to give a mild start to something like a formal opposition to the extravaganzas of the Arbitration propaganda. If discussion be provoked, the common people, who are accepting arbitration at its face value, will soon realize its limitations." Published at the end of 1907 under the title *Some Neglected Aspects of War*, the book sold out within four months and was hastily reprinted.[160]

In this volume, Mahan took the opportunity to add an introductory essay complaining that the cause of peace, to which he subscribed, was being jeopardized "by the exaggerations and oversights of its noisier followers."[161] He let fly at what he regarded as the arrogance, moralizing, simplistic reasoning, vitriol, judgmental tone, and unyielding tenor of advocates of universal arbitration and disarmament. He took particular aim at international lawyers for arrogating to themselves special authority to pronounce on the subject of war and law. Not only did lawyers mistakenly assume that law was the governing consideration, Mahan argued, but they demonstrably had given no thought to the nature or character of war. (The speeches by Choate and Rose given at The Hague rather tend to substantiate his accusation.) For Mahan, the principles of international law seemed abstract, and they too often overlooked the harsh economic realities confronting statesmen engaged in the exercise of power. To support his position, Mahan included a copy of a letter on the subject by the late General William T. Sherman.[162] Mahan of course had known Sherman.

Given the clear ignorance of lawyers on the subject of war, Mahan objected, why should the opinions of lawyers on the relationship between law and war be privileged as they demanded? They were exceeding the boundaries of their competence. In presenting his case, Mahan delivered an extended discussion on the role and place of the law in society, premised on the belief that the law was the servant of society, not its master. "We speak of law with bated breath, as though it were some self-existent Being; a reverence probably due to the superabundance of lawyers in representative governments. Law in truth is the creation of the state, of the people. It is a functionary, with methods and powers by them prescribed, as to any other official; and it depends for its efficiency upon the physical force behind it, of the state, of the organized people."[163]

What is more, he continued, "The mandates of law are simply the register of past decisions reached by the people upon precedent conditions; and when unprecedented conditions arise, law, unless ex post facto, is paralyzed, for want of mandate. A new decision must be taken; a new instruction issued. A large proportion of the questions embarrassed under honor and vital interests today are precisely in that inchoate condition, of non-decision and possibly even of dispute, which cannot be brought under the head of law."[164]

Though Mahan's critics tried to dismiss his views as the uninformed rantings of an antediluvian sea dog, ignorant of the law, his writings show that he understood a great deal more than they allowed and that he had looked a good deal more closely at the relevant parts than had most advocates of immunity. The evidence is clear that on this issue and at this time Mahan enjoyed measurably widespread influence and that his very different viewpoint on one of the leading issues of the day was acknowledged as well-grounded and legitimate. Most importantly, Mahan was correct in insisting that the question of immunity remained fundamentally a matter of policy, not of law, and that the questions it raised could not be resolved without possessing also an understanding of the character and conduct of war—and of international economics.

CHAPTER 10

TWILIGHT YEARS

(1908–14)

I become continually more and more convinced that the average man
can't tell—as years advance—when he has really got out of touch
with the times, & becomes a mere "wind-jammer"—to use a
naval expression for useless talk.

—ALFRED THAYER MAHAN, MARCH 12, 1901[1]

AFTER COMPLETING *Sea Power in Its Relations to the War of 1812*,
the first copies of which became available in November 1905, Mahan
resolved not to write another major monograph or undertake any
project that entailed significant new research. He rented out his New
York brownstone and travelled. Although he remained fit and active,
and his mind unimpaired, he was now sixty-six years old and increasingly feeling his age. His disinclination to undertake anything strenu-
ous was reinforced by a 20 percent boost in his naval pension on his
unexpected promotion to the rank of rear admiral (retired).[2] The extra
$1,000 per year translated into two fewer articles each year.

As we saw in chapter 9, Mahan spent most of 1906 concentrating on the immunity issue and the second Hague Peace Conference, producing two major articles on the subject that commanded
worldwide attention and respect. As he applied the final coats of
polish, he cast about for his next project. He considered, but quickly

304

rejected, reviving his old idea of producing a school textbook. Next he tried obtaining permission to take some chapters he contributed (in 1897) to Laird Clowes' *History of the Royal Navy* and expand them into a book, but Clowes' publisher refused to reassign him the copyright.[3]

In July 1906, aware that Mahan was contemplating how to occupy his time, Adm. Luce wrote him suggesting that he update and revise for publication his old War College lecture notes. Though composed mostly during the late 1880s, they were still being used at Newport as the basis of the foundational course on naval strategy.[4] "I have heard them read over each year (with a few exceptions) since they were first delivered and each time with increased interest," Luce told Mahan, adding, "You have made a great reputation by your work on Sea Power: this last work will be, in effect, the capstone, as it were, of the great monument you have reared—the summing up of all your studies in Naval Science. For I take it these lectures must sometime be published and it is far better that they should have a final revising by you, rather than by somebody else far less competent. You will then have done for naval warfare what Jomini did for warfare on land."[5] Clearly flattered, Mahan nevertheless politely declined, claiming he was too busy with other work at the moment to undertake the task.[6] Over the next several months, Luce pressed him several times to reconsider, but Mahan continued to make excuses, aware that the project was a far greater undertaking than Luce seemed to appreciate.[7] Besides, he was now genuinely busy writing his autobiography, something much more to his liking.[8]

Mahan completed his autobiography in the early summer of 1907. No sooner had he finished than Luce resumed badgering him to revise his lectures. Anticipating further excuses, and aware that Mahan had been stung by the poor reception given to *1812*, Luce deviously remarked that they would "contribute more to your reputation than many 'pot boilers' however desirable the latter may be. They (the strategy lectures) are the culmination of your exhaustive studies in Naval History."[9] Such blandishments did not work, however, and again Mahan rebuffed his old mentor.[10]

Luce's persistence and his seeming veneration for Mahan's strategy lectures raises an interesting question. Was the admiral's praise
mere flattery, or did he sincerely regard them as Mahan's finest work,
superior not only to his writings on contemporary affairs (his so-called
potboilers) but even to his sea power monographs? At once it should
be noted that Luce was not proposing that Mahan revise his lectures
for publication; he simply wanted updated versions for use at the
Naval War College. In other words, he seems to have regarded their
value as more pedagogical than scholarly, envisioning their use as a
primer for naval officers unaccustomed to thinking outside narrow
professional concerns. In Luce's opinion, nothing better was available
for this purpose.

Reading these lectures (or rather the revised copies, since the originals were destroyed), it seems pretty obvious why Luce so liked them.
The contained exactly his kind of history: filled with quotations from
Jomini and other military theorists, replete with immutable principles
of war, comparing and contrasting land and sea warfare throughout.
Indeed, in one of his periodic exhortations to Mahan Luce explicitly congratulated him for "unconsciously adopt[ing] the 'Comparative Method.' This was the scientific method of proceeding I tried to
explain in my paper of 1886. You will [therefore] see from this why I
want you to revise your lectures on strategy and bring us up to date."[11]
As readers will recall from chapter 2, this was the methodological
approach Luce pressed Mahan to utilize when he first started at the
War College back in 1886. This letter from Luce demonstrates that, a
quarter century later, the admiral remained wedded to his belief that
the principles of naval warfare could be scientifically deduced through
the "comparative method of history."[12]

Recalling that Mahan subsequently abandoned Luce's idiosyncratic methodology as quickly as he decently could (also related in
chapter 2), Mahan's unwillingness to revive his lectures becomes easier to fathom. By this stage of his life, he was much more interested
in scholarship than professional military education. Since compiling
these lectures, moreover, he had developed considerably as a historian. His old lectures might have been adequate for use at a service

institution but they would not pass muster with the literati, and he knew it. This is not to say that it was impossible to produce a work that would satisfy both constituencies. But in the case of these naval strategy lectures, to do the job properly would require reorganizing the material along very different lines and employing a very different logic. In effect, Mahan would have to undertake a complete rewrite and of course revisit all the sources he had visited more than twenty years before.[13] This would have represented an enormous undertaking, and anyone who has ever contemplated something similar will appreciate why Mahan was not keen.

It therefore is curious that a year later, in 1908, Mahan suddenly acceded to Luce's request. All of Mahan's biographers have remarked on this volte-face. Robert Seager attributed Mahan's reversal to a combination of vanity, a sense of obligation to his old mentor, and "a pervasive sense of duty to the War College"; William Livezey thought it strange; Capt. William Puleston came closest when he remarked that "Mahan acquiesced somewhat reluctantly, for kneading over old work did not appeal to him, and he could not take his thoughts off the current international situation."[14] But he erred in suggesting that Mahan "agreed with Luce that the lectures were the culmination of his studies in naval history and, as such, were his most valuable contributions to his own profession": in fact, read closely, this volume differed fundamentally from Mahan's previous work. Where all agree is that Mahan came to regret his decision, and the final product was undoubtedly the worst and most slapdash volume he ever published.[15]

Why then did Mahan go against his better judgment and decide to publish his old 1887 lectures? The answer was money. To begin with, between 1907 and 1908 Mahan's circumstances changed. First, his health collapsed. In the early spring of 1907, Mahan suffered what seems to have been either a mild heart attack or a minor stroke. His doctor ordered him to avoid exerting himself so much and to take a rest cure.[16] Writing from a German health spa a couple of months later, "crowded with cripples—like myself," Mahan told Bouverie Clark that "the physician here confirms in general terms the diagnosis, which I conceive to be that, as I am nearing sixty seven, wear and tear is evident; I must moderate my pace—literally and metaphorically."[17] A few months later, Mahan was diagnosed with prostate cancer. The initial prognosis seems to have been grim because we find Mahan writing to all his old friends contemplating his mortality.[18] Over the next six months he underwent three major operations.[19] It was many months—practically a year—before he was sufficiently recovered to resume his correspondence, let alone do any serious work. On November 18, 1907, in between operations, Mahan responded to yet another letter from Luce entreating him revise his lectures, saying he would consider the matter when he had the time but intimating that if he did, he expected to be properly compensated with the full pay of a rear admiral.[20] But this was far from a promise, and in any case Mahan spent most of following year convalescing while composing his religious memoirs. During the entire year he produced only a solitary lightweight article for *Collier's Weekly*. His correspondence with his publisher confirms that Mahan had nothing else significant on his literary horizon.

In early 1908 Mahan incurred a second shock, apparently financial. Interviewed in 1935, his daughter, Ellen, vaguely recalled that "my parents received a blow which altered everything for us. From my mother and father something had gone which they were never to get back."[21] Various historians have speculated as to what this might have been.[22] What seems most likely is that Mahan lost a chunk of his savings in the crash of 1907 (the aftereffects of which reverberated well into 1908). Possibly he had his money invested in the New York branch of the Bank of North America, which closed its doors in January 1908—the largest bank to collapse in more than a decade—with depositors getting back only 50 percent of their money.[23]

There is considerable circumstantial evidence to support the supposition of a serious financial setback. First, the family abandoned their plans to return to their fashionable Upper West Side brownstone (which had been rented out the previous three years), instead choosing to move permanently out of the expensive city to the then much cheaper far end of Long Island.[24] Second, in March 1908, Mahan did something he had never done before: he exploited his friendship with

President Roosevelt to ask for a political favor, specifically to endorse the appointment of his son, Lyle, as an assistant district attorney in New York City.[25] In the event, his son's application was unsuccessful and Mahan was obliged to subsidize him (and his family) while he established a new law practice in New York City. This would explain why, in April 1908, and despite not yet having fully recovered his health, Mahan suddenly became anxious to resume writing and making money.[26]

In May 1908 Mahan received a letter from Rear Adm. John P. Merrell, the current head of the Naval War College, offering him a position back in Newport. Merrell told him that his task would be to revise (and present) his old lectures on "naval strategy" and, where possible, to bring them up to date by incorporating lessons learned from the recent Russo-Japanese War. In making this offer, Merrell all but admitted that it was Luce who was really pulling the strings: "I was on the point of writing to you last year [1907] to ask you to undertake this revision when I learned through Admiral Luce of your illness, and did not carry out my intentions. Understanding that at present your health is much better, I venture to urge you that for the good of the College and the service you will undertake this work."[27]

Mahan replied immediately, agreeing to do the work on the understanding he would be paid for his trouble.[28] "I have to consider the pecuniary side," he apologized. "Up to my illness my pen has added to my income an amount of substantial importance to my family, and I hesitate to contract the obligation to write which orders would entail."[29] He also insisted that the college buy all the books that he would need and pay his research expenses and his postage.[30] There was a snag, however. Under naval regulations, if Mahan was recalled to active service, he would be paid as a captain—the rank at which he had retired—and not receive the pay of a rear admiral. To add insult to injury, the pay of a captain on the active list was more or less the same as the pension of a retired rear admiral, meaning that if Mahan went back on the active list he would be no better off, and indeed (thanks to the tax system) might end up worse off! Anyone who has worked for the federal government will recognize this unique incentive structure, though they may be surprised to learn that it has been around for so long.

Ultimately a compromise was reached. Merrell agreed to compensate Mahan through the Navy's system of allowances, what today government employees know as per diem and locality pay, while remaining at home on Long Island. This would give him roughly an extra $1,500 per year tax free. In addition, he would also be allowed to publish the lectures as a book and keep the royalties earned.[31] At the same time, the contracting parties agreed that Mahan could scale back on the deliverable: the lectures would be lightly revised instead of completely rewritten.[32] "Simple revision may be best," Mahan wrote Luce on June 17. "I had contemplated, vaguely, the preparation of a fairly elaborate treatise on the subject of Naval Warfare; but perhaps the old lectures, as a trial balloon, might be advisable first, in publication."[33] On this basis, Mahan returned to duty at the end of October 1908.[34] The task of revising his lecture notes took two years; he completed it shortly after his seventieth birthday.[35]

Mahan's *Naval Strategy Compared and Contrasted with the Principles and Practice of Military Operations on Land*, published in 1911, is a cocktail of contradictions, a confusing blend of old and new, unsystematic, unshaken, and unstirred. Mahan did the minimum work necessary, perhaps motivated to do so by the Naval War College adding considerably to his workload, having him do odd jobs in addition to what had been agreed while at the same time—despite the assurances given him beforehand—cutting his allowances by approximately one-third.[36] After he finished, a much-relieved Mahan wrote to his friend Bouverie Clark, "I will confess to you that the composing [of] it was the most perfunctory job I have ever done in book writing. There were very compelling reasons for undertaking it, but it alone of all my much writing [*sic*] was felt to be a burden."[37]

For the purposes of this study, a full-scale critique of *Naval Strategy* is not necessary. Far from being the culmination of his scholarship, it in fact represented a retrograde step. Even a perusal of the work (which is not recommended) makes clear that in glaring contrast to all of Mahan's previous books relating to naval history (and many of his articles on contemporary affairs), this volume was not organized around his concept of sea power. Instead, as indicated already, Mahan framed his arguments using Luce's idiosyncratic methodology dating from the early 1880s rather than his own explicated during the late 1880s and refined during the 1890s. This point is fundamental and has not before been recognized. Though *Naval Strategy* contains hints of sea power theory—"commercial value cannot be separated from military in sea strategy, for the greatest interest of the sea is commerce"—they are few and far between, clustered toward the end of the book, which we know from other sources mentioned in chapter 2 that he wrote slightly later than the others.[38]

Another important difference between *Naval Strategy* and Mahan's other work, and again reflecting the influence of Luce, is that the narrative and analysis focused on the intersection of strategy and operations (tilted strongly toward the latter) rather than between policy and strategy, where Mahan normally operated. This focus made the book much narrower in conception than his other work. He made practically no mention of international economics or their importance in the exercise of state power, which as we have seen became the key theme in his later work. If there was a single or constant thread running through his whole intellectual career, it was *not* the need for a battle fleet or command of the seas, as is often thought, but rather the need to understand the economic environment in which nations employ sea power. Furthermore, as the subtitle indicates, the majority of the text adapted "scientific" military theory to the study of war at sea.

Back in 1887, complying with Luce's instructions to follow Jomini and seek immutable principles of war, Mahan had endeavored to illustrate these general principles by supplying historical examples drawn from the annals of military history.[39] The chief drawback to this mechanistic approach was that it led to discussion of operations divorced from their relevant political context, a defect that during the early 1890s (and even the 1880s) Mahan came to see as problematic. Too many of his students at the Naval War College viewed him as reducing the conduct of war to rules of thumb.[40] When reading

Naval Strategy, therefore, it is surprising to find that Mahan retained so much Jominian scaffolding, strongly suggesting that his revisions to his old lectures were very light indeed. In the (new) introductory essay, Mahan sagely exhorted his readers never to forget the political context for operational decisions:

> The question, if merely one of military force, would be simple: the superior fleet dominates, if the margin of superiority be sufficient. It is the question of political relations which introduces perplexing factors. . . . Every naval officer should order his study, and his attention to contemporary events, abroad and at home, by the reflection that he may someday be an adviser of the Government, and in any case may beneficially affect events by his correct judgment of world-wide conditions. I have just stated a principle, namely, the necessity of including political—international—conditions in military projects.[41]

Internal content suggests this section was written in 1910 or 1911. In the (unrevised) pages that immediately followed, we find Mahan ignoring his own stricture and heralding Jomini as "my best military friend" and extolling his principles.[42] Yet in a subsequent (revised) chapter, Mahan denounced the Swiss theorist for dogmatism and overstating the importance of strictly adhering to principles:

> Maxims of war are not so much positive rules as they are the development and applications of a few general principles. They resemble the ever varying, yet essentially like, forms that spring from living seeds, rather than the rigid framework to which the free growth of a plant is sometimes forced to bend itself. But it does not therefore follow that there can be no such maxims, or that they have little certainty or little value. . . . The maxim, rooting itself in a principle, formulates a rule generally correct under the conditions; but the teacher must admit that each case has its own features—like the endless variety of the one human face—which modify the application of the rule, and may even make it at times wholly inapplicable.

It is for the skill of the artist in war rightly to apply the principles and rules in each case.[43]

The pages of the volume are filled with similar contradictions and inconsistencies, indicating that Mahan had not performed his revisions with care.[44] Accordingly, *Naval Strategy* needs to be viewed *not* as the final expression of Mahan's concept of sea power (in fact, the volume was not about sea power at all) but rather as the intellectual precursor to his ideas first set out in *Influence*. At most, therefore, *Naval Strategy* is of value in illustrating the development in Mahan's thinking between 1887 and 1910, for within the pages of the same volume readers can see the Mahan of 1887 side-by-side with the Mahan of 1911. Though perhaps interesting, the exercise is of limited practical utility.

OTHER WORK

After 1908, Mahan increasingly struggled with his writings on contemporary affairs as well. Although his output recovered—in 1911 he produced no fewer than ten essays for major journals (five for the *North American Review*)—they contained more reflections than analysis and few new arguments or insights. This is not to suggest that Mahan did a poor job or was merely repackaging old material (which, in truth, he was not averse to doing). The subjects he wrote about in 1911—the militarization of the Panama Canal, for instance, or the debate over President William Taft's international arbitration treaties—were topical and touched directly on leading political issues of the day. But for twenty years Mahan had been preaching on the importance of the Isthmian Canal, and for a decade he had been voicing his concern that arbitration was not an adequate substitute for diplomacy (by which he meant that legal systems were insufficiently robust or elastic to reconcile disputes between nations when their vital interests clashed). In other words, these articles were very much old (albeit respectable) wine in new bottles. Nevertheless, as compared with the pieces he wrote at the zenith of his powers between 1902 and 1907, they were unoriginal and pedestrian. In summary, Mahan's later work conjures a picture of an incredibly vital mind slowed down, hampered by physical setbacks, unable to operate for a sustained period at the level or speed it once had.

Interestingly, after 1908 Mahan tended to avoid writing on naval subjects or the perennial question of whether private property at sea should be "immune" from capture. During the London Naval Conference, an assembly of leading naval powers that met between December 1908 and February 1909 to try and codify international maritime law, he remained remarkably silent. Perhaps he was tired of dealing with a government, a public, and indeed a U.S. Navy unwilling or unable to engage in serious discussion of a subject so manifestly central to the exercise of state power and so vital to the republic's long-term interests. Even when discussing the subject with close naval friends, Mahan's engagement was usually halfhearted. "We will have to agree to differ about immunity of private property," he wrote British admiral William H. Henderson in February 1909.[45] Or perhaps Mahan realized that no one was listening? But he still followed political-economic affairs and, on occasion, showed keen insight into them. Writing to Henderson again at the end of 1910, for instance, he observed: "I don't clearly see how the naval situation of the world is going to turn out. The increasing power of the working classes seems bent on such social expenditures as make the burden of armaments nearly insupportable. By one means or another, your old age pensions, and our war pensions, etc. etc. in other countries, the resources of the countries are being mortgaged."[46] Though he no longer wrote on the subject, international maritime law remained of perennial interest to him and occasionally he found the energy to reenter the still ongoing fray over the immunity issue and score a telling point or two.

In November 1910, for instance, Mahan wrote to the *Times* of London neatly summarizing his latest thinking on the subject. Taking aim at a recent article that had argued "that 'completely disorganizing the conditions of business' constitutes 'a pressure of comparatively small importance' upon a nation at war," Mahan responded,

> I will venture the assertion that historically, this is not so; that "complete disorganization of business," which it is argued will

result from the exercise of the right of maritime capture, has always constituted a "very important," and often—if not always—a decisive "pressure." To say that the greatness and intricacy of modern industrial and commercial development will cause the pressure hereafter to be greater is reasonably probable, and may safely be prophesized. To bring the pressure of war to bear upon the whole population, and not merely upon the armies in the field, is the very spirit of modern warfare.[47]

Perhaps most striking of all was Mahan's prediction that the transformation in the global economic system consequent to industrialization, urbanization, and globalization would make the effects of sea power even more potent in the next war.[48]

After delivering his final lecture to the Naval War College on June 6, 1912, Mahan again found himself at a loss about what to do with himself.[49] He gave vent to his frustration (and perhaps amused himself) by writing viperous letters to the *New York Times*; he had, to use his own term, become a windjammer. Writing to Bouverie Clark from the south of France in March 1913, he acknowledged that "I am a hopeless old fogey"; travel now bored him, though only "seven years ago I loved seeing things."[50] Though he still possessed the passion to write, he was painfully aware that "my vogue is largely over—I am less in demand, and therefore must make work for myself, without security it will be wanted."[51] At the same time he was averse to writing more naval history (which sold easily).[52] "I am a little weary of that special form of authorship," he admitted to Henderson in November 1913.[53] He had said all he wanted to say on the subject; the genre was too narrow to command his interest.

Despite the research entailed, Mahan's literary ambitions extended to one more book, which he intended to be a serious piece of work. He envisioned "a history of the United States" during the long nineteenth century, looking at the friction between those who favored conventional (Western) expansion and those who saw the possibilities overseas—a sort of blending of Frederick Jackson Turner's frontier thesis with his own concept of sea power.[54] He had done some work in the direction back in 1900 when working on his textbook project (which of course he had abandoned after the publisher lost interest). In 1906 he certainly had flirted with the idea of returning to the man-uscript, and for a short period may well have done so. In any case, in early 1914 Mahan's friends arranged for him to be awarded a six-month fellowship at the Carnegie Institution in Washington, DC, so that he might conduct his research.[55] In November 1914, despite a recent heart attack, Mahan proceeded to Washington to take up his fellowship.[56] Shortly after his arrival, however, he suffered a relapse. On December 1, 1914, at the age of seventy-four, the master of sea power died.

CHAPTER 11

INTERPRETING MAHAN'S LEGACY

(1914–2021)

*Naval historians have troubled themselves little about the
connection between general history and their own particular topic,
limiting themselves generally to the duty of simple chroniclers
of naval occurrences.*

—ALFRED THAYER MAHAN, PREFACE TO *INFLUENCE*[1]

ALFRED THAYER MAHAN ASPIRED to be more than a historian; he
wanted to be an applied historian, and he wanted to be remembered.
Before his death in 1914, he sensed that most of his readers were
impatient with his economics-heavy arguments, preferring simpler
models of war that emphasized combat operations. He nevertheless
hoped that his concept of sea power would be of use to subsequent
generations. But his authority was not to last beyond his lifetime
and his later, more sophisticated work emphasizing the commercial
and economic aspects of sea power was very quickly forgotten. In
an otherwise unremarkable article that appeared in the *Yale Review*
directly after the 1922 Washington Naval Conference, William Stevens, a professor at the U.S. Naval Academy, found it extraordinary,
yet unsurprising, that "in all our newspaper and magazine discussion

of the Conference, the name of Mahan was strangely absent."[2] Eight years earlier, this would have been unthinkable.

Why, then, did appreciation for Mahan's corpus fade so quickly? There were three main reasons. First, after World War I there was a widespread perception that the fleets on all sides had contributed little to the final outcome. As is well known, after four and a half years there had been no decisive clash between rival battle fleets. The defining event of the war at sea was the near victory by Germany's U-boats. Furthermore, in the eyes of many, the British Royal Navy's vaunted prewar dominion of the ocean highways had counted for very little and failed to produce the decisive results that Mahan had promised. All this prompted suspicion that Mahan's ideas on sea power either were inapplicable to the modern age or simply had been wrong.

Second, World War I ended the first era of globalization. In the aftermath, the world that Mahan had observed and the problems he had contemplated no longer existed. Although the Western powers tried to restart the international economy, throughout the roaring twenties the engine of growth and prosperity coughed and spluttered. The dominating event of the 1930s, of course, was the Great Depression and the collapse of all semblance of prewar globalization. The world slid into nationalism and totalitarianism; across the globe protectionist tariffs soared, the movement of capital and people slowed to a dribble, and the future of the international economy trended unmistakably toward autarky and barter between trading blocks.[3] (One "lesson" of the war was the need to insulate national economies from economic "blockade."[4]) By the middle of the decade, the international economic landscape had changed beyond recognition, rendering much of Mahan's economic analysis not merely irrelevant but incomprehensible to those interested in contemporary international affairs and the exercise of national power.

The third reason for the eclipse of Mahan's concept of sea power was the result of the deliberate undermining of his scholarly credibility. In the *Yale Review* article just cited, the author observed that "little fault can be found with Mahan as a historian" and that "the main lines of his demonstration are beyond question."[5] Ten years later, opinions had drastically changed. There is deep irony here. For one thing, Mahan had sought contemporary relevance, yet he became the victim of those who came after him seeking relevance for their own work in their own time. For another, those scholars who attacked Mahan were among the last to read Mahan and recognize his interest in economics. Julius W. Pratt, for instance, a leading diplomatic historian, declared that Mahan's true significance was as an "expansionist" more than as a "navalist" and noted that while the text of *Influence* dealt with mainly military history, "its fundamental significance is economic."[6]

Far more damaging, however, was the assault on Mahan's scholarly reputation by Charles Beard, one of the most respected American historians of his generation.[7] Beard also sought contemporary relevance. Independently wealthy (thanks to the royalties earned on the textbooks he wrote), during the late 1920s he became convinced that the nation's intervention in World War I had been a mistake. He was anxious for the United States to disengage from the outside world in order to reduce the risk of being dragged into another foreign war. During Franklin Roosevelt's administrations, Beard wrote extensively in support of what he called "continentalism" and even testified before Congress as an expert witness on foreign affairs.[8] During the 1930s, Beard opposed calls by the U.S. Navy (backed by aggressive lobbying from the Navy League of the United States) for the fleet to build up to treaty-authorized levels. Viewing the Navy as an instrument of U.S. imperialism, Mahan as its prophet, and sea power as its creed, Beard demonized Mahan as a mere peddler of propaganda in support of the late nineteenth-century American expansionism he abhorred. The "distorter of history," he cried, "used history, economics, and religion to defend and justify his new [imperialistic] creed to America."[9] The entire concept of sea power, Beard sweepingly insisted, was false; history had been made by armies, not navies.[10]

Beard received help with his mission. In a thoroughly scurrilous and now forgotten essay published in 1934, Louis Hacker (a Marxist economic historian and one of Beard's protégés) reinforced the charges against Mahan as a tool of imperialistic capitalists and, for good measure, accused him of having been a warmonger. Avowing

that Mahan "knew nothing of economic and social history and theory" and castigating him for making "astounding historical errors,"
Hacker exclaimed that "to regard Mahan seriously as a great historian
or thinker is therefore an absurdity." In so doing, Hacker took special
aim at the first chapter in Mahan's original *Influence* volume, pointing
to the quasi-formula for sea power—the six principles—as prima facie
evidence of Mahan's shallow and doctrinaire intellect.[11]

Hacker's character assassination of Mahan and gross mischarac-
terizations of his arguments prompted Capt. William Puleston (U.S.
Naval Academy class of 1902) to write in defense of his hero. During
the 1930s, while serving a three-year term as the director of the Office
of Naval Intelligence, Puleston wrote a number of well-researched
essays culminating in a full-length biography of Mahan published in
1939.[12] In many ways, it is the best—or at any rate the least unsatisfac-
tory—of the four published Mahan biographies. Though not a man of
letters, Puleston enjoyed certain unique advantages. The Mahan children gave him access to their father's private papers, many of which
have since been lost or destroyed; he also benefited from conversations
with people who had worked with Mahan and knew him well, including Samuel Ashe, John Bassett Moore, and Edith Roosevelt (the wife
of Theodore Roosevelt).[13]

Puleston had an axe to grind with Hacker. The naval officer
insisted on Mahan's brilliance and his high reputation in his own time:
"By world consent, Mahan . . . was hailed as the naval philosopher of
his era. This was no mean tribute, nor was it yielded without contest,
for in England alone there was a host of writers on naval subjects and
a good half-dozen who, except for the appearance of Mahan, would
have been considered of the first rank. Mahan's brilliance, like Nelson's, dimmed the luster of many able contemporary commentators."[14]
Pushing back against Hacker's depictions of sea power as a determinis-
tic model, Puleston accurately countered that "while Mahan continually made use of the term 'principles' of strategy, it is plain that he used
the term in a less complete sense than is the dictionary acceptation
of the word 'principle' as something of eternal and universal application."[15] He also correctly identified that "Mahan proposed to occupy

the vacant field by 'putting maritime interests in the foreground' of an accurate outline of general history, being careful not to divorce them from their surroundings of cause and effect to show their reciprocal relations."[16] Puleston further noted that sea power consisted of two distinct dimensions—one naval and one commercial—pointing out that Mahan's first book was about "the effect of sea power upon the course of history, *and* the prosperity of nations."[17] So far, so good.

Yet Puleston stumbled in presenting his evidence. Overly anxious to salvage Mahan's reputation as a deep thinker on naval matters, he tended toward hagiographical assertion ahead of reasoned argument. Even when he did employ argument, he often buried his point in a mass of undifferentiated detail. He also fell into the trap of defining Mahan by what he wrote in *Influence* and discounted his subsequent work. While Puleston assessed the book as influential and important, his weak grasp of the political, economic, and social debates of the day prevented him from precisely explaining the nature of its influence and importance. Being just eight years old when the book was first published and not having studied the Progressive Era in any detail, Puleston's sense of the period in which Mahan lived and wrote was superficial at best. In consequence, he could not see, let alone relate, many of Mahan's arguments to the prevailing climate of opinion. As a naval officer, perhaps not surprisingly he also tended to privilege the naval, or combat-related, aspects of sea power ahead of its commercial and economic factors, in so doing twisting Mahan's original arguments. The net result of all this was to muddy the waters.

Puleston was also largely responsible, though inadvertently, for one of the most regrettable and persistent trends in interpretations of Mahan's work, which is to attach absurdly disproportionate importance to the introductory chapter of *Influence* as an indicator of Mahan's ideas about sea power. In his biography, Puleston remarked in passing that Mahan's first chapter provided "a synopsis of his whole sea power series, a statement of what he expected to prove upon close examination."[18] A year later, however, in a 1940 article for *Proceedings* titled "A Re-Examination of Mahan's Concept of Sea Power" (which in fact was about the implications of naval airpower), Puleston—likely working quickly and wanting a convenient summary of Mahan's ideas for a paper, the real focus of which lay elsewhere—presented the six "conditions" and three "elements" of sea power as the foundation of Mahan's sea power thesis, effectively promoting them to the same level of undeserved importance as Hacker had, and in so doing seeming to validate his charges.[19]

Soon after the appearance of the Puleston biography, several other scholars published work purporting to shed additional light on Mahan's thinking. Foremost were Harold and Margaret Sprout with *The Rise of American Naval Power*. As mentioned in chapter 1, the Sprouts approached Mahan as subordinate to the larger goal of charting the course of "American naval policy and development."[20] In so doing, moreover, they employed a presentist lens. That is to say, they sought practical lessons for contemporary application. They were not at all interested in understanding Mahan's arguments or the process by which he reached conclusions—to understand Mahan in his own terms, so to speak. Instead, they banged the square peg of the historical Mahan into the round hole of their contemporary agenda, which was to tell a story about the Navy's progress and importance to the American people as the international situation deteriorated around them.

Accordingly, they did not bother to examine Mahan's private correspondence or to contact Dudley Knox, who was responsible for the archives of the Navy Department, both of which were open to them.[21] The result was a superficial reading of Mahan that drained him of his complexity. Indeed, they needed him to be a static caricature rather than a sophisticated, dynamic thinker in order to answer the question that interested them, namely, what influence had Mahan exerted on the key contemporary policy makers, most notably Theodore Roosevelt, to whom they awarded the lion's share of the credit for the "rise" of the Navy.

Reviewing the Puleston volume in 1939, Harold Sprout took issue with the biographer's characterization of his subject as an important and original thinker, insisting (like Hacker) that Mahan had been an intellectual hack on a quest for the immutable principles of naval warfare, general in their application.[22] In dismissing Mahan and his work, Sprout was the first to compare him to Baron Antoine-Henri de Jomini, the notoriously mechanistic theorist of land warfare who is often unfavorably compared to Carl von Clausewitz.[23] Four years later, in 1943, Margaret Sprout hammered this argument home in her landmark essay "Mahan: Evangelist of Sea Power."[24] This is probably the most widely read and influential piece on Mahan ever published and a leading contender (within a strong field) to be identified as the most inaccurate. As such, it merits close attention.

MAKERS OF MODERN STRATEGY
AND MAHAN'S ENTOMBMENT

It is important to understand that Margaret Sprout's article was commissioned by Edward Mead Earle, another historian–turned–political scientist and a denizen of the Institute for Advanced Study at Princeton University who had a good claim to have founded the field of "strategic studies" in its modern form.[25] Earle was a man on a mission, being among the first in the United States to take alarm at the steady growth of totalitarian states across the globe. Perceiving their surging military strength to be a threat to critical U.S. interests, he wished—much like Mahan several decades earlier—to shake the United States out of its isolationism and help its leaders formulate a national strategy in response.

Beginning in 1939, Earle led a circle of Princeton scholars who met weekly to discuss trends in current events and their strategic implications with a view to producing work intended to influence public discussion and government policy.[26] An early topic of particular interest to the group was "the relation of American naval policy to world politics since 1890," a subject which of course mandated consideration of Mahan and his ideas.[27] The leading participants in these discussions included both Harold and Margaret Sprout, as well as the German *émigré* Herbert Rosinski (who for many years would teach at the Naval War College) and a young Bernard Brodie (who later became famous for his thoughts on strategy in the nuclear age).[28]

The textbook published under the title of *Makers of Modern Strategy* was the most famous product of Earle's efforts in the direction of influencing current policy. On its surface, this tome was a collection of historical essays exploring the ideas of the leading theorists of war since the Renaissance. Yet in the preface Earle frankly stated that his overarching goal was to instruct readers about "the causes of war and the fundamental principles which govern the conduct of war" as well as to comprehend the history of strategic thought, broadly defined as "the art of controlling and utilizing the resources of a nation or a coalition of nations—including its armed forces, to the end that its vital interests shall be effectively promoted and secured."[29] Translated, Earle had a double agenda for the book: to identify fundamental principles in order and to promote America's vital interests. Notably, this agenda did not include understanding the past as accurately as possible. The essays that Earle commissioned were subordinate to his agenda for the volume.

Once again, there was considerable irony here. Earle's agenda for the volume was in many ways similar to Mahan's in his own publications: to awaken the American people to an external danger they did not realize. Moreover, like Mahan, Earle's ideas about how to meet this external danger were inseparable from his ideas about the structure of U.S. society and the leading domestic political issues of the day.[30] But events (specifically World War I) occurring between Mahan's era and Earle's rendered the similarity between their projects and the sophistication of Mahan's invisible to Earle, as to most others in the 1930s. By ending the wave of globalization that so shaped Mahan's thinking about sea power, World War I threw his world out of all recognition to Earle's cohort, which was trying to make sense of the opposite phenomenon: the rise of autarky in a deglobalized world. The international economic contexts for their projects were practically opposites.

Unsurprisingly, Earle's agenda guided his selection of an author for the chapter on Mahan, a backstory that largely explains why Margaret Sprout's influential essay took the flawed form it did. First, it should be noted that Earle sought to include a chapter on Mahan not because he was impressed by Mahan's writings but because Mahan was an American. As Earle noted in the preface to the volume, "We have not produced a Clausewitz or a Vauban. Mahan is our only military theorist of comparable reputation."[31] Second, it seems likely that Earle never read Mahan closely and viewed his work with a jaundiced eye. Earle's mentor was Charles Beard (whom he addressed him in correspondence as "Uncle Charlie"), and who, as we have seen, regarded Mahan as an arch-imperialist and thus an enemy.[32]

When Earle first proposed the volume that became *Makers of Modern Strategy*, the naval specialists in his circle at Princeton—Margaret Sprout, Bernard Brodie, and Herbert Rosinski—were all contenders for writing the Mahan chapter. This presented Earle with a dilemma, for the three prospective candidates held drastically different views on the meaning and significance of Mahan's work. The Sprouts, of course, found Mahan singularly unimpressive. Brodie, it seems, held Mahan in similarly low regard, albeit for different reasons.[33] But after being recruited to work on the staff of the Chief of Naval Operations, he dropped out of the running. This left Rosinski, who was very much the odd man out: not only had he read Mahan far more closely than the others—as is apparent to anyone who reads his various essays—he held a radically different opinion on the subject.

Rosinski's disagreement with the Sprouts (and Brodie) turned on whether Mahan was better understood as a theorist or as a historian. That is, was Mahan more interested in identifying immutable principles of sea power that applied in all times and all places, like a theorist, or was he more interested in explaining how sea power had worked in different times and places, like a historian? As we have seen, the Sprouts asserted that he was the former. Rosinski, who at that time was preparing a manuscript (sadly never finished) on the development of naval thought, strongly disagreed.[34] "Theory to him [Mahan] was entirely subordinate to history; to the elucidation of concrete instances in the light of a few, a very few, general considerations," Rosinski insisted.[35] What is more, "the idea of abstracting these individual insights from their historical background and of integrating them into a systematic analysis of the whole complicated and paradoxical structure of naval warfare . . . was wholly foreign to him."[36] In effect, Rosinski was arguing that Mahan would have to be wrenched out of his real identity as a historian in order to be plugged into *Makers of Modern Strategy* as a theorist.

Additionally, Rosinski discerned the economic dimension within Mahan's sea power thesis and saw the importance of it. He noted that "It is blockade which really constitutes the corner-stone of naval warfare, while the fuller measure of command achieved by the complete destruction of the enemy's main forces forms merely its superstructure. This defensive function of blockade [*sic*], so often unduly disregarded compared with its offensive function as an instrument to bring economic pressure to bear upon our opponent, is stressed by Mahan throughout his writings."[37] But as one reads on, it becomes clear that although Rosinski could see that Mahan gave much importance to "economic pressure," he could not quite see why. He missed the connection between the political object of applying pressure on one's enemy and the potential of blockade to derange their economy through higher-order consequences; or if he did understand, then given the prevailing economic environment of the 1930s, he regarded the power of economic coercion as now minimal. In any case, Rosinski was not interested in delving deeper to understand, being equally guilty of plundering Mahan's writings to bolster his own theories.

So what? Manifestly, Rosinski's conception of Mahan was incompatible with Earle's conception of his volume. Put simply, Earle needed Mahan to be a theorist in order to make apples-to-apples comparisons with other theorists. Despite reservations about the Sprouts' work— after reading the proofs for *The Rise of American Naval Power*, Earle told "Uncle Charlie" (Beard) that "the book is not at all that it might be"—he chose Margaret to write the essay on Mahan, tasking her to provide an "appraisal of Mahan's place in the history of military thought."[38]

Margaret Sprout soon encountered difficulties along the lines predicted by Rosinski. In attempting to summarize Mahan's "theory" of sea power, she found that "[His] principal books and essays are history written with the focus of interest on sea power. His discussion of national policy, naval policy, naval strategy, and tactics therefore are not presented separately but are interwoven, largely at random, into a chronological narrative. A systemic appraisal of Mahan's place in the history of military thought requires the disentangling of many separate strands and the rearrangement in orderly manner."[39] Harold Sprout agreed. In a piece written some years later, he similarly grumbled,

> It is very hard to condense his [Mahan's] propositions into a short statement. A very prolific and prolix writer, I find him a very difficult theorist to interpret. He modified and qualified his opinions a good deal from time to time and nowhere did he set down in concise form—in a single article or in a single book—the main outlines of his thoughts. He scattered them through a series of naval histories and scores of magazine articles on technical naval subjects and on current affairs. One has to put together bits and pieces and make the best one can of it.[40]

By their own admission, therefore, in tackling Mahan's ideas, the Sprouts "put together bits and pieces" and rearranged them in an "orderly manner" to produce a manifestly artificial "Mahanian" theory. They failed to engage Mahan's concept of "sea power" on its own terms and instead shoehorned his words into their model of what they thought theory ought to look like. In so doing, moreover, they made no attempt to disguise their low opinion for Mahan's scholarship, which they scorned as consisting "entirely of rambling histories of naval warfare and popular magazine articles on current topics. One who plods through his massive literary output will find historical narratives, technical analyses of battles, discussions of strategy, tactics and weapons, homilies on ethics and on the white man's destiny to rule the world, odd mixtures of current events and political prophecy, interpretations of history, and a great deal of gratuitous advice to the makers of history."[41]

Desperate to locate Mahan within broader studies of military thought, the Sprouts derided as "anachronistic" his interest in political economy and international economics, as well as his insistence on studying the domestic imperatives behind strategy and policy formulation.[42]

They never wavered in this belief. During a lecture delivered at the Naval War College in 1953, for instance, Harold Sprout apologized to his audience that "time does not permit anything about the anachronistic character of Mahan's general thinking on economic policy patterns that support sea power. Almost all of his thinking on that subject comes right out of the seventeenth and eighteenth centuries."[43] He elaborated only to press his claim that "Mahan never achieved much sophistication in the economic field and in consequence his economic thinking was a century behind times"—the point being that Mahan's economic opinions could be safely disregarded.[44] What is particularly striking, fascinating even, is that the Sprouts possessed no conception whatsoever of sustained wealth generation by a society, let alone an appreciation of this as a factor in state power. The whole subject, so central to Mahan, was alien to them. For the Sprouts, therefore, sea power was a theorem of conflict and combat.

Returning to 1943, finding Mahan inconveniently unsystematic in his thinking, Margaret Sprout grasped at the first piece of systematic, theoretical flotsam she could find, which was the introductory chapter to *Influence*. Following Puleston's lead (in fact Louis Hacker's), she seized the formulaic "elements and factors" material at the beginning of *Influence* and none too gently fashioned it into a model of what she thought naval theory should look like, which was predictive and thus relevant to contemporary policy makers in much the same way that some people today deem international relations theory useful.

To support her portrayal of Mahan as a mechanistic theoretician, Margaret Sprout injected another mischievous but enduring myth into the bloodstream of Mahan scholarship, first floated by her husband four years earlier—namely, that Mahan was "Jominian."[45] Mahan was to the theory of war at sea, so to speak, what Jomini was to the theory of war on land. Of course, as we have seen, this assessment seems at first glance to possess merit. In the first thirteen pages of *Influence*, Mahan referenced and discussed "general" or "fundamental" principles of war no fewer than seventeen times, buttressed with explicit statements like "the old foundations of strategy so far remain, as though laid upon a rock."[46] This certainly sounds like Jomini. Closer examination, however, reveals that in the 528 pages that followed, Mahan discussed the "principles of war" less than a dozen more times. In the entire book, Jomini is actually mentioned but once in the text and once in a footnote, far less than might be supposed from Sprout's characterization.[47]

Indeed, when Mahan's oeuvre is surveyed as a whole rather than artificially reduced to a single chapter in a single book, it becomes clear that although he borrowed some ideas from Jomini, he subsequently returned many. In outlook and approach, Mahan was far from Jominian. His use of military theory in the construction of his concept of sea power more closely resembles surrounding scaffolding than internal framing—temporary and supportive rather than permanent and structural. Thus the Sprouts confused the scaffolding for the building. Had they looked more deeply in into the archives, furthermore, they would have found, as we saw in chapters 2 and 3, that Mahan had good reasons (his commanding officer's admiration for Jomini) for retaining much of this theoretical scaffolding in his first book, even at the cost of obscuring some of his own arguments.

The Sprouts also failed to note that in subsequent publications, Mahan progressively distanced himself from the Swiss theorist.[48] In his *Life of Nelson* (1897), for instance, Mahan described Jomini as "too absolute and pedantic in his insistence upon definite formulation of principles."[49] Two years later Mahan distanced himself yet further from Jomini, taking pains in *Lessons of the War with Spain* to correct misperceptions of his own views on the use of theory and the relative importance of principles and history in professional officer education.[50] In his *War of 1812* (1905), Jomini did not warrant so much as a mention. In his autobiography (1907), Mahan acknowledged his early debt to Jomini, though in carefully qualified terms, and went on to credit the work of others as having been more important sources of inspiration.[51]

The Sprouts' mischaracterization of Mahan as Jominian was thus doubly mischievous. Not only did they explicitly paint Mahan as mechanistic but they also implicitly presented his idea of sea power as focused on combat and war (like Jomini) rather than economics and peace. In fact, and not coincidentally, the further Mahan moved away from Jomini and military theory, the less focused on combat he became and the greater the importance he attached to the commercial and economic aspects of sea power. To the extent that Mahan can be considered a naval theorist at all, then, the better point of comparison in military theory is Clausewitz, Jomini's more sophisticated competitor, who insisted on the need to relate the military means of combat to political ends (except that Mahan would have pointed to political economy as the ultimate end).

LATER INTERPRETATIONS

Subsequent to the publication of Margaret Sprout's 1943 essay, the concept of sea power remained discredited and deemed unworthy of serious analysis. In a biography of Mahan published in 1947 under the hopeful yet misleading title of *Mahan on Sea Power*, William Livezey supplied only generic descriptions of Mahan's core concept, concluding that "for Mahan, sea power was the sum total of forces and factors, tools and geographical circumstances, which operated to gain command of the sea" and that "use and control of the sea was the central link in assisting a nation to achieve strength and wealth."[52] It was the sort of book that one finds unobjectionable yet from which one learns little new.

The next important entry in the Mahan canon was Robert Seager's *Alfred Thayer Mahan: The Man and His Letters* (1977). Seager arguably came to the subject better qualified than anyone before him. Though Seager was systematic and comprehensive in his research, providing facts and insights unavailable elsewhere, his analysis of the evidence was warped by what can only be described as a hatred for Mahan. The text of his biography is peppered throughout with contempt and sarcasm; Seager often seems more interested in scoring points against Mahan than in trying to illuminate what he had been trying to say.[53] As one reviewer sardonically remarked: "The biography is, as Seager admits, based largely on the available letters of Mahan and aspires to be a 'psychological' portrait. More of Seager's prejudice than Mahan's seems to be revealed."[54] As for the subject of sea power,

Seager mentioned the concept only to deride it as derivative and unoriginal. At its heart, he sneered, "was Captain Mahan's enumeration of the six basic conditions," which thereby again reared their ugly, seemingly Jominian heads.[55] Though Seager's biography was awarded a fistful of prizes, it very quickly became understood among Mahan scholars that the book, though useful, could not be relied on because it was so deeply flawed. Yet his judgments continue to be cited widely without qualification.

Seager's biography was followed nearly a decade later by the appearance of a new edition of *Makers of Modern Strategy* containing an updated essay on Mahan.[56] Amusingly, as had occurred forty years before, there was a tussle over who should write the chapter on Mahan between three candidates holding divergent views.[57] Peter Paret, the general editor, settled on Philip Crowl, the head of the Strategy and Policy Department at the Naval War College (where Seager had also spent time). As before, the editor's choice significantly, albeit inadvertently, influenced popular understandings of Mahan. Crowl came to his subject no more sympathetic to the man and his ideas than Margaret Sprout had been. He too saw Mahan as a doctrinaire thinker who was certain that "the study of history would permit the discovery of certain immutable principles in the field of human affairs comparable to the laws of science governing the physical universe. Specifically, he believed that from the study of naval history would emerge certain principles of maritime strategy, certain permanent truths of equal applicability today as yesterday, and tomorrow as today."[58] Crowl further agreed that Mahan's concept of sea power was unworthy of serious analysis, alleging that he coined the term "sea power" simply "to compel attention" (i.e., to sell books).[59] That said, however, he conceded that Jomini's influence over Mahan had been overstated, and he also felt that previous scholars had attached too much importance to Mahan's six factors. He even noted Mahan's considerable interest in economics.[60] Overall, Crowl's essay was neither a step forward nor well polished. His analysis was truncated, his thoughts undigested (note the tension between minimizing Mahan's six factors while still maintaining that Mahan was doctrinaire), and his arguments so incomplete that students with questions invariably return to Margaret Sprout looking for quick answers.[61]

The most serious weakness of the works by Seager and Crowl was their failure to integrate their study of Mahan into the wider historical literature on the era in which he lived—or, if one prefers, they neglected to incorporate into their studies of Mahan the latest scholarly understandings of his era. Unlike the first generation of Mahan scholars of the 1940s, they had available to them the important series of studies of the Gilded Age and the Progressive Era produced after World War II by William Appleman Williams and Walter LaFeber.[62] More than any other historians before them (or many since), they provided detailed explanations of how U.S. leaders of Mahan's era viewed the world and why they chose certain policy options rather than others.[63] But Seager and Crowl deliberately opted not to use the Wisconsin School's work, clearly a mistake given that Mahan's concept of sea power was built on a fundamentally political-economic worldview.

True, on its first appearance during the late 1950s and the 1960s, the new scholarship was rejected by most senior mainstream historians. The consensus view of U.S. history then held, inter alia, that U.S. expansion at the turn of the century had been a response to external geopolitical developments and, on balance, beneficial to the world. Williams especially turned this argument on its head, arguing that U.S. expansion had been a response to internal economic crisis—essentially a crisis of modern capitalism—and that it had been aggressively imperialistic in nature. It was not a flattering portrait. With McCarthyism still recent and the Cold War in full swing, "Wisconsinite" heterodoxy offended many and inspired suspicions of Marxist sympathies.[64] That Williams' and LaFeber's explanations of events relied heavily on economic arguments suggested to the legion of historians uncomfortable with the subject (as well as unfamiliar with what Marx actually wrote) that their scholarship was unsound—wholly irrespective of the quantity and quality of their research in the relevant primary sources of the period, which remains unsurpassed to this day.

By the late 1970s—certainly by the 1980s—the initial hostility to the ideas of the Wisconsin School had subsided to the point that most mainstream historians now viewed their scholarship as essential.[65] Not so among naval historians. In a retrospective on his career, John Lewis Gaddis, the distinguished Cold War historian who briefly taught at the Naval War College during the mid-1970s, recalled that "William Appleman Williams's *Tragedy of American Diplomacy* had been on the [reading] list, I was told, but had to be taken off because the war college students found it too convincing."[66] Both Seager and Crowl remained not merely skeptical but lastingly dismissive. The former's antagonism had very deep roots.[67] Seager not merely refused to utilize any Wisconsin scholarship in his study of Mahan, but whenever Williams and LaFeber published their thoughts on Mahan and his influence, he responded with broadsides of invective.[68] The real question, however, is not why Seager and Crowl so disliked Wisconsin School, or why their loathing went unchallenged by their peers, but rather why most naval historians continue to ignore so rich and relevant a body of work.[69] Like it or not, this scholarship provides an essential map for understanding the period; though others exist, they are not nearly so detailed or insightful.

It is difficult to escape the impression that most naval historians instinctively regard the subject of economics as distasteful and vaguely subversive. Such criticism is supported by the extent to which other important historiography is overlooked. Over the past forty years, economic historians have produced a literature on what they call the first era of globalization—the years between roughly 1870 and 1914. This must be read alongside the work of the Wisconsin School, whose members produced their major studies of the era before it became available and were writing, like Earle's group, when the world still had not recovered from the deglobalizing shock of World War I. With the concept of globalization, the meaning of many of Mahan's writings on international economics—which formerly were dismissed as anachronistic and incomprehensible—suddenly become visible and understandable.

This literature on globalization ought to be of special interest to naval historians because it pertains directly, far more so than industrialization, to what happens on the world's oceans—the Navy's domain.

Yet for the most part they have ignored it because it does not fit with their combat-centric model of sea power. They may pay lip service to globalization, but they (unlike Mahan) do not do the work to understand how business was conducted on a day-to-day level in a globalized world economy. Without such an understanding, they are in no position to explain the "mechanism of coercion" within economic warfare: that is, how navies might exert power over the global trading system to produce strategically significant results.

⁘⁘⁘⁘⁘⁘⁘⁘⁘⁘⁘⁘⁘⁘⁘⁘⁘⁘

Mahan was the Navy's first global strategist. He possessed the outlook and approach of a practitioner and historian rather than a theorist. But he was also much more than that. He possessed the courage to leave the comfort zone inhabited by his peers, the pursuit of operational excellence, for the study of the pursuit of national power. His interest was in understanding and solving the real-world problems that existed in the present or could be discerned on the horizon, but he also had a historian's cast of mind in that he became fascinated by serious historical research as an end in itself, not merely because it advanced a contemporary agenda. At the same time, he was engaged with the leading political issues of the day, which were substantially economic in nature. Either way, the key to understanding Mahan's writings is therefore to look at the world though his eyes and with his perception of how it worked.

Mahan possessed an uncommon worldview, seeing connections and relationships that others (both then and since) either missed or thought unimportant. Glaringly unsystematic in his approach, Mahan never intended *Influence* to be a treatise on or a contribution to the theory of war in the mold of Jomini or Clausewitz. In many ways Mahan was the antithesis of a theorist. Yet at the same time, except for a few short weeks during the Spanish-American War, he cannot be classified as a true practitioner because he never held a position of major responsibility. Though neither fish nor fowl, his thought is all the more interesting and worth grappling with as a result. Today, invoking Mahan risks inviting ridicule. But if we read Mahan with a view to his own intellectual journey, within his own historical context, mindful of his foibles and struggles in the public space with politicians and academics, we can only conclude that Mahan has modern and future meaning. Most importantly for readers today, they will encounter a profound thinker on the relationship between naval power, a multipolar globalized economy, and technologies transforming geopolitics at breakneck speed.

EPILOGUE

Magister Resurget?

How simple it all sounds; and undeniably "Strategy," in its principles, is among the simplest of conceptions. In the application of those principles there is more difficulty, as there is in the application of all knowledge to the emergencies of common life. Still, it is marvelous how absolutely simple, how perfectly comprehensible, are the great features of a campaign upon which have hung, perhaps the fates of empires, the humiliation or exaltation of a nation. . . . [So] where then is the difficulty, and why have there been so few great captains?

—ALFRED THAYER MAHAN, MARCH 4, 1897[1]

IN *THE INFLUENCE OF SEA POWER UPON HISTORY*, Alfred Thayer Mahan provided the world with a novel and coherent explanation for the purpose of navies. The book's central argument was that all previous historians had neglected to consider the importance of "sea power" in their accounts of the rise and fall of nations. History taught that national power was chiefly a function of sustained wealth generation, broadly defined, and that the single most valuable fount of wealth was overseas trade and its associated commerce. This occurred because, he argued, "both travel and traffic by water have always been easier and cheaper than by land."[2] Moreover, since all nations depended (to a greater or lesser degree) on international trade for their economic prosperity, it followed that any constriction in their access must undermine their economy and thus weaken their power potential. In time of war, he concluded, the command of the sea—the ability to guarantee or deny access to the global trading system—had proved vital.

The concept of sea power rested on fundamentally economic propositions. This was obscured, however, by Mahan's overly ambitious agenda for *Influence* combined with structural flaws in his argumentation, a function of his inexperience as a writer. Additionally, while Mahan was still conceptualizing his sea power thesis, Adm. Luce pressed him to employ Jomini's theory of land warfare as a template. Though Mahan found some of his ideas useful as intellectual scaffolding, he saw that the Swiss theorist's model was inapplicable to the study of war at sea because it lacked any political and especially economic foundations. From his own research, he had already discerned that in sea warfare strategic decision making was seldom governed by military considerations but more often by political goals, driven mostly by economic-commercial factors. Hence his insistence on the necessity, when looking at ostensibly naval decisions, always to examine the broader contexts. However, uncertainty and self-doubt, combined with pressure from Luce, caused him to retain some Jominian language in *Influence* and also to overemphasize the importance of battle *relative* to the political, economic, and commercial dimensions of sea power.

Another reason why so many readers of *Influence* have not recognized that economics lay at the heart of Mahan's concept of sea power is that in this first volume he only intuitively asserted the interconnections between naval action and economic consequences. That is to say, he struggled to explain clearly or convincingly how the naval interdiction of maritime commerce could generate significant economic pressure on an enemy polity sufficient to bring about an end to conflict on favorable terms. Only in his next book, *French Revolution and Empire* (1892), did Mahan expound clearly on the precise mechanisms of pressure, postulating that the first-order effects of commerce destruction by naval forces were amplified over time by second- and higher-order economic consequences for and within the enemy's economy.

Essentially, Mahan argued that British sea power corroded the Napoleonic Empire from within. The "noiseless pressure" of sea power cut France off from the outside world, wrecking imperial finances and provoking the cash-strapped state into arbitrary seizures of private property within its European dominions, which undermined its legitimacy in the eyes of its subjects. Acknowledging that these so-called higher-order consequences of naval commerce destruction were almost impossible to map, Mahan nevertheless insisted that it was possible to show that within Napoleon's empire socioeconomic derangement had occurred. What is more, no previous historian had offered any better explanation for this derangement. In effect, Mahan claimed for sea power a vast swath of previously unclaimed economic history. In his hands, the story of sea power was international and economic history writ large.

As an explanation of how sea power worked, this was certainly an improvement over the argument offered in *Influence*. It was not, however, a complete explanation, nor was it clear whether such circumstances and causal dynamics would recur in future conflicts under "modern conditions"—wars between urban, industrialized, economically interdependent societies. After his retirement from the Navy in 1896, Mahan contemplated this problem. By stages, his explanation of how naval force interacted with economic systems became more precise and sophisticated. Mahan came to recognize that the explosion in international trade during the nineteenth century, together with the growing dependence of modern urban-industrial societies on the smooth flow of that trade, had major implications for the application of sea power. These went far beyond mere supply-chain dependencies. Not only were there new pressure points for naval forces to target but the greater national dependence on global markets and greater interdependencies between nations—that is, globalization—meant greater sociopolitical vulnerability. In line with other thinkers of the time, Mahan doubted whether modern, urban-dwelling, wage-earning, industrial workers would long tolerate the resultant fall in their standards of living consequent to the derangement of their economy. "The intricate network of modern commerce," he thought, would thus likely *magnify* the potency of sea power.[3] This is what he meant when he wrote in 1910 that "to bring the pressure of war to bear upon the whole population, and not merely upon the armies in the field, is the very spirit of modern warfare."[4]

At the same time, Mahan came to see that navies had a dual role. On the one hand, "in the general scheme its [the Navy's] office is essentially defensive. It protects the economical processes which sustain national endurance, and thus secures the foundation on which the vigor of war rests."[5] On the other, "the object of a blockade proper is to embarrass the finances of a country by shutting its ports to foreign commerce, thus deranging one main feature of its general markets, and thereby bring confusion into the whole [economy]."[6] From this perspective, though combat might seem to be the essence of war, its character—certainly when fought at sea—was essentially economic (by other means). This was a sort of naval variation on Clausewitz's famous metaphor about land warfare: that its grammar was combat but its logic was political.

For the past six or seven decades, consideration of sea power, however defined, has been overshadowed by the notion that navies existed primarily to facilitate the projection of national power on land. The intellectual origins of naval "power projection" are found in the landmark 1954 essay by Samuel P. Huntington, "National Policy and the Transoceanic Navy."[7] Herein, his central argument was that a navy must be organized around a coherent, comprehensible, and above all relevant "strategic concept." He defined this term as "a description of how, when, and where the military service expects to Protect [*sic*] the nation against some threat to its security. If a military service does not possess such a concept, it becomes purposeless, it wallows about amid a variety of conflicting and confusing goals, and ultimately it suffers both physical and moral degeneration." He further insisted that "the resources which a service is able to obtain in a democratic society are a function of the *public support* of that service. The service has the responsibility to develop this necessary support, and it can only do this if it possesses a strategic concept which clearly formulates its relationship to the national security." Huntington averred that since the 1890s, the U.S. Navy had been expressing its raison d'être—its strategic concept—employing Mahan's idea of "acquiring command of the sea through the destruction of the enemy fleet." The accuracy of this assessment aside, Huntington went on to argue that since the end of World War II this was no longer appropriate. The multipolar world of yesteryear had been replaced with a bipolar world dominated by two superpowers, one a major land power and one a major sea power.

"This bipolarity of power around a land-sea dichotomy is the fundamental fact which makes the Mahanite concept inapplicable today," Huntington declared.[8] Where was the sense, he rhetorically wondered, in the United States investing scarce resources in maintaining a gigantic fleet when continental Russia possessed few maritime interests and practically no navy at all? Manifestly, it was "impossible, if not ridiculous" for the Navy to claim that is served as the nation's first line of defense. At the same time, what damage could the Navy inflict on Russia? Where was the mechanism of pressure? In short, what would Russia care that the U.S. Navy enjoyed undisputed command of the sea?

Because all "decisive actions will now take place on land," Huntington proceeded to argue, it followed that "the Navy can no longer accept [the] Mahanite definition of its mission. Its purpose now is not to acquire command of the sea but rather to utilize its command of the sea to achieve supremacy on the land. More specifically, it is to apply naval power to that decisive strip of littoral encircling the Eurasian continent. This means a real revolution in naval thought and operations."[9] Accordingly, instead of being organized for sea control, the U.S. Navy should reorganize to facilitate the projection of U.S. military (and air) power against vital littoral regions of Korea and Western Europe. Crudely put, Huntington concluded that the role of the Navy was merely to amplify the power of U.S. land and air forces by providing strategic mobility and, when appropriate, direct support.

In his view, this was the only coherent rationale for the existence of the Navy—the only plausible "strategic concept" to guide its force structure and justify itself to the American taxpayers.

It is unnecessary to expound on Huntington's mischaracterization of Mahan's arguments because his interpretive error does not matter. His central argument, that in the post-1945 world navies were incapable of generating strategically significant pressure against its enemies, applied to all variants of Mahanian thought—indeed to all "navalist" interpretations of what navies do. For policy makers, practitioners, and historians alike, Huntington's logic appeared impeccable and his conclusions unassailable, and for a time they were. After 1945, in effect the sea was not a separate medium but merely a highway to ferry forces onto land masses where the real action would happen. Accordingly, command of the sea gave way to power projection and the Navy became the handmaiden to land power.

Throughout the Cold War and beyond, the Navy remained wedded to power projection as its strategic concept, and Huntington's paper stood as a landmark for admirals, strategists, and policy makers. During the 1970s, however, cracks began to emerge in the logic underpinning power projection as the Navy's strategic concept, though at the time they were not apparently seen as structural. These cracks emerged because, in recommending power projection as the Navy's strategic concept, Huntington had made three key assumptions, both explicit and implicit, which gradually became less and less applicable.

First, he assumed that the United States enjoyed and would continue to enjoy uncontested command of the sea. By the 1970s, however, this was no longer the case. The Soviet Union possessed significant naval forces that endangered the Atlantic bridge.[10] Fortunately, at that time the United States possessed the economic and fiscal wherewithal to expand the Navy's combat forces while simultaneously sharpening its technological edge. After the collapse of the Soviet Union, the Navy resumed parroting the language of engaging in littoral regions to best affect U.S. geopolitical objectives (on land), issuing statements tellingly prefaced "From the Sea" or "Forward . . . from the Sea."[11]

Second, Huntington assumed that the United States would retain its absolute advantages in the economic, financial, and diplomatic spheres (he also implicitly assumed allies with significant conventional armies in the principal theatre of operations—Western Europe—would assist in a conflict). By the 1970s, however, the United States' military, financial, and economic superiority *relative to* its rivals had visibly shrunk. Those trends have only continued, and now the diplomatic strength of the United Sates has begun to erode as well, meaning that the assistance of allies cannot be taken for granted.

The third, and by far the most important, of Huntington's assumptions was that international trade would remain at 1950s levels and thus relatively unimportant as a factor in international politics. He supposed that most national economies (especially that of the United States) would remain practically autarkic and thus invulnerable to economic pressure by being cut off from the outside economic world. This obviously no longer holds true. The revitalization of global trade during the 1960s and 1970s led to structural changes in the world economy. International trade and thus access to the common increasingly began to matter—and to be seen to matter.[12] This meant that the power to regulate access once again became a weapon of some importance.

Adm. Elmo Zumwalt was the first to discern (albeit dimly) that this economic transformation opened the door to an array of new vulnerabilities and opportunities at sea, and that consequently the U.S. Navy might want to change the way it did business. In the spring of 1974, just after the first Oil Shock and toward the end of his tenure as Chief of Naval Operations, he remarked to a gathering of officials that "over the last six or seven years, while the United States has been preoccupied with Southeast Asia . . . major changes have been taking place within the world's economic structure." He went on to urge his colleagues "to take a look at the growing economic interdependence of nations and the impact which this interdependence is likely to have upon US policy."[13] Zumwalt's suspicion that the changing structure of the global economy had important strategic ramifications and his plea for further study, however, apparently went unheeded by his successor in office or anyone else inside the Navy Department. At least outwardly, the Navy remained—and still remains—unmoved.

Before he died, Huntington himself seems to have sensed the need for reconsideration of his theory, recognizing that the disintegration of the Soviet Union destroyed the bipolar structure of global power politics and thus one of his governing considerations. Though the United States remained the sole superpower, peerless and to all appearances unassailable, Huntington saw with remarkable perceptiveness and prescience that the United States was far from all-powerful. Writing in 1999, he perceived that contrary to what many others thought, it was not a unipolar new world because "the settlement of key international issues requires action by the single superpower but always with some combination of other major states." He predicted that within a couple of decades the era of "Pax Americana" would draw to close and be replaced with a multipolar world.[14] In other words, the United States would be relegated from being the solitary superpower to becoming merely the greatest of the Great Powers, and by implication it would be compelled to adopt a less expansive definition of its national security. Unlike what he had done a half century earlier, however, Huntington never joined up all of the pieces. He neither grasped the strategic implications of globalization nor considered the possibility of "weaponizing" global interdependency.[15]

/////////////////////////////

Today, none of the foundational assumptions underpinning Huntington's concept of power projection hold true. This is not a rebuke of Huntington, whose analysis was masterful for its time. But as he himself anticipated, "shifts in the international balance of power will inevitably bring about changes in the principal threats to the security of any given nation. These must be met by shifts in national policy and corresponding changes in service strategic concepts."[16] Like technology, he understood that strategic concepts can become obsolescent.

The naval leadership admits that it faces a peer competitor, which means that command of the sea in time of conflict cannot be taken for granted. Although the United States still remains a superpower, it increasingly resembles a "hollow hegemon," to borrow a later Huntingtonism.[17] There are questions as to whether the United States retains the economic wherewithal to wage a sustained conventional war of attrition on the far side of the Pacific, whether it remains possible to forge the necessary domestic-political consensus to wage a major war, and whether the fiscal capability for sustained operations still exists. Above all, since the mid-1980s the world has unmistakably entered a second era of globalization, an economic system characterized by insidious interdependence between national economies, with manufacturing supply chains that stretch around the world—85 percent of which (by volume) are transoceanic. Essential to the functioning of the global economic system are the undersea fiber-optic cables—within the Navy's domain—carrying the flows of data fundamental to all commercial activity. The global economic system is most vulnerable to manipulation at sea.

The defining characteristic of today's geostrategic environment is a globalized world economy with highly optimized, interlocking commercial systems that are critically dependent on timely and accurate information flows and smoothly functioning transportation systems (themselves also dependent on information). For reasons of cost, there is very little redundancy built into any of these systems. What is more, all are fundamentally dynamic in character. Stockpiles at the beginnings and the ends have been replaced with "just-in-time" supply chains that stretch around the world. Major failure at any single point in the entire interconnected web is likely to produce cascading failure throughout the global economy. In light of all the recent supply chain failures, which in the greater scheme of things are comparatively minor, the fragility of the system and the consequences of failure is glaringly apparent. All societies and all players hold a stake in the smooth running of the global economic system and recognize its importance to their security and prosperity, especially over the long term.

MAGISTER RESURGET?   345

In short, the present geoeconomic environment more closely resembles that of Mahan's day than that of the early Cold War. As was the case in the pre-1914 world, just-in-time ordering (then it was called "hand to mouth") has made the economies of the world worryingly susceptible to even slight disruptions in the maritime order. The efficiencies, conveniences, and lower prices for consumers made possible by globalization have magnified strategic vulnerability and, reciprocally, strategic opportunity. In recent years, the importance of sea trade to the United States' vital economic interests (and to those of its allies) has become ever clearer, and the threats ever greater. The deliberate interference in flows of international trade—especially in energy and food—have once again become a hallmark of geopolitical competition, in both peace and war.

Where does this leave us? Forty years ago, it was possible for the United States to build and maintain a fleet capable of both power projection and sea control missions, but no longer. Today, the Navy's coat must be cut from a much smaller piece of politically available fiscal cloth. Besides, as defining "strategic concepts," to borrow Huntington's still useful phrase, sea power and power projection are incommensurable: they pull in different directions. Whereas power projection models fold the sea into the domain of the land, sea power regards the sea as a separate and distinct domain from the land. Mahan maintained that sea power was an independent force in international affairs—a thing in and of itself—capable of contributing to the power of the state and generating significant political pressure. Huntington, by contrast, saw control of the sea as a means to the end of achieving politically decisive results on land, the only domain where he *believed* they could be achieved. Expressed in the modern vernacular, he subscribed to the "boots on the ground" argument.

The mechanisms of pressure for these two strategic concepts are quite different. Power projection conceptualizes the Navy's role solely in terms of combat, specifically combat by the Army on land. Huntington allowed that sometimes the sea might be a battleground, but only battle on land could generate decisive results. In addition, the power projection model explains everything in terms of combat and superior combat power; its deterrent capability in peacetime stems from its potency in wartime. To the contrary, Mahan insisted that the sea needed to be recognized as a distinct and separate domain, not as a mere subset of the land. More than that, he saw the Navy as something more than a combat force. He believed that sea power operated both in peace as well as in war: the sea was not merely a thoroughfare or an occasional battleground but part of a thriving economic organism that generated wealth, which Mahan regarded as the key long-term factor in global power.

Since the beginning of the twenty-first century, the United States has seen a marked deterioration of its relative strength in both military and especially economic terms. At the same time, the nation and the Navy now find themselves confronted by a determined and capable challenger. Yet discussion of the Navy's role in national security remains framed to a remarkable degree by the ideas and the language of the last Cold War, which ended decades ago. Judging from the Navy's pronouncements, it attaches little significance to the trident of economic coercion; it mentions the subject only in the most generalized terms, supplying no evidence that it has sought to determine (as Mahan did) the precise mechanisms by which such coercion works. It would seem either to have lost its interest in or actually forgotten that its enduring raison d'être is to safeguard the global trading system lying at the heart of the liberal international order. Apparently, the subject is deemed unworthy by a "warfighting force" grappling with its own sense of identity and purpose. Meanwhile, at home, support for the Navy wanes as laymen and taxpayers instinctively recognize that the world in which the strategic concept of power projection might apply no longer exists.

Though Mahan's concept of sea power is more than a century old, the time may have come for it be resurrected for a new age of international relations. From a sociopolitical perspective rather than a

purely naval one, economics-focused sea power—sea power proper—
is an offensive weapon of fearsome potential and a vital element in
national defense. It may be that in a future conflict, U.S. leadership
will choose not to wield the trident, but the Navy should at least think
about the possibility and prepare to defend against others who might.
One thing is certain: those who ignore the question of "why" navies
exist and focus instead on "what" a navy will fight with are doomed
to have neither the right ideas nor the tools to implement them when
the reckoning comes.

NOTES ABBREVIATIONS

1812   Alfred Thayer Mahan, *Sea Power in Its Relations to the War of 1812*, 2 vols. (Boston: Little, Brown, 1905)

ATM   Robert Seager, *Alfred Thayer Mahan: The Man and His Letters* (Annapolis, MD: Naval Institute Press, 1977)

FRE   Alfred Thayer Mahan, *The Influence of Sea Power upon the French Revolution and Empire, 1793–1812* (Boston: Little, Brown, 1892)

FSS   Alfred Thayer Mahan, *From Sail to Steam: Recollections of Naval Life* (New York: Harper and Brothers, 1907)

IGS   Jon Tetsuro Sumida, *Inventing Grand Strategy and Teaching Command: The Classic Works of Alfred Thayer Mahan Reconsidered* (Baltimore: Johns Hopkins University Press, 1997)

ISPH   Alfred Thayer Mahan, *The Influence of Sea Power upon History, 1660–1783* (Boston: Little, Brown, 1889)

LOC   Library of Congress, Manuscripts Division

LP   Alfred Thayer Mahan, *The Letters and Papers of Alfred Thayer Mahan*, edited by Robert Seager II and Doris D. Maguire, 3 vols. (Annapolis, MD: Naval Institute Press, 1975)

LWS   Alfred Thayer Mahan, *Lessons of the War with Spain, and Other Articles* (Boston: Little, Brown, 1899)

MMS1   Margaret Tuttle Sprout, "Mahan: Evangelist of Sea Power," in *Makers of Modern Strategy: Military Thought from Machiavelli to Hitler*, ed. Edward Mead Earle (Princeton, NJ: Princeton University Press, 1943)

MMS2   Philip Crowl, "Alfred Thayer Mahan: The Naval Historian," in *Makers of Modern Strategy: From Machiavelli to the Nuclear Age*, ed. Peter Paret (Oxford: Oxford University Press, 1986)

NE   Walter LaFeber, *The New Empire: An Interpretation of American Expansion, 1860–1898*, 35th anniversary edition with a new preface (Ithaca, NY: Cornell University Press, 1998)

NS   Alfred Thayer Mahan, *Naval Strategy Compared and Contrasted with the Principles and Practice of Military Operations on Land* (Boston: Little, Brown, 1911)

NWCR   *Naval War College Review*

NYT   *New York Times*

Roots William Appleman Williams, *The Roots of the Modern American Empire* (New York: Random House, 1969)

SECNAV *Report of the Secretary of the Navy, Being Part of the Message and Documents Communicated to the Two Houses of Congress* (Washington, DC: Government Printing Office)

SNA   Alfred Thayer Mahan, *Some Neglected Aspects of War*
                 (Boston: Little, Brown, 1907)

Sprouts   Harold Sprout and Margaret Sprout, *The Rise of*
                 American Naval Power, 1776–1918 (Princeton, NJ:
                 Princeton University Press, 1939)

Tragedy   William Appleman Williams, *The Tragedy of American*
                 Diplomacy (New York: W. W. Norton, 1959)

NOTES

PREFACE

1. Herbert Rosinski, "Mahan and World War II: A Commentary from the United States" (1941), in *The Development of Naval Thought: Essays by Herbert Rosinski*, ed. B. Mitchell Simpson III (Newport, RI: Naval War College Press, 1977), 20.
2. Julian S. Corbett, *Some Principles of Maritime Strategy* (London: Longmans, Green, 1911), 14.
3. A. T. Mahan, "The Principles of Naval Administration," *National Review* 41, no. 244 (June 1903): 554.

INTRODUCTION

1. Capt. A. T. Mahan, "Word Coinage," *New York Times* (hereafter *NYT*), August 25, 1901, SM22.
2. Alfred Thayer Mahan, *From Sail to Steam: Recollections of Naval Life* (New York: Harper and Brothers, 1907), 276 (hereafter cited as *FSS*).
3. Alfred Thayer Mahan to Arthur Twining Hadley, April 17 and April 28, 1905, series 1, box 58, RU 25, Arthur T. Hadley Papers, Sterling Library, Yale University (hereafter cited as Hadley Papers). From 1899, Hadley was president of Yale College. Mahan's friendship with Hadley and also with Henry Farnam, another Yale economist, is previously unknown.
4. Robert Seager, *Alfred Thayer Mahan: The Man and His Letters* (Annapolis, MD: Naval Institute Press, 1977), 564, 572–75 (hereafter cited as *ATM*).
5. Alfred Thayer Mahan, *Naval Strategy Compared and Contrasted with the Principles and Practice of Military Operations on Land* (Boston: Little, Brown, 1911) (hereafter cited as *NS*).
6. Point first noticed in Don Schurman, *The Education of a Navy* (Chicago: University of Chicago Press, 1965), 65n31.
7. Alfred Thayer Mahan, *The Influence of Sea Power upon History, 1660–1783* (Boston: Little, Brown, 1889), 25 (hereafter cited as *ISPH*).
8. Jon Tetsuro Sumida, *Inventing Grand Strategy and Teaching Command: The Classic Works of Alfred Thayer Mahan Reconsidered* (Baltimore: Johns Hopkins University Press, 1997), 28 (hereafter cited as *IGS*).

9. For example: Barry Hunt, "The Outstanding Naval Strategic Writers of the Century," *Naval War College Review* (hereafter cited as *NWCR*) 37, no. 5 (September–October 1984): 89; Philip Crowl, "Alfred Thayer Mahan: The Naval Historian," in *Makers of Modern Strategy: From Machiavelli to the Nuclear Age*, ed. Peter Paret (Oxford: Oxford University Press, 1986), 451 (hereafter cited as *MMS2*).

10. Alfred Thayer Mahan, *Lessons of the War with Spain, and Other Articles* (Boston: Little, Brown, 1899), 10–11 (hereafter cited as *LWS*).

11. Peter Karsten, *The Naval Aristocracy: The Golden Age of Annapolis and the Emergence of Modern American Navalism* (New York: Free Press, 1972), 337, 338–39; see also John Hattendorf, "Recent Thinking on the Theory of Naval Strategy," in *Maritime Strategy and the Balance of Power: Britain and America in the Twentieth Century*, ed. John Hattendorf and Robert Jordan (Basingstoke, UK: Macmillan, 1989), 137.

12. Arthur James Balfour to Lord Knollys, October 1, 1902, RA/VIC/MAIN/R22/121, King Edward VII correspondence, Royal Archives, Windsor Castle, Windsor, UK. Lord Knollys was private secretary to King Edward VII.

13. Theodore Roosevelt, "A Great Public Servant," *The Outlook* 109 (January 13, 1915): 85–86.

14. George Baer, *One Hundred Years of Sea Power: The U.S. Navy, 1890–1990* (Stanford, CA: Stanford University Press, 1994), 9.

15. C. Vann Woodward, "The Age of Reinterpretation," *American Historical Review* 66, no. 1 (1960): 1–19. The general concept, but not the phrase, can be traced to the work of Charles Beard (who Woodward knew and greatly admired), for which see Campbell Craig, "The Not-So-Strange Career of Charles Beard," *Diplomatic History* 25, no. 2 (Spring 2001): 251–74.

16. Theodore Roosevelt to Henry Cabot Lodge, June 5, 1905 (quoting Adams), as cited by William A. Williams, "Brooks Adams and Amercian Expansion," *New England Quarterly* 25, no. 2 (June 1952): 217–32.

17. Kevin O'Rourke and Jeffrey Williamson, *Globalization and History: The Evolution of a Nineteenth-Century Atlantic Economy* (Cambridge, MA: MIT Press, 1999), 2–5, 33–36; O'Rourke and Williamson, "When Did Globalisation Begin?," *European Review of Economic History* 6, no. 1 (April 2002): 23–50; Paul James and Manfred Steger, "A Genealogy of 'Globalization': The Career of a Concept," *Globalization* 11, no. 4 (2014): 417–34.

18. William Appleman Williams, *The Roots of the Modern American Empire* (New York: Random House, 1969), 348 (cited hereafter as *Roots*). For an interesting commentary, see also John A. Thompson, *A Sense of Power: The Roots of America's Global Role* (Ithaca, NY: Cornell University Press, 2015), 25–55.

19. James A. Field Jr., "Alfred Thayer Mahan Speaks for Himself," *NWCR* 29, no. 2 (Fall 1976): 47.

20. Geoffrey Till, "Alternative Routes and Command of the Sea," in *Maritime Strategy and the Nuclear Age*, ed. Geoffrey Till, 2nd ed. (London: Macmillan, 1984), 130.

21. Hew Strachan, "The Lost Meaning of Strategy," *Survival: Global Politics and Strategy* 43, no. 7 (2005): 33–54.

22. *NS*, 121–22.

23. A. T. Mahan, "Considerations Governing the Dispositions of Navies," *National Review* 39 (July 1902): 701–19.

24. *ATM*, 431, 452–54; *MMS2*, 453.

25. Suzanne Geissler, *God and Sea Power: The Influence of Religion on Alfred Thayer Mahan* (Annapolis, MD: Naval Institute Press, 2015).

26. The first biography is Charles Carlisle Taylor, *The Life of Admiral Mahan: Naval Philosopher* (London: John Murray, 1920); see also Capt. William D. Puleston, USN, *Mahan: The Life and Work of Captain Alfred Thayer Mahan, USN* (New Haven, CT: Yale University Press, 1939); William E. Livezey, *Mahan on Sea Power* (Norman: University of Oklahoma Press, 1947); *ATM*.

CHAPTER 1. MAHAN'S WORLD

1. Alfred Thayer Mahan to Samuel Ashe, August 14, 1883, as reproduced in Mahan, *The Letters and Papers of Alfred Thayer Mahan*, ed. Robert Seager II and Doris D. Maguire, 3 vols. (Annapolis, MD: Naval Institute Press, 1975), 1:558 (hereafter cited as *LP*).

2. *FSS*.

3. Cited in Herman F. Krafft and Walter B. Norris, *Sea Power in American History: The Influence of the Navy and the Merchant Marine upon American Development* (New York: Century Company, 1920), 298.

4. Frederick Drake, *The Empire of the Seas: A Biography of Rear Admiral Robert Wilson Shufeldt, USN* (Honolulu: University of Hawaii Press, 1984), 132.

5. Mahan to Ashe, May 15, 1875, *LP*, 1:433.

6. Mahan to Ashe, August 19 and 21, 1876, *LP*, 1:458.

7. Mahan to Ashe, December 21, 1882, *LP*, 1:543.

8. Alfred Thayer Mahan to Stephen B. Luce, September 4, 1884, *LP*, 1:577.

9. Don Schurman, "Mahan Revisited," in *Maritime Strategy and the Balance of Power: Britain and America in the Twentieth Century*, edited by John B. Hattendorf and Robert S. Jordan (Basingstoke, UK: Macmillan, 1989), 101.

10. Mahan to Ashe, November 13, 1880, *LP*, 1:486.

11. Mahan to Ashe, December 21, 1882, *LP*, 1:543.

12. Mahan to Ashe, April 30, 1879, *LP*, 1:473; November 26, 1879, *LP*, 1:476; November 13, 1880, *LP*, 1:486.

13. Mahan to Ashe, March 5 and 7, 1878, *LP*, 1:467.

14. An excellent entry point to the literature on the tariff in U.S. politics is Richard Franklin Bensel, *The Political Economy of American Industrialization, 1877–1900* (Cambridge: Cambridge University Press, 2000), esp. chap. 7.

15. Jay Sexton, *The Monroe Doctrine: Empire and Nation in Nineteenth-Century America* (New York: Hill and Wang, 2011), 169.

16. Daniel Wicks, "Dress Rehearsal: United States Intervention on the Isthmus of Panama, 1885," *Pacific Historical Review*, 49, no. 4 (November 1980): 586–87.

17. Mahan to Ashe, March 12, 1880, *LP*, 1:481.

18. *Report of the Secretary of the Navy, Being Part of the Message and Documents Communicated to the Two Houses of Congress* (Washington, DC: Government Printing Office, 1880), 24 (hereafter cited as *SECNAV*).

19. *SECNAV*, 1880, 25.

20. Sexton, *Monroe Doctrine*, 162–63, 176–79.

21. Sexton, 176–79.

22. Mahan to Ashe, December 21, 1882, *LP*, 1:543.

23. Mahan to Ashe, December 21, 1882, and March 11, 1885, *LP*, 1:544, 592.

24. Scott Mobley, *Progressives in Navy Blue: Maritime Strategy, American Empire, and the Transformation of US Naval Identity, 1873–1898* (Annapolis, MD: Naval Institute Press, 2018), 102–5.

25. Walter LaFeber, *The New Empire: An Interpretation of American Expansion, 1860–1898* (Ithaca, NY: Cornell University Press, 1998), 47–52 (hereafter cited as *NE*).

26. Mahan to Ashe, July 26, 1884, *LP*, 1:571–72.

27. For details of U.S. actions leading to the landing in Panama, see Wicks, "Dress Rehearsal," 581–605.

28. Mahan to Ashe, July 26, 1884, *LP*, 1:574.

29. Mahan to Ashe, July 26, 1884, *LP*, 1:574.

30. David Surdam, *Northern Naval Superiority and the Economics of the American Civil War* (Columbia: University of South Carolina Press, 2001).

31. George T. Davis, *A Navy Second to None: The Development of Modern American Naval Policy* (New York: Harcourt, Brace, 1940), xi.

32. Mahan to Ashe, March 11, 1885, *LP*, 1:593.

33. Mahan to Ashe, May 21, 1875, *LP*, 1:434; see also Mahan to Ashe, December 27, 1875, *LP*, 1:437.

34. Mobley, *Progressives in Navy Blue*, 147.

35. Paul E. Pedisich, *Congress Buys a Navy: Politics, Economics, and the Rise of American Naval Power* (Annapolis, MD: Naval Institute Press, 2016), 54–55.

36. *SECNAV*, 1881, 1.

37. Useful here is Pedisich, *Congress Buys a Navy*, 54–55.

38. Harold Sprout and Margaret Sprout, *The Rise of American Naval Power, 1776–1918* (Princeton, NJ: Princeton University Press, 1939), 183–89, hereafter cited as Sprouts). Yet the Sprouts' arguments were strikingly similar to those found in Louis M. Hacker and Benjamin B. Kendrick, *The United States since 1865* (New York: F. S. Crofts, 1932); see esp. 125–27. In turn, Hacker and Kendrick relied extensively on a book produced by two Naval Academy professors who have used Mahan's autobiography as their template: see Krafft and Norris, *Sea Power in American History*, chap. 21.

39. Davis, *Navy Second to None*, 28–55.
40. Sprouts, 183.
41. Sprouts, 186–87; but for a repudiation of Mahan, built on a mistaken analysis of his arguments, see "Author's Introduction to the 1966 Edition," iv.
42. Sprouts, 186; Davis, *Navy Second to None*, 37–38. For astute insight in to why *SECNAV* is circumventing the bureaus, see Drake, *Empire of the Seas*, 164–65.
43. Sprouts, 183–84.
44. Sprouts, 188–89.
45. Sprouts, 190.
46. Sprouts, 190.
47. First noted by Drake, *Empire of the Seas*, 164–65.
48. Davis, *Navy Second to None*, 56–61, 72–85.
49. Sprouts, "Author's Introduction to the 1966 Edition," i.
50. For example, Kenneth J. Hagen, *The People's Navy: The Making of American Sea Power* (New York: Free Press, 1991), 185–86; Timothy Wolters, "Recapitalizing the Fleet: A Material Analysis of Late-Nineteenth-Century U.S. Naval Power," *Technology and Culture* 52, no. 1 (January 2011): 103–26.
51. Hagen, *People's Navy*, 185–87; Mobley, *Progressives in Navy Blue*, 160–71; Pedisich, *Congress Buys a Navy*, 24–26; George Baer, *One Hundred Years of Sea Power: The US Navy, 1890–1990* (Stanford, CA: Stanford University Press, 1996), 10–11. A notable exception is Stephan Howarth, *To Shining Sea: A History of the United States Navy, 1775–1998* (Norman: University of Oklahoma Press, 1991), 225–26. Mobley too is uncomfortable with the logic yet follows it (*Progressives in Navy Blue*, 153–54).
52. Mahan to Ashe, August 14, 1883, *LP*, 1:558.
53. Mahan to Ashe, August 14, 1883, *LP*, 1:558.
54. Mahan to Ashe, July 6, 1883, *LP*, 1:554.
55. *FSS*, 7–8.
56. Mahan to Ashe, March 11, 1885, *LP*, 1:593.
57. Mahan to Ashe, March 11, 1885, *LP*, 1:593.
58. Mahan to Ashe, March 11, 1885, *LP*, 1:593.
59. Mahan to Ashe, September 8, 1887, *LP*, 1:642.
60. Sprouts, 186–87; Mobley, *Progressives in Navy Blue*, 125.
61. The Rodgers report (November 7, 1881) was printed as an appendix in *SECNAV*, 1881, 35; see also Mobley, *Progressives in Navy Blue*, 153; Hagen, *People's Navy*, 185–86.
62. Robert G. Angevine, "The Rise and Fall of the Office of Naval Intelligence, 1882–1892: A Technological Perspective," *Journal of Military History* 62, no. 2 (April 1998): 293.
63. Naval Appropriation Act, August 5, 1882, 22 STAT 296, chap. 391, 291–92; see also *SECNAV*, 1883, Appendix 2, Reports of the Naval Advisory Board, 52–82.
64. Drake, *Empire of the Seas*, 312–15; yet see *SECNAV*, 1885, 40.

65. Norman Friedman points out that the bureaus initially refused to submit designs to the Schufelt board. See Friedman, *US Cruisers: An Illustrated Design History* (Annapolis, MD: Naval Institute Press, 1984), 18.

66. Chandler to Hon. J. Warren Keifer (Speaker of the House), January 2, 1883, transmitting recommendations of the Naval Advisory Board concerning unarmored naval vessels, Executive Documents of the House of Representatives, 47th Congress, 2nd session, Ex. Doc. No. 32. See also Mobley, *Progressives in Navy Blue*, 143, 156–57, 167; Hagen, *People's Navy*, 187.

67. *SECNAV*, 1883, 3.

68. *SECNAV*, 1883, 3.

69. Friedman, *Cruisers*, 15.

70. Christopher Renfrew, *Home Squadron: The US Navy and the North Atlantic Station* (Annapolis, MD: Naval Institute Press, 2014), 43; Leonard Alexander Swann, *John Roach, Maritime Entrepreneur: The Years as Naval Contractor, 1862–1886* (Annapolis, MD: U.S. Naval Institute, 1965).

71. Davis, *Second to None*, 43; Pedisich, *Congress Buys a Navy*, 27, 38.

72. Drake, *Empire of the Seas*, 312.

73. Friedman, *Cruisers*, 22.

74. *SECNAV*, 1884, 4–5.

75. Friedman, *Cruisers*, 14.

76. *SECNAV*, 1885, 19–27.

77. Thomas Heinrich, *Ships for the Seven Seas: Philadelphia Shipbuilding in the Age of Industrial Capitalism* (Baltimore, MD: Johns Hopkins University Press, 1997), 112–21.

78. *SECNAV*, 1885, 19.

79. *SECNAV*, 1885, 27–41.

80. *NYT*, December 5, 1885, 4.

81. See *SECNAV*, 1889, appendix 1 on staffing.

82. Whitney to Chairman J. D. Cameron, July 27, 1886, as cited in Angevine, "Rise and Fall," 299.

83. Friedman, *Cruisers*, 25.

84. Angevine, "Rise and Fall," 303, is important here.

85. Friedman, *Cruisers*, 16–20; Angevine, "Rise and Fall," 294; Michael E. Vlahos, "The Making of an American Style," in *Naval Engineering and American Seapower*, ed. Randolph W. King (Baltimore: Nautical and Aviation Publishing Company of America, 1989), 3–32.

86. *SECNAV*, 1885, 19, 27–47.

87. A theme developed by Williams in *The Contours of American History* (Cleveland: World Publishing Company, 1961).

88. *Roots*, 23–25.

89. Jeffrey Williamson, *American Growth and the Balance of Payments, 1820–1913* (Chapel Hill: University of North Carolina Press, 1964), table B-9.

90. Morton Rothstein, "America in the International Rivalry for the British Wheat Market, 1860–1914," *Mississippi Valley Historical Review* 47, no. 3 (December 1960): 402; Rothstein, "Centralizing Firms and Spreading Markets: The World of International Grain Traders, 1846–1914," *Business and Economic History* 17 (1988): 103–13.

91. *Roots*, 20.

92. Rothstein, "America in the International Rivalry," 403.

93. Williams touches on this (*Roots*, 20–23) but does not develop the theme or supply price data.

94. Kevin O'Rourke and Jeffrey Williamson, *Globalization and History: The Evolution of a Nineteenth-Century Atlantic Economy* (Cambridge, MA: MIT Press, 1999), 95–96.

95. For more on the working of the international grain trade during this period and a more complete survey of the literature, see Nicholas A. Lambert, *The War Lords and the Gallipoli Disaster: How Globalized Trade Led Britain to Its Worst Defeat of the First World War* (Oxford: Oxford University Press, 2021), chap. 1.

96. *Roots*, 20–27.

97. *Roots*, 27–46, 238–50, 319–48.

98. *Roots*, 29–30, 236–38, 264–68.

99. *Roots*, 236.

100. *Roots*, 21, 238–39; Commo. Robert W. Shufeldt, "The Relation of the Navy to the Commerce of the United States: A Letter Written by Request to Hon. Leopold Morse, M.C., Member of Naval Committee, House of Representatives" (Washington, DC: J. L. Ginck, 1878). Shufeldt retired due to age in 1884.

101. *Roots*, 29.

102. For an interesting commentary of this subject, see David Dixon Porter to Stephen Luce, March 14, 1889, reel 7, Rear Adm. Stephen B. Luce Papers, Library of Congress, Washington, DC (hereafter Luce Papers, LOC).

103. *Roots*, 310, 346.

104. Thomas Coode, "Southern Congressmen and the American Naval Revolution, 1880–1898," *Alabama Historical Quarterly* (Fall–Winter 1968): 92–94.

105. Coode, 94.

106. Coode, 95.

107. Peter Trubowitz, *Defining the National Interest: Conflict and Change in American Foreign Policy* (Chicago: University of Chicago Press, 1998), 43–52.

CHAPTER 2. NAVAL INSTRUCTOR

1. *FSS*, 273–74.

2. Frederick Drake, *The Empire of the Seas: A Biography of Rear Admiral Robert Wilson Shufeldt, USN* (Honolulu: University of Hawaii Press, 1984), 153–59.

3. Ronald Spector, *Professors of War: The Naval War College and the Development of the Naval Profession* (Newport, RI: Naval War College Press, 1977), 12.

4. John Hattendorf, "Stephen B. Luce: Intellectual Leader of the New Navy," in *Admirals of the New Steel Navy: Makers of the American Naval Tradition, 1880–1930*, ed. James Bradford (Annapolis, MD: Naval Institute Press, 1990), 3.

5. Rear Adm. Bradley A. Fiske, "Stephen B. Luce: An Appreciation," *Proceedings* 43/9/175 (September 1917). All issues of *Proceedings* are digitized and are available at http://www.usni.org.

6. Alfred Thayer Mahan to John G. Walker, October 13, 1888, *LP*, 1:661. For earlier expression of this view, see Cdr. A. T. Mahan, "Naval Education," *Proceedings* 4/5/9 (1879): 349.

7. Spector, *Professors of War*, 12.

8. Further developed in Jon Tetsuro Sumida, "The Relationship between History and Theory in *On War*: The Clausewitzian Ideal and Its Implications," *Journal of Military History* 65, no. 2 (April 2001): 333–54.

9. *IGS*, 20–23.

10. Stephen B. Luce, "On the Study of Naval History (Grand Tactics)," *Proceedings* 13/2/41 (April 1887): 175–201.

11. Scott Mobley, *Progressives in Navy Blue: Maritime Strategy, American Empire, and the Transformation of US Naval Identity, 1873–1898* (Annapolis, MD: Naval Institute Press, 2018), 142.

12. Robert Shufeldt to Richard W. Thomson, January 16, 1878, as quoted in Drake, *Empire of the Seas*, 166.

13. Adm. D. D. Porter to George M. Robeson, November 7, 1874, in *SECNAV*, 1874.

14. For a helpful and concise discussion of "strategy" and the U.S. Navy, see Mobley, *Progressives in Navy Blue*, 2–4, 12–13, 83–89.

15. Stephen B. Luce, "War Schools," *Proceedings* 9/5/27 (December 1883): 633–57. Luce first aired his Naval War College idea in 1877 but found no interest. My thanks to Scott Mobley for this information.

16. Stephen B. Luce to William Chandler, March 8, 1884, Luce Papers.

17. Spector, *Professors of War*, 20–27; John Hattendorf and John D. Hayes, eds., *The Writings of Stephen B. Luce* (Newport, RI: Naval War College, 1975), 53. For Luce's recollections on the subject, see Stephen B. Luce to William Chandler, February 21, 1905, folder 5, NWC file, Naval Historical Foundation Collection, Library of Congress, Washington DC; and Stephen B. Luce to Alfred Thayer Mahan, July 15, 1907, box 2, folder 2, RG 28, U.S. Naval War College Archives, Newport, RI (hereafter cited as Naval War College Archives).

18. *ATM*, 161–63, 185–87.

19. See James C. Rentfrow, *Home Squadron: the U.S. Navy on the North Atlantic Station* (Annapolis, MD: Naval Institute Press, 2014), 50–63, 96–98, 109. For an earlier suggestion that "Luce had hoped for a symbiotic relationship with the North Atlantic Squadron" and the Naval War College, see James A. Field, "Alfred Thayer Mahan Speaks for Himself," *NWCR*, Fall 1976, 55.

20. Hattendorf and Hayes, *Writings of Stephen B. Luce*, 69. Note that Luce's paper on grand tactics (see note 9 of this chapter) distinguishes between evolutionary tactics (maneuver) and grand tactics, or tactics of battle.

21. Hew Strachan, "Maritime Strategy: Historical Perspectives," *RUSI Journal* 152, no. 1 (February 2007): 29–33. On the changed meaning of the word "strategy" over time, see Strachan, "The Lost Meaning of Strategy," *Survival* 47, no. 3 (July 2006): 33–54; Strachan, "Strategy and the Limitation of War," *Survival* 50, no. 1 (January 2008): 31–54.

22. Stephen B. Luce, "On the Study of Naval Warfare as a Science," *Proceedings* 12/4/39 (October 1886): 527–46.

23. Hattdendorf and Hayes, *Writings of Stephen B. Luce*, 46.

24. Luce, "On the Study of Naval Warfare."

25. Luce.

26. Articulated most clearly in Azar Gat, *The Development of Military Thought: The Nineteenth Century* (Oxford: Oxford University Press, 1991), 173–84, esp. 176; see also Spector, *Professors of War*, 9, 17–20, 44.

27. Luce, "On the Study of Naval Warfare," 530.

28. Luce, 534.

29. Luce, 532.

30. Luce, 531–32.

31. Luce, 531.

32. Luce, 534–35.

33. Luce, "Naval Administration III," *Proceedings* 29/4/108 (September 1903): 820.

34. Luce, "On the Study of Naval History," 175–201.

35. Luce, 534–35.

36. Luce, 533.

37. Luce, 533. For Mahan seeking clarification of his instructions, see Alfred Thayer Mahan to Stephen B. Luce, September 4, 1884, *LP*, 1:577.

38. Mahan to Luce, September 4, 1884.

39. Letter to the authors cited in Herman F. Krafft and Walter B. Norris, *Sea Power in American History: The Influence of the Navy and the Merchant Marine upon American Development* (New York: Century Company, 1920), 298.

40. U.S. House of Representatives, Investigations of the Navy Department, 44th Cong., 1st sess., 1876, Rept. No. 784.

41. *IGS*, 17–19.

42. Alfred Thayer Mahan to Charles Scribner's Sons, April 12, 1883, *LP*, 1:347. A detailed history of this book found in Alfred Thayer Mahan to Samuel Ashe, July 6, 1883, *LP*, 1:554.

43. Caspar Goodrich to Charles Sperry, March 5, 1906, box 3, folder 13, RG 1, U.S. Naval War College Archives, Newport, RI.

44. Caspar Goodrich to Stephen B. Luce, February 12, 1884, MSC-10, box 1, folder 1, Rear Adm. Stephen B. Luce Papers, U.S. Naval War College Archives (hereafter Luce Papers, NWC).

45. Mahan to Luce, September 4, 1884, *LP*, 1:577.

46. Mahan to Luce, September 4, 1884, *LP*, 1:577.

47. Mahan to Luce, September 4, 1884, *LP*, 1:577.

48. Mahan to Luce, September 4, 1884, *LP*, 1:577.

49. Albert Gleaves, *Life and Letters of Rear Admiral Stephen B. Luce, U.S. Navy, Founder of the Naval War College* (New York: G. P. Putnam's Sons, 1925), 180; also Alfred Thayer Mahan to Stephen B. Luce, November 5, 1884, LP 1:581, references Luce to Mahan, September 30, 1884.

50. See Mahan to Luce, November 2, 1885, *LP*, 1:616.

51. Mahan to Luce, May 13, 1885, *LP*, 1:603.

52. Mahan to Luce, May 13, 1885, *LP*, 1:603.

53. William Mathews to Stephen B. Luce, March 23, 1885, MSC-10, box 1, folder 2, Luce Papers, NWC.

54. Mahan to Luce, May 16, 1885, *LP*, 1:606, in reply to letter from Luce of April 6, 1885.

55. Mahan to Luce, May 16, 1885, *LP*, 1:606.

56. Alfred Thayer Mahan to SECNAV, May 15, 1885, *LP*, 1:605.

57. William C. Whitney to Stephen B. Luce, July 27, 1885, box 1, folder 33, RG 1, Naval War College Archives.

58. Mahan to Luce, September 2, 1885, *LP*, 1:613.

59. Mahan to Luce, October 16, 1885, *LP*, 1:614.

60. Mahan to Luce, May 16, 1885, *LP*, 1:606.

61. Mahan to Luce, September 4, 1884, *LP*, 1:577.

62. Between 1878 and 1880, Mahan served as head of the ordnance department at the Naval Academy when Foxhall Parker was superintendent.

63. Stephen B. Luce, "Report of the Superintendent Naval War College" [*sic*], September 30, 1885, box 1, RG 1, Naval War College Archives.

64. Gat, *Development of Military Thought*, 179; *ATM*, 166, 173.

65. Mahan to Ashe, February 2, 1886, *LP*, 1:625.

66. Mahan to Luce, April 24, 1886, *LP*, 1:628.

67. Mahan to Luce, May 1, 1886, *LP*, 1:630.

68. *ATM*, 164, 166, 170–71.

69. Mahan to Luce, November 3, 1885, *LP*, 1:616–17; Mahan to Luce, November 19, 1885, *LP*, 1:618.

70. Mahan to Luce, November 14, 1885, *LP*, 1:617; Henri Martin, *Histoire de France depuis les temps recules jusqu'en 1789*, rev. 4th ed., 16 vols. (Paris: Furne, 1861–1865). The four volumes spanning the period from 1661 to 1789 were translated from the edition into English by Mary L. Booth and published under the title *Martin's History of France in the Age of Louis XV*, 4 vols. (Boston: Walker, Fuller & Co., 1864–1867). These were the editions Mahan used.

71. *FSS*, 280–81.

72. *FSS*, 282–83.

73. *IGS*, 28–32, 101.

74. Mahan to Luce, January 6, 1886, *LP*, 1:619.

75. Mahan to Luce, January 18, 1886, *LP*, 1:621.

76. Mahan to Luce, January 22, 1886, *LP*, 1: 622–23.

77. Mahan to Luce, January 22, 1886, *LP*, 1:623.

78. Mahan to Luce, January 22, 1886, *LP*, 1:624.

79. Mahan to Luce, January 22, 1886, *LP*, 1: 623.

80. Mahan to Ashe, January 13, 1886, *LP*, 1:621.

81. Mahan to Ashe, February 2, 1886, *LP*, 1:624–25.

82. Between March and the first fortnight in April, Mahan was ill with malarial fever and unable to work.

83. Mahan to Luce, April 24, 1886, *LP*, 1:628.

84. Mahan to Luce, April 7, 1886, *LP*, 1:626–27. For return of the paper, see Mahan to Luce, May 1, 1886, *LP*, 1:631.

85. Mahan to Luce, April 24, 1886, *LP*, 1:628.

86. Mahan to Luce, May 1, 1886, *LP*, 1:630.

87. Typed copy of "Fleet Battle Tactics," with note in Mahan's hand stating the original was written April/May 1886 and never revised. Rear Adm. Alfred T. Mahan Papers, MSC-017, box 1, folder 2, Naval War College Archives.

88. Mahan to Luce, May 6, 1886, *LP*, 1:632.

89. Mahan to Luce, May 31, 1886, *LP*, 1:632.

90. Mahan to Luce, May 6, 1886, *LP*, 1:632.

91. Report of Naval War College, October 19, 1886, box 1, folder 7, RG 1, Naval War College Archives.

92. John D. Hayes, "Stephen B. Luce and the Beginnings of the U.S. Naval War College," *NWCR* 23, no. 5 (January 1971): 58; Gleaves, *Life and Letters of Rear Admiral Stephen B. Luce*, 181.

93. Mahan to Ashe, October 3, 1886, *LP*, 1:635.

94. Mahan to Ashe, October 3, 1886, *LP*, 1:635.

95. Mahan to Ashe, September 8, 1887, *LP*, 1:641.

96. Stephen B. Luce to J. S. Barnes, August 5, 1889, Luce Papers, LOC; Lt. John F. Meigs to Stephen B. Luce, October 27, 1888, MSC-10, box 1, folder 1, Luce Papers, NWC.

97. For instance, October 3, 1886 (*LP*, 1:635); September 8, 1887 (*LP*, 1:641); January 12, 1888 (*LP*, 1:647); August 10, 1888 (*LP*, 1:653).

98. Spector, *Professors of War*, 50–70; *ATM*, 181–85.

99. Don Shurman, "Mahan Revisited," in *Maritime Strategy and the Balance of Power: Britain and America in the Twentieth Century*, ed. John B. Hattendorf and Robert S. Jordan (New York: St. Martin's Press, 1988), 103.

100. The impact of Jomini upon Mahan is recognized as exaggerated by Peter Karsten, *The Naval Aristocracy: The Golden Age of Annapolis and the Emergence of Modern American Navalism* (New York: Free Press, 1972), 326–47, and in *MMS2*, 450–51. By contrast, Robert Seager saw Mahan as Jominian (*ATM*, 168–70); George Baer regarded Mahan as mildly Jominian (*One Hundred*

Years of Sea Power: The US Navy, 1890–1990 [Stanford, CA: Stanford University Press, 1996], 14); and Jon Tetsuro Sumida says Mahan is not at all Jominian (*IGS*, 23–24).

101. *SECNAV*, 1887, 163, reproducing Alfred Thayer Mahan to John G. Walker, October 4, 1887.
102. *SECNAV*, 1887, 163, reproducing Mahan to Walker, October 4, 1887.
103. For Luce employing Mahan's arguments, see Stephen B. Luce to Banjamin F. Tracy, March 19, 1889, Luce Papers, LOC.
104. Mahan to Scribner's, September 4, 1888, *LP*, 1:657–58.
105. Stephen B. Luce to Lt. John F. Meigs, October 29, 1888, Luce Papers, MSC-10, box 1, folder 1, Naval War College Archives.
106. Luce to Meigs, October 29, 1888.
107. Luce to Barnes, August 5, 1889, Luce Papers, LOC; see also Mahan to Luce, August 1, 1889, *LP*, 1:700.
108. Luce to Tracy, March 14, 1889, Luce Papers, LOC.

CHAPTER 3. INFLUENCE

1. *ISPH*, iii.
2. Lyle Mahan and John Hattendorff, "My Parents, Rear Admiral and Mrs. Alfred Thayer Mahan," *NWCR* 43, no. 4 (Autumn 1990): 86.
3. Alfred Thayer Mahan to Stephen B. Luce, September 21, 1889, *LP*, 1:707.
4. Mahan to Luce, October 7, 1889, *LP* 1:712. For further details, see Alfred Thayer Mahan to James McIntyre, January 7, 1909, *LP*, 3:274. McIntyre took over the editorship of Little, Brown after the death of James B. Brown in 1908.
5. James Soley was, from 1885 to 1889, a civilian instructor on international law; from 1890 to 1893, Assistant Secretary of the Navy; and from 1893, partner in the New York law firm headed by Secretary of the Navy Benjamin F. Tracy.
6. Mahan to Luce, October 7, 1889, *LP*, 1:712.
7. Mahan to Luce, October 16, 1889, *LP*, 1:714; the letter did not reach Luce until the end of the month, for which see Stephen B. Luce to Lt. John F. Meigs, October 29, 1888, Luce Papers, LOC.
8. Remarks by Captain Mahan on "Our Future Navy" by Rear Adm. Stephen B. Luce, *Proceedings*, 15/4/51 (October 1889): 554.
9. *ISPH*, 524.
10. *ISPH*, v–vi.
11. *ISPH*, 21.
12. *ISPH*, v.
13. *ISPH*, iii.
14. *MMS2*, 450–51.
15. *IGS*, 27n6, but not explicitly developed.
16. *ISPH*, 50, 53.
17. *ISPH*, 95–97.

18. *ISPH*, 95–96.

19. *ISPH*, 98.

20. *ISPH*, 225.

21. *ISPH*, 1.

22. *ISPH*, 1.

23. *ISPH*, 25.

24. *ISPH*, 25.

25. *ISPH*, 26.

26. *ISPH*, 26.

27. *ISPH*, 25.

28. *ISPH*, 138.

29. *ISPH*, 197–200.

30. *ISPH*, 198.

31. *ISPH*, 200.

32. *ISPH*, v, vi, 28.

33. *ISPH*, vi.

34. *ISPH*, vi.

35. *ISPH*, 88–89; emphasis added.

36. *ISPH*, 90–91.

37. Mahan to Luce, January 22, 1886, *LP*, 1:623.

38. *ISPH*, 102; emphasis added.

39. *ISPH*, 205.

40. *IGS*, 32.

41. For Mahan's similar struggle to define "principles," see Donald M. Schurman, *The Education of a Navy: The Development of British Naval Strategic Thought, 1867–1914* (London: Cassell, 1965), 72–75.

42. *ISPH*, 7.

43. *ISPH*, 8.

44. *ISPH*, 22–23.

45. Seen clearly in *NS*, 121–22.

46. *ISPH*, 23, repeated on 89.

47. *ISPH*, 191.

48. *ISPH*, 201.

49. *ISPH*, 208.

50. *ISPH*, 225–26.

51. *ISPH*, 254.

52. *ISPH*, 295.

53. *ISPH*, 297.

54. *ISPH*, 28.

55. *ISPH*, 82; see also 93, 107, 317.

56. *ISPH*, 8, 31.

57. *ISPH*, 506; see also 509–10.

58. *NS*, 203–4.

59. *ISPH*, 283.
60. *ISPH*, 288; see also 339–40, 520–21.
61. *ISPH*, 288.
62. *ISPH*, 539–40.
63. *ISPH*, 31–32, 530, 539–40.
64. *ISPH*, 132.
65. *ISPH*, 132–33.
66. *ISPH*, 339.
67. *ISPH*, 136.
68. *ISPH*, 132.
69. *ISPH*, 193.
70. *ISPH*, 196.
71. *ISPH*, 131–36.
72. *ISPH*, 194.
73. *ISPH*, 138.
74. Arne Røksund, *The Jeune École: The Strategy of the Weak* (Leiden: Brill, 2007); another with a good grasp of *jeune école* theory is David Olivier, *German Naval Strategy, 1856–1888: Forerunners to Tirpitz* (New York: Frank Cass, 2004).
75. *ISPH*, 138.
76. Jan Martin Lemnitzer, *Power, Law and the End of Privateering* (London: Palgrave Macmillan, 2014).
77. *ISPH*, 138.
78. *ISPH*, 339–41, 478–85.
79. *ISPH*, 31.
80. *ISPH*, 539. For similarly explicit statements condemning *guerre de course*, see 401 and 468.
81. *ISPH*, 500.
82. *ISPH*, 90–91.
83. *ISPH*, 76.
84. *ISPH*, 86.
85. *ISPH*, 87; see also 90–91.
86. Theodore Roosevelt, reviews of *ISPH* and of Alfred Thayer Mahan, *The Influence of Sea Power upon the French Revolution and Empire, 1793–1812* (Boston: Little, Brown, 1892) (hereafter cited as *FRE*), *Political Science Quarterly* 9, no. 1 (1893): 171–72.
87. *ISPH*, 84–97.

CHAPTER 4. BENJAMIN TRACY AND THE QUESTION OF INFLUENCE

1. *SECNAV*, 1891, 31.
2. *Roots*, 320.
3. *Roots*, 27–46, 245–50, and esp. 332–44.
4. *Roots*, 319–32; *NE*, 102–17.

5. *NE*, 122; Benjamin F. Cooling, *Benjamin Franklin Tracy: Father of the Modern American Fighting Navy* (Hamden, CT: Shoe String Press, 1973), 70–73.

6. Editorial, *NYT*, March 4, 1889, 4.

7. Cooling, *Benjamin Franklin Tracy*, 44.

8. Cooling, 63.

9. Cooling, 65.

10. Commo. W. P. McCann's report appears in *Proceedings* 16/2/53 (April 1890). Also useful here is "Cruisers and Warships," *NYT*, January 30, 1890, 2. For George Davis and the Sprouts attaching great importance to this board, see George T. Davis, *A Navy Second to None: The Development of Modern American Naval Policy* (New York: Harcourt, Brace, 1940), 86–88; Sprouts, 211–12.

11. Eugene Hale to Benjamin Franklin Tracy, September 22 and October 20, 1889, both in box 3, Benjamin Franklin Tracy Papers, Library of Congress, Washington, DC (hereafter cited as Tracy Papers).

12. Rear Adm. Stephen B. Luce, "Our Future Navy," *North American Review* 149 (July 1889): 54–65.

13. Cooling, *Benjamin Franklin Tracy*, 70.

14. David Dixon Porter to Stephen B. Luce, March 14, 1889, reel 7, Luce Papers, LOC.

15. Porter to Luce, March 21, 1889, reel 7, Luce Papers, LOC.

16. "The President's Trip," *NYT*, August 15, 1889, 1; "The Proposed Navy," *NYT*, August 22, 1889, 1.

17. Hale to Tracy, September 22, 1889, box 3, Tracy Papers. These cruisers were the *Raleigh* (Norfolk Navy Yard) and *Cincinnati* (Brooklyn Navy Yard).

18. Sprouts, 207; *NE*, 123. Davis, *Navy Second to None*, 93, uses the same word to describe the Tracy program but with quite a different meaning.

19. "Our Navy," *NYT*, December 2, 1889, 4.

20. French Chadwick to Benjamin Franklin Tracy, December 26, 1889, as cited in Cooling, *Benjamin Franklin Tracy*, 78.

21. *SECNAV*, 1889, 10–12.

22. Charles Boutelle to Stephen B. Luce, n.d. [December 26, 1889], reel 7, Luce Papers, LOC.

23. Davis, *Navy Second to None*, 91, more generally 56–60, 74, 77, 91–94; Margaret Tuttle Sprout, "Mahan: Evangelist of Sea Power," in *Makers of Modern Strategy: Military Thought from Machiavelli to Hitler*, ed. Edward Mead Earle (Princeton, NJ: Princeton University Press, 1943), 436 (hereafter cited as *MMS1*); and Cooling, *Benjamin Franklin Tracy*, 78.

24. George Baer, *One Hundred Years of Sea Power: The US Navy, 1890–1990* (Stanford, CA: Stanford University Press, 1996), 1; emphasis added.

25. Sprouts, 207; see also *MMS1*, 436. Davis, *Navy Second to None*, 94–99, is just as bad.

26. Alfred Thayer Mahan to Stephen B. Luce, December 3, 1889, *LP*, 1:718.

27. Paul E. Pedisich, *Congress Buys a Navy: Politics, Economics, and the Rise of American Naval Power* (Annapolis, MD: Naval Institute Press, 2016), 76; Scott Mobley, *Progressives in Navy Blue: Maritime Strategy, American Empire, and the Transformation of US Naval Identity, 1873–1898* (Annapolis, MD: Naval Institute Press, 2018), 174; Cooling, *Benjamin Franklin Tracy*, 74; *MMS2*, 470–71, 471n96; Baer, *One Hundred Years of Sea Power*, 1–2. The notable exception is Ronald Spector, *Professors of War: The Naval War College and the Development of the Naval Profession* (Newport, RI: Naval War College Press, 1977), 48.
28. *SECNAV*, 1889, 14, table 1.
29. Luce to Boutelle, December 28, 1889, reel 7, Luce Papers, LOC.
30. *SECNAV*, 1887, ix; *SECNAV*, 1888, 16.
31. "Our Navy," 2.
32. The other eight being upgraded monitors. "Our Navy," 2.
33. "Our Navy," 2.
34. *SECNAV*, 1889, 4.
35. *SECNAV*, 1889, 10–12.
36. *SECNAV*, 1889, 5.
37. *SECNAV*, 1889, 4.
38. *SECNAV*, 1889, 5. See also *SECNAV*, 1891, 31.
39. For Mahan's dislike of naval militia, see *IGS*, 47–48.
40. *SECNAV*, 1889, 13.
41. "To Strengthen the Navy: Converting Merchant Vessels into Cruisers," *NYT*, January 12, 1890, 11; "Our Auxiliary Navy," *NYT*, May 23, 1892, 4.
42. Andrew Gibson and Arthur Donovan, *The Abandoned Ocean: A History of United States Maritime Policy* (Columbia: University of South Carolina Press, 2000), 53, 64–99; Randolph W. King, ed., *Naval Engineering and American Seapower* (Baltimore: Nautical and Aviation Publishing Company of America, 1989). I am indebted to Scott Mobley for bring this book to my attention.
43. The best (and only good) summary of the postbellum story is found in Edward Crapol and Howard Schonberger, "The Shift to Global Expansion, 1865–1900," in *From Colony to Empire: Essays in the History of American Foreign Relations*, ed. W. A. Williams (New York: J. Wiley, 1972), 157–68. For older though still useful accounts, see Rear Adm. William S. Benson, *The Merchant Marine* (New York: Macmillan, 1923); and Paul M. Zeis, *American Shipping Policy* (Princeton, NJ: Princeton University Press, 1938).
44. *Roots*, 263–64.
45. Gibson and Donovan, *Abandoned Ocean*, 82–83.
46. Gibson and Donovan, *Abandoned Ocean*, 84.
47. Winthrop L. Marvin, *The American Merchant Marine: Its History and Romance, from 1620 to 1902* (New York: Charles Scribner's Sons, 1902), 422–29; William Wallace Bates, *American Marine: The Shipping Question in History and Politics* (Boston: Houghton Mifflin, 1893), 411–15.

48. *NE*, 108–9.
49. *Roots*, 328.
50. President Benjamin Harrison, First Annual Message, December 3, 1889, The American Presidency Project, https://www.presidency.ucsb.edu/documents/first-annual-message-14.
51. President Benjamin Harrison, State of the Union address, December 3, 1889.
52. "American Shipping," *NYT*, December 5, 1889, 4.
53. Editorial, *NYT*, December 4, 1889, 4; "Mr. Harrison's Message," *NYT*, December 5, 1889, 9; "American Shipping," *NYT*, December 8, 1889, 12.
54. "Appeals for Subsidies," *NYT*, January 23, 1890, 6. Also "Pleading for Subsidies," *NYT*, January 24, 1890, 2; "A Convert from Subsidies," *NYT*, February 13, 1890, 4.
55. "Subsidies for Shipping," *NYT*, March 17, 1890, 1.
56. Crapol and Schonberger, "Shift to Global Expansion," 166.
57. Editorial, *NYT*, December 19, 1890, 4; editorial, *NYT*, January 8, 1891, 4.
58. Editorial, *NYT*, January 8, 1891, 5.
59. Crucial House votes were on February 27 and 28, 1891.
60. "The Ship Subsidy Fraud," *NYT*, November 20, 1891, 1. Subsequent useful articles are "Liberal Subsidies to American Steam Lines Advocated," *NYT*, September 6, 1892, 1; "Subsidies and Free Ships," *NYT*, December 8, 1892, 4.
61. *SECNAV*, 1892, 34–35.
62. Benjamin F. Cooling, *Grey Steel and Blue Water Navy* (Hamden, CT: Archon Books, 1979), 90–98.
63. Boutelle to Luce, n.d. [December 26, 1889], reel 7, Luce Papers, LOC.
64. Boutelle to Luce, March 1, 1890, reel 7, Luce Papers, LOC.
65. Boutelle to Luce, March 6, 1890, reel 7, Luce Papers, LOC.
66. Boutelle to Luce, March 6, 1890, reel 7, Luce Papers, LOC.
67. *SECNAV*, 1890, 37; *SECNAV*, 1892, 31–32.
68. I am indebted to Capt. Scott Mobley for this information.
69. For a thoughtful discussion, see Peter Karsten, "The Nature of 'Influence': Roosevelt, Mahan and the Concept of Sea Power," *American Quarterly* 23, no. 4 (October 1971): 585–600.
70. Porter to Luce, March 14, 1889, reel 7, Luce Papers, LOC.
71. Alfred Thayer Mahan to John F. Pratt, September 28, 1889, *LP*, 1:710–11; Mahan to John G. Walker, September 30, 1889, *LP*, 1:711; Mahan to Colby Chester, October 8, 1889, *LP*, 1:713–14.
72. For the report on the strategic study of the Pacific Northest, see Mahan to Colby Chester, October 18, 1889, *LP*, 1:714–15.
73. Mahan to Luce, October 7, 1889, *LP*, 1:711–13.
74. Covering letters to complimentary copies: Alfred Thayer Mahan to William Henderson, May 5, 1890; Mahan to Luce, May 7, 1890, *LP*, 2:9; Mahan to Benjamin Franklin Tracy, May 10, 1890, *LP*, 2:9–10.
75. *FSS*, 303.

76. For reference to secret instructions, see Mahan to Tracy, September 6, 1890, *LP*, 2:18–19.

77. Cooling, *Benjamin Franklin Tracy*, 99, 120, 133.

78. Robert G. Angevine, "The Rise and Fall of the Office of Naval Intelligence, 1882–1892: A Technological Perspective," *Journal of Military History* 62, no. 2 (April 1998): 307n78.

79. Alfred Thayer Mahan to Cdr. Charles H. Davis, August 23, 1890, *LP*, 2:17, and esp. December 23, 1890, *LP*, 2:35–36; Mahan to Luce, October 27, 1890, *LP*, 2:29; Mahan to Luce, December 20, 1890, *LP*, 2:33–34. Charles H. Davis was brother-in-law to Henry Cabot Lodge and chief of the ONI from September 1889 to August 1892.

80. Mahan to Luce, October 27, 1890, *LP*, 2:29.

81. *FSS*, 269–70.

82. *FSS*, 269n1; emphasis added.

83. *ATM*, 227–30.

84. *ISPH*, 86.

85. Capt. A. T. Mahan, "The United States Looking Outward," *Atlantic Monthly* 66 (December 1890): 816–24; emphasis added.

86. *FSS*, 270.

87. Mahan to Luce, September 3, 1901, *LP*, 2:734.

88. Mahan to Tracy, December 7, 1892, LP, 2:89.

89. Mahan to Tracy, May 12, 1891, *LP*, 2:46. In January 1891, Mahan was offered command of the *Boston* but refused it (*LP*, 2:38).

90. Mahan to Tracy, January 23, 1892, *LP*, 2:91.

91. Mahan to Luce, January 28, 1892, *LP*, 2:64; Mahan to Luce, January 5, 1892, *LP*, 2:62. Also important is Alfred Thayer Mahan to John M. Brown, June 1, 1893, *LP*, 2:109.

92. *FSS*, 312; Mahan to Luce, January 5, 1892, *LP*, 2:62.

93. Cooling, *Benjamin Franklin Tracy*, 67.

94. *SECNAV*, 1890, 10.

95. *SECNAV*, 1891, 14; *SECNAV*, 1892, 31–32. For an earlier speech by Tracy, see "The Ships We Want Not the Kind We Are Getting," *Scientific American* 65, no. 16 (October 17, 1891): 240.

96. *SECNAV*, 1892, 11, 32.

97. Cooling, *Grey Steel and Blue Water Navy*, 69–70; Thomas Heinrich, *Ships for the Seven Seas: Philadelphia Shipbuilding in the Age of Industrial Capitalism* (Baltimore, MD: Johns Hopkins University Press, 1997), 113–17.

98. *SECNAV*, 1893, 37.

99. Hilary Herbert to Alfred Thayer Mahan, October 4, 1893, cited in Charles Carlisle Taylor, *The Life of Admiral Mahan: Naval Philosopher* (London: John Murray, 1920), 33.

CHAPTER 5. REVISED INFLUENCE

1. *FRE*, 2:105.
2. Alfred Thayer Mahan to Henry Cabot Lodge, May 19, 1890, P525, reel 6, Henry C. Lodge Papers, Massachusetts Historical Society, Boston (hereafter cited as Lodge Papers).
3. See Theodore Roosevelt to Horace Scudder, July 24, 1890, in *Letters of Theodore Roosevelt*, 8 vols., ed. Elting Morison and John Blum (Boston: Harvard University Press, 1951–54), 1:229.
4. Alfred Thayer Mahan to Stephen B. Luce, September 17, 1890, *LP*, 2:19–20.
5. Mahan to Luce, September 17, 1890, *LP*, 2:19, 20.
6. Alfred Thayer Mahan to Horace Scudder, September 23, 1890, *LP*, 2:22.
7. Mahan to Scudder, October 11 and 13, 1890, *LP*, 2:28, 29.
8. *ATM*, 226, 225.
9. *ATM*, 224–26.
10. Richard F. Bensel, *The Political Economy of American Industrialization, 1877–1900* (Cambridge: Cambridge University Press, 2000), 475–76.
11. Bensel, 465.
12. Bensel, 466.
13. Randall G. Holcombe, "Veterans Interests and the Transition to Government Growth: 1870–1915," *Public Choice* 99, no. 3/4 (1999): 319.
14. Paul E. Pedisich, *Congress Buys a Navy: Politics, Economics, and the Rise of American Naval Power* (Annapolis, MD: Naval Institute Press, 2016), 93.
15. *Roots*, 320–27.
16. *NE*, 21.
17. *Roots*, 27–46, 245–50, and esp. 332–38.
18. *Roots*, 321.
19. Bensell, *Political Economy of American Industrialization*, 476–78, 488–500; *NE*, 113–21; *Roots*, 327–35.
20. *Roots*, 320, 333–37.
21. Theodore Roosevelt to Benjamin Tracy, November 30, 1892, box 23, Tracy Papers.
22. *Roots*, 327–30, 337–40.
23. Bensell, *Political Economy of American Industrialization*, 478–79, 488–92; *Roots*, 337–40.
24. Capt. A. T. Mahan, "The United States Looking Outward," *Atlantic Monthly* 66 (December 1890): 816–24.
25. Mahan, 816–17.
26. Mahan to Scudder, October 11, 1890, *LP*, 2:28.
27. Mahan, "United States Looking Outward," 818.
28. Mahan, 816. See also map of commercial routes for the Naval War College, August 23, 1890, *LP*, 2:18.
29. Mahan to Luce, April 4, 1890, *LP*, 2:1.
30. Mahan to Luce, April 4, 1890, *LP*, 2:1.

31. Mahan to Luce, April 9, 1890, *LP*, 2:2.
32. Mahan to Luce, April 9, 1890, *LP*, 2:2.
33. Mahan to Luce, October 27, 1890, *LP*, 2:29.
34. Mahan to Luce, December 20, 1890, *LP*, 2:33.
35. Mahan to Luce, December 20, 1890, *LP*, 2:33.
36. Mahan to Luce, December 31, 1890, *LP*, 2:37.
37. *FSS*, 282.
38. *FRE*, iv–v.
39. *FRE*, 1:376–77; see also 2:220.
40. *FRE*, 1:342, 409.
41. *FRE*, 1:iii, 1.
42. *FRE*, 2:394, 404. For further evidence that Mahan saw his argument as original, see Mahan to Scudder, September 26 and October 8, 1890, *LP*, 2:26, 27.
43. *FRE*, 1:109.
44. Alfred Thayer Mahan to George Clarke, November 5, 1892, *LP*, 2:84, 85.
45. Mahan explains the logic of his chapter structure in *FRE*, 2:201–2.
46. *FSS*, 310.
47. *FRE*, 2:386–90.
48. *FRE*, 1:1.
49. *FRE*, 1:185; emphasis added.
50. *FRE*, 2:337.
51. *FRE*, 2:242.
52. *FRE*, 1:109, but see also 1:217.
53. *FRE*, 2:253.
54. *FRE*, 2:288–89.
55. *FRE*, 2:252–57. These former French colonies became important markets for British exports (1:170, 326–29, 390). See also A. T. Mahan, "The Isthmus and Sea Power," *Atlantic*, September 1893, in Mahan, *The Interest of America in Sea Power* (Boston: Little, Brown, 1897), 67.
56. *FRE*, 2:372–73; see also Jon Sumida, "Alfred Thayer Mahan, Geopolitician," *Journal of Strategic Studies* 22, no. 2 (1999): 5.
57. *FRE*, 2:374.
58. Alan Beyerchen, Clausewitz, Nonlinearity, and the Unpredictability of War," *International Security* 17, no. 3 (Winter 1992–93): 59–90.
59. *FRE*, 2:373.
60. Alfred T. Mahan, "Possibilities of an Anglo-American Reunion," *North American Review* 159, no. 456 (November 1894): 561.
61. A. T. Mahan, "Strategic Features of the Gulf of Mexico and the Caribbean Sea," *Harper's Magazine*, October 1897, 272.
62. Mahan; see also *FRE*, 1:11–14.
63. *FRE*, 2:212–71.
64. *FRE*, 2:289.
65. *FRE*, 2:197–203, 375–76.

66. *FRE*, 2:223.
67. *FRE*, 2:257.
68. *FRE*, 2:223–28.
69. *FRE*, 2:230–35.
70. *FRE*, 218.
71. *FRE*, 205–6.
72. *FRE*, 2:11–15.
73. *FRE*, 1:170–79, 396, 401, 2:11–14, 219–20, 271, 341–51, 371–74, 376–80, 396–410.
74. *FRE*, 2:14.
75. *FRE*, 2:184.
76. *FRE*, 2:256.
77. *FRE*, 2:288–89, 303, 322–29.
78. *FRE*, 2:298.
79. *FRE*, 2:349–50.
80. *FRE*, 1:396, 2:11–15, 299–300, 333–40, 349.
81. *FRE*, 2:374–75.
82. *IGS*, 113.
83. *ISPH*, 539–40.
84. Theodore Roosevelt, review of *FRE*, *Political Science Quarterly*, 9, no. 1 (March 1894): 171–72.
85. Roosevelt, review of *FRE*.
86. Anonymous [John Knox Laughton], "Captain Mahan on Maritime Power," *Edinburgh Review* 172 (October 1890): 420–53. For Laughton's confusion of terminology, see 436, 439, 442.
87. Anonymous, 442.
88. *ISPH*, 7–8.
89. *IGS*, 43.
90. A. T. Mahan, "The Future in Relation to American Naval Power," *Harper's Monthly*, June 1895, reprinted in Mahan, *The Interest of America in Sea Power, Present and Future* (Boston: Little, Brown, 1897), 149.
91. *IGS*, 43–44, 52–56.
92. *FRE*, 2:197.
93. *FRE*, 2:352.
94. *FRE*, 2:352–53.
95. Other antinomies found at *FRE*, 1:130, 2:105.
96. *FRE*, 2:356–57.
97. *FRE*, 2:235.
98. Alfred Thayer Mahan to John Knox Laughton, March 21, 1893, fol. 3, LGH 13, box 3, John Knox Laughton Papers, National Maritime Museum, Greenwich, CT (hereafter cited as Laughton Papers). See also Capt. A. T. Mahan, "Principles of Naval Administration," *National Review*, June 1903, 6–7, 20–21.

99. Mahan to Scudder, April 21, 1891, *LP*, 2:44; Alfred Thayer Mahan to Bouverie Clark, May 22, 1891, *LP*, 2:47–48.
100. Mahan to Clarke, November 5, 1892, *LP*, 2:83–85.
101. Alfred Thayer Mahan to John Brown, June 9, 1893, *LP*, 2:110.
102. Mahan to Brown, June 9, 1893, *LP*, 2:110.
103. *FSS*, 313.

CHAPTER 6. PROPHET IN EXILE

1. Brooks Adams, "The Decay of England," in *America's Economic Supremacy* (New York: Harper, 1947), 134.
2. Alfred Thayer Mahan to Bouverie Clark, May 22, 1891, *LP*, 2:47.
3. Alfred Thayer Mahan to Horace Scudder, February 3, 1892, *LP*, 2:94.
4. *ATM*, 328.
5. Mahan to Scudder, November 22, 1892, *LP*, 2:85–86.
6. Mahan to Scudder, February 3, 1893, *LP*, 2:94.
7. Alfred Thayer Mahan to Walter Hines Page, October 28, 1903, *LP*, 3:41; Alfred Thayer Mahan to Andrew McLaughlin, December 17, 1902, *LP*, 2:46.
8. For subsequent attempts by Page to recruit Mahan, see Mahan to Page, July 23, 1897, *LP*, 2:520.
9. Burton J. Hendrick, *The Life and Letters of Walter H. Page*, 3 vols. in 6 parts (Garden City, NY: Doubleday Page, 1924), 1:51–52.
10. Capt. A. T. Mahan, "Hawaii and Our Future Sea Power," *Forum*, March 1893, reprinted in Mahan, *The Interest of America in Sea Power, Present and Future* (Boston: Little, Brown, 1897), 51.
11. Mahan, 52.
12. Mahan, 47–49.
13. Capt. A. T. Mahan, "The Isthmus and Sea Power," *Atlantic*, September 1893, reprinted in Mahan, *Interest of America in Sea Power*, 78.
14. Mahan, 66.
15. Mahan to Clark, May 22, 1891, *LP*, 2:47.
16. *ATM*, 246–47. See also Theodore Roosevelt to Alfred Thayer Mahan, May 1, 1893, in *Letters of Theodore Roosevelt*, 8 vols., ed. Elting Morison and John Blum (Boston: Harvard University Press, 1951–54), 1:315; Henry Cabot Lodge to Stephen B. Luce, January 22, 1894, MSC-10, box 1, folder 2, Luce Papers, NWC.
17. *ATM*, 251–53.
18. Alfred Thayer Mahan to BuNAV, April 18, 1893, *LP*, 2:102.
19. Roosevelt to Anna Roosevelt Cowles (sister), June 3, 1894, in Morison and Blum, *Letters of Theodore Roosevelt*, 1:382.
20. Alfred Thayer Mahan to Stephen B. Luce, May 6, 1909, *LP*, 3:299.
21. Alfred Thayer Mahan to Sir George Clarke, July 29, 1894, *LP*, 2:305.
22. Alfred Thayer Mahan to John M. Brown, May 31, 1893, *LP*, 2:107.
23. Alfred Thayer Mahan to Sam Ashe, November 24, 1893, *LP*, 2:181–83.

24. Alfred Thayer Mahan to wife, September 22 and November 18, 1893, *LP*, 2:156, 178.

25. Mahan to wife, April 14, 1894, *LP*, 2:258.

26. Mahan to wife, January 11, 1894, *LP*, 2:205.

27. Alfred Thayer Mahan to Helen Mahan (daughter), February 18, 1894, *LP*, 2:229. See also Mahan to Clarke, January 29, 1895, *LP*, 2:394–95.

28. Mahan to wife, July 24, 1894, *LP*, 2:303.

29. Mahan to Scudder, September 12, 1893, *LP*, 2:153; Mahan to wife, April 14, 1894, *LP*, 2:258.

30. Mahan to wife, June 29, 1894, *LP*, 2:292.

31. Mahan to wife, October 5 and November 1, 1894, *LP*, 2:343, 355.

32. Mahan to wife, February 22 and 23, 1894, *LP*, 2:234.

33. Mahan to wife, November 1, 1894, *LP*, 2:355.

34. Mahan to Luce, May 6, 1909, *LP*, 3:299.

35. Mahan to wife, August 1, 1893, *LP*, 2:128.

36. Alfred Thayer Mahan to Gouverneur Ogden, August 31, 1893, quoting letter received from Cmdr. Bowman H. McCalla, *LP*, 2:144–45.

37. Hilary Herbert to Alfred Thayer Mahan, October 4, 1893, cited in Charles Carlisle Taylor, *The Life of Admiral Mahan: Naval Philosopher* (London: John Murray, 1920), 33.

38. *SECNAV*, 1893, 37. Norman Friedman also is persuaded of Tracy's commitment to *guerre de course*, for which see Friedman, *US Cruisers: An Illustrated Design History* (Annapolis, MD: Naval Institute Press, 1984), 29, 35, 40.

39. Mahan to wife, February 9, 1894, *LP*, 2:223.

40. For Mahan's unhappiness with the paper, see Mahan to Clarke, July 19, 1894, *LP*, 2:305.

41. Alfred Thayer Mahan, "Possibilities of an Anglo American Reunion," *North American Review* 159, no. 456 (November 1894): 556, 559.

42. Mahan, 561.

43. Mahan, 563; emphasis added.

44. Mahan to wife, May 22, 1894, *LP*, 2:274–76; Alfred Thayer Mahan to Col. J. B. Sterling, July 18, 1894, *LP*, 2:301–2.

45. Alfred Thayer Mahan, "Blockade in Relation to Naval Strategy," *Journal of the Royal United Services Institute* 39, no. 313 (November 1895): 1063, 1067. Mahan thought that blockade in the age of steam would be far more difficult than it had been in the age of sail, but other technological developments would mitigate the damage corsairs at sea might inflict.

46. Mahan, 1064.

47. Mahan, 1064.

48. Mahan, 1062.

49. Mahan, 1064.

50. Mahan, 1064.

51. Mahan, 1064.

52. Mahan, 1064.

53. Azar Gat, *The Development of Military Thought: The Nineteenth Century* (Oxford: Oxford University Press, 1991), 181.

54. Speech by Senator John T. Morgan, *Congressional Record* 27 (1895), 1929.

55. Speech by Senator John T. Morgan, 1950.

56. Speech by Senator John T. Morgan, 1950.

57. Speech by Senator John T. Morgan, 1950. After Morgan's speech, Mahan's work was frequently cited in Congress, arguably signifying universal approval of Mahan's ideas. For corroboration of this interpretation, at least with respect to Henry Cabot Lodge, see William C. Widenor, *Henry Cabot Lodge and the Search for an American Foreign Policy* (Berkeley: University of California Press, 1980), 89.

58. Mahan to Clark, June 14, 1895, *LP*, 2:419.

59. Mahan to Brown, April 11, 1896, *LP*, 2:450.

60. "Capt. Mahan, USN, Retired," *NYT*, November 18, 1896, 16.

61. Mahan to Ashe, January 3, 1897, *LP*, 2:482.

62. Mahan to Sterling, April 17, 1896, *LP*, 2:452.

63. Mahan, *Interest of America in Sea Power*.

64. Mahan to Luce, December 5, 1896, *LP*, 2:474.

65. Mahan to Ashe, November 24, 1893, and November 7, 1896, *LP*, 2:181, 470.

66. Mahan to wife, August 4, 1893, *LP*, 2:130–32.

67. Mahan to wife, August 5, 1893, *LP*, 2:132.

68. A. T. Mahan, "Diplomacy and Arbitration," in *Armaments and Arbitration; or, The Place of Force in the International Relations of States* (New York: Harper and Bros., 1912), 36–38.

69. Alfred Thayer Mahan to Henry W. Farnam, June 15, 1897, box 170, folder 1897, Henry W. Farnam Papers, MS 203, Sterling Library, Yale University (hereafter Farnam Papers); Farnam to Mahan, June 17, 1897, fol. 154, box 205, folder 3, Farnam Papers.

70. Ellen Mahan to Henry W. Farnam, June 16, 19, and 24, 1897, box 170, folder 1897, Farnam Papers.

71. See especially Arthur T. Hadley, *Railroad Transportation: Its History and Its Laws* (New York: G. P. Putnam's Sons, 1885); Hadley, *Economics: An Account of the Relations between Private Property and Public Welfare* (New York: G. P. Putnam's Sons, 1896).

72. Alfred Thayer Mahan to Arthur Twining Hadley, April 17, 1905, series 1, box 58, RU 25, Hadley Papers.

73. The Centenary Association, *Reports, Constitution, By-laws and List of Members of the Century Association* (New York: Knickerbocker Press, 1901). Hadley joined in 1894 and Mahan in 1896; both were also active members of the American Philosophical Society (for which see *American Philosophical Society* 44, no. 181 [August 1905]: 249–67), the Episcopal Church, and the Mark Twain Memorial Committee (*NYT*, November 14, 1910).

74. Mahan to Ashe, November 7, 1896, *LP*, 2:470.

75. Richard F. Bensel, *The Political Economy of American Industrialization, 1877–1900* (Cambridge: Cambridge University Press, 2000), 370–71, 394–96.

76. Gretchen Ritter, *Goldbugs and Greenback: The Antimonopoly Tradition and the Politics of Finance in America, 1865–1896* (Cambridge: Cambridge University Press, 1997), 58–61, 190–94.

77. Bensell, *Political Economy of American Industrialization*, 434.

78. Mahan to Ashe, November 7, 1896, *LP*, 2:470.

79. Mahan to Ashe, January 3, 1897, *LP*, 2:482–83.

80. Mahan to Ashe, January 3, 1897, *LP*, 2:482.

81. Mahan to Brown, August 31 and September 8, 1896, *LP*, 2:466, 467.

82. Mahan to Brown, August 31, 1896, *LP*, 2:466.

83. William Appleman Williams, *The Tragedy of American Diplomacy* (New York: W. W. Norton, 1959), 29 (hereafter cited as *Tragedy*).

84. *NE*, 85, 94; see also Walter LaFeber, "A Note on the 'Mercantilist Imperialism of Alfred Thayer Mahan," *Mississippi Valley Historical Review* 48, no. 4 (1962): 674–85. LaFeber specifically targeted Harold Sprout and Margaret Sprout, William Livezey (the author of the third Mahan biography), and Foster Rhea Dulles (doctorial supervisor of Robert Seager, author of the fourth Mahan biography).

85. Sprouts, 207; *NE*, 58–61, 123.

86. *NE*, 62–101. William Appleman Williams identifies the same four intellectuals in *The Contours of American History* (London: Jonathan Cape, 1961), 364–65.

87. *NE*, 62–63.

88. *NE*, 80, 85–90, 95–101.

89. Roosevelt to Mahan, August 2, 1900, reproduced in Richard W. Turk, *The Ambiguous Relationship: Theodore Roosevelt and Alfred Thayer Mahan* (Westport, CT: Greenwood Press, 1987), 126.

90. Williams, *Contours of American History*, 365. See also *Tragedy*, 30–32; *NE*, 63–72.

91. Brooks Adams, "New Struggle for life among Nations," in *America's Economic Supremacy*, 89.

92. *NE*, 79; Brooks Adams, *The Law of Civilization and Decay: An Essay on History* (London: Macmillan, 1897). For the connection between Turner and Adams, see William A. Williams, "Brooks Adams and American Expansion," *New England Quarterly* 25, no. 2 (1952): 217–32; Williams, *Contours of American History*, 364–67; Brooks D. Simpson, *The Political Education of Henry Adams* (Columbia: University of South Carolina Press, 1996).

93. Brooks Adams, "England's Decadence in the West Indies," in *America's Economic Supremacy*, 107.

94. Adams, 134.

95. Adams, 134. For Adams' preference for Continental ahead of maritime systems, see 71–72, 78, 100, 112, 127, 132.

96. For Lodge's perspective on Conant, see Widenor, *Henry Cabot Lodge*, 87–94.

97. Carl Parrini, "Charles A. Conant, Economic Crises and Foreign Policy, 1896–1903," in *Behind the Throne: Servants of Power to Imperial Presidents, 1898–1968*, ed. Thomas McCormick and Walter LaFeber (Madison: University of Wisconsin Press, 1993), 35–66.

98. Charles A. Conant, *The United States in the Orient: The Nature of an Economic Problem* (Boston: Houghton Mifflin, 1900). This book was an expansion of a series of articles Conant produced for the *Forum*, the *Atlantic*, and the *North American Review*.

99. Gary Marotta, "The Economics of American Empire: The Views of Brooks Adams and Charles Arthur Conant," *American Economist* 19, no. 2 (Fall 1975): 34–37.

100. For a good contemporary example, see Henry George, "Overproduction," *North American Review* 137 (December 1883): 584–93.

101. Charles A. Conant, "The Economic Basis of Imperialism," *North American Review* 167 (September 1898): 326.

102. Conant, 329–31.

103. Conant, 327–30.

104. Conant, 330.

105. Carl Parrini and Martin Sklar, "New Thinking about the Market, 1896–1904: Some American Economists on Investment and the Theory of Surplus Capital," *Journal of Economic History* 43, no. 3 (September 1983): 559–78; Carl Parrini, "Theories of Imperialism," in *Redefining the Past: Essays in Diplomatic History in Honor of William Appleman Williams*, ed. Lloyd Gardner (Corvallis: Oregon State University Press, 1986), 65–83; Williams, *Contours of American History*, 349–89.

106. Readers interested in further details are referred to the articles by Carl Parrini and Martin Sklar cited in note 105.

107. Conant, "Economic Basis of Imperialism," 327.

108. Conant, 337–40.

109. Conant, 338.

110. Capt. A. T. Mahan, "Current Fallacies upon Naval Subjects," *Harper's Monthly*, June 1898, reprinted in *LWS*, 300–301.

111. Alfred Thayer Mahan, "The Relations of the United States to Their New Dependencies," in *LWS*, 246–47; emphasis added.

CHAPTER 7. RETURN TO DUTY

1. *LWS*, 12.

2. Capt. A. T. Mahan, *Naval Administration and Warfare: Some General Principles with Other Essays* (Boston: Little, Brown, 1908), 64.

3. See Alfred Thayer Mahan to SECNAV (Charles Bonaparte), June 26, 1906, *LP*, 3:161; see also postscript, Alfred Thayer Mahan to Stephen B. Luce, July 11, 1906, *LP*, 3:163. For further details, see Alfred Thayer Mahan to George Dewey, September 5, 1906, *LP*, 3:174–75.

4. Alfred T. Mahan, "The Work of the Naval War Board of 1898: A Report to the General Board of the Navy," October 29, 1906, 1–2, copy in file ON (strategy and tactics), box 3, file 401.2, RG 80, National Archives and Records Administration, Washington, DC, and College Park, MD (hereafter cited as NARA).

5. "Transactions of the Naval War Board and Secret Service," in appendix to the report of the Chief of the Bureau of Navigation, Navy Department, *SECNAV*, 1898, 33–34.

6. William J. Barnette to Stephen B. Luce, February 5, 1906, plus a misfiled letter from Barnette to Luce (n.d.), fols. 600–601, reel 10, Luce Papers, LOC. For a broader discussion of this subject, see John T. Kuehn, *America's First General Staff: A Short History of the Rise and Fall of the General Board of the Navy, 1900–1950* (Annapolis, MD: Naval Institute Press, 2017), 47–54.

7. David Trask, *The War with Spain in 1898* (New York: Macmillan, 1981), 88.

8. Trask, 88, 89, x.

9. Contrast the thoroughness of his treatments of the Secretaries of the Navy and the Army: Trask, 79, 146.

10. Alfred Thayer Mahan to Seth Low, June 28, 1900, *LP*, 2:690.

11. Wendell Garrett, "John Davis Long, Secretary of the Navy, 1897–1902," *New England Quarterly*, September 1958, 291–311.

12. Garrett, 296.

13. John D. Long, *The New American Navy*, 2 vols. (New York: The Outlook Company, 1903), 1:vii.

14. The subject was studied the previous year by a board under the presidency of Rear Adm. Francis Ramsey; entry 98, Records of the Office of the Chief of Naval Operations, RG 38, NARA.

15. The characterization of Sicard comes from Mahan to Luce, October 7, 1889, *LP*, 1:713.

16. Rear Adm. Montgomery Sicard to SECNAV, June 30, 1897, letter books, entry 98, RG 38, NARA.

17. Trask, *War with Spain in 1898*, 78; see also 72–78. Also useful here is John A. Grenville, "American Naval Preparations for War with Spain, 1896–1898," *Journal of American Studies* 2, no. 1 (April 1968): 33–47.

18. Trask, *War with Spain in 1898*, 21–25; see also *Tragedy*, 40–45.

19. Theodore Roosevelt to John D. Long, January 14, 1898, cited in *Letters of Theodore Roosevelt*, ed. Elting Morison and John Blum, 8 vols. (Boston: Harvard University Press, 1951–54), 1:759.

20. John D. Long diary, January 13, 1898, fol. 18, vol. 78, John D. Long Papers, Massachusetts Historical Society, Boston (hereafter cited as Long Papers); see also Theodore Roosevelt to Henry Cabot Lodge, September 24, 1897, P490, reel 2, Henry Cabot Lodge Papers, Massachusetts Historical Society, Boston (hereafter cited as Lodge Papers).

21. Long diary, February 2, 1898, fol. 57, vol. 78, Long Papers.

22. Trask, *War with Spain in 1898*, 81.

23. Long diary, February 25 and February 5, 1898, fols. 93 and 60, vol. 78, Long Papers.

24. Theodore Roosevelt to Stephen B. Luce, August 13, 1897, fol. 171, reel 9, Luce Papers, LOC.

25. Theodore Roosevelt to Benjamin Tracy, April 18, 1898, box 23, Tracy Papers.

26. *Tragedy*, 41.

27. Alfred Thayer Mahan to John M. Brown, February 25, 1898, *LP*, 2:543.

28. Long, *New American Navy*, 2:58–59.

29. For a summary of the literature, see Philip Zelikow, "Why Did America Cross the Pacific? Reconstructing the U.S. Decision to Take the Philippines, 1898–99," *Texas National Security Review* 1, no. 1 (November 2017): 36–67.

30. Trask, *War with Spain in 1898*, 82–83. On March 16, 1898, the U.S. Navy purchased two cruisers, a gunboat, and a torpedo boat from the United Kingdom, plus another torpedo boat from Germany.

31. Long, *New American Navy*, 1:162.

32. Long diary, March 12 and April 21, 1898, fols. 108 and 137, vol. 78, Long Papers.

33. Roosevelt to Long, April 11 and April 15, 1898, fols. 40.8 and 40.11, vol. 40, Long Papers. Roosevelt noted that the naval militia from Pennsylvania was not of much use and the one from Georgia was hopeless. Roosevelt to Long, April 15, 1898, fol. 40.11, vol. 40, Long Papers.

34. With now-president Theodore Roosevelt and Rear Admirals Crowninshield and Baker.

35. Roosevelt to Long via L. H. Finney (private secretary to Long), April 7, 1898, fol. 40.6, vol. 40, Long Papers.

36. Mahan Report to the General Board of the Navy, October 29, 1906, 1, file ON (strategy and tactics), box 3, file 401.2, RG 80, NARA.

37. Arent Crowninshield to Henry Cabot Lodge, September 24, 1898, P-525, reel 12, Lodge Papers.

38. William Chandler to John D. Long, March 10, 1898, fol. 39.11, vol. 39, Long Papers.

39. Long diary, April 22, 1898, fol. 138, letter book, vol. 78, Long Papers.

40. Alfred Thayer Mahan to Leo Maxse, May 16, 1904, *LP*, 3:98.

41. Mahan to Roosevelt, May 1 and May 6, 1897, *LP*, 2:505–6, 507.

42. For indications that Roosevelt may have met with Mahan once or twice during these weeks, see Roosevelt to Mahan, January 3, 5, and 8, 1898, as reproduced in an appendix to Richard W. Turk, *The Ambiguous Relationship: Theodore Roosevelt and Alfred Thayer Mahan* (Westport, CT: Greenwood Press, 1987), 121.

43. Roosevelt to Mahan, March 10, 1898, series 2, reel 315, Theodore Roosevelt Papers, Library of Congress, Washington, DC (hereafter cited as Roosevelt Papers).

44. Trask, *War with Spain in 1898*, 72–79.

45. Turk, *Ambiguous Relationship*, 34.

46. William McKinley, Second Annual Message, December 5, 1898, Miller Center, University of Virginia, https://millercenter.org/the-presidency/presidential-spee ches/december-5-1898-second-annual-message. The maximum effective fighting force of the U.S. Navy during the war, separated into classes, was as follows: 4 battleships of the first class, 1 battleship of the second class, 2 armored cruisers, 6 coast-defense monitors, 1 armored ram, 12 protected cruisers, 3 unprotected cruisers, 18 gunboats, 1 dynamite cruiser, 11 torpedo boats plus 14 miscellaneous craft, 11 auxiliary cruisers, 28 converted yachts, 27 converted tugs, 19 converted colliers, 15 revenue cutters, 4 lighthouse tenders, and 19 miscellaneous vessels.

47. Roosevelt to Mahan, March 14, 1898, series 2, reel 315, Roosevelt Papers.

48. Roosevelt to Mahan, March 21, 1898, series 2, reel 315, Roosevelt Papers. For reference to the plans sent to Mahan for comment, see Roosevelt to Mahan, March 16, 1898, series 2, reel 315, Roosevelt Papers.

49. Secretary of the Navy John D. Long to Rear Adm. Montgomery Sicard, Com- mander, North Atlantic Station, March 23, 1898, Records of Naval Operating Forces, RG 313, entry 47, NARA.

50. Roosevelt to Mahan, March 24, 1898, series 2, reel 315, Roosevelt Papers.

51. Alfred Thayer Mahan to Col. John B. Sterling, March 4, 1898, *LP*, 2:545.

52. Roosevelt to Mahan, March 24, 1898.

53. Long diary, April 12, 1898, fol. 134, vol. 78, Long Papers. A clipping from the *Newport Herald*, February 24, 1898, rumored that Sicard might retire owing to ill health; Long diary, vol. 39, Long Papers.

54. Long diary, April 20, 1898, fol. 136, vol. 78, Long Papers.

55. Long diary, April 25, 1898, fol. 143, vol. 78, Long Papers.

56. Roosevelt to Long, May 6, 1898, fol. 41.3, vol. 41, Long Papers.

57. Turk, *Ambiguous Relationship*, 35.

58. Alfred Thayer Mahan to John D. Long via David Dixon Porter (Paris), April 29, 1898, *LP*, 2:551.

59. Capt. William D. Puleston, USN, *Mahan: The Life and Work of Captain Alfred Thayer Mahan, USN* (New Haven, CT: Yale University Press, 1939), 186.

60. Long diary, May 9, 1898, fol. 161, vol. 78, Long Papers.

61. Mahan to Luce, August 31, 1898, *ATM*, 2:592. On May 20, Captain Barker quit the War Board to take command of the recommissioned cruiser *Newark*. Long diary, May 20, 1898, fol. 179, vol. 78, Long Papers.

62. Mahan to Long, May 10, 1898 (on stationery of Office of the Naval War Board), fol. 41.6, vol. 41, Long Papers.

63. Long diary, May 19, 1898, fol. 177, vol. 78, Long Papers.

64. *ATM*, 369–70; Paul E. Pedisich, *Congress Buys a Navy: Politics, Economics, and the Rise of American Naval Power* (Annapolis, MD: Naval Institute Press, 2016), 115–16.

65. Alfred Thayer Mahan to George Clarke, May 24, 1898, *LP*, 2:556.

66. Stephen B. Luce to Henry Cabot Lodge, May 24, 1898, fol. 385, reel 9, Luce Papers, LOC.

67. Luce to Lodge, May 24, 1898, fol. 385, reel 9, Luce Papers, LOC.

68. Lodge to Luce, May 27, 1898, fols. 386 and 387, reel 9, Luce Papers, LOC.

69. Lodge to Luce, May 27, 1898.

70. Roosevelt to Lodge, September 21, 1897, in *Selections from the Correspondence of Theodore Roosevelt and Henry Cabot Lodge*, 2 vols. (New York: C. Scribner's Sons, 1925), 1:278–79.

71. French Chadwick to John D. Long, April 30, 1898, fol. 40.24, vol. 40, Long Papers.

72. Malcolm Muir, "French Ensor Chadwick: Reformer, Historian and Outcast," in *Admirals of the New Steel Navy*, ed. James C. Bradford (Annapolis, MD: Naval Institute Press, 1990), 103–4; see also French Chadwick, "Naval Department Organization," *Proceedings* 20/3/71 (1894).

73. Long diary, May 11 and [May 14, 1898], fols. 165 and 171, vol. 78, Long Papers.

74. BuNAV [Arent Crowninshield] to Long, June 30, 1898, fol. 42.16, vol. 42, Long Papers.

75. Copy, John D. Long to Walter Allen (*Boston Herald*), June 30, 1902, fol. 164, reel 10, Luce Papers, LOC.

76. BuNAV [Crowninshield] to Long, June 30, 1898.

77. Lodge to Luce, April 7, 1897, fol. 86, reel 9, Luce Papers, LOC.

78. French Chadwick, *The Relations of the United States and Spain: The Spanish-American War*, 2 vols. (New York: C. Scribner's Sons, 1911), 2:359.

79. George Dewey, *Autobiography of George Dewey: Admiral of the Navy* (New York: Scribner, 1913), 167. For Dewey's long-standing dislike of Crowninshield, see Ronald Spector, *Admiral of the New Empire: The Life and Career of George Dewey* (Baton Rouge: Louisiana State University Press, 1974), 138–39.

80. Crowninshield is named but not discussed in Peter Karsten, *The Naval Aristocracy: The Golden Age of Annapolis and the Emergence of Modern American Navalism* (New York: Free Press, 1972), 88; see also Kuehn, *America's First General Staff*, 47–54.

81. Long to Sicard, March 23, 1898.

82. For Trask's broad concurrence, see *War with Spain in 1898*, 84–85.

83. *LWS*, 107.

84. *LWS*, 44–46, 54, 62, 68–69, 93, 99.

85. Alfred Thayer Mahan to Montgomery Sicard, May 19, 1898, correspondence of the Naval War Board, entry 194, RG 80, NARA; see also Trask, *War with Spain in 1898*, 84–86.

86. Mahan to Sicard, May 19, 1898.

87. Mahan to Clarke, May 25, 1898, *LP*, 2:556.

88. Roosevelt to Mahan, June 27, 1911, series 2, reel 367, Roosevelt Papers, as cited in Turk, *Ambiguous Relationship*, 160, and expanded on in Roosevelt, *Theodore Roosevelt: An Autobiography* (New York: Scribner's, 1920), 214–17.

89. Alfred Thayer Mahan, *Sea Power in Its Relations to the War of 1812*, 2 vols. (Boston: Little, Brown, 1905), 1:316 (hereafter cited as *1812*).

90. For instance, see Mahan, memorandum to Naval War Board, July 18, 1898, recommending against an attack on Puerto Rico as premature, in *LP*, 2:565; see also Office of Naval War Board, July 21, 1898, fol. 43.16, vol. 43, Long Papers, recommending against an attack on the Canary Islands or Ceuta (a Spanish enclave on the North African coast).

91. Mahan, "The War on the Sea and Its Lessons," *McClure's Magazine* 12 (November 1898– April 1899): 358, reproduced in *LWS*, 109.

92. Appendix, "Transactions of the Naval War Board and Secret Service," in *Report of the Chief of the Bureau of Navigation, Navy Department, 1898* (Washington, DC: Government Printing Office, 1898), 33–34; see also George O. Squier, "The Influence of Submarine Cables upon Military and Naval Supremacy," *Proceedings* 26/4/96 (October 1900).

93. Alfred Thayer Mahan, 1906 report, 5–6, file ON (strategy and tactics), box 3, file 401.2, RG 80, NARA.

94. Kenneth C. Wenzer, "The Naval War Board of 1898," *Canadian Military History* 25, no. 1 (2016): 9–10.

95. Trask, *War with Spain in 1898*, 125–26.

96. Mahan to Clarke, August 17, 1898, *LP*, 2:579.

97. Long diary, May 26, 1898, fol. 186, vol. 78, Long Papers.

98. Long to his wife, June 19, 1898, fol. 229, vol. 78, Long Papers.

99. Long to his wife, June 19, 1898.

100. Long to his wife, July 14, 1898, fol. 275, vol. 78, Long Papers.

101. Mahan to Low, June 28 and August 7, 1900, *LP*, 2:690, 292; Mahan to Long, June 17, 1901, *LP*, 2:727–28.

102. Lodge to Mahan, July 23, 1898, P-525, reel 12, Lodge Papers.

103. William Day was promoted from assistant to principal secretary of state on April 26, 1898, and remained in office until September 16, 1898.

104. Lodge to Roosevelt, June 24, 1898, in Roosevelt, *Letters of Theodore Roosevelt*, 1:680–83; also in P-490, reel, 2 Lodge Papers.

105. Naval War Board to Secretary, August 22, 1898, E371 (Boards and Commissions), vol. 1, Naval Records Collections of the Office of Naval Records and Library, RG 45, NARA.

106. Puleston interviewed John B. Moore for his Mahan biography. See *Mahan*, viii and 192–93.

107. Mahan to Clarke, August 17, 1898, *LP*, 2:579. Until 1891, Moore had been third secretary at the State Department but left to assume the chair in international law at Columbia University.

108. Personal recollections of Admiral Mahan, address given at the grave of Mahan on September 27, 1940, commemorating the one hundredth year of his birth, box 298, John Bassett Moore Papers, Library of Congress, Washington, DC (hereafter cited as Moore Papers).

109. Mahan to Lodge, July 12, 1898, P525, reel 12, Lodge Papers.

110. Long diary, July 6, 1898, fol. 265, vol. 78, Long Papers.

111. Mahan to Long, July 23 and 28, 1898, fols. 43.18 and 43.21, vol. 43, Long Papers; Long to his wife, August 7, 1898, fol. 317, vol. 79, Long Papers.

112. *ATM*, 405–6.

113. Mahan to Luce, August 31, 1898, fol. 288, reel 9, Luce Papers, LOC.

114. For more details on naval administrative reform, see Ronald Spector, *Professors of War: The Naval War College and the Development of the Naval Profession* (Newport, RI: Naval War College Press, 1977), 133–40.

115. Luce to Mahan, August 25, 1898, fol. 454, reel 9, Luce Papers, LOC.

116. Mahan to Luce, August 31, 1898, fol. 288, reel 9, Luce Papers, LOC.

117. Mahan to Luce, August 31, 1898.

118. Alfred Thayer Mahan to Robert U. Johnson, May 17, 1898, *LP*, 2:552.

119. Mahan to Long, October 4, 1898, *LP*, 2:605–6.

120. Adm. Pascual Cervera y Topete, *The Spanish-American War: A Collection of Documents Relative to the Squadron Operations in the West Indies* (Washington, DC: Government Printing Office, 1899); Cervera y Topete, *Views of Admiral Cervera regarding the Spanish Navy in the Late War* (Washington, DC: Government Printing Office, 1898).

121. Yet he alluded to this in *LWS*, viii.

122. *LWS*, v–vi.

123. *LWS*, 157.

124. Mahan, 1906 report, conclusion D, 16. ON (strategy and tactics), box 3, file 401.2, RG 80, NARA.

125. *LWS*, 16.

126. *LWS*, 46; see also 72–74.

127. The first pair of articles for *McClure's Magazine* had already been set in type, for which see Mahan to Brown, November 24, 1898, *LP*, 2:615.

128. *LWS*, 102–9.

129. *LWS*, 102–3.

130. *LWS*, 106.

131. *LWS*, 53, 70–72, 102–9.

132. *LWS*, 107.

133. Chadwick, *Relations of the United States and Spain*, 2:322–26.

134. Chadwick, 2:322–26.

135. Trask, *War with Spain in 1898*, chap. 6.

136. Editorial, *NYT*, November 15, 1898, 6.

137. "War and Business," editorial, *NYT*, May 5, 1897, 6.

138. Henry Lee Higginson to John D. Long, April 28, 1898, fol. 40.12, vol. 40, Long Papers.

139. In December 1902, Charles Henry Butler was appointed reporter of the Supreme Court.

140. "Commerce and War," editorial, *NYT*, November 15, 1898, 6.

141. Mahan to Brown, November 27, 1898, *LP*, 2:616.

142. Charles H. Stockton, "The Capture of Enemy Merchant Vessels at Sea," *North American Review* 168 (February 1899): 206–11.
143. "Capt. Mahan on Commerce and War," editorial, *NYT*, November 19, 1898, 6.
144. "Capt. Mahan on Commerce and War," 6.
145. Capt. Alfred T. Mahan, "Possibility of an Anglo-American Reunion," *North American Review* 159 (November 1894): 563.
146. For the editors' rebuttal of Mahan's argument, see "Capt. Mahan on Commerce and War," 6. For Mahan's reply, see Mahan, "Commerce and War," *NYT*, November 23, 1898, 6; Butler, "A Reply to Capt. Mahan," *NYT*, November 27, 1898, 4.
147. *FRE*, 2:235.
148. President McKinley, State of the Union address, December 5, 1898.
149. "Private Property at Sea," editorial, *NYT*, December 6, 1898, 8. See also editorial number 3 (no title) of December 24, *NYT*, 1898, 6.
150. For a good summary, see William R. Hawkins, "Captain Mahan, Admiral Fisher and Arms Control at The Hague, 1899," *Naval War College Review* 39, no. 1 (January 1986): 78; see also Stephen Barcroft, "The Hague Peace Conference of 1899," *Irish Studies in International Affairs* 3, no. 1 (1989): 55–68.
151. Frederick Holls to Andrew Dickson White, April 4, 1899, reel 77, Andrew Dickson White Papers, Cornell University Library, Ithaca, NY (hereafter cited as White Papers). White would lead the delegation to The Hague, with Holls accompanying him as secretary.
152. Andrew Dickson White to Willard Fiske, April 10, 1899, White Papers. See also White to Holls, March 21, 1899, and reference in Holls to White, April 4, 1899, White Papers, mentioning that Francis Patton, president of Princeton University, had already turned down the job.
153. Holls to White, April 4, 1899, reel 77, White Papers.
154. For Mahan's nomination, see John Hay to William McKinley, March 18, 1899, John Hay Papers, reel 1, vol. 2, Library of Congress, Washington, DC (hereafter cited as Hay Papers). For Mahan's closeness to Hay at this time, see Tyler Dennett, review of "The Problem of Asia and Its Effect upon International Policies by Alfred Thayer Mahan," *Foreign Affairs* 13, no. 3 (April 1935): 464–72.
155. "Private Property at Sea," editorial, *NYT*, July 7, 1899, 6. For the effort being half-hearted, see Andrew Dickson White to F. D. White (son), July 10, 1899, reel 78, White Papers.
156. Andrew Dickson White to John Hay, June 7, 1899, reel 78, White Papers; Hay to White, July 8, 1899, reel 78, White Papers.
157. Andrew Dickson White, diary entry for June 19, 1899, in White, *Autobiography of Andrew Dickson White*, 2 vols. (New York: The Century Company, 1917), 2:317; see also entries for June 22 (2:319), July 22 (2:338), July 24 (2:339), and July 29 (2:347). These entries in the published edition, however, do not correspond to those in the diary, for which see 1899 diary, reel 132,

1408–10, White Papers. For an early summary of Mahan's position, see A. T. Mahan, "The Peace Conference and the Moral Aspect of War," *North American Review* 169 (October 1899): 443–47, reprinted *LWS*, 207–41.

158. White, *Autobiography of Andrew Dickson White*, entry for July 29, 1898, 2:347. Again, this entry is not found in the original diary.

159. White to Hay, August 8, 1899, reel 78, White Papers. For further expressions of unhappiness with Mahan, and also with Clement Newel and Seth Low, who sided with Mahan, see Holls to White, September 21, 1899, reel 79, and Holls to White, March 15, 1901, reel 83, both in White Papers.

CHAPTER 8. THE RECASTING OF SEA POWER

1. *LWS*, 237–38.
2. "Captain Mahan Sails for New York," *NYT*, August 13, 1899, 1.
3. Alfred Thayer Mahan to James R. Thursfield, June 17, 1899, *LP*, 2:637.
4. Alfred Thayer Mahan to John Brown, February 15, 1897, *LP*, 2:492; Alfred Thayer Mahan to Charles Wingate, May 23, 1897, *LP*, 2:510.
5. Mahan to Brown, June 27, 1899, *LP*, 2:641.
6. Henry Adams, *History of the United States of America*, 9 vols. (New York: C. Scribner's Sons, 1890).
7. Adam Smith is referenced in the text of *1812*, 1, 9, 10, 49, 59.
8. Mahan to Brown, May 9, 1901, *LP*, 2:723–24.
9. For Mahan seeing 1870 as an economic watershed, see *FSS*, 266–69.
10. Alfred Thayer Mahan to John Knox Laughton, December 25, 1900, fol. 91, LGH 14, John Knox Laughton Papers, National Maritime Museum, Greenwich, CT (hereafter cited as Laughton Papers).
11. Mahan to Brown, April 15 and May 9, 1901, *LP*, 2:716–17, 723–24.
12. Mahan to Brown, December 13, 1901, *LP*, 2:738–39.
13. Mahan to Brown, April 15, 1900, *LP*, 2:688.
14. Alfred Thayer Mahan to Bouverie Clark, February 8, 1902, *LP*, 3:8–10.
15. Alfred Thayer Mahan to Leo Maxse, December 26, 1901, *LP*, 2:742–44.
16. Mahan to Maxse, April 10, 1902, *LP*, 3:17.
17. Mahan to Maxse, December 26, 1901, *LP*, 2:742–44.
18. Mahan to Maxse, June 20, 1902, *LP*, 3:30.
19. Henry Cabot Lodge to Theodore Roosevelt, March 30, 1901, in *Selections from the Correspondence of Theodore Roosevelt and Henry Cabot Lodge*, 2 vols. (New York: C. Scribner's Sons, 1925), 2:486.
20. Theodore Roosevelt to Alfred Thayer Mahan, March 18, 1901, series 2, reel 325, Roosevelt Papers.
21. Parliamentary Papers, HC Deb September 2, 1895, vol. 36, col. 1485, George Goschen (First Lord of the Admiralty).
22. Arthur James Balfour to Lord Knollys, September 23, 1902, RA/VIC/MAIN/R22/117, King Edward VII correspondence, Royal Archives, Windsor Castle, Windsor, UK.

23. Alfred Thayer Mahan to wife, August 2, 1893, *LP*, 2:131. Mahan met Balfour, H. H. Asquith, and John Morley for lunch. For his staying in touch with Balfour, see Arthur James Balfour to George Goschen, December 15, 1899, fol. 228, 231, Add.MS. 49706, British Library, London; Arthur James Balfour to Alfred Thayer Mahan, December 20, 1899, fol. 249, Add.MS. 49742, British Library, London.

24. Balfour to Mahan, December 20, 1899.

25. Balfour to Knollys, September 23, 1902; Balfour to Knollys, October 1, 1902, RA/VIC/MAIN/R22/121, Royal Archives.

26. Balfour to Knollys, October 1, 1902, RA/VIC/MAIN/R22/121, Royal Archives. The chair was finally given to John B. Bury. Ironically, Bury was an exponent of "history as science."

27. Thomas J. McCormick, *China Market: America's Quest for Informal Empire, 1893–1901* (Chicago: Quadrangle Books, 1967), 32.

28. Roosevelt to Lodge, August 17, 1897, in *Selections from the Correspondence of Theodore Roosevelt*, 1:271–72.

29. Charles A. Conant, "The Economic Basis of 'Imperialism,'" *North American Review* 167 (September 1898): 326–40.

30. Brooks Adams, "New Struggle for Life among Nations," in *America's Economic Supremacy* (New York: Harper, 1947), 89; see also William A. Williams, "Brooks Adams and American Expansion," *New England Quarterly* 25, no. 2 (June 1952): 218–20, esp. 218n34.

31. *LWS*, 157; Alfred Thayer Mahan to Henry Cabot Lodge, February 7, 1899, *LP*, 2:627.

32. A. T. Mahan, *The Problem of Asia and Its Effect upon International Policies* (Boston: Little, Brown, 1900), 158.

33. *LWS*, vii–viii.

34. Alfred Thayer Mahan, "Considerations Governing the Dispositions of Navies," *National Review*, July 1902, reprinted in Mahan, *Retrospect and Prospect: Studies in International Relations, Naval and Political* (Boston: Little, Brown, 1907), 146–47.

35. Mahan to Maxse, May 27, 1903, *LP*, 3:27; Alfred Thayer Mahan to William H. Henderson, June 1, 1902, *LP*, 3:28.

36. Gerald T. White, "Economic Recovery and the Wheat Crop of 1897," *Agricultural History* 13, no. 1 (January 1939): 13–21; McCormick, *China Market*, 53; see also 22–39.

37. McCormick, *China Market*, 63.

38. McCormick, 139.

39. Williams, "Brooks Adams and American Expansion," 223.

40. Mahan to Brown, April 15, 1900, *LP*, 2:688.

41. Alfred Thayer Mahan to William McKinley, September 2, 1900, *LP*, 2:693.

42. Thomas Otte, *The China Question: Great Power Rivalry and British Isolation 1894–1905* (Oxford: Oxford University Press, 2007).

43. Charles A. Conant, "Russia as a World Power," *North American Review* 168, no. 507 (February 1899): 178–90; also useful is Conant, "The Development of Credit," *Journal of Political Economy* 7, no. 2 (March 1899): 161–81.

44. Carl Parrini, "Charles A. Conant, Economic Crisis and Foreign Policy, 1896–1903," in *Behind the Throne: Servants of Power to Imperial Presidents, 1898–1968*, ed. Thomas McCormick and Walter LaFeber (Madison: University of Wisconsin Press, 1993); Carl Parrini and Martin Sklar, "New Thinking about the Market, 1896–1904: Some American Economists on Investment and the Theory of Surplus Capital," *Journal of Economic History* 43, no. 3 (September 1983): 559–67.

45. Conant, "Russia as a World Power," 178.

46. Conant, 190.

47. Charles A. Conant, "The Struggle for Commercial Empire," *Forum*, June 1899, 427.

48. Charles A. Conant, "The United States as a World Power: The Nature of the Economic and Political Problem," *Forum*, July 1900, 608.

49. Conant, 620.

50. Capt. A. T. Mahan, "The Problem of Asia (III)," *Harper's Magazine*, May 1900, 938.

51. Mahan to Roosevelt, March 12, 1901, reproduced in Richard W. Turk, *The Ambiguous Relationship: Theodore Roosevelt and Alfred Thayer Mahan* (Westport, CT: Greenwood Press, 1987), 128.

52. Mahan to Maxse, March 7, 1902, *LP*, 3:12.

53. During 1902, Mahan produced three major articles discussing the Russia problem: "Motives to Imperial Federation" (May 1902), "Considerations Governing the Dispositions of Navies" (July 1902), and "The Persian Gulf and International Relations" (September 1902). All three are reproduced in Mahan, *Retrospect and Prospect*.

54. *IGS*, 91; Alfred T. Mahan, "Possibilities of an Anglo-American Reunion," *North American* Review 159, no. 456 (November 1895): 557.

55. Ivan S. Bloch, edited by William Stead, *The Future of War in Its Technical, Economic, and Political Relations: Is War Now Impossible?* (New York: Doubleday & McClure, 1899), xvi–xvii.

56. Andrew Dickson White, diary entry, May 22, 1899, in White, *Autobiography of Andrew Dickson White*, 2 vols. (New York: The Century Company, 1917), 262. For presentation copies to all delegates, see Calvin Davis, *The United States at the Second Hague Peace Conference: American Diplomacy and International Organization, 1899–1914* (Durham, NC: Duke University Press, 1975), 23.

57. Mahan, "The Problem of Asia (II)," *Harper's Magazine*, March 1900, 748–49.

58. Mahan, "Problem of Asia (III)," 936. This idea is also found in *1812*, 2:126–27.

59. A. T. Mahan, "Considerations Governing the Dispositions of Navies," *National Review* 39 (July 1902): 144–45; see also Mahan to Maxse, February 21 and May 23, 1902, *LP*, 3:11, 25–26.

60. Mahan, 149.
61. Mahan, 144–45.
62. Mahan, 194.
63. Mahan, "The Submarine and Its Enemies," *Collier's Weekly* 39 (April 6, 1907): 17–21.
64. Mahan, "Considerations Governing the Dispositions of Navies," 171.
65. Mahan, "The Persian Gulf and International Relations," *National Review*, September 1902, reprinted in Mahan, *Retrospect and Prospect*, 209–51.
66. Mahan, 249; emphasis added.
67. H. J. Mackinder, "The Geographical Pivot of History," *Geographical Journal* 23, no. 4 (April 1904): 421–37. For Mackinder's conceptualization of his paper as a "formula," see 422 and 442.
68. Mackinder, 433.
69. John Hay to Alfred Thayer Mahan, November 23, 1904, fol. 669, reel 2, Rear Adm. Alfred Thayer Mahan Papers, Library of Congress, Washington, DC (hereafter cited as Mahan Papers). Both attended the July 1904 Imperial Federation League dinner, where Mahan was the guest of honor. For Mahan's previous awareness of Mackinder's article, see Mahan to Maxse, June 17, 1904, *LP*, 3:98–99.
70. Mackinder, "Geographical Pivot of History," 434, 442–43.
71. Mackinder, 434, 443.
72. Mahan to Maxse, June 17, 1904, *LP*, 3:99.
73. Mahan, *Problem of Asia*, 38.
74. Mahan.
75. Mahan to Clark, December 19, 1902, *LP*, 2:47–48.
76. Mahan to John Brown, February 15, 1897, *LP*, 2:492.
77. Alfred Thayer Mahan to Stephen B. Luce, May 12, 1903, *LP*, 3:61.
78. Capt. A. T. Mahan, "American Naval Power," reprinted in Mahan, *The Interest of America in Sea Power, Present and Future* (Boston: Little, Brown, 1897), 149.
79. Mahan, 150.
80. Luce to Mahan, January 3, 1903, fol. 398, reel 10, Luce Papers, LOC.
81. Mahan to Luce, January 13, 1903, *LP*, 3:52.
82. Mahan to Laughton, September 25, 1903, fol. 115r, LGH 15, Laughton Papers.
83. Mahan, letter to the editor of the *New York Times*, August 31, 1914, *LP*, 3:542.
84. *1812*, 2:227.
85. *FSS*, 317; see also Mahan to Brown, January 1, 1907, *LP*, 3:200.
86. Mahan to Luce, January 13, 1903, fol. 398, reel 10, Luce Papers, LOC.
87. Mahan to Luce, January 13, 1903.
88. *1812*, 2:208–9.
89. Mahan to Brown, December 13, 1903, *LP*, 3:80–81.
90. Mahan to Maxse, August 21, 1903, *LP*, 3:72.
91. Mahan to Maxse, February 7, April 28, and June 11, 1903, *LP*, 3:58–59, 59–60, 63–64.

92. Mahan to Maxse, November 22, 1904, *LP*, 3:109.

93. Alfred Thayer Mahan to John Bassett Moore, March 30, 1905, *LP*, 3:127.

94. Mahan to Brown, January 1, 1907, *LP*, 3:200.

95. Alfred Thayer Mahan to Arthur Twining Hadley, April 17 and 28, 1905, series 1, box 58, RU 25, Hadley Papers; Hadley to Mahan, April 18, 1905, fol. 441, series 1, box 107, RU 25, Hadley Papers.

96. Eli F. Heckscher, *The Continental System: An Economic Interpretation* (Oxford: Oxford University Press, 1922), 30; see also 45, 100n1.

97. Lance E. Davis and Stanley L. Engerman, *Naval Blockades in Peace and War: An Economic History since 1750* (Cambridge: Cambridge University Press, 2006), 74nn76–77.

98. Mahan to Brown, December 13, 1903, *LP*, 3:80–81.

99. William Dudley, "Alfred Thayer Mahan on the War of 1812," in *The Influence of History on Mahan: The Proceedings of a Conference Marking the Centenary of Alfred Thayer Mahan's* The Influence of Sea Power upon History, 1660–1783, ed. John B. Hattendorf (Newport, RI: Naval War College Press, 1991), 149.

100. Mahan to Brown, December 13, 1903, *LP*, 3:80–81; Alfred Thayer Mahan to Andrew McLaughlin, January 3, 1905, *LP*, 3:115.

101. *1812*, 1:284–85; emphasis added.

102. *1812*, 1:285.

103. *1812*, 1:285.

104. *1812*, 1:285.

105. *1812*, 1:286.

106. See also *1812*, 2:126–28, 177–213, 285–97.

107. *1812*, 1:297.

108. "The hands of Zerubbabel have laid the foundation of this house; his hands shall also finish it; and thou shalt know that the Lord of hosts hath sent me unto you. For who hath despised the day of small things? for they shall rejoice." Zechariah 4:9–10 (KJV).

109. *FSS*, 317–19; *1812*, 1:i.

110. *1812*, 2:21.

111. *1812*, 2:127.

112. *1812*, 1:289.

113. *1812*, 2:221.

114. *1812*, 2:21–22.

115. *1812*, 2:222.

116. *1812*, 2:208; also 1:289–96, 2:126–27.

117. For similar thoughts in earlier work, see *FRE*, 2:184; *ISHP*, 208.

118. Sprouts, 86.

119. Wade G. Dudley, *Splintering the Wooden Wall: The British Blockade of the United States, 1812–1815* (Annapolis, MD: Naval Institute Press, 2003).

120. Useful summaries of all the literature are found in a pair of articles by Kevin O'Rourke: "The Worldwide Economic Impact of the French Revolutionary

and Napoleonic Wars, 1793–1815," *Journal of Global History* 1 (2006): 123–49; and esp. "War and Welfare: Britain, France, and the United States 1807–14," *Oxford Economic Papers* 59, supp. (2007): i8–i30.

121. Douglass North, *The Economic Growth of the United States, 1790–1860* (Englewood Cliffs, NJ: Prentice-Hall, 1961), 38; see also 66–68.

122. North, 56.

123. Davis and Engerman, *Naval Blockades in Peace and War*, 102.

124. O'Rourke, "War and Welfare," i.10.

125. See folder of correspondence between Mahan and Moore, box 10, Moore Papers.

126. *1812*, 1:146–48, 291–97.

127. *1812*, 1:144–45.

128. *1812*, 1:145.

129. Capt. William D. Puleston, USN, *Mahan: The Life and Work of Captain Alfred Thayer Mahan, USN* (New Haven, CT: Yale University Press, 1939), 265.

130. Mahan to Roosevelt, October 24, 1906, *LP*, 3:190.

131. Puleston, *Mahan*, 261.

132. Review by Galliard Hunt, *American Historical Review*, July 1906, 924–26. For Mahan's reply, see Alfred Thayer Mahan to the American Historical Association, July 25, 1906, *LP*, 3:167.

133. Theodore Roosevelt to James Jeffrey Roche (U.S. Consul, Genoa, Italy), March 7, 1906, in *Letters of Theodore Roosevelt*, 8 vols., ed. Elting Morison and John Blum (Boston: Harvard University Press, 1951–54), 5:173.

134. For an excellent summary of the differences, see Michael T. Corgan, "Mahan and Theodore Roosevelt: The Assessment of Influence," *NWCR* 33, no. 6 (1980): 91.

135. Turk, *Ambiguous Relationship*, 63.

CHAPTER 9. THE QUIXOTIC CRUSADE

1. Philip H. Sheridan, *The Personal Memoirs of P. H. Sheridan, General United States Army*, 2 vols. (New York: Charles Webster & Co., 1888), 1:487–88.

2. *1812*, 2:106.

3. *ISPH*, 1.

4. For the novelty and importance of this development in international relations, see Jan Martin Lemnitzer, *Power, Law and the End of Privateering* (Houndmills, UK: Palgrave Macmillan, 2014).

5. Andrew White cited in Carlton Savage, *Policy of the United States toward Maritime Commerce in War*, 2 vols. (Washington DC: Department of State, 1934), doc.152, June 20, 1899, 1:494. For White's views on immunity, see Calvin DeArmond Davis, *The United States and the Second Hague Peace Conference: American Diplomacy and International Organization, 1899–1914* (Durham, NC: Duke University Press, 1975), 28.

6. For the anti-U.S. character of the Declaration of Paris and the backstory to the Marcy Amendment, see Jan Martin Lemnitzer, *Power, Law and the End of Privateering*, 75–95. Also useful is Rear Adm. Charles Stockton, "The Declaration of Paris," *American Journal of International Law* 14, no. 3 (July 1920): 356–68.

7. For the instructions issued April 18, 1899, see *Foreign Relations of the United States* (Washington, DC: Government Printing Office, 1899), 511–13; see also Samuel B. Crandall, "Exemption of Private Property at Sea from Capture," *Columbia Law Review* 5, no. 7 (November 1905): 487–99.

8. Davis, *United States and the Second Hague Peace Conference*, 92–102.

9. A. T. Mahan, "The Peace Conference and the Moral Aspect of War," *North American Review* 169, no. 515 (October 1899): 433–47. For a good summary of the aspirations of the peace movement and the history surrounding the Permanent Court of Arbitration, see Davis, *United States and the Second Hague Peace Conference*, 29–34, 149–61, 251–72.

10. Alfred Thayer Mahan to Leo Maxse, January 24, 1902, *LP*, 3:5–6.

11. James Brown Scott, ed., *Instructions to the American Delegates to the Hague Peace Conferences and Their Official Reports* (Oxford: Oxford University Press, 1916), 62.

12. "The Hague Conference," *NYT*, September 26, 1904, 8; "Appeals to the Public to Support Arbitration," *NYT*, June 4, 1904, 6.

13. For Roosevelt's cultivation of the peace lobby, see Davis, *United States and the Second Hague Peace Conference*, 51–54, 92–118. For the popular misunderstanding of Roosevelt's message, see Eliot Cohen, *The Big Stick: The Limits of Soft Power and the Necessity of Military Force* (New York: Basic Books, 2017), ix–xiii.

14. John Hay diary, 23 October 23, 1904, reel 1, Hay Papers.

15. "Europe Skeptical about Peace Congress," *NYT*, September 27, 1904, 1.

16. "The President's Peace Conference," *NYT*, September 28, 1904, 8; "The New Hague Conference," *NYT*, October 22, 1904, 8.

17. Dispatch dated November 2, 1904, quoted in Davis, *United States and the Second Hague Peace Conference*, 115.

18. Hay notes in his diary that he dictated the letter on October 10, 1904; reel 1, Hay Papers.

19. Scott, *Instructions to the American Delegates*, 59; "The Hague Conference to Place Peace Congress: Text of Hay's Letter Calling Second Convention," *NYT*, October 31, 1904, 1.

20. John Hay diary, October 10, 1904, reel 1, Hay Papers.

21. "No Hague Conference Yet," *NYT*, December 1, 1904, 2.

22. "Hague Conference Shelved," *NYT*, December 24, 1904, 2.

23. Alfred Thayer Mahan to Theodore Roosevelt, December 27, 1904, *LP*, 3:112.

24. Mahan to Roosevelt, December 27, 1904, *LP*, 3:113.

25. Mahan to Roosevelt, December 27, 1904, *LP*, 3:113.

26. Theodore Roosevelt, Third Annual Message, December 7, 1903. Miller Center, University of Virginia, https://millercenter.org/the-presidency/presidential-speeches/december-7-1903-third-annual-message.

27. Theodore Roosevelt to John Hay, August 29, 1904, in *Letters of Theodore Roosevelt*, 8 vols., ed. Elting Morison and John Blum (Boston: Harvard University Press, 1951–54), 4:913.

28. Keith Neilson, "'A Dangerous Game of American Poker': The Russo-Japanese War and British Policy," *Journal of Strategic Studies* 12, no. 1 (March 1989): 63–87.

29. Roosevelt to Mahan, December 29, 1904, fol. 62, series 2, reel 336, Roosevelt Papers.

30. Hay to Roosevelt, December 31, 1904, box 5, reel 4, Hay Papers.

31. Hay to Roosevelt, December 31, 1904.

32. John Hay makes no mention of Mahan or his letter during the period from December 29, 1904, through January 1, 1905. *Note*: The diary entry for January 1, 1905, is not on the microfilm and the originals must be requested.

33. Theodore Roosevelt to William Howard Taft, July 3, 1905, and Roosevelt to Henry Cabot Lodge, July 11, 1905, in Morison and Blum, *Letters of Theodore Roosevelt*, 4:1260 and 1271; see also Davis, *United States and the Second Hague Peace Conference*, 112.

34. Alfred Thayer Mahan to Elihu Root, April 20, 1906, *LP*, 3:157; see also reference to Mahan sending Roosevelt a copy of Loreburn's article on the subject in Alfred Thayer Mahan to John Knox Laughton, January 31, 1906, fol. 137, LGH 15, Laughton Papers; Mahan to Maxse, May 10, 1907, *LP*, 3:211.

35. Mahan finished the final chapter on July 22, 1905, for which see *LP*, 3:133.

36. Mahan to Roosevelt, September 9, 1905, *LP*, 3:139.

37. For reply, see Roosevelt to Mahan, September 21, 1905, in Richard W. Turk, *The Ambiguous Relationship: Theodore Roosevelt and Alfred Thayer Mahan* (Westport, CT: Greenwood Press, 1987), 137.

38. Theodore Roosevelt to Elihu Root, September 14, 1905, in Morison and Blum, *Letters of Theodore Roosevelt*, 5:25.

39. Scott, *Instructions to the American Delegates*, 65; see also Philip Jessup, *Elihu Root*, 2 vols. (New York: Dodd, Mead, 1938), 2:68.

40. Mahan to Maxse, September 14, 1905, *LP* 3:141. For Mahan's relatives in France, see Alfred Thayer Mahan to Little, Brown, October 8, 1905, *LP*, 3:145.

41. Mahan to Laughton, January 31, 1906, fol. 136, LGH 15, Laughton Papers.

42. Mahan to Laughton, January 31, 1906. *Note*: Mahan highlights this point in *1812*, 1:144–48.

43. Alfred Thayer Mahan to James R. Thursfield, January 31, 1906, *LP*, 3:155.

44. For the text, see Scott, *Instructions to the American Delegates*, 66–68; immunity is item 3c. Russia wanted the conference convened in July 1906, but the United States and other countries replied this was too soon. See telegram, Elihu Root to Whitelaw Reid, April 6, 1906, and reply of April 7, 1906, reel 176, Whitelaw Reid Papers, Library of Congress, Washington, DC (hereafter cited as Reid Papers).

45. Mahan to Root, April 20, 1906, *LP*, 3:157. See also Immunity of Commerce in War 1906 (subject file), fol. 282, Mahan Papers.

46. The enclosure is reproduced in *LP*, 3:623–26.

47. Root to Mahan, May 21, 1906, Department of State, Domestic letter CCXC [290], 628, 629, RG 59, State Department Archives, NARA, copy in box 9, Papers of Rear Adm. Charles Sperry, Library of Congress, Washington, DC (hereafter cited as Sperry Papers).

48. For the early history of this body, see John T. Kuehn, *America's First General Staff: A Short History of the Rise and Fall of the of the General Board of the U.S. Navy, 1900–1950* (Annapolis, MD: Naval Institute Press, 2017), chap. 4.

49. SECSTATE to SECNAV, May 21, 1906, copy in box 9, Sperry Papers.

50. Endorsement 1 of May 23, 1906.

51. General Board report No. 438 of June 20, 1906, copy in box 9, Sperry Papers.

52. General Board report No. 438 of June 20, 1906, 28.

53. General Board report No. 438 of June 20, 1906, 10.

54. General Board report No. 438 of June 20, 1906, 20–23.

55. Private letter from William J. Barnette to Alfred Thayer Mahan, member of General Board, July 27, 1906. fol. 677, reel 2, box 2, Mahan Papers. The voting members of the board were Adm. George Dewey, Rear Adm. George Converse (BuNAV), Capt. John P. Merrell (Naval War College), Capt. Raymond P. Rodgers (ONI), Capt. Richard Wainwright, Capt. William J. Barnette, and Capt. William B. Potter. Capt. William Smith was suspended from duty following his court-martial for the grounding of the *Connecticut* (*NYT*, October 25, 1907).

56. A/SECNAV to SECSTATE, October 6, 1906 [received October 8], ref. 21950–2, fol. 165, Numerical File 1466, roll 165, RG 59, State Department Archives, NARA, forwarding General Board to SECNAV, September 28, 1906, GB No. 438, fol. 696, Numerical File 1466, RG 59, State Department Archives, NARA.

57. General Board to SECNAV, September 28, 1906, 5.

58. Mahan in fact was invited to discuss the thinking behind setting up of the Naval War Board, for which see Alfred Thayer Mahan to George Dewey, July 29, 1906, *LP*, 3:169. For his keeping this meeting, see Alfred Thayer Mahan to William S. Sims, August 6, 1906, *LP*, 3:170.

59. Mahan to Roosevelt, August 14, 1906, fol. 252, Numerical File 805, RG 59, State Department Archives, NARA.

60. Mahan to Roosevelt, incorrectly dated by Seager as July 20, 1906, *LP*, 3:164–65; the original is Mahan to Roosevelt, August 14, 1906.

61. Mahan to Roosevelt, August 14, 1906.

62. For amplification of this point, see Mahan to Maxse, October 17, 1906, *LP*, 3:181.

63. Roosevelt to Mahan, August 16, 1906, series 2, reel 342, Roosevelt Papers; Roosevelt to Mahan, August 16, 1906, fol. 256, Numerical File 805, RG 59, State Department Archives, NARA.

64. William Loeb (Roosevelt's secretary) to Robert Bacon, August 24, 1906, fol. 248, Numerical File 805, RG 59, State Department Archives, NARA, stamped September 5, 1906.

65. Davis, *United States and the Second Hague Peace Conference*, 118–25.

66. Theodore Roosevelt to Whitelaw Reid, August 7, 1906, series 2, vol. 74, reel 346, Roosevelt Papers. For evidence that Mahan was corresponding with Reid much earlier, see Alfred Thayer Mahan to Whitelaw Reid, August 10, 1903, *LP*, 3:71.

67. Roosevelt to Reid, July 29, 1907, fol. 151, series 2, vol. 74, reel 346, Roosevelt Papers.

68. See also Mahan to Maxse, April 30, 1907, *LP*, 3:210.

69. Roosevelt to Mahan, October 22, 1906, in Turk, *Ambiguous Relationship*, 148.

70. Mahan to Maxse, August 21, 1906, *LP*, 3:172.

71. Mahan to Maxse, October 17, 1906, *LP*, 3:181; Mahan to Maxse, January 22, 1907, *LP*, 3:204.

72. Mahan to Maxse, November 9, 1906, *LP*, 3:191.

73. Mahan to Maxse, January 22, March 5, and April 15, 1907, *LP*, 3:204–5, 207, 209.

74. Mahan to Maxse, October 17 and November 9, 1906, *LP*, 3:181–82, 192.

75. Charles H. Stockton, "Would Immunity from Capture, during War, of Non-Offending Private Property upon the High Seas Be in the Interest of Civilization?," *American Journal of International Law* 1, no. 4 (October 1907): 930–43, copy in box 6, Ms.COLL-56, Papers of Rear Adm. Charles Stockton, U.S. Naval War College Archives, Newport, RI (hereafter cited as Stockton Papers).

76. Charles Sperry to his son, March 1, 1906, and to Alice[?], March 7, 1906, box 5, Sperry Papers; see also Elisha J. Babcock (Root's secretary) to Sperry, February 28, 1906, box 9, Sperry Papers; Sperry to Lt. Cdr. Frank Marble, March 13, 1906, Sperry Papers.

77. Elihu Root to Charles Bonaparte, March 23, 1906, Domestic letters sent, vol. 289, fol. 20, RG 59, State Department Archives, NARA; Theodore Roosevelt to Joseph H. Choate, October 10, 1906, box 16, Joseph H. Choate Papers, Library of Congress, Washington, DC (hereafter cited as Choate Papers). It seems that Choate was recommended for the position by Senator Henry Cabot Lodge. Roosevelt to Lodge, August 19, 1905, in *Selections from the Correspondence of Theodore Roosevelt and Henry Cabot Lodge*, 2 vols. (New York: C. Scribner's Sons, 1925), 1:174.

78. Charles H. Stockton, *The Laws and Usages of War at Sea: A Naval War Code* (Washington, DC: Government Printing Office, 1900), copy in Ms.COLL-56, Stockton Papers. Stockton arrived back in Washington, DC, on January 6, 1906, and was employed at miscellaneous duties until his retirement as rear admiral in October 1907. In December 1909 he was recalled to service and appointed first delegate to the London Naval Conference.

79. Sperry to Alice[?], March 7, 1906, and to his son, May 13, 1906. box 5, Sperry Papers.

80. Charles H. Stockton, "Capture of Enemy Vessels at Sea," *North American Review* 168, no. 507 (February 1899): 206–11.

81. For Sperry's possession of Marcy's private papers, see Naval War College receipt, "Deposited for Safekeeping the Wlm L Marcy Papers (Property of Mrs. Sperry)," May 7, 1907, box 7, Sperry Papers.

82. Sperry his to son, November 5, 1906, Sperry Papers.

83. Charles Sperry to Robert Bacon, December 15, 1906, and Charles Sperry to Raymond L. Rogers (then chief of naval intelligence and member of the General Board), May 7, 1907, both in folder Hague Correspondence and Orders, box 9, Sperry Papers.

84. Root to Reid, October 24, 1906, reel 176, Reid Papers. This probably was the letter Reid showed the British foreign secretary, Sir Edward Grey, early the following month, for which see Edward Grey to Edward Durant, November 6, 1906, in G. P. Gooch and Harold Temperley, eds., *British Documents on the Origins of the War, 1898–1914*, vol. 8, *Arbitration, Neutrality and Security* (London: HMSO, 1932), 197–98.

85. Alvin Adee to James Brown Scott, December 27, 1906, and James Brown Scott to Robert Bacon, January 23, 1907, both fol. 732, Numerical File 1466, roll 165, RG 59, State Department Archives, NARA.

86. Robert Bacon to Frank Taussig, January 25, 1907, fol. 718, Numerical File 1466, roll 165, RG 59, State Department Archives, NARA.

87. Bacon to Sperry, December 23, 1906, folder marked Hague Correspondence and Orders, box 9, Sperry Papers.

88. Davis to Sperry, December 12, 1906, folder August–December 1906, box 9, Sperry Papers. For Adee's opposition, see Davis, *United States and the Second Hague Peace Conference*, 139.

89. Elihu Root, "The Need of Popular Understanding of International Law," *American Journal of International Law* 1, no. 1 (January 1907): 1–3.

90. It is telling that half the articles in the April 1907 issue of the *American Journal of International Law* are on arbitration.

91. Benjamin Coates, *Legalist Empire: International Law and American Foreign Relations in the Early Twentieth Century* (Oxford: Oxford University Press, 2016), 88–92; Davis, *United States and the Second Hague Peace Conference*, 29–34, 149–61.

92. Frederic Kirgis, "Elihu Root, James Brown Scott and the Early Years of the AJIL," *American Society of International Law* 90 (March 1996): 141.

93. Charles Sperry to Lt. Cdr. Frank Marble, March 13, 1906, box 9, Sperry Papers.

94. "Minutes: Meeting of the American Commission to the Second Hague Conference, Held April 20, 1907, in the Diplomatic Room of the Department of State," para 1, box 21, Choate Papers; original in Numerical File 40, roll 5, fols. 446–93, RG 59, State Department Archives, NARA. Present at the meeting were Secretary of State Elihu Root, Assistant Secretary of State Robert Bacon, Gen. Horace Porter, Rear Adm. Charles Sperry, Brig. George B. Davis, Hon. William Buchanan, Chandler Hale, James B. Scott, and Charles H. Butler.

95. "Minutes," para. 16.

96. "Minutes," para. 17.

97. "Minutes," paras. 17–19. For Sperry's strongly held and deeply considered views on the question of contraband, see Sperry to his son, July 28, 1906 [Grand Hotel des Themes, Vichy] and November 5, 1906, box 9, Sperry Papers; Sperry to Bacon, December 15, 1906, folder Hague Correspondence and Orders, box 9, Sperry Papers.

98. Sperry to Bacon, December 15, 1906, box 9.

99. "Minutes," para. 20. For an amplification of Sperry's views in the obsolescence of much international law, see Sperry to Bacon, 15 December 1906, box 9, Sperry Papers.

100. "Minutes," para. 22.

101. "Minutes," paras. 34–35.

102. "Minutes," para. 35.

103. Joseph H. Choate to Elihu Root, May 7, 1907, fol. 585, Numerical File 40/229, RG 59, State Department Archives, NARA; Choate to Root, May 10 and 15, 1907, and Root to Choate, May 31, 1907, fol. 917, Numerical File 40/288, RG 59, State Department Archives, NARA.

104. Choate to his son Jo, May 30, 1907, box 8, Choate Papers.

105. Choate to Root, May 7, 1907, fol. 585, containing seven-page memorandum ["Mr. Choate's suggestions upon the subject of the immunity of private property on the high seas"], fol. 589, roll 5, Numerical File 40/229, RG 59, State Department Archives, NARA.

106. For instance: Andrew Carnegie to Joseph H. Choate, July 1, 1907, box 21, Choate Papers, and Andrew White (Cornell) to Joseph H. Choate, August 12, 1907, box 21, Choate Papers.

107. Choate to Root, May 7, 1907, fol. 585, containing seven-page memorandum.

108. Choate to his son, Jo, May 30, 1907. For the subsequent issue of instructions, see Instructions Issued to U.S. Delegates, May 31, 1907, fol. 48, Numerical File 40, roll 6, RG 59, State Department Archives, NARA.

109. Scott, *Instructions to the American Delegates*, 81–82.

110. Scott, 84.

111. Mahan to Maxse, April 30, 1907, *LP*, 3:210.

112. Mahan to Maxse, May 30, 1907, *LP*, 3:213.

113. Mahan to Maxse, May 30, 1907, *LP*, 3:213–14.

114. These articles are produced in Alfred Thayer Mahan, *Some Neglected Aspects of War* (Boston: Little, Brown, 1907), 57–93 (hereafter cited as *SNA*).

115. *SNA*, 69–79.

116. *SNA*, 72.

117. *SNA*, 78–80.

118. *SNA*, 73. The biblical quote is from Matthew 6:24.

119. *SNA*, 58

120. *SNA*, 59.

121. *SNA*, 71–72.

122. *SNA*, 157–93.

123. Memorandum prepared by Admiralty Plans Division in consultation with Dr. (Alexander) Pearce Higgins [Professor of Law at Cambridge University], signed Capt. Cyril Fuller, by Director of Plans, December 2, 1918, "Freedom of the Seas," ADY, December 2, 1918, ADM1/8545/312. Edited version submitted to the Cabinet under CAB 21/307.

124. *SNA*, 157.

125. *SNA*, 165.

126. *SNA*, 162–67.

127. *SNA*, 169.

128. *SNA*, 167.

129. *SNA*, 171.

130. *SNA*, 179.

131. *SNA*, 190.

132. Davis gives a good summary of the U.S. position in *United States and the Second Hague Peace Conference*, 135–61; Bernard Semmell, *Liberalism and Naval Strategy: Ideology, Interest and Sea Power during the Pax Britannica* (Winchester, MA: Allen & Unwin, 1986), 157–58; Coates, *Legalist Empire*, 87.

133. Joseph H. Choate to James Brown Scott, December 8, 1909, box 21, Choate Papers.

134. Sir Ernest Satow diary, June 2, 1907, fol. 23, PRO 30/33/16/10, Ernest Satow Papers, National Archives, Kew (hereafter cited as Satow Papers).

135. Mahan to Maxse, July 30, 1907, *LP*, 3:221.

136. Eyre Crowe to Leo Maxse, May 16, 1907, fol. 528, Maxse Ms., Chichester Record Office, Chichester, UK.

137. Mahan to Maxse June 28, 1907, *LP*, 3:216; see also Mahan to Maxse, May 30, 1907, *LP*, 3:213–14.

138. Alexander Thayer Mahan to Stephen B. Luce, July 1907, *LP*, 3:217.

139. Reid to Roosevelt, June 7, 1907, reel 74, Reid Papers.

140. Scott, *Instructions to the American Delegates*, 72.

141. Reid to Roosevelt, July 19, 1907 (received July 29), reel 75, Reid Papers. For Reid's report, see telegram, June 5, 1907, U.S. Embassy to Root, reel 74, Reid Papers. For the official U.S. record, see State Department, fol. 77, Numerical File 40, roll 6, RG 59, State Department Archives, NARA. For the British report of the conversation, see Satow diary, June 12, 1907, fol. 25, PRO 30/33/16/10, Satow Papers. For Satow's poor opinion of Choate, see Satow diary, June 14, 1907, fol. 26, June 27, 1907, PRO 30/33/16/10, Satow Papers.

142. Roosevelt to Reid, July 29, 1907, fol. 151, series 2, vol. 74, reel 346, Roosevelt Papers.

143. Sperry to his son, October 6 and September 6, 1907, box 5, Sperry Papers.

144. Satow diary, June 14, fol. 26; June 24, fol. 30; June 26, fol. 31r; June 27, fol. 33; July 10, fol. 38r; and July 13, 1907, fol. 40, PRO 30/33/16/10, Satow Papers.

145. Roosevelt to Carnegie, April 5, 1907, reported in *NYT*, April 5, 1907. See also "Andrew Carnegie's Pleas for Peace," *NYT*, April 7, 1907, SM1.

146. Roosevelt to Reid, November 13, 1905, Roosevelt Papers.

147. Davis, *United States and the Second Hague Peace Conference*, 165–67.

148. "The Afternoon Session: Mayor, Gov. Hughes, Secretary Root and Mr. Carnegie Speak," *NYT*, April 16, 1907, 1.

149. Davis, *United States and the Second Hague Peace Conference*, 155, 167.

150. Roosevelt to Root inviting Root and Carnegie to lunch, March 18, 1907, box 195, Elihu Root Papers, Library of Congress, Washington, DC (hereafter cited as Root Papers); Roosevelt to Root, July 2, 1907, in Morison and Blum, *Letters of Theodore Roosevelt*, 5:699–700.

151. Root wrote Roosevelt's message in 1907 (Jessup, *Elihu Root*, 2:68).

152. Jessup, *Elihu Root*, 2:76–77.

153. Choate to Root, November 20, 1907, box 49, Root Papers.

154. Frederic Kirgis, "Elihu Root, James Brown Scott and the Early Years of the ASIL," *American Society of International Law* 90 (March 1996): 139–43.

155. Kirgis.

156. Coates, *Legalist Empire*, 90, also notes this.

157. Mahan to Laughton, September 6, 1907, fol. 146, LGH 15, Laughton Papers.

158. Mahan to Laughton, September 6, 1907.

159. Alfred Thayer Mahan to Julian Corbett, August 12, 1907, *LP*, 3:223.

160. Mahan to Little, Brown, March 13, 1908, *LP*, 3:238.

161. *SNA*, xxi.

162. *SNA*, 52–53.

163. *SNA*, xviii–xix.

164. *SNA*, xix.

CHAPTER 10. TWILIGHT YEARS

1. Alfred Thayer Mahan to Theodore Roosevelt, March 12, 1901, *LP*, 2:707.

2. Alfred Thayer Mahan to Sir George Clarke, January 15, 1907, *LP*, 3:203.

3. Alfred Thayer Mahan to John M. Brown, September 29, 1906, *LP*, 3:176.

4. For Mahan's admission that most of his lectures were written in 1887, see *NS*, 155; see also 102.

5. Stephen B. Luce to Alfred Thayer Mahan, July 9, 1906, fol. 332, Luce Papers, LOC.

6. Mahan to Luce, July 11, 1906, *LP*, 3:163.

7. Mahan to Luce, December 15 and 21, 1906, *LP*, 3:198, 199.

8. Mahan to Brown, September 27, 1906, *LP*, 3:176; Alfred Thayer Mahan to Harper & Brothers, August 29, 1906, *LP*, 3:173.

9. Luce to Mahan, July 15, 1907, NWC file, Naval Historical Foundation Collection, Library of Congress; Mahan to Luce, July 11, 1906, *LP*, 3:163.

10. Mahan to Luce, July 20, 1907, box 2, folder 2, RG 28, Luce Papers, NWC.

11. Luce to Mahan, July 15, 1907.

12. Stephen B, Luce, "On Naval Strategy," July 17, 1902, box 2, folder 8, RG 14, Luce Papers, NWC; Luce, "History of the NEWC," August 20, 1906, box 2, folder 1, RG 28, Luce Papers, NWC.

13. See Mahan to Luce, June 17, 1908, *LP*, 3:250.

14. *ATM*, 545–47; William Livezey, *Mahan on Sea Power* (Norman: University of Oklahoma Press, 1947), 311; Capt. William D. Puleston, USN, *Mahan: The Life and Work of Captain Alfred Thayer Mahan, USN* (New Haven, CT: Yale University Press, 1939), 281–82.

15. Puleston, 315.

16. Mahan to Clarke, May 20, 1907, *LP*, 3:212.

17. Mahan to Clarke, May 20, 1907, *LP*, 3:212.

18. Mahan to Luce, July [8], 1907, *LP*, 3:216–17.

19. Alfred Thayer Mahan to Samuel Ashe, September 9, 1907, *LP*, 3:227–28; Alfred Thayer Mahan to Bouverie Clark, October 31, 1907, *LP*, 3:233; Mrs. Mahan to Stephen B. Luce, December 3 and 12, 1907, *LP*, 3:235; also Mahan to Clark, September 11, 1908, *LP*, 3:263; Mahan to Ashe, November 30, 1908, *LP*, 3:270; Alfred Thayer Mahan to Adm. William H. Henderson, May 17, 1910, *LP*, 3:341. For the third operation, see Alfred Thayer Mahan to James F. Rhodes, April 11, 1908, *LP*, 3:241.

20. Mahan to Luce, November 18, 1907, *LP*, 3:233–34; more explicitly demanded in Alfred Thayer Mahan to John P. Merrell, June 5, 1908, *LP*, 3:248.

21. "Recollections of Ellen Kuhn Mahan, c. 1937–1938," reprinted in *LP*, 3:728.

22. Suzanne Geissler, *God and Sea Power: The Influence of Religion on Alfred Thayer Mahan* (Annapolis, MD: Naval Institute Press, 2015), 165.

23. "Syndicate Cash for Morse Depositors," *NYT*, April 10, 1908, 3, and April 11, 1908, 11.

24. Mahan to Clark, December 14, 1906, *LP*, 3:197; Mahan to Henderson, January 19, 1907, *LP*, 3:203–4. Both letters indicate an intent to return to New York in 1908. Mahan to Little, Brown, November 11, 1908, *LP*, 3:269, indicates the change in plan.

25. Theodore Roosevelt to Alfred Thayer Mahan, March 27, 1908, in Richard W. Turk, *The Ambiguous Relationship: Theodore Roosevelt and Alfred Thayer Mahan* (Westport, CT: Greenwood Press, 1987), 150.

26. Mahan to Brown, April 17 and May 9, 1908, *LP*, 3:241–22, 244–45; Mahan to Luce, April 6, 1908, *LP*, 3:239.

27. Merrell to Mahan, May 29, 1908, box 3, RG 1, Naval War College Archives.

28. Mahan to Merrell, June 5, 1908, *LP*, 3:248.

29. Mahan to Luce, November 18, 1907, *LP*, 3:233–34.

30. Mahan to Merrell, May 31, 1909, *LP*, 3:304; Alfred Thayer Mahan to Raymond Rodgers, April 16, 1910, *LP*, 3:338.

31. Mahan to Little, Brown, January 30, 1911, *LP*, 3:373.

32. "I find that Revision takes the shape rather of Expansion." Mahan to Merrell, July 23, 1909, *LP*, 3:306.

33. Mahan to Luce, June 17, 1908, *LP*, 2:250.

34. Mahan to Merrell, October 19, 1908, and Merrell to Mahan, October 21, 1908, NWC file, Naval Historical Foundation Collection, Library of Congress; John P. Merrell to John E. Pillsbury (BuNAV), October 21, 1908, makes clear that as of this day Mahan was still not well enough to write.

35. Mahan to Merrell, November 17, 1908, *LP*, 3:269. On completion of his lecture notes, see Mahan to Rodgers, April 14, 1910, *LP*, 3:337.

36. *ATM*, 548, 556–59.

37. Mahan to Clark, March 12, 1912, *LP*, 3:447.

38. *NS*, 302–3.

39. *FSS*, 282–83.

40. Puleston, *Mahan*, 297–98.

41. *NS*, 18.

42. *NS*, 107, 200–221. The first half of *Naval Strategy* in particular contains a great deal of turgid prose, yet some passages sparkle (e.g., 228–30).

43. *NS*, 300.

44. *IGS*, 99–117 argues that Mahan saw discussion of principles as possessing some value, as a kind of entry level (101) survey course. This may be how Mahan justified it to himself but he neglected to define his terms with clarity, and this does not excuse the contradictions in *Naval Strategy*.

45. Mahan to Henderson, February 16, 1909, HEN 3/284, Adm. William H. Henderson Papers, National Maritime Museum, Greenwich, UK (hereafter cited as Henderson Papers).

46. Mahan to Henderson, December 26, 1910, HEN 3/370, Henderson Papers.

47. Capt. A. T. Mahan, "On the Immunity from Capture of Private Property at Sea," *Times* (London), November 4, 1910, 5.

48. Captain Mahan, "The Origins of the European War," interview with the *New York Evening Post*, August 3, 1914, reprinted in *LP*, 3:698–700; Capt. A. T. Mahan, "Sea Power in the Present European War," *Leslie's Illustrated Weekly*, August 20, 1914, *LP*, 3:706–10.

49. Mahan to Ashe, June 7, 1912, *LP*, 3:464.

50. Mahan to Clark, March 24 and October 6, *LP*, 3:492, 510.

51. Mahan to Clark, March 24, 1913, *LP*, 3:492.

52. Mahan to Clark, October 23, 1913, *LP*, 3:511–12.

53. Mahan to Henderson, November 7, 1913, *LP*, 3:513.

54. Alfred Thayer Mahan to John Bassett Moore, May 4 and June 1, 1912, *LP*, 3:456, 461; Alfred Thayer Mahan to Franklin Jameson, April 27, 1912, *LP*, 3:523–24.

55. Alfred Thayer Mahan to Robert Woodward, January 29, 1914, *LP*, 3:517.

56. Mahan to Clark, October 1, 1914, *LP*, 3:549.

CHAPTER 11. INTERPRETING MAHAN'S LEGACY

1. *ISPH*, v.

2. William O. Stevens, "Scrapping Mahan," *Yale Review* 12, no. 3 (April 1923): 533.

3. Harold James, *The End of Globalization: Lessons from the Great Depression* (Cambridge, MA: Harvard University Press, 2002).

4. Michael Barnhart, *Japan Prepares for Total War: The Search for Economic Security, 1919–1941* (Ithaca, NY: Cornell University Press, 1988).

5. Stevens, "Scrapping Mahan," 528, 529.

6. Julius W. Pratt, *The Expansionists of 1898: The Acquisition of Hawaii and the Spanish Islands* (Chicago: Quadrangle Books, 1964), 13.

7. Charles Beard, "Our Confusion over Naval Defense," *Harper's Magazine*, February 1932; Beard, *The Navy: Defense or Portent* (New York: Harper Bros., 1932), 18–21. For a useful overview of Charles Beard's ideas, see Campbell Craig, "The Not-So-Strange Career of Charles Beard," *Diplomatic History* 25, no. 2 (Spring 2001): 251–74; see also William Appleman Williams, "A Note on Charles Austin Beard's Search for a General Theory of Causation," *American Historical Review* 62 (October 1956): 59–80.

8. Arthur Skop, "The Primacy of Domestic Politics: Eckart Kehr and the Intellectual Development of Charles A. Beard," *History and Theory* 13, no. 2 (May 1974): 123. Also useful is Thomas C. Kennedy, "Beard vs. F.D.R. on National Defense and Rearmament," *Mid-America: An Historical Quarterly* 50 (January 1968): 22–40.

9. Charles Beard, *A Foreign Policy for America* (New York: Alfred A. Knopf, 1940), 45; see also 36–42, 74–75.

10. Beard, 74–75.

11. Louis M. Hacker, "The Incendiary Mahan: A Biography," *Scribner's Magazine* 95 (April 1934): 263–68, 311–20 (the quote is found on 312–13); see also Louis Hacker and Burton Kendrick, *The United States since 1865* (New York: F. S. Crofts and Co., 1932), 127, 352–58. Yet twenty-five years later, it is interesting to note, Hacker significantly modified his assessment of Mahan in his four-page foreword to the 1957 reprint edition of *Influence* (New York: Hill and Wang, 1957).

12. Capt. William D. Puleston, USN, *Mahan: The Life and Work of Captain Alfred Thayer Mahan, USN* (New Haven, CT: Yale University Press, 1939).

13. Puleston, v–vi.

14. W. D. Puleston, "Mahan: Naval Philosopher," *Scribner's Magazine* 96 (September 1934): 295.

15. W. D. Puleston, "Broad-Minded Mahan: The Admiral Who Balanced the Value of Land and Sea Forces," *Army Ordnance* 15, no. 89 (March 1935): 277.

16. Puleston, *Mahan*, 93.

17. Capt. W. D. Puleston, "A Re-Examination of Mahan's Concept of Sea Power," *Proceedings* 66/9/451 (September 1940): 1230.

18. Puleston, *Mahan*, 95.

19. Puleston, "Re-Examination of Mahan's Concept of Sea Power." Note the change of the object applied to the term "synopsis."

20. Sprouts, v; see also the preface to the 1966 edition, i.

21. Charles Tansill, review of Harold Sprout and Margaret Sprout, *Rise of American Naval Power*, *Journal of Modern History* 11, no. 4 (December 1939): 537–38.

22. Harold Sprout, review of Puleston, *Mahan: The Life and Work of Captain Alfred Thayer Mahan, USN*, *American Political Science Review* 33, no. 5 (October 1939): 907–8.

23. Sprout, review of Puleston, *Mahan: The Life and Work of Captain Alfred Thayer Mahan, USN*.

24. *MMS1*.

25. David Ekbladh, "Present at the Creation: Edward Mead Earle and the Depression-Era Origins of Security Studies," *International Security* 36, no. 3 (Winter 2011/12): 107–41; Michael Finch, "Edward Mead Earle and the Unfinished Makers of Modern Strategy," *Journal of Military History* 80, no. 3 (July 2016): 781–814; Dexter Fergie, "Geopolitics Turned Inwards: The Princeton Military Studies Group and the National Security Imagination," *Diplomatic History* 43, no. 4 (September 2019): 644–70. Also useful here is Thomas R. Pollock, "The Historical Elements of Mahanian Doctrine," *NWCR* 35, no. 4 (July 1982): 44–49.

26. Ekbladh, "Present at the Creation," 119.

27. Finch, "Edward Mead Earle," 788.

28. Bernard Brodie, *A Layman's Guide to Naval Strategy* (Princeton, NJ: Princeton University Press, 1942); Herbert Rosinski, "Command of the Sea" (1939) and "The Development of Naval Thought" (1941), both appearing in *Brassey's Naval Annual* (London: William Clowes and Sons, 1941); see also Mitchell Simpson, ed., *The Development of Naval Thought: Essays by Herbert Rosinski* (Newport, RI: Naval War College Press, 1977).

29. Edward Mead Earle, ed., *Makers of Modern Strategy: Military Thought from Machiavelli to Hitler* (Princeton, NJ: Princeton University Press, 1943), viii.

30. See esp. Fergie, "Geopolitics Turned Inwards."

31. Earle, *Makers of Modern Strategy*, ix.

32. Edward Mead Earle to Charles Beard, December 13, 1938, Beard Correspondence file, box 13, Edward Mead Earle Papers, Seely Mudd Library, Princeton University, Princeton, NJ (hereafter cited as Earle Papers); see also Edward Mead Earle to Herbert Richmond, December 20, 1944, box 36, file 2, MC020, Earle Papers.

33. Bernard Brodie to E. M. Earle, November 17, 1944, Brodie Correspondence file, MC020, Earle Papers. See also Brodie's review of *MMS1* in *American Journal of International Law* 38, no. 4 (October 1944): 754–55. I am indebted to John Kuehn for a copy of this hard-to-obtain review.

34. Notes on "Mahan 1938," box 7, folder 3, Professor Herbert Rosinski Papers, MSC-091, series V, U.S. Naval War College Archives, Newport, RI. See also Herbert Rosinski's review in (U.S. Army) *Infantry Journal*, December 1943, 57–59. I am indebted to John Kuehn for a copy of this document.

35. Rosinski, "Command of the Sea," 21.

36. Rosinski, 21.

37. Rosinski, 6.

38. Earle to Uncle Charlie (Beard), December 13, 1938, Beard Correspondence file, box 13, MC020, Earle Papers.

39. *MMS1*, 417–18.

40. Harold Sprout, "Geopolitical Theories Compared," *NWCR* 7, no. 1 (January 1954): 23.

41. Harold Sprout and Margaret Sprout, *Foundations of International Politics* (Princeton, NJ: Van Nostrand, 1962), 318; see also 324–26.

42. Sprout, "Geopolitical Theories Compared," 19–36.

43. Sprout, 26.

44. Sprout, 26. For the flaws in the Sprouts' assessment of Mahan as a mercantilist, see Walter LaFeber, "A Note on the Mercantilist Imperialism of Alfred Thayer Mahan," *Mississippi Valley Historical Review* 48, no. 4 (1962): 674–85; William A. Williams, "The Age of Mercantilism: An Interpretation of the American Political Economy, 1763 to 1828," *William and Mary Quarterly* 15, no. 4 (October 1958): 419–37.

45. Thomas R. Pollock, "The Historical Elements of Mahanian Doctrine," *NWCR* 35, no. 4 (July 1982): 44–49; William E. Livezey, *Mahan on Sea Power* (Norman: University of Oklahoma Press, 1947), 43–44, 308, 356.

46. *ISPH*, 88.

47. *ISPH*, 21, 89n8.

48. *IGS*, 67–68.

49. A. T. Mahan, *The Life of Nelson*, 2 vols. (Boston: Little, Brown, 1897), 1:235.

50. *LWS*, 3–15; see also 298–300.

51. *FSS*, 278–78, 282–83.

52. Livezey, *Mahan on Sea Power*, 304, 345.

53. *ATM*, xi.

54. Michael T. Corgan, "Mahan and Theodore Roosevelt: The Assessment of Influence," *NWCR* 33, no. 6 (1980): 91. For further examples of Seager's prejudice, see Suzanne Geissler, *God and Sea Power: The Influence of Religion on Alfred Thayer Mahan* (Annapolis, MD: Naval Institute Press, 2015), 29–38.

55. *ATM*, 206; see also 145–46, 165–66, 174–75.

56. *MMS2*, 5.

57. The other competitors were Don Schurman and Theodore Ropp (conversations with Don Schurman).

58. Philip Crowl, "The Strategist's Short Catechism: Six Questions without Answers," in *Military Strategy*, comp. Anthony W. Gray Jr. and Eston T. White (Washington, DC: National Defense University, 1983), 94–95. Originally published under the same title in *The Harmon Memorial Lectures in Military History Number Twenty* (U.S. Air Force Academy, Colorado, 1978).

59. *MMS2*, 451, 442–54.

60. *MMS2*, 455.

61. *MMS2*, 455–59, 462–63.

62. William Appleman Williams was a graduate of the U.S. Naval Academy (class of 1944) who served with distinction in the Pacific theater until invalided out of the service for combat wounds sustained at Okinawa. He was of the generation that could never, under any circumstances, publicly denigrate the service he loved. He always wore his class ring. I thank Professor Lloyd Gardner for this information.

63. Katherine C. Epstein, "The Conundrum of American Power in the Age of World War I," *Modern American History* 2, no. 3 (2019): 345–65; see also Anthony R. Hopkins, *American Empire: A Global History* (Princeton, NJ: Princeton University Press, 2018), 340–41.

64. The story is told in Jonathan M. Wiener, "Radical Historians and the Crisis in American History, 1959–1980," *Journal of American History* 76, no. 2 (September 1989): 399–434.

65. Jay Sexton, *The Monroe Doctrine: Empire and Nation in Nineteenth-Century America* (New York: Hill and Wang, 2011), 5.

66. George Fujii, ed., "H-Diplo Essay 208—John Lewis Gaddis on Learning the Scholar's Craft: Reflections of Historians and International Relations Scholars," March 27, 2020, https://networks.h-net.org/node/28443/discussions/6029287/h-diplo-essay-208-john-lewis-gaddis-learning-scholar%E2%80%99s-craft.

67. Seager earned his doctorate in history in 1956 from The Ohio State University, where he studied under Foster Rhea Dulles, first cousin to Alan and John Foster Dulles. Foster Rhea Dulles was one the earliest critics of Williams (which is a story in itself), for which see his dismissive review of *The Tragedy of American Diplomacy* in the "Other Recent Publications" section of *American Historical Review* 64, no. 4 (1959): 1022–23.

68. Robert Seager, "Alfred Thayer Mahan: Christian Expansionist, Navalist, and Historian," in *Admirals of the New Steel Navy: Makers of the American Naval Tradition, 1880–1930*, ed. James Bradford (Annapolis, MD: Naval Institute Press, 1990), 24–72.

69. The exceptions being Benjamin Cooling and Scott Mobley.

EPILOGUE

1. Alfred Thayer Mahan, series of lectures given to the Lowell Institute, Lecture 1, March 4, 1897, 22, Speech File, Naval Warfare, Mahan Papers.

2. *ISPH*, 25.

3. A. T. Mahan, "Belligerent Merchant Shipping," *National Review* 39 (June 1907): 536.

4. A. T. Mahan, "The Immunity from Capture of Private Property at Sea," *Times* (London), November 4, 1910, 15.

5. A. T. Mahan, "Considerations Governing the Dispositions of Navies," *National Review* 39 (July 1907): 712.

6. Capt. A. T. Mahan, "The Submarine and Its Enemies," *Collier's Weekly* 39 (April 6, 1907): 17–21.

7. Samuel P. Huntington, "National Policy and the Transoceanic Navy," *Proceedings* 80/5/615 (May 1954).

8. Huntington.

9. Huntington.

10. Adm. Thomas B. Hayward, "The Future of U.S. Sea Power," *Proceedings* 105/5/915 (May 1979).

11. Sean O'Keefe, Frank B. Kelso, and Carl E. Mundy, "From the Sea," *Proceedings* 118/11/1077 (November 1992); John H. Dalton, Jeremy M. Boorda, and Carl E. Mundy, "Forward . . . from the Sea," *Proceedings* 120/12/1102 (December 1994).

12. Richard N. Cooper, *The Economics of Interdependence: Economic Policy in the Atlantic Community* (New York: McGraw-Hill, 1968).

13. Daniel J. Sargent, *A Superpower Transformed: The Remaking of American Foreign Relations in the 1970s* (Oxford: Oxford University Press, 2015), 174.

14. Samuel P. Huntington, "The Lonely Superpower," *Foreign Affairs* 78, no. 2 (March–April 1999): 37.

15. Samuel P. Huntington, "Globalization and Culture," lecture given in Seoul, South Korea, July 12, 1999, https://koreajoongangdaily.joins.com/2003/01/04/features/Globalization-and-Culture-by-Prof-Samuel-Huntington/1872356.html; Huntington, "The Clash of Civilizations?," *Foreign Affairs*, 72, no. 3 (Summer 1993): 22–49. For weaponing the system, see Nicholas Lambert, *Planning Armageddon: British Economic Warfare and the First World War* (Cambridge, MA: Harvard University Press, 2012); Henry Farrell and Abraham L. Newman, "Weaponized Interdependence: How Global Economic Networks Shape State Coercion," *International Security* 44, no. 1 (Summer 2019): 42–79.

16. Huntington, "National Policy and the Transoceanic Navy."

17. Huntington, "Lonely Superpower," 37.

Archival Sources

BRITISH LIBRARY, LONDON
Arthur James Balfour

CORNELL UNIVERSITY LIBRARY, ITHACA, NY
Andrew Dickson White

LIBRARY OF CONGRESS, WASHINGTON, DC
Joseph H. Choate
Admiral of the Navy George Dewey
John Hay
Rear Adm. Stephen B. Luce
Rear Adm. Alfred Thayer Mahan
John Bassett Moore
Naval Historical Foundation
Adm. David Dixon Porter
Whitelaw Reid
Theodore Roosevelt
Elihu Root
Rear Adm. Charles Sperry
Benjamin Franklin Tracy
Rear Adm. John G. Walker

MASSACHUSETTS HISTORICAL SOCIETY, BOSTON
Henry C. Lodge
John D. Long

NATIONAL ARCHIVES, KEW, UK
Ernest Satow

NATIONAL ARCHIVES AND RECORDS ADMINISTRATION, WASHINGTON, DC, AND COLLEGE PARK, MD

Naval Records Collections of the Office of Naval Records and Library, RG 45
Records of Naval Operating Forces, RG 313
Records of the Office of the Chief of Naval Operations, RG 38
U.S. Navy Archives, RG 80
U.S. State Department Archives, RG 59

NATIONAL MARITIME MUSEUM, GREENWICH, UK

Adm. William Henderson
John Knox Laughton
James R. Thursfield

NAVAL HISTORY AND HERITAGE COMMAND, WASHINGTON, DC

Admiral of the Navy George Dewey
Capt. William D. Puleston

PRINCETON UNIVERSITY, PRINCETON, NJ (SEELY MUDD LIBRARY)

Edward Mead Earle

ROYAL ARCHIVES, WINDSOR CASTLE, WINDSOR, UK

King Edward VII correspondence

U.S. NAVAL WAR COLLEGE ARCHIVES, NEWPORT, RI

RG 1, RG 14, RG 15, RG 16, RG 28
Rear Adm. Stephen B. Luce (MSC-10)
Rear Adm. Alfred T. Mahan (MSC-017)
Professor Herbert Rosinski (MSC-091)
Rear Adm. Charles Stockton (Ms.COLL-56)

YALE UNIVERSITY, NEW HAVEN, CT (STERLING LIBRARY)

Henry W. Farnam
Arthur T. Hadley

INDEX

About the Author

Nicholas A. Lambert completed his undergraduate and graduate degrees at Oxford University. He was the Class of 1957 Chair at the U.S. Naval Academy from 2016 to 2018. His previous books include *Sir John Fisher's Naval Revolution* (1999), *Planning Armageddon: British Economic Warfare and the First World War* (2012), and *The War Lords and the Gallipoli Disaster: How Globalized Trade Led Britain to Its Worst Defeat of the First World War* (2021).

The **Naval Institute Press** is the book-publishing arm of the U.S. Naval Institute, a private, nonprofit, membership society for sea service professionals and others who share an interest in naval and maritime affairs. Established in 1873 at the U.S. Naval Academy in Annapolis, Maryland, where its offices remain today, the Naval Institute has members worldwide.

Members of the Naval Institute support the education programs of the society and receive the influential monthly magazine *Proceedings* or the colorful bimonthly magazine Naval History and discounts on fine nautical prints and on ship and aircraft photos. They also have access to the transcripts of the Institute's Oral History Program and get discounted admission to any of the Institute-sponsored seminars offered around the country.

The Naval Institute's book-publishing program, begun in 1898 with basic guides to naval practices, has broadened its scope to include books of more general interest. Now the Naval Institute Press publishes about seventy titles each year, ranging from how-to books on boating and navigation to battle histories, biographies, ship and aircraft guides, and novels. Institute members receive significant discounts on the Press' more than eight hundred books in print.

Full-time students are eligible for special half-price membership rates. Life memberships are also available.

For more information about Naval Institute Press books that are currently available, visit www.usni.org/press/books. To learn about joining the U.S. Naval Institute, please write to:

Member Services
U.S. Naval Institute
291 Wood Road
Annapolis, MD 21402-5034
Telephone: (800) 233-8764
Fax: (410) 571-1703
Web address: www.usni.org